THE ROMANCE OF THE GRAIL

The healing of King Pellean

THE ROMANCE
OF THE GRAIL

A STUDY OF THE STRUCTURE AND GENESIS
OF A THIRTEENTH-CENTURY ARTHURIAN
PROSE ROMANCE

by

FANNI BOGDANOW

*M.A., Ph.D., Lecturer in French
in the University of Manchester*

MANCHESTER UNIVERSITY PRESS
BARNES & NOBLE, INC., NEW YORK

First published

in the United States

1966

Barnes & Noble, inc.

105 Fifth Avenue, New York 3

Printed in Great Britain by Butler & Tanner Ltd, Frome and London

Acknowledgments

IN inscribing on the dedication page the name of Professor Eugène Vinaver I wish to express to him my very deep and sincere gratitude for all the generous and invaluable help he has given me in the preparation of this book. At every stage of the work he has allowed me to turn to him for advice and encouragement. There is not a problem that we have not discussed together, not a page that he has not read and re-read and criticized with insight and kindliness. If there is anything of value in this study, it is due in no small measure to his inspiring guidance and vision.

My thanks are also due to Dr F. Whitehead who first introduced me to medieval studies and the complex problems of Arthurian romance. Both as a teacher and as a colleague he has always been ready with help and advice and has given unstintingly of his time. I owe much to his wide and generous learning.

I likewise wish to thank Professor J. P. Collas for numerous valuable suggestions; Dr E. Kennedy for putting at my disposal H. O. Sommer's unpublished material on the *Demanda*; Mrs J. M. Sutcliffe, Assistant Secretary of the Manchester University Press, for much useful advice; and the publishers of the *University of Texas Studies in English* and of *Romania* for permission to use some of the material which originally appeared in those journals. Finally I wish to express my appreciation to the Bretey Fund Committee of the University of Manchester for its generous grant which has made the publication of this book possible.

F. B.

Manchester, 1965

Contents

Plates

Author and Publishers are grateful to the Bibliothèque Nationale, Paris, for permission to reproduce the Plates.

Abbreviations

ALMA	*Arthurian Literature in the Middle Ages, a collaborative history*, ed. R. S. Loomis (Oxford, Clarendon Press, 1959, 1961).
Löseth, *Analyse*	*Le roman en prose de Tristan. . . analyse critique d'après les manuscrits de Paris* (Bibliothèque de l'École des Hautes Études, fasc. 82, Paris, 1891).
Lot, *Étude*	*Étude sur le Lancelot en prose* (Bibliothèque de l'École des Hautes Études, fasc. 226; Paris, 1918; reprinted with a supplement, Champion, 1954).
La Mort le Roi Artu or *Vulgate Mort Artu*	*La Mort le Roi Artu, roman du XIIIe siècle*, ed. J. Frappier (Paris, Droz, 1936).
Magne, P. *D.*	Portuguese *Demanda do Santo Graal*, ed. A. Magne (Rio de Janeiro, 1944).
Pauphilet, *Études*	*Études sur la Queste del Saint Graal* (Paris, Champion, 1921).
Pickford, *Évolution*	*L'Évolution du roman arthurien en prose vers la fin du moyen âge d'après le manuscrit 112 du fonds français de la Bibliothèque Nationale* (Paris, Nizet, 1960).
Vettermann, *Die Balen-Dichtungen*	*Die Balen-Dichtungen und ihre Quellen*, Beihefte zur *ZRPh*, LX (Halle, 1918).
Vinaver, *Études*	*Études sur le Tristan en prose* (Paris, Champion, 1925).
Vinaver, *Works*	*The Works of Sir Thomas Malory*, ed. E. Vinaver (Oxford, Clarendon Press, 1947, 1948, 3 vols.).
Vulgate *Queste*	*La Queste del Saint Graal, roman du XIIIe siècle* ed. A. Pauphilet (CFMA, Paris, 1923, 1949).
Vulgate Version	*The Vulgate Version of the Arthurian Romances*, ed. H. O. Sommer (The Carnegie Institute of Washington, Publication no. 74, Washington, 1908–16). I, *L'Estoire del Saint Graal*; II, *L'Estoire de Merlin*; III, IV, V, *Le Livre de Lancelot del Lac*; VI, *Les Aventures ou la Queste del Saint Graal* and *La Mort le Roi Artu*; VII, *Supplement: Le Livre d'Artus*; VIII, *Index of Names and Places*.
Wechssler	*Über die verschiedenen Redaktionen des Robert von Borron zugeschriebenen Graal–Lancelot–Cyklus*, E. Wechssler (Halle, 1895).

II. *Periodicals*

    AR   *Archivum Romanicum*
    ASNSL   *Archiv für das Studium der neueren Sprachen und Literaturen*

BBSIA	*Bulletin Bibliographique de la Société Internationale Arthurienne*
BJRL	*Bulletin of the John Rylands Library*
MA	*Le Moyen Age*
Med. Aev	*Medium Aevum*
MPh.	*Modern Philology*
PMLA	*Publications of the Modern Language Association of America*
R	*Romania*
RFE	*Revista de Filologia Española*
RH	*Revista de Historia*, São Paulo
RI	*Revista Investigações*, São Paulo
RR	*Romanic Review*
Spec.	*Speculum*
ZFSL	*Zeitschrift für französische Sprache und Literatur*
ZRPh.	*Zeitschrift für romanische Philologie*
UTSE	*University of Texas Studies in English*

III. *Other abbreviations*

CFMA	Classiques Français du Moyen Age
SATF	Société des Anciens Textes Français
TLF	Textes Littéraires Français
B.N. fr.	Bibliothèque Nationale, fonds français

IV. *Note on the use of references*

For all quotations from the Huth MS. references are to the Gaston Paris edition. Folio references are only given if the manuscript reading differs from the reading given by G. Paris.

In notes, line references are preceded by 'l', paragraph references by '§', and for page references the number alone is given.

Addenda

p. 50 n. 1. *The Cambridge MS. f. 272a has the same reading as the Huth MS. except for the following variants:* (*7 lines from the top*) qu'il n'out laeins riens lassié fors de s'espee; (*9 lines from the top*) *Camb. om.* ja.

p. 51 n. 1. *The Cambridge MS. f. 278a agrees with the Huth MS. except for the following variants:* q'il s'entreblessassent mie grantment . . . lor force e lor pooir qu'a paines il porroit sustenir lor escuz e lor espeez. *In addition the Camb. MS. omits:* ne che n'estoit pas grans merveilles". There are numerous other passages in the *Baladros* which have been modified, usually in order to make the narrative more coherent.

p. 78 n. 4. MSS. B.N. fr. 99 (ff. 533c–536d), Chantilly 646 (ff. 384b–388b) and New York, Pierpont Morgan 41 (ff. 137d–140c) have replaced the *Tristan* account of the knighting of Perceval by the one from the Vulgate *Lancelot.* (Cf. Löseth, 239 n. 3.) The Leningrad MS. breaks off before reaching this point.

p. 92 n. 7. *D*, § 22 and Sp. *D*, Ch. XX end with a remodelled version of Vulgate *Queste*, 14, ll. 16–23. The prose *Tristan* reproduces this Vulgate passage later, after its account of Tristan's arrival in the field where the tournament is being held.

p. 93 n. 1. Later in *D*, §§ 43–4, Sp. *D*, Chs. XL–XLI, at a point corresponding to Vulgate *Queste* 26, l. 5, the ugly damsel who had brought the bleeding sword to Arthur's court, returns and once more warns Gauvain against entering the Quest of the Grail.

p. 95 n. 1. One of the episodes added by the *Tristan* and the *Demanda*, the Cayphas story, is also in MS. 112, *Livre* IV, ff. 179d–180c.

p. 95 n. 4. MS. 112, *Livre* IV, ff. 138d–139b has a summary of the account of Galaad's meeting with Tristan.

p. 96 n. 3. MS. 112, *Livre* IV, ff. 146d–147d contains the story of the death of the *beste glatissant* as in MS. 343 and *D*.

p. 96 n. 4. Palamedes' and Esclabor's death is in MS. 112, *Livre* IV, ff. 147d–150c.

p. 215 n. 3. See also Vinaver, 'La Mort de Roland', *Cahiers de Civilisation Médiévale, Université de Poitiers*, VII (1964) 133–43.

p. 241 n. 215. *D* Tor, el fijo de Dares (*B* omits Siena MS., lines 213–15).

INTRODUCTION

The Literary Tradition
behind the 'Roman du Graal'

THE thirteenth century was one of the most fruitful periods in the history of medieval French narrative fiction. It was the time when the verse romances of the twelfth century were turned into prose, and when writers were no longer content to produce a series of unconnected romances as did Chrétien de Troyes,[1] but wished to combine them in coherent groups, making them part of a larger scheme and filling in where necessary gaps in the tradition. Chrétien de Troyes, who wrote a number of verse romances, knew of Wace's *Brut*,[2] which includes an account of Arthur's life and death adapted from Geoffrey of Monmouth's *Historia Regum Britanniae*, but while using in all his romances the same Arthurian décor and making Arthur preside over the Round Table—introduced for the first time by Wace—Chrétien did not attempt to establish a sense of continuity or relationship between any of his romances. It is true that in two of them, his *Yvain* and *Lancelot*, the adventures of one of the knights, Gauvain, appear to

---

[1] Christian von Troyes, *Sämtliche erhaltene Werke nach allen bekannten Handschriften*, herausgegeben von Wendelin Förster (Halle, Niemeyer, 1884–1932): I *Cligés* (1884), II *Yvain* (1887), III *Erec* (1890), IV *Karrenritter* (*Lancelot*) und *Wilhelmsleben* (Guillaume d'Angleterre) (1899), V *Der Percevalroman* (*Li contes del Graal*) ed. Alfons Hilka (1932). More recently there have appeared in the CFMA: *Les Romans de Chrétien de Troyes édités d'après la copie de Guiot* (Bibl. Nat. fr. 794): I *Erec et Enide*, Mario Roques (1955), II *Cligés*, A. Micha (1957), III *Le Chevalier de la Charrette*, M. Roques (1958), IV *Le Chevalier au Lion* (*Yvain*), M. Roques (1960). The *Perceval* has been published in the TLF series by William Roach: *Le Roman de Perceval ou le Conte du Graal*, publié d'après le ms. fr. 12576 de la Bibl. Nat. (Genève, Droz, Lille, Giard, 1956). For the most recent comprehensive account of Chrétien's works see J. Frappier, *Chrétien de Troyes* (Connaissance des Lettres, Paris, Hatier, 1957, 2nd. ed. 1961), and Frappier, 'Chrétien de Troyes', *ALMA*, Ch. 15.

[2] *Le Roman de Brut de Wace*, ed. I. D. O. Arnold (SATF): I (1938), II (1940). The Arthurian section of Wace's *Brut* has been published separately: *La Partie Arthurienne du Roman de Brut, édition avec introduction, glossaire, notes et bibliographie* by Arnold and M. M. Pelan, Paris, Klincksieck, 1962. On Wace and his major source, Geoffrey of Monmouth's *Historia Regum Britanniae* (1136) and *Vita Merlini*, see *ALMA*, Chs. 8 and 9.

interlock in the sense that in the *Yvain* Gauvain is prominent at the beginning and end only, and so is free for a time to play an active part in the rescue of Guenevere.[1] There is nothing, however, in the two romances to suggest that Chrétien intended the one to be a sequel to the other. Neither does Chrétien in any of his romances deal with the birth or death of Arthur, for he had no intention of producing a comprehensive history of Arthur's kingdom.

The idea of a coherent scheme of romances first occurred to Robert de Boron, a Burgundian knight whose literary activity falls between the years 1191 and 1212.[2] Robert de Boron planned a trilogy of verse romances, to which he gave the collective title *li livres dou Graal*,[3] which was to cover the whole history of both the Grail and Arthur's kingdom. Of this trilogy only the first part, the *Joseph* or *Le Roman de l'Estoire dou Graal*, and 502 lines of the second part, the *Merlin*, have been preserved in their original verse form in a unique late thirteenth-century manuscript, B.N. fr. 20047.[4] But both the *Joseph* and the *Merlin* were subsequently re-written in prose, and we possess numerous manuscripts of the prose version.[5] Robert de Boron was essentially

---

[1] Cf. *ALMA*, Ch. 15, 180–1. Gauvain, of course, plays an important part in all Chrétien's romances, but this does not make his work into a cycle.

[2] Most critics would now agree that Robert de Boron wrote after Chrétien de Troyes and knew his *Perceval*. For a discussion of the problems raised by Robert and for further bibliographical references, see W. A. Nitze, 'Messire Robert de Boron: Enquiry and Summary', *Spec.*, XXVIII (1953) 279–96; Micha, 'Deux Études sur le Graal: II, Le Livre du Graal de Robert de Boron', *R*, LXXV (1954) 316–34; P. Le Gentil, 'The Work of Robert de Boron and the Didot Perceval' in *ALMA*, Ch. 19; J. Marx, 'Robert de Boron et Glastonbury', *MA*, LIX (1953) 69–86.

[3] Robert refers to his work as the *livres dou Graal* in his *Merlin* (see *Merlin, roman en prose du XIIIe siècle, publié avec la mise en prose du poème de Merlin de Robert de Boron d'après le manuscrit appartenant à M. Alfred Huth*, par Gaston Paris et Jacob Ulrich (SATF, 2 vols., Paris, 1886) I, 47–8: 'Et tes livres, por chou que tu en as fait et feras de moi et d'aus, quant tu seras alés et mors, si avra a non tous jours mais li *Livres dou Graal*, et sera moult volentiers oïs.'

[4] Robert de Boron, *Le Roman de l'Estoire dou Graal*, ed. W. A. Nitze (CFMA, 1927).

[5] For a list of MSS. of the prose *Joseph* and the prose *Merlin*, see B. Woledge, *Bibliographie des romans et nouvelles en prose française antérieurs à 1500* (Genève, Droz, Lille, Giard, 1954) 69–70, 82–3. For a classification of the *Merlin* MSS., see A. Micha, 'Les manuscrits du *Merlin* en prose de Robert de Boron', *R*, LXXIX (1958) 78–94 and 145–74. The prose *Joseph* has been published by George Weidner, *Joseph d'Arimathie, der Prosaroman von Joseph von Arimathie mit einer Einleitung über die handschriftliche Überlieferung* (Oppeln, 1881) and by William Roach, 'The Modena Text of the prose Joseph d'Arimathie', *RPh.*, IX (1955–6)

a builder of stories, anxious to elucidate and expand in a coherent manner the material at his disposal. Chrétien de Troyes in his *Conte del Graal* had made no attempt to explain the origin of the Grail. Robert de Boron, who intended to write a well-constructed trilogy, began his work with an account of the early fortunes of the Grail. Putting the Grail into the context of pious legend and using for this purpose material derived from the *Gesta Pilati*, the *Vindicta Salvatoris* and the *Cura Sanitatis Tiberii*,[1] he invented in his *Joseph* a story according to which the Grail was the Vessel of the Last Supper and was after the crucifixion given by Pilate to Joseph of Arimathea who used it to catch the last drops of Christ's blood. Joseph carefully hid the holy vessel, but when after Christ's resurrection Joseph was thrown into prison, Christ appeared before him in a great light, bearing the precious vessel, and told him that only three men, including himself, were ever to have the vessel in their care. Many years later Vespasian, having been miraculously cured of leprosy, went to Jerusalem to avenge Christ and freed Joseph from prison, who, together with a small company, including his sister Enygeus and her husband Bron, went to live in distant lands where, one day, at the prompting of the Holy Ghost, he set up the Grail Table in memory of the Last Supper. Later, also in obedience to the voice of the Holy Spirit, Joseph entrusted the holy vessel to the care of Bron who, with his wife and twelve sons, moved westwards, presumably to Britain, to preach the Christian faith and await the coming of the third and last Grail guardian, Bron's grandson.[2] In the second part of the trilogy, the *Merlin*, which is linked to the *Joseph* by a series of references, Robert de Boron set himself the task of bridging the chronological and material gap between the story of the Grail in apostolic times and the achievement of the Grail adventure in the time of King Arthur. Basing himself on Geoffrey of Monmouth's *Historia Regum Britanniae* and *Vita Merlini*,[3] but remodelling and

---

313–42. The prose *Merlin* was incorporated into the Vulgate Cycle and the Post-Vulgate *Roman du Graal* (see below, 6, 11) and has been published as part of these works (see *Vulgate Version*, II, 1–88; *Merlin*, ed. G. Paris, I, 1–146).

[1] On the sources of the *Joseph*, see Le Gentil, in *ALMA*, 254–6.

[2] There is a contradiction in Robert's *Joseph* concerning the identity of the 'third man'. At one point Robert says that Bron's son is to be the third Grail guardian (see *Joseph*, ed. Nitze, ll. 2535–6), but later he states that the last Grail guardian will be Alain's son, i.e. Bron's grandson (see *Joseph*, ed. Nitze, ll. 2791–6).

[3] On the sources of Robert's *Merlin* and his methods of composition, see P. Zumthor, *Merlin le prophète* (Lausanne, 1943) 132–58; Micha, 'L'origine de la

elaborating his sources freely so as to make his borrowings fit into his narrative scheme, Robert de Boron relates how Merlin, born of an incubus and a virgin, was able both to know the past and to foretell the future, a power of which he gave evidence from the age of two and which enabled him to know the history of Joseph of Arimathea and his descendants which he dictated to Blaise; how Uther, after the death of his brothers Moine and Pandragon, took the name Utherpendragon, became king of Britain and on Merlin's advice established the Round Table with its Perilous Seat on the model of the Grail Table set up by Joseph of Arimathea; how at a Christmas feast at Carduel, Utherpendragon fell in love with Ygerne, the wife of the Duke of Tintagel, who refused his love but was deceived when thanks to Merlin's enchantments Utherpendragon took the shape of her husband the night that the Duke was killed in battle; how Utherpendragon married Ygerne two months after conceiving Arthur and how, in order to conceal Arthur, Merlin gave the child immediately after its birth to a foster-father, Auctor, with whose son, Keu, Arthur grew up; and finally how, after Utherpendragon's death, Arthur proved his right to the throne by drawing his sword from the anvil which appeared on Christmas day outside the church at Carduel, but had to wait until the following Whitsuntide before being crowned as the barons refused at first to accept an unknown youth as their king. The third part of the trilogy, relating how Perceval, Bron's grandson, achieved the Grail adventure and how, after Arthur and his kingdom had been destroyed through the treachery of Mordred, Merlin retired to his *esplumoir* and was never seen again, has only been preserved in prose in the Didot and Modena manuscripts.[1] This prose *Perceval* may be a *remaniement* of a verse romance by Robert de Boron, but it seems more likely that it was composed directly in prose by a writer who wished to fulfil certain forecasts in the *Joseph* and the *Merlin*, and thus complete the trilogy.[2]

Table du Graal et de la Table Ronde chez Robert de Boron', *RPh.*, IX (1955) 173–7; Micha, 'La Table Ronde chez Robert de Boron et dans la *Queste del Saint Graal*', in *Les Romans du Graal dans la littérature des XIIe et XIIIe siècles* (Editions du CNRS, Paris, 1956) 119–36; Vinaver, 'King Arthur's Sword or the Making of a Medieval Romance', *BJRL*, XL, no. 2, March 1958, 513–26; Micha, 'The Vulgate *Merlin*' in *ALMA*, 319–22.

[1] The prose Perceval of these two manuscripts has been edited by W. Roach: *The Didot Perceval, according to the manuscripts of Modena and Paris*, Philadelphia, 1941.

[2] A number of critics, in particular E. Brugger and W. Roach, believe that

This tendency to combine in coherent groups gave rise to the composition between 1215 and 1230 of a second cycle of very much greater dimensions, the so-called Vulgate or 'pseudo-Map' cycle of Arthurian prose romances, in which the Grail theme is for the first time combined with the story of Lancelot's love for Guenevere.[1] In its completed form the Cycle counted five branches, totalling some 4000 quarto pages in modern print. The first branch, the *Estoire del Saint Graal*, consists of an elaborated and much expanded version of Robert de Boron's *Joseph*. Whereas Robert de Boron's *Joseph* ends with Bron's departure for the West and tells us nothing about the evangelization of Britain, leaving in fact a gap of some 400 years between the time of Joseph and that of Utherpendragon, the *Estoire del Saint Graal* takes the narrative much further. Joseph, after being freed from prison by Vespasian, goes together with his wife, his son Josephés and a small company to the Orient, taking with them nothing except the Holy Grail which they transported in an Ark; after converting many Saracens, Joseph and his people come in a miraculous way to Britain where they establish the Christian faith by preaching and by force; Josephés who had been consecrated Bishop by Christ himself entrusts at his death the Grail to his nephew Alain who goes to the Terre Foraine; its ruler, Alfasim, after being converted, has the Grail castle built, and gives it the name of Corbenic. Finally, the author of the *Estoire del Saint Graal* takes the

---

the Didot-*Perceval* is a reworking of a verse poem by Robert (see Roach, ed. cit. 113–25, and bibliographical references given there). Other critics, however, notably Bruce, Pauphilet, Le Gentil and Micha, suggest that the Didot-*Perceval* was written directly in prose and is not based on a hypothetical verse *Perceval* by Robert (see Bruce, *Evolution*, II, 1–7, 104–11, and *RR*, IV (1913) 448–51; Pauphilet, 'Le roman en prose de Perceval', in *Mélanges d'Histoire du Moyen Age offerts à M. Ferdinand Lot*, Paris, Champion (1925) 603–18; Micha, 'Deux Études sur le Graal', *R*, LXXV (1954) 334–52; Le Gentil, in *ALMA*, 259–62). The theory that the prose *Perceval* does not derive from a verse romance by Robert seems to me the more probable hypothesis, for the prose *Perceval* contains much material adapted from the First Continuation of Chrétien's *Perceval*, which is later in date than Robert's work, and if we remove these episodes from the Didot-*Perceval* there is very little left and it is difficult to imagine what Robert's *Perceval* would have contained.

[1] The whole of the Vulgate Cycle has been published by H. O. Sommer: *Vulgate Version*. Some of the branches of the Cycle have been edited separately (see 6, 7, notes). On the date of the Cycle, see Lot, *Étude sur le Lancelot en prose* (Paris, 1918 and 1954) 126–40, and 'Sur la date du *Lancelot* en prose', *R*, LVII (1931) 137–46. Frappier, *Étude*, 124–38 and 432–3, would place the composition of the *Lancelot-Graal* between 1215 and 1235.

B

story down to the time of King Pelles, Lancelot's grandfather on the maternal side.[1] The second branch, the *Estoire de Merlin*, consists of the prose rendering of Robert de Boron's *Merlin* followed by a pseudo-historical sequel, referred to by modern scholars as the Vulgate *Merlin* continuation. In this section, which covers the first three and a half years of Arthur's reign, we are told how the barons rebelled against Arthur as they could not believe Merlin when he said that Arthur was really Utherpendragon's son; how with the help of Merlin Arthur overcame the rebel barons and the Saxons who had invaded the country; and how Merlin was beguiled and entombed by the woman he loved.[2] The third branch, the *Lancelot* proper, by far the largest part of the Cycle, consists of three sections, the *Enfances Lancelot* or *Galeaut*, which deals with the youth of Lancelot, his friendship with Galeaut, and the awakening of Lancelot's love for Guenevere; the *Charrette*, which is a prose rendering of Chrétien de Troyes' romance of that name; and the *Agravain* which serves as a transition to the next branch of the Cycle, the *Queste del Saint Graal*, predicting as it does the messianic rôle of Galaad, the pure knight, who in the *Queste* will replace his father, Lancelot, as the greatest knight in the world, and achieve the high adventure of the Grail from which Lancelot, because of his sinful love, will be excluded.[3] For in the *Queste del Saint Graal*,

---

[1] Besides Sommer's edition of the *Estoire del Saint Graal* there is one by E. Hucher who used the Le Mans MS. 354: *Le Saint Graal ou le Joseph d'Arimathie, première branche des romans de la Table Ronde, publié d'après des textes et des documents inédits*, Le Mans, 3 vols., 1874–8, and one by F. J. Furnivall, based on Brit. Mus. MS. Royal 14 E. iii: *Seynt Graal, or the Sank Ryal. The History of the Holy Graal, partly in English verse, by Henry Lonelich Skynner. . . and wholly in French prose, by Sires Robiers de Borron*, . . . printed for the Roxburghe Club (London, I, 1861, II, 1863). On the *Estoire del Saint Graal*, see Frappier, 'The Vulgate Cycle', in *ALMA*, 313–15; Lot, *Étude*, 204–14; Bruce, *Evolution*, I, 374–94; Myrrha Lot-Borodine, 'Le Symbolisme du Graal', *Neophilologus*, XXXIV (1950) 65–79, and 'Les apparitions du Christ aux messes de l'*Estoire* et de la *Queste del Saint Graal*', *R*, LXXII (1951) 202–23.

[2] On the Vulgate *Merlin* continuation, see Micha, 'The Vulgate *Merlin*' in *ALMA*, 319–24; and the series of articles by Micha on different aspects of the work: 'L'épreuve de l'épée', *R*, LXX (1948–9) 37–50; 'L'épisode de la bataille des Romains', *R*, LXXII (1951) 310–23; 'La Suite-Vulgate du *Merlin*, Étude littéraire', *ZRPh.*, LXXI (1951) 33–59; 'Les sources de la Vulgate du *Merlin*', *MA*, LVIII (1952) 299–345; 'La Composition de la Vulgate du *Merlin*', *R*, LXXIV (1953) 199–220.

[3] Besides Sommer's edition we have an edition of the beginning of the work by students of E. Wechssler in the *Marburger Beiträge zur romanischen Philologie* (1911–17); G. Hutchings has published the *Charrette* portion (*Le roman en prose de*

in contrast to the early parts of the *Lancelot*, courtly love and earthly chivalry will be condemned, and only the pure will succeed.[1] The last branch of the Cycle, the *Mort Artu*, relates how the discovery of Lancelot and Guenevere's love, which until then had been kept secret from Arthur, wrought dissension among the knights of the Round Table and thus enabled the traitor Mordred to destroy Arthur and his kingdom.[2] Although there is a marked difference in spirit between the *Queste del Saint Graal* and portions of the other parts of the Cycle, most critics would agree that the *Lancelot* proper in its final form, the *Queste* and the *Mort Artu*, form an indissoluble whole. All three branches are part of a biographical romance of Lancelot and are the work if not of one man, at least of a group of men working under the guidance of an 'architect' who supplied the general framework.[3] The

---

Lancelot du Lac, Le conte de la Charrette, Paris, Droz, 1938); E. Kennedy is preparing an edition of the first part of the prose *Lancelot* for the Clarendon Press, Oxford. For the most recent account of the prose *Lancelot*, see Frappier, 'The Vulgate Cycle' in *ALMA*, 294–302, and bibliographical references given there. On the manuscripts of the Vulgate *Lancelot* see A. Micha, 'Les manuscrits du *Lancelot* en prose', *R*, LXXXI (1960) 145–87; LXXXIV (1963) 28–60, 478–99; 'La tradition manuscrite du *Lancelot* en prose', *R*, LXXXV (1964) 292–318, 478–517; 'Tradition manuscrite et versions du *Lancelot* en prose', *BBSIA*, 14 (1962) 99–106; 'Lancelot au verger de Corbenic', *MA*, LXIX (1963) 381–90.

[1] The *Queste* has been edited, apart from H. O. Sommer, by F. J. Furnivall (London, Roxburghe Club, 1864) and by Pauphilet (CFMA, 1923, 1949). For a discussion of the problems raised by the *Queste*, see in particular Pauphilet, *Études sur la Queste del Saint Graal*, Paris, 1921; E. Gilson, 'La Mystique de la grâce dans la Queste del Saint Graal', *R*, LI (1925) 321–7 (reprinted in Gilson, *Les Idées et les Lettres*, Paris, 2nd. ed. 1955, 59–91); M. Lot-Borodine, *Trois essais sur le roman de Lancelot du Lac et la Quête du Saint Graal*, Paris, Champion, 1919, and *De l'amour profane à l'amour sacré* (Paris: Nizet, 1961), Ch. VIII. For further bibliographical references, see Frappier, in *ALMA*, 302–7.

[2] Besides Sommer's edition of the *Mort Artu*, there are three others: J. D. Bruce, *Mort Artu, an Old French prose romance of the XIIIth century. . . now first edited from MS. 342 (fonds français) of the Bibliothèque Nationale, with collations from some other MSS.* (Halle: Niemeyer, 1910), and two by Frappier, one with variant readings (*La Mort le Roi Artu, roman du XIIIe siècle*, Paris, Droz, 1936) and one without (TLF, Genève, Droz, Lille, Giard, 1954; 2nd. ed., Genève, Droz, Paris, Minard, 1956; 3rd. ed., 1959). For a general study of the work, see Frappier, *Étude*. The *Estoire de Merlin* and the *Mort Artu* both revive the chronicle tradition of Arthur initiated by Geoffrey of Monmouth's *Historia Regum Britanniae* and Wace's French adaptation of the latter, *Le Roman de Brut*.

[3] Before Lot's study of the Vulgate Cycle (*Étude sur le Lancelot en prose*) it was assumed that the Cycle was the work of an indefinite number of authors. Lot

Estoire del Saint Graal and the *Estoire de Merlin*, on the other hand, are later additions supplied by writers who, on the model of Robert de Boron's work, wished to round off and complete the Cycle by providing a counterbalance to the last two branches.[1]

The Vulgate Cycle, which illustrates so well the cyclic process, represents, however, by no means the final stage of the development of the Arthurian prose romances. The twelfth-century verse romance of Tristan was likewise turned into prose in the thirteenth century and this prose *Tristan* became linked with the Lancelot and Guenevere story and the Grail theme.[2] Tristan's lineage is traced back to the days

showed, however, that it has a unity of structure and subject matter, and he attributed the whole, with the exception of the *Estoire de Merlin*, to one author. This view has not been accepted by all scholars. Brugger, Bruce and Pauphilet assume that the various sections are the work of individual authors and were put together subsequently by *remanieurs* who added incidents to link up the separate romances (see Brugger's articles 'L'Enserrement Merlin', *ZFSL*, XXIX (1905)–XXXV (1909); Bruce, *Evolution*, I, 398–442; Bruce, 'The Composition of the Old French Prose *Lancelot*', *RR*, IX (1918) 241–68, 353–95, X (1919) 48–66, 97–122; Pauphilet, *Le Legs du Moyen Age*, Melun, Librairie d'Argences (1950) 212–17. Frappier, however, has suggested that while the *Lancelot*, the *Queste* and the *Mort Artu* are the work of separate authors, the man who wrote the *Lancelot* had an outline of the whole trilogy in mind and guided the authors of the *Queste* and *Mort Artu* (see Frappier, *Étude*, 122–46 and 440–55; and in *ALMA*, 315–17). Frappier rejects Lot's theory of the unity of authorship because there are differences of spirit between the various sections. In a recent study, however, Micha ('L'Esprit du *Lancelot-Graal*', *R*, LXXXII (1961) 357–78) has suggested that the differences in spirit are not so much due to different authors as to the fact that we are shown in the *Lancelot-Graal* the evolution of Lancelot's character. There is no reason therefore for attributing the *Lancelot*, *Queste* and *Mort Artu* to three different authors. Vinaver expressed a similar view in *Malory*, 70–8 and in *The Tale of the Death of King Malory by Sir Thomas Malory*, Oxford, Clarendon Press (1955) ix–xi.

[1] According to Lot (*Étude*, 125) the *Estoire del Saint Graal* was written by the same author as the rest of the *Lancelot-Graal* cycle, and if not before the whole *Lancelot* proper, at least before the *Agravain*, the *Queste* and the *Mort Artu*. Mme Lot-Borodine expressed the same opinion in 'Le Double Esprit et l'Unité du Lancelot en prose' (first published in *Mélanges . . . offerts à M. F. Lot*, 477–90, reprinted as an Appendix to the revised edition of Lot's *Étude* (1954) 443–56 and in her *De l'amour profane à l'amour sacré*, Ch. VI), and in various articles dealing with aspects of the *Estoire del Saint Graal* (see her *De l'amour profane*, Ch. VIII; *Neophilologus*, XXXIV (1950) 65–79; *R*, LXXII (1951) 202–23). Pauphilet (review of Lot's *Étude* in *R*, XLV (1918) 521–7) and Frappier (*Étude*, 55–9), on the other hand, consider the *Estoire del Saint Graal* a late addition to the Cycle, and not the work of the author of the Vulgate *Queste*.

[2] The Archetype of the early *Tristan* poems has not survived. We possess in

of Joseph of Arimathea, and Tristan, after fleeing to Logres to escape the wrath of King Mark, becomes one of Lancelot's closest friends, is made a knight of the Round Table, takes part in the Quest of the Grail and, like his friend, is unable to achieve the high adventure because of his sin of luxury. The prose *Tristan*, of which some fifty manuscripts have survived, exists for us today in two main forms, the First Version and the Second or Enlarged Version.[1] The Second Version differs from the First mainly in that it relates in full certain adventures referred to briefly in the latter, includes a long account of Mark's comic adventures in Logres, and incorporates the whole of the *Queste del Saint Graal*, whereas the First Version only gives an outline of it, concentrating instead on Tristan's own adventures in the Quest. But the Grail theme is no mere intrusion in either the First or Second

---

French only two fragmentary versions, that of Béroul, the most recent editions of which are by A. Ewert (*The Romance of Tristan*, Oxford, Blackwell, 1939) and by E. Muret (*Le roman de Tristan, poème du XIIe siècle*, 4e édition revue par L. M. Defourques, CFMA, 1947), and that of Thomas, edited by J. Bédier (*Le roman de Tristan par Thomas, poème du XIIe siècle*, SATF, 1902–5, 2 vols.; reprinted 1961 and distributed by Pollard, Old Marston, Oxford) and by B. H. Wind (*Les fragments du Tristan de Thomas*, Leiden, Brill, 1950; new edition of same in the TLF series, Genève, Droz, Paris, Minard, 1960). For a study of the early Tristan poems, see F. Whitehead in *ALMA*, 134–43. The prose *Tristan* has so far not been edited in its complete form. Bédier in vol. II of his edition of Thomas' poem published *Les parties anciennes* of the prose *Tristan* from MS. B.N. fr. 103 and 757; other partial editions of the prose *Tristan* are: F. C. Johnson, *La grant ystoire de Monseignor Tristan 'Li Bret'*, London and Edinburgh, Oliver and Boyd, 1942: R. L. Curtis, *Le Roman de Tristan en prose*, tome 1, München, 1963 (Max Hueber Verlag); E. S. Murrel, 'The Death of Tristan from Douce MS. 189', *PMLA*, XLIII (1928) 343–83. Löseth has summarized the prose *Tristan* in his *Analyse*. This work he supplemented later by *Le Tristan et le Palamède des manuscrits français du British Museum, Étude critique* (Videnskabs-Selskabets Skrifter II. Hist.-Filos. Klasse, 1905, no. 4, Christiana) and *Le Tristan et le Palamède des manuscrits de Rome et de Florence* (Videnskabs-Selskabets Skrifter II. Hist.-Filos. Klasse, 1924, no. 3, Christiana). For a study of the prose *Tristan* and bibliographical references, see Vinaver, *Études*; idem, *Le Roman de Tristan et Iseut dans l'œuvre de Thomas Malory* (Paris: Champion, 1925); 'The prose *Tristan*' in *ALMA*, 339–47; *Works* I, lxix–lxxv, III, 1422–37.

[1] On the two versions of the prose *Tristan*, see Vinaver, *Études*, 23–33. The First Version of the prose *Tristan* was written shortly after the Vulgate Cycle, and the Second Version dates from *c.* 1250 (see Vinaver, *Études*, 23, 28–30, *ALMA*, 339, and 'Un chevalier errant à la recherche du sens du monde: Quelques remarques sur le caractère de Dinadan dans le Tristan en prose', in *Mélanges de Linguistique romane et de philologie médiévale offerts à M. Maurice Delbouille*, Bruxelles, 1964, II, 677–86).

Version of the prose *Tristan*. Whereas in the Vulgate Cycle the Grail Quest is undoubtedly the central portion of the work and serves to show that earthly chivalry alone is not sufficient, in the prose *Tristan* the Grail Quest has less an ideological function than a structural purpose. It serves to prepare for the death of Tristan and Yseut. In the poetic versions, Tristan dies in Brittany of a wound received in his fight with Bedenis. In the prose *Tristan*, however, Tristan dies at the hands of his rival, King Mark. Now to lead up to this new ending, the prose writer relates that Tristan and Yseut, after fleeing from Cornwall, found refuge in Lancelot's castle, Joieuse Garde. Later, when all the companions of the Round Table, including Tristan, were engaged on the Quest of the Grail, Mark invaded Logres and forced Yseut to return with him to Cornwall. But Tristan, unable to live without Yseut, abandoned the Quest and followed her to Cornwall where, one day, while he was harping a lay in Yseut's room, Mark killed him by stabbing him in the back.[1] Thus the Grail Quest, which originally was unconnected with the Tristan story, becomes an integral part of the prose romance. The scribes of certain prose *Tristan* manuscripts endeavoured, moreover, to carry the process of integrating the Tristan and Lancelot-Grail material still further by adding, after Tristan's death, an account of Arthur's death and the destruction of the Round Table.[2]

The combination of such contrasting themes as the Grail Quest and the Lancelot and Guenevere story produced in the Vulgate Cycle an inevitable clash of ideologies. This *double esprit* on which modern scholars have so often commented did not escape the attention of medieval readers either, and a short time after the completion of the Vulgate Cycle and the First Version of the prose *Tristan*, but before the Second Version, a *remanieur* revised the Vulgate Cycle so as to produce a more homogeneous composition in which Arthur rather than Lancelot was the central character and themes derived from the First Version of the prose *Tristan* were combined with the material adapted from the Vulgate so as to form a closely knit and unified whole. This 'new Arthuriad' which in the manuscripts is wrongly attributed to Robert de Boron, used to be referred to by scholars as

---

[1] On the account of Tristan's death in the prose *Tristan*, see Vinaver, *Études*, 17–20.

[2] MS. B.N. fr. 24400 adds a summary of the Death-of-Arthur story, and MS. B.N. fr. 758 appends at the end of the *Tristan* the whole of the *Mort Artu* (see Löseth, *Analyse*, 407, n. 2, and § 619).

the 'pseudo-Robert de Boron' cycle, but to give the work a more positive status I have ventured to call it the Post-Vulgate *Roman du Graal* or the Post-Vulgate Grail romance, a title by which the medieval *remanieur* himself refers to the work at several points.[1]

Unlike the Vulgate Cycle or prose *Tristan*, the Post-Vulgate Arthuriad has not been preserved in its complete form in any one manuscript, but has to be reconstructed from the scattered fragments that have survived, some of which are still unpublished and have only recently come to light. From internal evidence it is clear that the Post-Vulgate *Roman du Graal* originally began with an account of the early history of the Grail—a version of the *Estoire del Saint Graal* similar to the Vulgate Version. This was followed, as in the latter, by the prose rendering of Robert de Boron's *Merlin* and by an account of Arthur's early wars against the rebel kings adapted from the Vulgate *Merlin* continuation. To the story of Arthur's wars is then added a new series of adventures not in the Vulgate *Merlin* sequel and known formerly as the *Suite du Merlin* of the Huth MS., the only MS. that at one time was known to contain this part of the romance.[2] The incidents which make up the Post-Vulgate *Merlin* sequel serve to foreshadow and prepare for events in the later sections of the work and include such episodes as Arthur's begetting of Mordred, the revelation of Arthur's parentage, his combat with Pellinor, the obtaining of Escalibor from a hand in a lake, the wars against Rion and Lot, the tragic tale of Balain, Arthur's marriage with Leodogan's daughter, the quests of Gauvain, Tor and Pellinor, the story of Merlin and Niviene, and the triple adventures of Gauvain, Yvain and Le Morholt. In addition to the Huth MS., which is incomplete at the end, three other

[1] On the Post-Vulgate *Roman du Graal*, see my article in *ALMA*, 325–35. The author of the *Roman du Graal* refers to his book as the *Estoire dou Saint Graal* or *Haute Escriture del Saint Graal* not only in the *Suite du Merlin* (Huth *Merlin*, I, 280, II, 57, 61, 173; *Die Abenteuer Gawains*, 55), but also in some of the other sections. Thus the Post-Vulgate *Queste* refers at one point to the whole as the *Estoire del Saint Graal*: 'Et de celes aventures qu'il trouverent adonc ne fait pas mencion l'*Estoire del Saint Grahaal*, pour ce que trop i couvenist a demorer qui tout voxist conter quant qu'il lor avenoit' (MS. B.N. fr. 343, f. 75b). Our author borrowed the title, it seems, from Robert de Boron who refers to his work as the *Livres dou Graal* (Huth *Merlin*, I, 48) (see above, 2, n. 3).

[2] Published by G. Paris and J. Ulrich under the title, *Merlin, roman en prose du XIIIe siècle* (SATF, Paris, 1886, 2 vols.). The Tale of Balain has been published separately (*Le roman de Balain*, ed. M. D. Legge, with an introduction by E. Vinaver, Manchester University Press, 1942). For the history of the Huth MS., see below, 23–4.

MSS. of the *Suite du Merlin* are now known, MS. B.N. fr. 112, *Livre* II,
ff. 17b–58b, which contains a portion of the end of the romance,[1] the
single folio preserved in the State Archives of Siena,[2] and the Cambridge MS. identified by Professor Vinaver in 1945, which is more
complete than the Huth MS. and is preceded by all the earlier sections
of the work—the *Estoire del Saint Graal*, the prose rendering of
Robert de Boron's *Merlin* and the rebellion of the kings.[3] There exist
also two foreign adaptations of the work, the Spanish *Baladro del Sabio
Merlin* and Malory's *Tale of King Arthur*.[4] No branch corresponding
to the *Lancelot* proper of the Vulgate Cycle formed part of the *Roman
du Graal*, but in order to supply a transition to the last sections of his
work, the Post-Vulgate versions of the *Queste* and *Mort Artu*, our
author adapted from the *Agravain* section of the Vulgate *Lancelot* and
from the First Version of the prose *Tristan* a number of incidents
which he combined with his own inventions. These episodes include
the account of how Lancelot went out of his mind when Guenevere
banished him from court after she had found him with King Pelles'
daughter, the story of Galaad's youth, Perceval's youth and other
episodes which link up with the *Suite du Merlin* or look forward to the
Post-Vulgate *Queste*. This part of the romance, until recently unknown to scholars, is preserved in two manuscripts, B.N. fr. 112,
Livre III, and B.N. fr. 12599.[5] The Post-Vulgate versions of the
Queste and *Mort Artu* which conclude the *Roman du Graal* are based
on the corresponding sections of the Vulgate Cycle, but have been
remodelled. New episodes have been added to link up with the *Suite du
Merlin*, and some of the original *Queste* and *Mort Artu* episodes have
been revised or omitted so as to make the Post-Vulgate versions of
these works fit in with the *remanieur's* conception of his Arthuriad.
No MS. contains the whole of the Post-Vulgate *Queste*, but fragments

---

[1] MS. B.N. fr. 112 consists of three volumes bound in one, numbered *Livre* II,
Livre III and *Livre* IV. The 112 *Suite* fragment, which begins at a point corresponding to vol. II, 228, of the Gaston Paris edition, has been published by H. O.
Sommer (*Die Abenteuer Gawains, Ywains und Le Morholts mit den drei Jungfrauen,
... nach der allein bekannten HS. Nr. 112 der Pariser National Bibliothek, Beihefte
zur ZRPh.*, XLVII, 1913).

[2] Published by Micha in *R*, LXXVIII (1957) 37–45.

[3] See Vinaver, *Works*, III, 1277–9 and 'La genèse de la *Suite du Merlin*' in
Mélanges ... offerts à Ernest Hoepffner (Paris: Les Belles Lettres, 1949), 295–300.

[4] Vinaver, *Works*, I, 1–180. For editions of the *Baladro*, see below, 26.

[5] Now edited by F. Bogdanow under the title, *La Folie Lancelot, Beihefte zur
ZRPh.*, 109 (Max Niemeyer Verlag, Tübingen, 1965).

of it have been preserved in B.N. fr. 112, *Livre* IV and B.N. fr. 343. A number of MSS. of the Second Version of the prose *Tristan* incorporate the Post-Vulgate *Queste*, modifying, however, some of its incidents and adding material from the First Version of the prose *Tristan*.[1] We also have a Spanish and a Portuguese translation of a later version of the Post-Vulgate *Queste*,[2] the *Demanda del Sancto Grial* and the *Demanda do Santo Graal*.[3] Of the Post-Vulgate *Mort Artu* two small fragments—Guenevere's death and Mark's destruction of Camalot after Arthur's death—have been preserved in French in B.N. fr. 340, but both the Spanish and Portuguese *Demandas* end with translations of the Post-Vulgate *Mort Artu*.[4]

It is possible to date the Post-Vulgate *Roman du Graal* fairly precisely, for the prose romance of *Palamède* which was in existence by 1240 contains a clear reference to the final incident of our work, Mark's destruction of Camalot. This means that the Post-Vulgate *Roman du Graal* was composed before 1240, but after 1230, the *terminus ad quem* of the Vulgate Cycle.[5]

Various attempts have been made by scholars to reassemble the *disjecta membra* of the Post-Vulgate *Roman du Graal*, but critics differ greatly in their views. The only point on which they seem to agree is that the various sections of the *Roman du Graal* are a 'labyrinth of fantastic adventures' put together without design or purpose.[6] That this should be the prevalent view is in no way surprising, for, as Professor Vinaver has pointed out,[7] generations of critics seem to have been unable to appreciate the inner mechanism of the thirteenth-century prose romances. With very few exceptions, scholars have tended to treat all medieval romances 'either as the antecedents of the modern psychological novel or as survivals of a forgotten pre-literary

---

[1] For details, see below, 22 and Ch. IV.

[2] For a discussion of the relationship of the Spanish and Portuguese versions to the French texts, see below, Ch. IV.

[3] For a list of the editions of the Spanish and Portuguese *Demandas*, see the Bibliography below.

[4] On the Post-Vulgate *Mort Artu*, see below, Ch. VI.

[5] For further details on the dating of the Post-Vulgate *Roman du Graal*, see Appendix I.

[6] Bruce, *Evolution*, I, 464.

[7] Vinaver, 'A la recherche d'une poétique médiévale', *Cahiers de Civilisation Médiévale*, *Université de Poitiers*, II, no. 1 (1959) 1–16; *Tristan et Iseut à travers le temps*, Discours de MM. Maurice Delbouille, Eugène Vinaver et Denis de Rougemont lors de la réception de M. Eugène Vinaver à l'Académie le 16 décembre 1961 (Bruxelles: Palais des Académies, 1961) 13–26.

civilization'.[1] They expected them to conform to the same canons of composition as classical literature, and when they found that in some of them action was not subordinated to psychology and that episodes, instead of having a well-defined beginning, middle and end, seemed at once to be the continuation of preceding incidents and the starting point of further events, they condemned them as collections of incoherent fragments of narrative, as 'creuses et monotones invraisemblances'.[2] Moreover, they believed that the most complete and most perfect form of a work necessarily represented the original version, 'que le "beau" et le primitif n'en font qu'un, que la supériorité d'une forme donnée de l'œuvre est synonyme de sa priorité dans le temps'.[3] The possibility that some *remanieurs* could improve on their sources was not considered; literary creation was conceived of 'as an essentially destructive process'.[4] As a result the genesis and relationship of a large number of texts, including our own, was completely misunderstood. Rudolf Tobler, for instance, finding that the prose version of the tale of Saint Julian was more cogent than the poem, argued that the latter was derived from the prose redaction, although the reverse was obviously the case,[5] while Bédier, considering Thomas' treatment of the love potion preferable to Béroul's and Eilhart's, suggested that the latter were based on a common source which had altered the original.[6] In the same way, Wechssler and his followers, unable to see

---

[1] Vinaver, 'King Arthur's Sword', *BJRL*, XL (March, 1958) 526.

[2] Huth *Merlin*, ed. G. Paris, lxix.

[3] Vinaver, 'A la recherche d'une poétique médiévale', 10.

[4] Vinaver, 'The Dolorous Stroke', *Med. Aev.*, XXV (1956) 176.

[5] Vinaver, 'Flaubert and the Legend of Saint Julian', *BJRL*, XXXVI, no. 1 (Sept. 1953) 237, n. 3.

[6] Bédier, *Le roman de Tristan par Thomas*, SATF, II, 236–9. Vinaver has shown, however, that it is Béroul and Eilhart who preserve the original version of the love potion (see 'The love potion in the primitive Tristan romance' in *Medieval Studies in memory of Gertrude Schoepperle Loomis* (Paris, Champion, New York, Columbia University Press, 1927) 75–86; *Tristan et Iseut à travers le temps*, 13–26; and 'A la recherche d'une poétique médiévale', 10–11, where, speaking of Thomas, Vinaver remarks: 'Libre à nous de trouver son récit supérieur à celui de Béroul; ce qui nous est interdit, c'est d'en conclure à son authenticité'). Numerous other examples could be added. For instance, in the Oxford *Roland* the reader is not told what happened to Durandal after Roland's vain attempt to break the sword when he felt his death approaching; one of the rhymed versions, however, Châteauroux and V⁷, relates how Roland cast his sword into a stream, while the *Karlamagnus saga*, the Provençal *Ronçasvals* and the *Roman de Galien* explain how Charlemagne cast the sword in the first into a stream, and in the second two into a lake. As these later texts fill an obvious gap in the narrative, Bédier assumed

any significance in the extant fragments of the *Roman du Graal*, assumed that they must have formed part of a lost 'pseudo-Robert de Boron cycle' of romances written before the Vulgate and truncated by three successive redactors.[1] Later scholars took the view that the texts in question were based on the Vulgate, but they too failed to see how they developed and dismissed them as 'a clumsy imitation'.[2]

Such theories might well have continued to hold the field if it were not for Vinaver who in a series of memorable studies has shown the errors of fact underlying them.[3] He has suggested that medieval literature did not develop in retrogression, but that constructive forces lie behind its changing forms. The prose romances in particular, he indicated, are neither the result of indiscriminate accumulation of unrelated episodes, nor yet of a process of 'gradual decomposition'.[4] Successive writers, far from mutilating their themes or adding episodes haphazardly, strove to elaborate and expand their material in a consistent manner so as to eliminate incoherencies and produce spacious and harmonious compositions.[5] They were not concerned with a

---

that they have preserved an earlier narrative and that the Oxford version altered at this point the original version: 'Plus on examine, plus on se persuade que la version *O* n'est pas la version primitive' (Bédier, *Les Légendes Epiques*, III, 388–390, n. 1). But there can be no doubt that the later texts invented the theme of Durandal being cast into a lake in order to satisfy the reader's curiosity as to the fate of the sword. There are numerous other passages, too, in the rhymed versions which are more satisfying than the Oxford redaction. For this reason another scholar, Maurice Delbouille, suggested that for these particular passages the rhymed versions and not the Oxford *Roland* have preserved the original redaction (M. Delbouille, *Sur la genèse de la Chanson de Roland*, Bruxelles, 1954, 1–32). But once again it could be shown that the 'belle ordonnance de l'ensemble', the 'parfait enchaînement des laisses' (21) which Delbouille supposes to have been the work of the primitive *Roland* poem is in the passages he cites the work of the later *remanieurs* who filled out the Oxford version so as to avoid certain incoherences and make the transitions from *laisse* to *laisse* smoother.

[1] For a detailed account of Wechssler's theory, see below, 42–6.

[2] Bruce, *Evolution*, I, 458–79; Frappier in *ALMA*, 318. For a detailed account of these theories see below, 46–8.

[3] Vinaver, 'A la recherche d'une poétique médiévale', 1–16; 'King Arthur's Sword', 513–26; 'The Dolorous Stroke', 175–80; 'Flaubert and the Legend of Saint Julian', 228–44; *Tristan et Iseut à travers le temps*, 13–26; *Le Roman de Balain* (ed. Legge), ix–xxx; *Works*, I, xlvii–liii.

[4] Vinaver in *Le roman de Balain*, xvii.

[5] Vinaver, 'The Dolorous Stroke', 170–80; cf. P. Le Gentil, 'Réflexions sur la création littéraire au Moyen Age', *Cultura Neolatina*, Anno XX, fasc. 2–3 (1960) 129–40.

carefully worked-out psychology of the characters, but sought to motivate action on a purely structural plane, 'through the matter itself, by adding antecedents to hitherto unexplained events'.[1]

Hence both the peculiar structure of the prose romances—the interweaving of episodes—and their prodigious, yet coherent growth.[2] The Vulgate Cycle, for example, though it now consists of five branches, originally only had three—the *Lancelot* proper, the *Queste del Saint Graal* and the *Mort Artu*. The other two, the *Estoire del Saint Graal* and the *Estoire de Merlin*, were added to provide a prehistory of the Grail and the early history of Arthur's kingdom.[3] The various incidents, too, which the authors of the Vulgate Cycle derived from their sources were expanded and remodelled to fit them into their new context and to remove obscurities. When, for instance, Chrétien's *Charrette* was incorporated to form the middle portion of the *Lancelot* proper, new sequences of events were added to the previous section, the *Enfances Lancelot* or *Galeaut*, so as to prepare for and elucidate some of the *Charrette* episodes. One of these was the theme of the exiles in Gorre. According to Chrétien, Gorre was the land 'don nus estranges ne retorne'[4] accessible only by means of two dangerous bridges, the *Pont Evage* and the *Pont de l'Espee*. Meleagant, the son of the king of Gorre, who comes to Arthur's court at the beginning of the poem, announces that the exiles in Gorre can only be freed if a knight succeeds in defending the Queen against him. Later when Lancelot crosses the Sword Bridge to rescue the Queen, the exiles are allowed to return to Logres,[5] but no attempt is made either here or

---

[1] Vinaver in *Le roman de Balain*, xxiii. Cf. ibid., xiii.

[2] Lot in his *Étude* noticed of course that the prose *Lancelot* consisted of a series of interwoven incidents, but, as Vinaver has pointed out, Lot obviously did not realize the significance of this technique (see 'A la recherche d'une poétique médiévale', art. cit., 14, n. 52: 'La signification de cet art semble pourtant lui avoir échappé. Dans le chapitre intitulé *Défauts et mérites littéraires*, il juge le *Lancelot* en prose comme s'il s'agissait de la *Comédie humaine* ou des *Rougon Macquart*, lui reprochant entre autres d'avoir raté en quelques occasions la *scéne à faire* susceptible de motiver l'action sur le plan psychologique. Ce reproche est un éloge: dans un roman comme le *Lancelot*, il est normal que l'enchaînement structural tienne lieu de l'enchaînement psychologique').

[3] The same principle of backward expansion underlies of course also the development of the epic cycles. A good example is furnished by the evolution of the *Guillaume d'Orange* cycle, see Bédier, *Les Légendes épiques*, I (Paris: Champion, 1926) 428–64.

[4] *Le Chevalier de la Charrette*, ed. M. Roques, l. 641.

[5] Ibid., ll. 29–79, 3897–3923.

earlier on to explain why none of Arthur's people had been able to leave Gorre before. Now the prose writer elucidates all this by giving an account of the history of Gorre at the point where Baudemagus, the king of Gorre, is appointed seneschal of Galeaut's lands. We are told that when Urien was king of Gorre, Utherpendragon made war on him as he refused to do homage. But the war was unsuccessful, and so one day when Urien set out for Rome disguised as a pilgrim, Utherpendragon captured him and threatened to hang him if he did not give up his land. Urien refused none the less, and Baudemagus, anxious to save his uncle's life, surrendered Gorre. Later Urien reconquered his country and made Baudemagus king. As Gorre had been greatly impoverished through Utherpendragon, Baudemagus decided to repeople his land 'de la gent Uterpendragon'.[1] For this purpose he had two wooden bridges built, and anyone who crossed them had to swear to remain in Gorre until delivered through the prowess of a single knight. When there were enough people in the country, the two bridges were replaced by the underwater bridge and the sword bridge.[2] The sequel, a seemingly trivial incident, was not added without purpose either, but serves to prepare for the opening incident of the *Charrette* section. Meleagant, who had come with his father to see Lancelot, took a dislike to him and deliberately wounded him at the next tournament.[3] Later, after hearing that Lancelot had accused him of treachery, Meleagant went to Arthur's court to challenge Lancelot, but as the latter was not there, he announced, as in Chrétien, the condition on which the exiles could be freed.[4] Thus by lengthening the narrative threads left incomplete by Chrétien, the prose writer succeeded in linking the *Charrette* section to the preceding part of the story.

This is only one small example of how the Vulgate elaborated its sources. The same methods of composition are equally evident in the other sections of the Cycle. The episodes which the author of the *Estoire del Saint Graal* added to his remodelled account of Robert de Boron's *Joseph* are nearly all either 'sequels' to incidents referred to in the *Lancelot* and the *Queste*, or serve to elucidate themes not adequately explained in these earlier branches of the Cycle. Thus the whole of Mordrain's life story—his war with Tolomer, his conversion, his journey to Britain to free Joseph and Josephés from Crudel's prison, as well as his misadventure on approaching the Grail too closely, are

[1] *Vulgate Version*, IV, 40.   [2] Ibid., 39–41.
[3] Ibid., 41–3.   [4] Ibid., 157–8.

developments of references in the *Queste*.[1] Similarly the story of
Alfasim explains the origin of the 'palais aventureux' of the *Lancelot*
and the *Queste*.[2]

Equally significant is the fact that after the Cycle was formed it still
continued to evolve. Some *remanieurs* attempted to give it a better
form and shape by adding incidents to balance other episodes and by
elucidating puzzling events. Thus one group of *Lancelot* manuscripts
inserts a detailed account of Gauvain's adventures on the way to the
Pont Evage so as to balance Lancelot's adventures on the way to the
Pont de l'Espee.[3] Another group (X) expands a reference into a long
series of incidents intended to complete themes introduced earlier in
the *Lancelot* and to prepare for one of the episodes in the *Mort Artu*.
The latter, it will be remembered, relates that when Mador de la Porte
accused the Queen of having poisoned his brother, none of Arthur's
knights was willing to champion her cause, but no explanation is given
for this unchivalrous conduct. Now at the point where the majority of
Lancelot manuscripts say that they will not relate the adventures of the
knights of the Round Table in their last quest of Lancelot,[4] group X
gives a detailed account of the adventures[5] and announces that as the
knights did not find Lancelot for a long time, the Queen was very
angry with them and so alienated their sympathies: 'Et pour la grant
villonie que elle leur en dist au repairier l'en cuillirent en si grant hayne
qu'ilz lui faillirent au besoing la ou Mador de la Porte l'apella de
murtre voiant toute la court du roy, dont elle [eust] (MS. ot) esté
destruite si Dieu et la grant proesce de Lancelot ne fust qui l'en delivra
si comme li contes le devisera ça avant apertement'.[6] In this way not

---

[1] Vulgate *Queste*, ed. Pauphilet, 32–5, 83–6; *Vulgate Version*, I, 21–30, 42–66,
73–5, 84–6, 88–107, 232–44. The *Queste* expands themes derived from Robert de
Boron's *Joseph* by adding references to further events in the time of Joseph of
Arimathea, and it is these references which the *Estoire del Saint Graal* in its turn
develops (cf. Micha, 'La Table Ronde chez Robert de Boron et dans la *Queste del
Saint Graal*', 129).

[2] *Vulgate Version*, I, 287–9.

[3] Ibid., 182–95. Hutchings (*Le conte de la Charrette*, 122–31) first pointed out
that Gauvain's adventures found in MSS. B.N. fr. 112, 114–16 and Brit. Mus. Add.
10293 are a late addition.

[4] *Vulgate Version*, V, 383: 'Et dura ceste queste ·ii· ans et plus, ne onques
d'aventure qui lor avenist en la voie ne parole mie li contes ci endroit.'

[5] Printed in *Vulgate Version*, V, 413–74, from Harley MS. 6342. Other manuscripts which contain these adventures are: Rylands French MS. 1, ff. 140d–164b;
MSS. B.N. fr. 120, ff. 495a–510c; B.N. fr. 342, ff. 5c–39d; B.N. fr. 115–16, ff. 569d–
593d.   [6] MS. B.N. fr. 120, f. 495a.

only the Mador de la Porte episode is elucidated, but the connexion between the *Lancelot* and the *Mort Artu* is strengthened. Similarly yet another *remanieur* replaced part of the *Estoire de Merlin* by a new continuation, now known as the *Livre d'Artus*, so as to prepare more adequately for some of the themes of the later 'branches' of the Cycle.[1] The prose *Tristan* reveals the same constructive tendencies. When the prose writer remodelled the poetic versions of the *Tristan*, he combined them with new material, some of which he invented and some of which he derived from the Vulgate. But the alterations and additions that he made, far from being haphazard, served above all, as Vinaver has shown, to rationalize and elucidate the various themes.[2] The history of Tristan's ancestors, for instance, which Gaston Paris described as 'aussi ennuyeuse que longue et inutile... farcie de réminiscences mythologiques, et de fictions d'une monotone absurdité'[3] not only balances the events after Tristan's death, but prepares for themes in the later sections of the romance. In the poetic versions, Mark's character is almost as noble as Tristan's and the impossibility of a material conflict between them forms the essence of the tragedy. The prose writer, however, anxious to have a more tangible action, represents Mark as a villain who constantly seeks to harm Tristan.[4] Now the 'prehistory' explains why Mark was so treacherous: he descended from a long line of wicked ancestors, and his father, Felix, in particular, was a very evil king.[5] The narrative, moreover, is so conceived as to elucidate also another theme, the tribute which Cornwall has to pay to Ireland.[6] When Thanor, who ruled over Cornwall

---

[1] The *Livre d'Artus* has been preserved in part in a single manuscript, B.N. fr. 337. It forms vol. VII of Sommer's *Vulgate Version*. On the *Livre d'Artus* see F. Whitehead and R. S. Loomis in *ALMA*, Ch. 25. Bruce, noticing that the *Livre d'Artus* related in detail certain episodes referred to briefly in the prose *Lancelot*, assumed wrongly that the former was one of the sources of the *Lancelot*; see *RR*, IX (1918) 263–4, 265, n. 58, and below, 183.

[2] See Vinaver, *Études*, 5–20; idem, *Le Roman de Tristan et Iseut dans l'œuvre de Thomas Malory*, 99–109; idem, *Works*, I, lxix–lxxv. Schoepperle (*Tristan and Isolt*, Frankfurt and London, 1913, 9–10, 111, 280–1, 439–46) and others thought that the prose *Tristan* derived in part from a version of the *Tristan* prior to that of the poems, but Vinaver has made it clear that all the episodes where the prose *Tristan* differs from the corresponding incidents in the poems are due to the prose writer's desire to bring the action down to a concrete level (see in particular, *Études*, 11–20, and his chapter on the prose *Tristan* in *ALMA*, 339–47).

[3] Gaston Paris, 'Note sur les romans relatifs à Tristan', *R*, XV (1886) 601–2.

[4] See Vinaver, *Études*, 13–17; *Works*, III, 1448–9.   [5] Löseth, *Analyse*, § 19.

[6] The primitive Tristan poem as represented by Eilhart does not explain why

in the time of Sadoc, Bron's eleventh son,[1] was attacked by Pelyas, king of Leonois, he tried unsuccessfully to obtain help from his overlord, King Galderich of France, and so asked King Gonosor of Ireland to intervene. The latter agreed, but on condition that Cornwall should pay tribute to him: 'Dont fu la pais faite et establie entr'aus si que cascuns ot sa terre tout quitement et fu establis li treus de chiaus de Cornuaille au roi d'Irlande et dura dusques au tans de Tristan, ki puis s'en combati au Morhaut et l'ocist ensi coume l'estoire le devisera cha avant.'[2]

Similarly, many of the other additions are not without purpose. Thus the story of how both Tristan and Mark fell in love with Segurades' wife, and how Mark became very angry when the latter spurned his advances but accepted Tristan's, is intended to explain the circumstances in which Mark first came to hate Tristan.[3] On the other hand, the tournament held before the Chastel de la Lande in Ireland serves to remotivate the love theme. In the poems, Tristan and Yseut love each other because of 'un boivre' which they drank. The prose writer preferred, however, as Vinaver has suggested, a more 'adventurous'[4] motivation and so invented the tournament where Tristan, seeing that Palamedes loved Yseut, 'out of sheer love of rivalry promptly decided to become Yseut's knight'.[5] Equally instructive is the story of Perceval's youth which precedes the account of his journey to Cornwall where he freed Tristan from Mark's prison.[6] Chrétien, who first deals with the theme, does not name Perceval's father, but states that he was wounded 'parmi la jambe'[7] and died out of sorrow when his two eldest sons were killed.[8] The *Lancelot* proper, which remodelled Chrétien's account of Perceval's youth, introduces one of Perceval's brothers, Agloval, but does not tell us any more than did Chrétien how the other brothers had been killed.[9] Now the prose

---

Cornwall had to pay tribute to Ireland, but Thomas gives an explanation which differs, however, from that of the prose *Tristan*.

[1] According to Robert de Boron, Bron's eleventh son was called Alain.

[2] Vienna, Bib. Nat. MS. 2542, f. 3c; Löseth, *Analyse*, § 13. Cf. Curtis, *Le Roman de Tristan*, § 142.

[3] Löseth, *Analyse*, § 34; Curtis, op. cit., §§ 356–76.

[4] Vinaver, *Works*, I, lxxi.

[5] Ibid., loc. cit.; Löseth, *Analyse*, §§ 30–1; Curtis, op. cit., §§ 319–40.

[6] Löseth, *Analyse*, §§ 308–17.

[7] *Le roman de Perceval*, ed. W. Roach (TLF, 1956), l. 436.

[8] Ibid., ll. 408–83.

[9] *Vulgate Version*, V, 383–6.

Tristan, which combines details from both Chrétien and the *Lancelot*, not only identifies Perceval's father as Pellinor, but adds a new theme, the feud between Gauvain and Pellinor's line, to explain how Perceval's father and brothers were killed:[1] Pellinor slew Gauvain's father, King Lot, and Gauvain consequently hated the whole of Pellinor's lineage and killed both Pellinor and two of his sons, Lamorat and Drian.[2] Löseth thought that the prose *Tristan* copied the details about Perceval's brothers from an independent 'roman biographique sur les fils de Pelinor',[3] but there can be no doubt that it was the author of the First Version of the prose *Tristan* who invented the theme so as to make the Perceval story more coherent.[4]

It could also be shown that many of the differences between the various prose *Tristan* manuscripts are due to the desire of *remanieurs* to make episodes more coherent and more complete, but enough has been said to suggest that neither the Vulgate Cycle nor the prose *Tristan* grew up haphazardly. Now the *Roman du Graal*, which was written after the Vulgate Cycle and the First Version of the prose *Tristan*, represents no exception in the development of the Arthurian prose romances. Once this romance has been reconstructed, it will be seen that it forms a closely-knit and coherent whole. The Post-Vulgate author, who drew freely for his themes on the earlier romances, did not simply accumulate episodes, but sought to produce a compact and coherent Arthurian history in which the various events of Arthur's reign were more adequately motivated than in the versions at his disposal. And to achieve this he used, as Vinaver has indicated, the same methods as other thirteenth-century writers: he expanded and

[1] The story of Perceval's youth has been edited from one of the prose *Tristan* manuscripts, B.N. fr. 757, by A. Hilka, 'Die Jugendgeschichte Percevals im Prosa-Lancelot und im Prosa-Tristan', *ZRPh.*, LII (1932) 513–36.

[2] Löseth, *Analyse*, §§ 302–7.

[3] Löseth, *Analyse*, 236, n. 5.

[4] The *Roman du Graal* will later expand the story of Perceval's father still further so as to remove obscurities that still remain in the prose *Tristan* account (see below, 173). It is interesting to note that the *Livre d'Artus* also tries to explain how Perceval's brothers were killed, but its account differs from that of the prose *Tristan* (see *Vulgate Version*, VII, 237–44). The Vulgate *Queste* (ed. Pauphilet, 72–3) mentions that Perceval's brothers were slain 'par lor outrage', but does not relate in what circumstances. Bruce (*RR*, IX, 265, n. 58) suggests therefore that the *Queste* reference is based on the *Livre d'Artus* or that a 'lost metrical romance is more likely the source of both'. It is clear, however, that the *Livre d'Artus* invented its account of the death of Perceval's brothers so as to elucidate the *Queste* reference.

c

elucidated themes through their antecedents.[1] But like the earlier romances, the *Roman du Graal* continued to develop once it was constituted. Various *remanieurs* attempted to eradicate inconsistencies in the *Suite du Merlin* and to strengthen the links between the different parts by inventing new episodes in the *Queste* section. Moreover, later prose romances, especially the Second Version of the prose *Tristan*, made in their turn use of the *Roman du Graal* and modified incidents derived from the latter. The result is that there now exists a complicated relationship between the various texts which it was virtually impossible to disentangle before Vinaver had pointed out the principles underlying the development of the prose romances. Now, however, that we are beginning to be aware of the constructive forces which determined the growth of medieval narrative fiction, it should be possible to attempt both a fresh reconstruction and a fresh evaluation of the Post-Vulgate Arthuriad.

[1] Vinaver in *Le roman de Balain*, xi-xxii; *Works*, III, 1265–73; 'La genèse de la *Suite du Merlin*', 296–8.

CHAPTER I

The Known Texts of the 'Suite du Merlin'

THE prose romance known as the Huth *Merlin* or the *Suite du Merlin* was first published in 1886 by Gaston Paris and Jacob Ulrich, who had at their disposal a unique early fourteenth-century manuscript then belonging to Alfred Huth and now in the British Museum.[1] This manuscript, which contains also the prose renderings of Robert de Boron's *Joseph* and *Merlin*,[2] was found in 1869 by Paulin Paris[3] among the books belonging to the late Comte de Corbière (1767–1853),[4] whose library had been acquired after his death by a Paris bookseller, Bachelin-Deflorenne. Realizing that the manuscript was not without interest, Paulin Paris brought it to the attention of F. J. Furnivall, who recognized it as the 'long-lost and long-sought book of Balin le Sauvage, which Malory used in his immortal *Morte d'Arthur*, the book which neither Southey nor any other student of Arthur romances could find'.[5] After an unsuccessful attempt to locate further manuscripts of the *Suite du Merlin*,[6] Furnivall encouraged a London book-collector, Henry Huth, to purchase the Bachelin manuscript. Henry Huth proposed to publish it and had it transcribed for

[1] Add. 38117. It was part of a bequest by Alfred Huth of 50 books and manuscripts to the British Museum in 1910.

[2] The prose *Joseph* occupies ff. 1–18c, the prose *Merlin* ff. 18d–74a and the *Suite du Merlin* ff. 74a–226b of the new foliation.

[3] The MS. belonged in the seventeenth century to Du Cange who used it in the compilation of his *Glossarium ad Scriptores mediae et infimae latinitatis* (1678). In the margin of folio 1 of the MS. is written: 'Messire Robert de Bourron est auteur de ce roman. Il se dit compagnon en armes de messires Helies qui a fait celuy de Lancelot du Lac.' Below this is the following note: 'L'écriture et la remarque en dessus est de la main du fameux Du Cange d'Amiens.' In his Introduction to the Huth *Merlin* (I, ii, n. 2), Gaston Paris lists some of the words which Du Cange took from the MS. for his *Glossarium*.

[4] The name Corbière has been written in the margin of the first folio of the MS.

[5] Quoted from *The Huth Library, a catalogue of the printed books, manuscripts, autograph letters and engravings collected by Henry Huth, with collations and bibliographical descriptions*, by W. C. Hazlitt and F. S. Ellis (London, 1880), III, 954.

[6] Furnivall sent a summary of the *Suite du Merlin*, furnished by Paulin Paris, to various public libraries, in the hope that they might contain further MSS. of the work. This summary was published in the *Huth Library*, III, 954–7.

this purpose by Mrs Cooper, but his plans did not materialize, and his heir, Alfred H. Huth, authorized the Société des Anciens Textes Français to produce an edition of the text.[1]

The Huth MS., which was copied by a Picard scribe, is incomplete: several leaves have been lost[2] and the latter portion of the *Suite du Merlin* has been omitted. In 1895 Eduard Wechssler found in a fifteenth-century compilation of Arthurian prose romances, MS. B.N. fr. 112, a fragment of the *Suite du Merlin*, the beginning of which overlaps with the end of the Huth MS. and which concludes the series of adventures left unfinished by the latter.[3] It was published subsequently by H. O. Sommer under the title of *Die Abenteuer Gawains, Ywains und Le Morholts mit den drei Jungfrauen.*[4]

In 1945 a new manuscript of the *Suite du Merlin* came to light when a London bookseller offered to the Syndics of the Cambridge University Library a fourteenth-century manuscript purporting to be a 'history of the Grail'.[5] Vinaver examined it on behalf of the Library and found that in reality it contained not only the *Estoire del Saint Graal*, but also the prose *Merlin* and the *Suite du Merlin*.[6] The Library then bought the manuscript, which now bears the number Add. 7071. According to its previous owner, Mr G. Dent, the manuscript was found by his grandfather in an old hide trunk at Ribston Hall, Wetherby, Yorks., together with a number of old deeds and seals relating to the property, some of which go as far back as the twelfth century.[7] Most of the manuscript is the work of a fourteenth-century Anglo-Norman scribe, but folios 269–73, 276 and 335–43 recto were replaced in the fifteenth century by vellum leaves of the same size on which an English scribe copied the corresponding portions of the text. It seems that at one time the manuscript was in the possession of someone acquainted with Malory's works, for on f. 199 recto we find, as Vinaver has pointed out, the following note written in an early sixteenth-century hand: *Ci commence le livre que Sir Thomas Malori chevalier reduce in Engloys et fuist emprente par William Caxton.* On f. 158 recto

---

[1] Mrs Cooper's transcription formed the basis for the G. Paris and J. Ulrich edition (cf. Huth *Merlin*, Introduction, v). It was also used by E. Hucher (see *Le Saint Graal*, Le Mans, 1874–8, I, 335–65).

[2] Folio 1 is missing; one leaf is missing after folio 101 and two after folio 133.

[3] See above, 12, n. 1.   [4] *Beihefte zur ZRPh*, XLVII (1913).

[5] Folios 269r–273r, 276r–276v and 335r–343r have been replaced by fifteenth-century leaves.

[6] *The Estoire del Saint Graal* occupies ff. 1–158b, the prose *Merlin* ff. 159a–202d and the *Suite du Merlin* ff. 202d–343b.   [7] See Vinaver, *Works*, III, 1277–9.

are written, also in an early sixteenth-century hand, the names of Thomas Jachson, Robert Constable and Thomas Ballyns, but it has not been possible to identify them.[1] The Cambridge MS. is of considerable importance for the study of the *Suite du Merlin*, for it continues beyond the point where the Huth MS. breaks off[2] and fills all the lacunae of the latter. Moreover, it includes, after the story of Arthur's coronation, an episode not found in the Huth MS.—an account of Arthur's wars against the rebel kings adapted from the Vulgate *Merlin* continuation.[3] For the portions of the text extant in both MSS., now the one, now the other preserves the better reading.[4]

A further small fragment of the *Suite du Merlin* is preserved in the State Archives of Siena, Italy. It consists of two un-numbered parchment folios written in a thirteenth-century hand. Most of the fragment is well preserved, though in one or two places the writing has become effaced due to the fact that in the seventeenth century it formed the covers of a law court register. It is written mainly in Francien and contains a portion of the *Suite du Merlin* corresponding to pp. 64–72 of the second volume of the Gaston Paris edition. Its interest lies in the fact that it appears to preserve a state of the text closer to the original than do the Huth and Cambridge MSS.[5]

There exist also two non-French versions of the *Suite du Merlin*, Malory's *Tale of King Arthur*[6] and the Spanish *Baladro del Sabio Merlin*. The former begins with the later portion of the *Merlin* proper and includes, like the Cambridge MS., an account of the rebellion of the kings. It is not a literal translation, but a free adaptation: in many places Malory has altered his French source in accordance with his own narrative technique,[7] and has substituted for the ending found in MS. B.N. fr. 112 a conclusion of his own.[8]

Only two early printed editions have survived of the Spanish trans-

---

[1] On f. 343v are some Latin verses with musical annotations.

[2] The Cambridge MS. breaks off at a point corresponding to p. 48 of Sommer's edition of the 112 fragment, with the words *dedenʒ cil piere. Sire, fait il, si vous.*

[3] For details, see below, 31–9.

[4] See Vinaver, *Works*, III, 1278–9, and 'La genèse de la *Suite du Merlin*', *Mélanges... Hoepffner*, 299.

[5] See my article in *R*, LXXXI (1960) 188–98, and for an edition of the fragment, below, 228–41.   [6] Vinaver, *Works*, I, 1–180.

[7] See Vinaver, *Malory*, 29–42; *Works*, I, xlviii–iv, and III, 1265–1359.

[8] See Whitehead, 'On certain episodes in the fourth book of Malory's *Morte Darthur*', *Med. Aev.*, II (1933) 199–216.

lation, *El Baladro del sabio Merlin con sus profecias*, Burgos, 1498, and *El Baladro del sabio Merlin: Primera parte de la Demanda del Sancto Grial*, Sevilla, 1535.[1] The first of these, of which one copy has survived,[2] was known to Gaston Paris who published, in an Appendix to the Huth *Merlin*, extracts from it forwarded to him by Menendez Pelayo,[3] but it is only recently that the text has been made generally available by Pedro Bohigas.[4] The 1535 edition, of which several copies are known to exist,[5] was first brought to the attention of scholars by Otto Klob in 1902.[6] It was reprinted five years later by Bonilla y San Martin.[7]

[1] It appears there existed two further editions of the *Baladro*, one published in Sevilla, 1500 and the other in Toledo, 1515 (see Entwistle, *The Arthurian Legend in the Literatures of the Spanish Peninsula*, London and Toronto, 1925, 153–4). A fragment of the *Merlin* proper has been preserved in MS. 2–G–5 in the Palace Library, Madrid. The fragment, which occupies ff. 282v–296v, was discovered by Otto Klob and published by K. Pietsch: *Spanish Grail Fragments, Modern Philology Monographs* (Chicago, 1924), I, 55–81. The scribe who copied the *Merlin* fragment in MS. 2–G–5 must have known a complete manuscript of the *Suite du Merlin*, for at the point where he breaks off, he announces certain episodes of the *Suite du Merlin*—Arthur's vision, how the *beste glatissant* came to drink at a fountain, how Merlin told Arthur the meaning of his vision and the nature of the *beste glatissant*, and how Merlin revealed to Arthur his parentage: 'Quedan otras muchas cosas de escrevir del libro de Josep e de Merlin por la grand prolixidat que aqui non se escriven. E de commo sonno un suenno el rrey Artus, e esso mismo Merlin. De una bestia que se llamava ladrador, de commo venia a bever a la fuente. E de commo se fallara ende el rrey Artus sin cavallo, e le veniera un su escudero. E de commo veniera ende Merlin e le desposiera el suenno, e que fuera de aquella bestia. E se maravillava el rrey del su dezir. De commo dexiera al rrey cuyo fijo fuera. E en esto estava Merlin en semejança de moço. E de commo le dezia el rrey que era el diablo. E se fue e torno ende commo viejo Adan' (Pietsch, I, 80–1).
[2] This copy, once in the possession of the Marquis de Pidal, Madrid, is now in Oviedo University Library.   [3] Huth *Merlin*, I, lxxxi–xci.
[4] *El Baladro del Sabio Merlin segun el texto de la edicion de Burgos de 1498*, ed. P. Bohigas, 3 vols., Barcelona, 1957, 1961, 1962.
[5] *La Demanda del Sancto Grial. Primera Parte: El Baladro del Sabio Merlin con sus profecias. Segunda Parte: La Demanda del Sancto Grial con los maravillosos fechos de Lanzarote y de Galaz su hijo* (Sevilla, 1535). One copy is in the Palace Library, Madrid, another in the Advocates' Library, Edinburgh, and a third in the Bibliothèque Nationale. A fourth copy of the 1535 *Baladro*, bound up with the 1515 Toledo edition of the *Demanda del Sancto Grial*, is in the British Museum.
[6] Klob, 'Beiträge zur Kenntnis der spanischen und portugiesischen Gral-Litteratur', *ZRPh.*, XXVI (1902) 177–85.
[7] *La Demanda del Sancto Grial... Libros de Caballerias. Primera Parte: Ciclo arturico* (Nueva Biblioteca de Autores Españoles, 6, Madrid, 1907).

The 1498 and 1535 editions are collateral versions: each omits accidentally a portion of the narrative preserved in the other.[1] Both Spanish versions begin their narrative with the prose *Merlin* and are, as far as they follow their French source, a fairly close translation of a manuscript similar to the Huth MS. They conclude the narrative, how-ever, with an expanded account of Merlin's death,[2] and insert additional episodes after Arthur's coronation and in the middle of the Balain story.[3] Gaston Paris and all subsequent critics thought that these incidents derive from a lost French *Conte del Brait*,[4] but as I shall indicate later, it is very likely that the episodes in question are the inventions of a late *remanieur* of the *Suite du Merlin* or of the Spanish compiler.[5]

Like the Vulgate *Merlin* continuation, the *Suite du Merlin* is an account of the early history of Arthur's kingdom. Both presuppose Robert de Boron's prose *Merlin* and take up the narrative from the

[1] Both editions divide the narrative into chapters, but the chapter divisions do not occur at the same point in the two texts. The 1498 edition (*B*) omits after Ch. XIII the equivalent of Ch. LXXXI of the 1535 edition (*D*), after Ch. XXIX, 86, l. 46, it omits the content of *D*, Chs. CCLXII–CCCIII, and after Ch. XXX, 114, l. 503, the equivalent of *D*, Chs. CCCXIV end to CCCXV. These lacunae correspond to Huth *Merlin*, I, 89–90, Huth *Merlin*, II, 1–68 and Huth *Merlin*, II, 96–8. *D*, on the other hand, omits after Ch. CCCXXIII the equivalent of Chs. XXXV, 19, l. 123–XXXVIIbis of *B*, which corresponds to Huth *Merlin*, II, 146–191. In addition *D*, Ch. CCLXI is found in *B* in vol. III, 62, after what corresponds to *D*, Ch. CCCXXIII. There are also some minor differences between the two editions. For the most important of these, see notes to the following sections of Bohigas' edition of *B*: Chs. I, ll. 143–7, 172–90, II, 174–93, XII, 7–10, 14–15, 42, XIII, 1–14, XV, 46–9, 77, XVIII, 67–8, XIX, 7–20, XX, 431, XXII, 7–15, 299, 300–25, XXIV, 307, XXVII, 68–70, XXIX, 178–80, 193, 221–7, XXX, 1–150, 201, XXXI, 5–12, 21–5, XXXII, 246–9, XXXIII, 28, 66–70, XXXVIII, 718–24, 732–75. See also Bohigas' study of the *Baladro* in vol. III, 159–86.

[2] Both Spanish *Baladros* omit the episodes which in the French *Suite du Merlin* follow the reference to Merlin's death, i.e. they omit Huth *Merlin*, II, 198 ff.

[3] In addition, at the point where Merlin tells Arthur about the *beste glatissant* (Huth *Merlin*, I, 160), the *Baladros* alone give an account of the birth of the *beste* adapted from the *Demanda del Sancto Grial*, while earlier on, in the *Merlin* proper, both *Baladros* insert prophecies ultimately derived from Geoffrey of Monmouth's *Historia*. Neither the Huth nor Cambridge MS. contains these prophecies, but they are found, in the same place, in the Didot MS. of the *Merlin* (see *The Didot Perceval*, ed. W. Roach, 6–7, n. 6). For a detailed account of all the additional episodes in the *Baladros*, see Bohigas, 1498 *Baladro*, III, 165 ff.

[4] See Huth *Merlin*, I, lxxv–lxxix.

[5] See below, 51–9, and my article in *R*, LXXXIII (1962) 383–99.

point where the latter leaves off, Arthur's coronation;[1] but while the Vulgate is little more than a chronicle of Arthur's wars against the rebel kings and the Saxons, the *Suite du Merlin* is an Arthurian romance in the proper sense. It relates how, shortly after Arthur's coronation, Lot's wife, the Queen of Orkney, comes to Arthur's court with her four sons, the eldest of whom, Gauvain, is aged ten, and how Arthur, not knowing that the Queen is really his sister, falls in love with her and begets Mordred. After the Queen of Orkney's return to her country Arthur has a frightening vision and the following day, while out hunting, sees the *beste glatissant* and meets Merlin who tells him of his incest, promises to make known to the people that he is Utherpendragon's rightful heir and explains the vision he had as signifying that a child as yet unborn will one day destroy him and his kingdom.

At a court held eight days later at Carduel Ygerne is forced through Merlin's stratagem to reveal Arthur's parentage, and during the feast celebrating this *connissanche*, a squire brings a dead knight to court. The following day Giflet, after being knighted, sets out to avenge the dead knight on Pellinor. Meanwhile, twelve messengers from the emperor of Rome come to demand tribute, but are defied by Arthur. As Giflet was unsuccessful, Arthur secretly leaves court at night to do combat with Pellinor, but his sword breaks in the battle and only Merlin's timely arrival saves him. In order to procure for Arthur a sword that will serve him all his life, Merlin takes him to a lake in the middle of which a hand holds up a sword which a damsel fetches by walking over an invisible bridge.

On his return to court Arthur gives his sister Morgain in marriage to King Urien, and their son Yvain is conceived. After the wedding Arthur goes to Carlion and there one day, while he is at table, a messenger from King Rion comes to demand Arthur's beard, but Arthur refuses this request. When the time approaches that the 'evil child' is to be born, Arthur has all the children born on May-day sent to Logres, but Lot's son, Mordred, escapes him, for the boat bearing him is shipwrecked and Nabur le Desree, in whose country Mordred lands, brings him up together with his son Sagremor. The children collected by Arthur are exposed on the sea in a rudderless boat, but they arrive safely at Amalvi, where they are cared for by King Oriant.

---

[1] The *Suite du Merlin* presupposes not only Arthur's coronation, but assumes also the existence of other events related in the *Merlin*, in particular the birth of Merlin, the latter's relationship to Utherpendragon, the foundation of the Round Table and Arthur's birth.

One day after this King Rion invades Logres and besieges Tarabel. Within three months Arthur's men assemble at court and the day they are to set out to meet King Rion, Balain, a poor Northumbrian knight, comes to court and achieves the adventure of the *espee as estranges renges*, but incurs Arthur's displeasure by killing a damsel in his presence. In order to win back his favour, he captures his enemy, King Rion, with the help of Merlin's advice. But Arthur's war is not yet over: Nero, King Rion's brother, leads Rion's men and is joined by Lot who wishes to avenge his little son Mordred. In the battles many of Arthur's knights distinguish themselves, but none more than Balain. Lot is killed by Pellinor, and his son Gauvain, aged eleven, swears to avenge his father.

About this time, Morgain's son Yvain is born and Merlin becomes acquainted with Morgain who is eager to learn his magic arts, but does not return his love. Arthur entrusts the magic scabbard of his sword to his sister's care, but it soon becomes a bone of contention between them. Balain, after many misadventures, finally comes to King Pellean's castle, where he involuntarily strikes the Dolorous Stroke which inaugurates the marvels of Logres and maims King Pellean who cannot be healed until the coming of Galaad. Then, after further misfortunes, Balain comes within a year of having obtained the *espee as estranges renges* to a castle where he is forced to joust with a knight living on a nearby island. His opponent is no other than his own brother, but neither recognizes the other until both are mortally wounded. After the two brothers have been buried, Merlin does many enchantments on the island, which is henceforth known as the *Isle Merlin* or the *Isle de merveilles*.

On Merlin's return to court, Arthur decides to marry Guenevere, and the latter's father, the king of Carmelide, sends the Round Table to Camalot. On his wedding day Arthur knights Gauvain, now aged eighteen, and Tor, 'li fieus a Arés', who, as Merlin reveals later, is really the son of Pellinor and a *villaine*. During the feast following the wedding, a strange adventure happens at court: a stag followed by a hound and the *damoisele chaceresse*, Niviene, appear; the stag, wounded by the hound, runs off, while two knights seize the hound and the damsel. On Merlin's advice, Gauvain, Tor and Pellinor set off in search of the stag, the hound and the damsel respectively. After various adventures, lasting three days, the three knights return to court, each bringing with him the object of his quest.

Arthur asks Niviene to stay at his court and Merlin soon falls in love with her and teaches her many of his magic arts, but his love is not returned. When Niviene's father recalls her to Northumberland, Merlin accompanies her and is entombed by her on the way. In the meantime Arthur successfully repulses the attack of five kings. Various knights are elected to the Round Table to replace those killed in the battle; Baudemagus, grieved to see Tor given a seat in preference to him, leaves court.

Morgain, who hates Arthur and seeks his death, succeeds in pitting him in battle against her lover Accalon to whom, more than a year ago, she gave Escalibor. Only Niviene's timely arrival, who casts a spell on Accalon, saves Arthur. During the same time Morgain attempts also to murder her husband Urien in his sleep and is only prevented from doing so by her newly knighted son Yvain. Thereupon Arthur banishes her and Yvain from court, but she contrives to steal the magic scabbard once more and casts it into a lake when pursued by Arthur.

Gauvain accompanies Yvain and on the third day they are joined by Le Morholt. The following day they meet three damsels sitting by a fountain, who promise to show them the adventures of the country. The three knights thereupon depart, but promise to meet again at the fountain in a year's time. Meanwhile, Morgain makes a final attempt to kill Arthur by sending him a poisoned cloak, but Niviene, in disguise, warns Arthur of the danger.[1] Gauvain, accompanied by one of the damsels, comes to the *plaine adventureuse*, where he learns of Arcade's cruelty to her lover Pelleas and helps the latter to win his lady's hand. Le Morholt, after a number of adventures, comes to the *Perron du Cerf* where his lady is killed and he himself wounded by a lance that strikes them.[2] Soon he meets Gauvain and both are bewitched by a lady whose love they scorn. Then they come to the *Roche aux Pucelles* onto which they are enticed by the twelve Ladies of the Rock, who keep them captive in a state of enchantment. Yvain, after suffering the same misfortune at the *Perron du Cerf* as Le Morholt, returns at the end of the year to the fountain to await his companions, but learns from a damsel that they are on the *Roche aux Pucelles*. He makes his way there, but is unable to rescue them and after his return to court tells Arthur of their misfortune. The latter, convinced that Merlin alone will be able to help, orders knights to go in quest of him. Tor and Aglant meet Baudemagus from whom they learn that Merlin's last prophecy before his death was that Gaheriet alone would be able to free the captives. After

---

[1] The Huth MS. breaks off at this point.
[2] The Cambridge MS. breaks off at this point.

being knighted, Gaheriet departs from court and after numerous adventures finally comes to the *Roche aux Pucelles*. When Gauvain and Le Morholt have been freed, they are greatly surprised to hear that they have been on the rock for more than a year and a half. Gauvain returns at once to court, and Le Morholt, after a combat with five of Arthur's knights, goes back to Ireland where eight days later he is joined by Gaheriet, who is to stay there until Le Morholt goes to Cornwall to seek tribute.[1]

The narrative, as outlined above, is common to the Huth and Cambridge versions of the *Suite du Merlin* as far as they go, but there is, as I have already indicated above, one important difference between them: whereas in the Huth MS. the account of Arthur's coronation is followed immediately by the initial episode of the *Suite* proper, the arrival of the Queen of Orkney at Arthur's court and the conception of Mordred, in the Cambridge MS. Arthur's coronation is followed first by an account, taken over from the Vulgate *Merlin* continuation, of Arthur's wars against the rebel kings.[2] Neither the 1498 nor the 1535 *Baladro* contain the account of the rebellion, but Malory has a version of it similar to, though considerably shorter than that preserved in the Cambridge MS.[3] Since Malory and the Cambridge MS. differ in certain details, Vinaver originally suggested that both go back to a common source which represents the original form of the *Suite du Merlin*.[4] More recently R. H. Wilson has denied that there was anything in Malory's account of the rebellion which could not be derived from the Cambridge MS.[5] But the mere fact that the text used by Malory may

---

[1] The 112 *Suite* fragment published by Sommer ends at this point.

[2] Cambridge MS., ff. 202d–230a. The Cambridge MS. reproduces the Vulgate account, in a somewhat modified form, up to the point where Galeschin sends a message to his cousin Gauvain (*Vulgate Version*, II, 88–128). Then it gives a brief summary of the main events of the later part of the Vulgate together with some fresh incidents intended to lead up to the beginning of the *Suite* proper: the rebel kings repent and return to their country to fortify their towns against the Saxons. Arthur, Ban and Boors help Leodogan to defeat Rion, after which they return to Logres. A reconciliation between Arthur and the barons takes place and together they drive out the Saxons. Then Ban and Boors return to their respective countries. Galeschin delivers his message and Lot's wife sets out for Arthur's court with her four sons.

[3] Vinaver, *Works*, I, 16–41.

[4] Ibid., III, 1277–80, 1291 n. 36, ll. 1–26, 1292, n. 39, ll. 1–41; Vinaver, 'La genèse de la *Suite du Merlin*', *Mélanges... Hoepffner*, 295–300.

[5] R. H. Wilson, 'The rebellion of the Kings in Malory and in the Cambridge

have been identical in this instance with the Cambridge MS. does not affect the main point at issue. In Vinaver's view the *Suite du Merlin* was originally preceded, as it is in the Cambridge MS., by the *Estoire del Saint Graal*, a prose rendering of Robert de Boron's *Merlin*, and a remodelled account of the Vulgate rebellion section.[1] Wilson, on the other hand, thinks that the *Suite du Merlin* was composed as an entirely independent work, roughly in the form in which we find it in the Huth MS.; the rebellion section of the Cambridge MS. was, in his opinion, a later interpolation. There is, however, strong textual evidence against this last contention.[2]

Wilson's main argument is based on certain contradictions which he finds between the rebellion section and the *Suite* proper. Some of the discrepancies concern only minor details, such as can be found in all prose romances, and it could be argued equally plausibly that they betray the hand of the original author, for an interpolator could have avoided them without much trouble.[3] Others, seemingly of a more fundamental nature, turn out, on closer examination, not to be contradictions at all. Wilson notes, for instance, that 'in the Vulgate portion of the Cambridge MS. Arthur's parentage is made known shortly after his accession, when the kings question his right to the throne and Merlin tells them about Uther and Ygerne. But later, in the *Suite* proper, Merlin makes the revelation as if for the first time, and it is then publicized by Ulfin's charge against Ygerne for concealing the facts.'[4] It can be shown, however, that in reality the two scenes are not mutually exclusive. The barons rebel against Arthur in the first place

---

Suite du Merlin', *UTSE*, XXXI (1952) 13–26 and 'The Cambridge *Suite du Merlin* re-examined', *UTSE*, XXXVI (1957) 41–51.

[1] Vinaver, *Works*, III, 1277–9, and 'La genèse de la *Suite du Merlin*', 295–300.

[2] I first set forth my views on this subject in *UTSE*, XXXIV (1955) 6–17. Wilson's 1957 article is a reply to mine, but his arguments have not convinced me, and I restate above my main reasons for considering the rebellion section to be part of the original version of the *Suite du Merlin*.

[3] See Wilson, *UTSE*, XXXI (1952) 18–19, *UTSE*, XXXVI (1957) 47–9. Similar minor discrepancies are found within the *Suite* proper. For instance at one point Sagremor is described as the son of Nabur (Huth *Merlin*, I, 206), but in a later portion of the narrative he is referred to as the son of the king of Hungary and nephew of the emperor of Constantinople as in the Vulgate *Merlin* continuation (*Die Abenteuer*, 131). For a more detailed discussion of the whole problem, see my article, 'The rebellion of the Kings in the Cambridge MS. of the *Suite du Merlin*', *UTSE*, XXXIV (1955) 6–17.

[4] Wilson, *UTSE*, XXXI (1952) 19.

because they do not believe Merlin's statement that he is Utherpendragon's son.[1] It is true that they finally make peace with him, but they do so for purely strategic reasons and the Cambridge MS. says distinctly that they are still perturbed by the uncertainty as to his origin: *ceo lor en pesoit pur ceo qu'il n'estoient pas certain de lui*.[2] If they are ever to accept Arthur whole-heartedly, they will have to be told again who he is and the final revelation scene in the *Suite du Merlin* is therefore a necessary part of the narrative.

The position with regard to Arthur is similar. He has been informed about his parentage on three different occasions by Merlin;[3] but Merlin's revelations had so little effect that at the beginning of the *Suite* proper he does not recognize Lot's wife as his sister and has an incestuous affair with her.[4] Hence the scenes in the *Suite du Merlin* in which Arthur still appears to be sceptical about Merlin's account of his origin.[5] They fit in well with the earlier scenes in the rebellion section, but are too heavy for the narrative as it stands in the Huth MS. Moreover, contrary to what Wilson suggests, the Cambridge *Suite du Merlin* does not reveal Arthur's parentage 'as if for the first time'. It often refers back to the earlier revelations of Arthur's origin in the rebellion section. Thus when Merlin tells Arthur about his father and mother, he remarks in the Cambridge MS. that he has already told him this once before: 'Jeo te die verraiement que li rois Utherpendragon fu tes peres e t'engendra en Ygraine, la roine, *si com autre foiz le t'ai dit*; mais ele n'estoit pas adonc roine.'[6] The phrase in italics is not in the Huth-*Baladro* version.[7] Similarly, when Ulfin publicizes the charge against Ygerne, the people recall that formerly there was a lively debate on the subject:

Lors lieve une grant noise e une grant fierté en la court, car li pover e li riche qui de ceste chose orent oïe la parole, comencerent tut a parler e dient que Ulfin pooit bien dire voir, *e que autre foiz fu li desbas mult grant e maint grant*

---

[1] Cambridge MS., ff. 203a–204b; *Vulgate Version*, II, 88–91.
[2] Cambridge MS., f. 229b. The remark is not in the Vulgate.
[3] Cambridge MS., ff. 203a–204b; f. 207b; f. 214a–b; *Vulgate Version*, II, 88–91, 96, 106–7.
[4] Huth *Merlin*, I, 147–8.
[5] Huth *Merlin*, I, 153–7, 161–2.
[6] Cambridge MS., f. 234a–b.
[7] Huth *Merlin*, I, 162; Bonilla, 1535 *Baladro*, Ch. CLII, 58a; Bohigas, 1498 *Baladro*, I, 203, ll. 510–12.

mal en deust estre fait, e que la roine est bien digne de mort resceiver, quant ele avoit ensi overé.[1]

The allusion is not in the Huth-*Baladro* version.[2] It is obvious what has happened: Huth and the *Baladro* omitted the allusions to the earlier scenes after the rebellion section had been cut out. The real contradiction lies, in fact, not in the successive revelation scenes, but in Arthur's ignorance of his parentage at the beginning of the *Suite* proper. It is made even more acute, as Wilson has pointed out, by the way in which the Cambridge MS. prepares for the arrival of Lot's wife at Arthur's court: she has heard that Arthur is her brother, but finds it difficult to believe and decides to go to court with her four sons *pur savoir e conoistre ent la verité*.[3] As she is thus anxious to discover her relationship to Arthur, Wilson argues rightly that 'it is preposterous that she should accept his love before finding anything out'.[4] But the reason for this apparent absurdity is simply that the author of the *Suite du Merlin* was anxious to give prominence to the incest theme, even at the price of an inconsistency. In the Vulgate, Mordred's birth is mentioned twice: after Arthur's first victory over the rebel kings, Merlin tells Arthur that Lot has five sons, one of whom, Mordred, was begotten by Arthur when he was a squire in London.[5] Later, when dealing in more detail with Lot's family, the Vulgate redactor explains that Arthur unwittingly committed incest after Utherpendragon's death while the barons were assembled at Carduel to elect a new king.[6] The Cambridge MS. omits both passages and reports the incest at the beginning of the *Suite* proper. If the Cambridge MS. had kept the Vulgate account, all contradiction would have been avoided between the rebellion section and the *Suite* proper. It seems, therefore, that the original author deliberately altered the Vulgate account for artistic reasons: in the Vulgate the incest theme is lost in a mass of other material; in the *Suite du Merlin* it not only serves to motivate and explain Arthur's death,[7] but becomes the starting point of a long sequence of events.[8]

But what is perhaps even more important is that certain incidents and allusions in the *Suite* proper presuppose events related in the re-

---

[1] Cambridge MS., ff. 235d–236a.
[2] Huth *Merlin*, I, 168; Bonilla, 1535 *Baladro*, Ch. CLIV, 59b; Bohigas, 1498 *Baladro*, p. 208, l. 125–p. 209, l. 127.
[3] Cambridge MS., f. 229d.   [4] Wilson, *UTSE*, XXXI (1952) 25.
[5] *Vulgate Version*, II, 96.   [6] Ibid., II, 128–9.
[7] See below, 143–5.   [8] See below, 172–4.

bellion section. According to the *Suite* proper, Leodogan owned the Round Table and gave it to Arthur as a wedding present; in the *Merlin*, the Round Table belongs to Utherpendragon.[1] Only the rebellion section explains this apparent discrepancy: it relates, as does the Vulgate *Merlin* continuation, that after Utherpendragon's death the knights of the Round Table left Logres because of the *desleauté* in that country and went to serve Leodogan.[2]

Similarly, the *Suite du Merlin* introduces Ban as if the reader were already acquainted with him and his affairs. As Merlin and Niviene pass through Benoic, war is raging there. They come to the castle of Trebes, and Helaine, Ban's wife, explains that Claudas does them harm whenever he can. In the Cambridge MS. she adds 'e tuz jors avoms eu guere a lui'.[3] Merlin comforts Helaine by predicting that her son Lancelot will one day overcome Claudas.[4] Now in the rebellion section, Ban and Boors play a considerable rôle. On Merlin's suggestion they do homage to Arthur and help him in his wars. Their own troubles with Claudas are also mentioned. Ban had built a castle on a piece of ground which Claudas claimed as his, but Ban denied the validity of his claim. 'E pur ceo comença entre eus la guere e la haine mult grant e mult mal que dura mult longement, e tant com il vesquirent n'orent pais ensemble.'[5] As Arthur's messengers, Ulfin and Bretel, pass through Ban's land, Claudas has just been defeated by Ban, but the author predicts that Claudas will take revenge later: 'Si en fu Claudas mult enpoveriz e amatiz durement, si se tint tut coies qu'il n'osa riens forfaire en lor tere de grant tens; mais puis le greva il plus que il li, si com vus orrez deviser el liver ça avant.'[6] It looks as if the *Suite du Merlin* has taken up this reference.

Again, Arthur's desire to marry Guenevere is more readily intelligible if we assume that the rebellion section preceded the *Suite du Merlin*. In the latter Arthur explains to Merlin that his barons reproach him for not being married. Merlin, too, counsels him to marry and when he asks Arthur if he has any one in mind, Arthur at once replies that he loves Guenevere. If he cannot have her, he will not marry at all

[1] Huth *Merlin*, II, 61–2; ibid., I, 95–8.
[2] Cambridge MS., ff. 204d–205a and f. 229a; *Vulgate Version*, II, 92.
[3] Cambridge MS., f. 301d.
[4] Huth *Merlin*, II, 142–4; Cambridge MS., ff. 301c–302a.
[5] Cambridge MS., f. 208a. The Vulgate *Merlin* continuation (*Vulgate Version*, II, 98, ll. 14–16) does not say that the wars between Ban and Claudas were continuous.
[6] Cambridge MS., f. 208b–c; see also *Vulgate Version*, II, 98, ll. 38–41.

(*e si jeo ne l'ai, jeo n'averai ja femme*).[1] There is nothing in the *Suite* proper to suggest that Arthur has previously heard of Guenevere, and his prompt reply is startling. The rebellion section explains his reaction. There Merlin has already told Arthur about Guenevere and advised him, shortly after his coronation, to help Leodogan, king of Carmelide, in his war against Rion, partly to prevent Rion from overrunning his own country and partly because he would thus win the hand of Leodogan's beautiful daughter Guenevere.[2] In the Vulgate *Merlin* continuation, Arthur sees Guenevere during the Carmelide expedition, and Leodogan eventually suggests that they should marry.[3] In the Cambridge MS., however, Guenevere's illness prevents Arthur from seeing her during his stay in Carmelide:

E avoit non Guenevere. E pur la grant beauté que li rois oï dire que en lui estoit la veist voluntiers li rois Artus, s'il peust; mais ele estoit malade, si c'onques tant com li rois fu iluc ne la peust veoir, [ne ne] la peust conoistre,[4] dont il fu moult dolenz e coruciez, car volunters se fust de lui acointés pur le grant bien qu'il oï dire de lui.[5]

The author of the *Suite du Merlin* has obviously remodelled the Vulgate account in order to postpone the marriage and prepare for events which occur in the *Suite* proper.[6]

[1] Cambridge MS., f. 280c; Huth *Merlin*, II, 61.

[2] Cambridge MS., f. 205c; *Vulgate Version*, II, 92.

[3] *Vulgate Version*, II, 156–9, 216–9, 299.

[4] The MS. reads: veoir dont il la peust conoistre.

[5] Cambridge MS., f. 229a.

[6] In his 1957 article (43–4), Wilson states that 'The presence of the Round Table at Carmelide, Arthur's interest in Guenevere, and the war against Claudas in Benoic, all very likely are present in the *Suite* because its author had read the related accounts in the *Estoire de Merlin*, which are also reproduced in the rebellion section of Cambridge. But to have read them, he does not need to have written this section. There is no indication that the passages "presuppose" the rebellion section in the sense that the author expected his readers to connect them with it. They occur much later (fifty folios or more), and unlike the passages concerning Arthur's parentage, they include no references to what happened "autrefoiz".' I would point out that the fact that the episodes are separated some 50 folios from the rebellion section is irrelevant. Furthermore, in the account of Claudas' wars there *is* in the Cambridge MS. a reference back to what happened 'formerly' (see above, 35). But most important of all is the fact that without the events in the rebellion section the incidents in the *Suite* lose much of their significance. The author *did* expect the reader to connect the incidents in the *Suite* with the corresponding ones in the rebellion section, and it is only reasonable to assume that he had in fact adapted the rebellion section.

Wilson's further argument that the presence of the rebellion section would

Equally revealing is Arthur's reply to Merlin when the latter, in the shape of a young boy, tells him whose son he is. In the Cambridge MS. he says:

En non Deu! fait li rois, si cil fu mes peres de qui tu paroles, jeo ne puis faillir a estre prodomes; car de li ai jeo tant oï parler qu'il fu si prodomes qu'il ne puist pas issir de li mauvaisse heirs, si merveille ne fust, *e asseʒ autre foiʒ le m'a home dit.* Et certes, si il est bien voirs, si le creroient ja bien a envis li prodome de ceste tere, *ne croire nel voelent. E en ai eu a eus mainte foiʒ mainte grant debat envers les greignors barons de ceste païs e n'en fusse venus a chef, si ne fust une mult grant aventure que me vint; car Merlin, qui tote siet, m'aida a maintenir ma guerre envers eus. Car il ne volent croire que jeo doie estre rois, ne teus com tu dis. Ensi le me dist Merlin autre foiʒ.*[1]

Huth and the *Baladro* have only:

... se mierveilles ne fust. Et ciertes, se il estoit bien voirs, si le creroient ja moult [a] envis li preudomme de cest païs.[2]

The interesting thing is that while the Huth-*Baladro* version omits the obvious allusion to the rebellion section, it still preserves Arthur's remark that the barons would be most unwilling (*moult a envis*) to believe that he is their rightful heir; and this remark is uncalled for unless, in the light of his past experiences, Arthur has reason to assume the worst.[3] Nor can there be any doubt that the passage in the

---

introduce a contradiction into the account of Arthur's marriage is not correct either. In his 1952 article (19) Wilson wrote: 'In the Vulgate, part of Merlin's plan for helping Leodogan is that Arthur should marry the old king's heiress, Guenevere. Yet, according to the *Suite* proper, the marriage is at Arthur's initiative, and Merlin would oppose it because of the future scandal with Lancelot, except that he knows he cannot resist Arthur's love'. Merlin does *not* try, however, to dissuade Arthur from the marriage. All he says when he hears that Arthur loves Guenevere is that if he did not love her so much, he would counsel him to take another wife; and yet, he adds, her beauty will enable him one day to recover his lands when he thinks all is lost. Obviously, the sole purpose of Merlin's remark is to allow the author to make a veiled reference to future events. Arthur does not even understand Merlin: 'Ceo dist il pur Galeheut qui devint ses homes liges e li rendi sa terre la ou il avoit tute gaigné. E tut ceo fist il pur l'amur de Launcelot. Li rois n'entendi pas a ceo que Merlin li dit adonc, car trop estoit obscure. Si avint ele puis tut ensi cum Merlin le devisa, si com ceste estoire le conte qui del Saint Graal est devisé' (Cambridge MS., f. 280c; Huth *Merlin*, II, 61).

[1] Cambridge MS., f. 232b–c.
[2] Huth *Merlin*, I, 156; Bonilla, 1535 *Baladro*, Ch. CXLIX, 55b; Bohigas, 1498 *Baladro*, I, 195, ll. 259–63.
[3] Wilson (*UTSE*, XXXVI, 44–5) remarks that 'a envis' has not only the meaning 'unwillingly', but also 'with difficulty'. It should be noted, however, that

D

Cambridge MS., omitted in the Huth-*Baladro* version, is authentic. Merlin's energetic reply—he tells Arthur he will make the barons certain about this matter so that they will know *de voir* who he is[1]—is more readily intelligible if, as in the Cambridge MS., Arthur has explained at length his troubles with the barons.

There are many other allusions to Arthur's difficulties with the barons, most of which were removed in the Huth-*Baladro* version after the rebellion section had been cut out. When Merlin reveals himself to Arthur he says: 'Sachez que jeo sui Merlin, li bons devins, que taunt mester t'ai eu en mainte bosoigne',[2] but in the Huth-*Baladro* version the reference has been replaced by a general statement: 'Sachés que je sui Merlin, li boins devins, dont tu as tantes fois oï parler.'[3] In the context, both readings are equally possible.

Similarly, when Merlin warns Arthur that Lot is preparing to attack him, he adds in the Cambridge MS. that Lot will be accompanied by many of the barons who were formerly against him:

... que, quant vus irrez a la bataille contre ces gent demain, ausi com les homes le roi Rion, que li rois Loth d'Orquenie vus vendra au devant entre lui e sa compaignie, *a tout grant plenté des barons que autre foiʒ ount esté encontre vus*, quant li autre vus serront au devant.[4]

The allusion could not be plainer and has been omitted in the Huth MS. and the *Baladro*.[5]

This evidence suggests that the author of the *Suite du Merlin*, having reproduced Robert de Boron's *Merlin* in its entirety, summarized some parts of the Vulgate *Merlin* continuation, and then went on with his own composition.[6] A later redactor (the author of the source

---

'unwillingly' is the primary meaning, and that in all the examples cited by Tobler-Lommatzsch the meaning 'with difficulty' is only given when 'unwillingly' does not fit the context. In the present case, however, it makes no difference to my argument whether we translate 'with difficulty' = 'hardly', or 'unwillingly'.

[1] Huth *Merlin*, I, 156; Cambridge MS., f. 232c.

[2] Cambridge MS., f. 234a.

[3] Huth *Merlin*, I, 162; Bonilla, 1535 *Baladro*, Ch. CLII, 58a; Bohigas, 1498 *Baladro*, I, 202, ll. 502–3.

[4] Cambridge MS., f. 255d.

[5] Huth *Merlin*, I, 246; Bonilla, 1535 *Baladro*, Ch. CCXII, 83a; Bohigas, 1498 *Baladro*, II, 33, ll. 326–30.

[6] There are also traces of the Vulgate *Merlin* continuation in the *Suite* proper. See Vetterman, *Die Balen-Dichtungen*, 223–4, 271–5, who noticed, for instance, that the Vulgate was the source of the *Suite*'s account of Arthur's war with Lot and Rion; she might have added that Rion's message to Arthur demanding his

of the Huth MS. and the *Baladro*) realized that the rebellion section was different both in spirit and subject matter from the new narrative, and deliberately left it out. But what the work as a whole may thus have gained in unity of tone, some parts of it lost in consistency and such loose threads as were left in it point to the conclusion that the story of Arthur's wars against the rebel kings formed part of the original composition.

beard was also borrowed from the Vulgate and not from Geoffrey of Monmouth. Other points of contact between the Vulgate *Merlin* continuation and the *Suite* proper have been noticed by Micha, 'Les sources de la Vulgate du Merlin', VII, 1952, 325 n. 33, and 337 n. 50. G. Paris, who also noticed several correspondencies between the two *Merlin* continuations, wrongly dismissed them as mere coincidences (see Huth *Merlin*, I, lxiv–lxviii).

CHAPTER II

The Theories concerning the 'Suite du Merlin'
and the 'pseudo-Robert de Boron' Cycle

THE *Suite du Merlin*, such as I have described it, is neither a complete nor a self-contained work. It is part of a larger whole, but critics are far from unanimous in their views as to the nature and development of the compilation to which it belongs. Gaston Paris, who was the first to deal with the problem, thought that the *Suite du Merlin* was the second part of a trilogy, the first part of which was a prose rendering of Robert de Boron's *Joseph* and *Merlin* (such as is found in the Huth MS. before the *Suite*), and the third a version of the *Queste del Saint Graal*, now lost, followed by an abbreviated redaction, also lost, of the *Mort Artu*. This version of the *Queste* was, in his view, probably older than the Vulgate:

Il est donc probable que la *Queste* attribuée à Gautier Map est un remaniement d'une *Queste* plus ancienne, mise sous le nom de Robert de Boron, qu'a connue l'auteur de *Tristan*, et à laquelle se réfère notre roman, dont elle devait former sinon seule, au moins essentiellement la troisième partie.[1]

Gaston Paris did not consider the *Suite du Merlin* and the *Queste–Mort Artu* as the work of the same author, but assumed that shortly after the composition of Robert de Boron's trilogy, the *Perceval* was replaced by a Galaad *Queste*, and that another redactor then composed the Huth *Suite*, independently of the Vulgate *Merlin* continuation, in order to join the *Joseph* and the *Merlin* to the new *Queste*. The whole was attributed to Robert de Boron and divided into three equal parts, the last of which only had a logical beginning.[2]

In 1887, a year after the publication of the Huth *Merlin*, Gaston Paris was able to substantiate his views in at least one point. In that year Karl von Reinhardstöttner published the first seventy folios of a hitherto virtually unknown text, the Portuguese *Demanda do Santo Graal*, contained in MS. 2594 of the National Library in Vienna, which includes both a version of the *Queste* differing from the Vulgate and an abbreviated redaction of the *Mort Artu*.[3] Gaston Paris found some

---

[1] Huth *Merlin*, I, lix.   [2] Huth *Merlin*, I, lxii–lxix.
[3] *A Historia dos cavalleiros da mesa redonda e da demanda do santo Graal* (Berlin,

interesting links between the Portuguese *Demanda* and the *Suite du Merlin* and concluded that the former represented in foreign dress the missing third part of the Huth compilation:

> On peut donc être assuré que nous possédons dans la version portugaise la troisième partie de la compilation dont le ms. Huth nous a conservé les deux premières.[1]

Gaston Paris proposed to examine in more detail the relationship of the *Suite du Merlin* and the Portuguese *Demanda* when the whole of the latter was published; but Reinhardstöttner did not complete his edition, and it was not until 1944 that the Portuguese *Demanda* was published in its entirety by a Brazilian scholar, Augusto Magne.[2] Another important discovery was made in 1895 by Eduard Wechssler who found large fragments of the French original of the *Demanda Queste* in MSS. B.N. fr. 112 and 343, and in certain manuscripts of the Second Version of the prose *Tristan*, and a small portion of the *Demanda Mort Artu* in one of the MSS. of the compilation of Rusticien de Pise, MS. B.N. fr. 340.[3] Some years later, in 1902 and 1907 respectively, Otto Klob and H. O. Sommer found Spanish versions of the Portuguese *Demanda*, printed in Sevilla, 1535, and Toledo, 1515, preceded by Spanish translations of the *Suite du Merlin*.[4] But the first critic to deal

---

1887). The Vienna MS. is mentioned for the first time by Jos. Mone (*Anzeiger für Kunde der deutschen Vorzeit*, VII. Jahrgang (Karlsruhe, 1838), 551, but he gives no indication of its contents. Later, Ferdinand Wolf referred to it on several occasions: *Über die Lais, Sequenzen und Leiche* (Heidelberg, Leipzig, 1841), 240–2; *Primavera y flor de romances o colecciom de los mas viejos y mas populares romances castellanos publicada con una introduccion y notas* (Berlin, 1856), I, lxxxiv, n. 28; *Studien zur Geschichte der spanischen und portugiesischen Nationalliteratur* (Berlin, 1859), 502–3 n. 2; and especially *Über Raoul de Houdenc und insbesondere seinen Roman Meraugis de Portlesguez*, Denkschriften der kaiserlichen Akademie der *Wissenschaft in Vienna*, Philos.-Hist. Klasse, 14 (Vienna, 1865), 183–94. In the latter work Wolf describes the manuscript, indicates its contents and studies the passages in which Meraugis figures. In his opinion it formed the third part of some redaction of the prose *Lancelot*.

[1] Review of Reinhardstöttner's edition, in *R*, XVI (1887) 585.
[2] Magne, *P. D.* The first volume of a second revised edition by Magne appeared in 1955.
[3] Wechssler, 11–13, 17–18.
[4] See Klob, 'Beiträge zur Kenntnis der spanischen und portugiesischen Gral-Literatur', *ZRPh.*, XXVI (1902) 184–5, and Sommer, 'The *Queste* of the Holy Grail', *R*, XXXVI (1907) 369–402, 543–90. Klob discovered also a fragment of the Spanish *Demanda Mort Artu* in MS. 2–G–5 of the Palace Library, Madrid (ff. 298v–300v). It has been edited by Karl Pietsch: *Spanish Grail Fragments*, I,

with the problem after Gaston Paris was Richard Heinzel, who devoted a section of his treatise *Über die französischen Gralromane*, 1891, to the relationship of the *Suite du Merlin* and the Portuguese *Demanda*. He found a number of discrepancies between them, from which he concluded that the Portuguese *Demanda* had not been preserved in its original form. Unlike Gaston Paris, he did not consider the *Demanda Queste* older than the Vulgate, but thought that both were derived from a common source. Moreover, on account of certain allusions he thought that the 'pseudo-Boron' cycle in its original form began with the *Estoire del Saint Graal* and included a *Conte del Brait* and a prose *Lancelot*, but that a later scribe omitted the last two branches and substituted the *Joseph* for the *Estoire del Saint Graal*.[1]

E. Wechssler, who was the first to have most of the relevant texts at his disposal, went even further. In his 'Habilitationsschrift' and his *Sage vom heiligen Gral*, published in 1895 and 1898 respectively, he put

---

83–9. The 1535 edition of the *Demanda* was reprinted in 1907 by Bonilla together with the 1535 *Baladro*. There are no episodic differences between the 1515 and 1535 editions of the Spanish *Demandas*. On the other hand, the Spanish and Portuguese *Demandas* differ greatly, the Spanish having omitted many episodes which are not only in the Portuguese *Demanda*, but also in the French versions. The question of the relationship of the Spanish and Portuguese *Demandas* has caused much controversy. Some scholars, notably Pietsch, op. cit., I, xvi–xxxvii, and Entwistle, op. cit., 172–4, thought that the Portuguese *Demanda* is a translation from the Spanish. Rodrigues Lapa, *A Demanda do Santo Graal. Prioridade do texto português* (Lisboa, 1930) and C. E. Pickford, 'La priorité de la version portugaise de la *Demanda do Santo Graal*', *Bulletin Hispanique, Annales de la Faculté des Lettres de Bordeaux*, LXIII (1961) 211–16 argued, however, that the Portuguese version is based directly on the French, while the Spanish is a translation from the Portuguese. Bohigas, *Los textos españoles*, 56, 81–94, maintained the theory of Spanish priority, but in his review of Lapa's book, *RFE*, XX (1933) 180–5, accepted the theory of Portuguese priority. More recently, however, Bohigas, 1498 *Baladro* (III, 189–93), suggests that the whole question of the relationship of the two versions needs to be examined afresh. From my own comparison of the Spanish and Portuguese versions with the French texts, it is clear that the Portuguese is on the whole closer to the French than is the Spanish, but there are cases where the Spanish is closer to the French. This means that the Spanish and Portuguese versions are both derived from a text which was nearer to the French than either of them is. But whether this earlier text was written in Spanish or Portuguese is a problem which only a Hispanist can resolve. (For a detailed bibliography of the *Demandas*, see *Los textos españoles*, 24–9.)

[1] Richard Heinzel, *Über die französischen Gralromane*, Denkschriften der kaiserlichen Akademie der Wissenschaft in Vienna, Philos.-Hist. Klasse, XL (Vienna, 1892) 162–71.

forward the view that there existed originally an *Ur-Lancelot-Graal* cycle, which consisted of five branches: an *Estoire del Saint Graal*, the prose *Merlin*, a prose *Lancelot*, a *Queste del Saint Graal* and a *Mort Artu*. Two independent redactors, he contended, subsequently wrote continuations to the *Merlin*, one producing what we now know as the Vulgate *Merlin* continuation, and the other the *Suite du Merlin*. They also revised the other branches and in this way were formed two separate cycles, one of which was attributed in part to Walter Map, and the other wholly to Robert de Boron. The main characteristic of the 'pseudo-Boron' cycle, to which the *Suite du Merlin* belonged, was that it included much prose *Tristan* material: 'Das wesentliche Merkmal, wodurch sich der Pseudorobert vom Pseudomap trennt, ist die Aufnahme Tristans und der andern Hauptpersonen seines Sagenkreises.'[1]

The original 'pseudo-Boron' cycle or *Redaktion A*, consisting of six branches—the *Estoire del Saint Graal*, the *Merlin*, the *Suite du Merlin*, the *Lancelot*, the *Queste del Saint Graal* and the *Mort Artu*—was, Wechssler argued, shortened subsequently by two successive redactors: the first shortened redaction (B) lost the *Lancelot*, while the second (C) lost the *Estoire del Saint Graal*. Moreover, the individual branches of the successive cycles were shortened so as to make the cycles fall into three equal parts.[2] The *Suite du Merlin*, it seems, suffered particularly heavily, for soon after it was written some compiler composed the *Conte del Brait* with extracts from the *Suite du Merlin*, and redactor B, in order to avoid unnecessary repetitions, omitted from the *Suite du Merlin* most of the episodes taken over by the *Conte del Brait*.

In Wechssler's view none of the three redactions have survived in their complete form. The 1498 Spanish *Baladro* was, he thought, a

[1] Wechssler, 5. See also idem, *Die Sage vom heiligen Gral in ihrer Entwicklung bis auf Richard Wagners Parsifal* (Halle, 1898) 125–9.

[2] The first trilogy, redaction B, was in Wechssler's view constituted as follows:

1. *Estoire del Saint Graal*
2. *Merlin* followed by the *Suite du Merlin*
3. *Queste del Saint Graal* followed by the *Mort Artu*.

The second trilogy, redaction C, took on the following form:

1. *Merlin* followed by the beginning of the *Suite du Merlin* (end of vol. 1 of the Gaston Paris edition)
2. Rest of the *Suite du Merlin*
3. *Queste del Saint Graal* followed by the *Mort Artu*.

translation of the greater part of the *Conte del Brait*,[1] while Malory's *Tale of King Arthur*, which contains some proper names and a few details not in the Huth MS., was derived from *Fassung* A of the *Suite du Merlin*.[2] The fragment of the *Suite du Merlin* contained in MS. B.N. fr. 112 belongs to redaction B, while the Huth MS., which has omitted the end of the triple adventures, represents redaction C.[3] Sections of the *Queste del Saint Graal* incorporated into the Second Version of the prose *Tristan* derive from redaction A,[4] while the Portuguese *Demanda* and portions of the *Queste* contained in MSS. B.N. fr. 112 and 343 belong to redaction B.[5] The description of the tournament of Louvezerp found in certain MSS. of the prose *Tristan* and the account of Galaad's conception and Lancelot's madness as found in some of the prose *Tristan* MSS.[6] and in Malory's Books XI and XII are fragments of the 'pseudo-Boron' *Lancelot*.[7] Finally, the Portuguese translation of the *Estoire del Saint Graal* contained in MS. 643 of the Torre do Tombo, Lisbon, may represent the *Estoire* of redaction A.[8]

Gaston Paris who reviewed Wechssler's 'Habilitationsschrift' in 1895 welcomed his work and considered his findings on the whole reasonable:

Je me borne en général au rôle de rapporteur; le contrôle des faits et des idées exigerait des recherches que je ne puis faire actuellement; mais je suis heureux de dire dès aujourd'hui que, sur presque tous les points qu'il aborde, M. Wechssler me semble avoir fait de véritables découvertes et en avoir tiré un parti excellent.[9]

---

[1] Wechssler, 37–51.   [2] Ibid., 22–37.
[3] Ibid., 7–10.   [4] Ibid., 16–18.
[5] Ibid., 10–16.   [6] MS. Brit. Mus. Add. 5474.
[7] Wechssler, 18–21.

[8] Ibid., 14. The Portuguese translation of the *Estoire* bears the following title: *Livro de Josep Abaramatia intetulado a primeira parte da Demanda do Santo Grial*. The manuscript was first described by F. A. de Varnhagen in 1846 (see his *Cancioneirinho de trovas antigas* [Vienna, 1872] 164–9). It was reported lost by Reinhardstöttner (see his Introduction to the Demanda, x), but Jules Cornu informed Wechssler that the manuscript was still in the Torre do Tombo in Lisbon. Later Klob described it in some detail (see 'Beiträge zur Kenntnis der spanischen und portugiesischen Gral-Literatur', art. cit. 170–6). Klob discovered also a Spanish fragment of the *Josep* in MS. 2–G–5 of the Palace Library in Madrid (ff. 252r–282r). See *ZRPh.*, XXVI, 185–8. It has been edited by K. Pietsch (*Spanish Grail Fragments*, I, 1–54).

[9] Gaston Paris, review of *Über die verschiedenen Redaktionen*, in *R*, XXIV (1895) 472–3.

He suggested, however, that Wechssler's theories might well be veri-
fied by an examination of the Huth *Suite du Merlin*.
In a series of articles beginning in 1906, E.
Brugger expounded at
length his own views on the origin of the common source of the
'pseudo-Boron' and 'pseudo-Map' cycles. He accepted the theory of
the three redactions with one reservation: in his view, the original
'pseudo-Boron' cycle, *Redaktion* A, was already in the form of a trilogy,
the *Estoire del Saint Graal* forming the first branch, the prose *Merlin*
followed by the *Suite du Merlin* the second, and the *Lancelot, Queste*
and *Mort Artu* the third. He examined the 1535 edition of the Spanish
translation of the *Suite du Merlin*, which was unknown to Wechssler,
and found that it derived in the main from redaction C, but contained
also some episodes from the *Conte del Brait*, which like Wechssler he
regarded as a collection of excerpts from redaction A of the *Suite*.
Besides what he thought was a Spanish version of the greater part of the
'pseudo-Boron' *Lancelot* he found a smaller fragment, in French, in
the prose *Tristan* MS. B.N. fr. 12599.[1] H. O. Sommer, on the
other hand, while also believing that the 'pseudo-Boron' cycle was
derived from the same source as the Vulgate, maintained, in a number
of publications beginning in 1907, that there was never more than one
redaction of the former, and that it was cast from the outset in the form
of a trilogy, consisting of (1) the *Estoire del Saint Graal* followed by
the *Merlin*, (2) the *Suite du Merlin* and (3) the *Demanda Queste* followed by the *Mort Artu*.[2] But he failed to support his theory by any
solid arguments.[3] Vettermann, writing in 1918, agreed in her turn with
Wechssler's theory of the three redactions.[4] Independently of Brugger

[1] E. Brugger, 'L'Enserrement Merlin. Studien zur Merlinsage', *ZFSL*, XXIX
(1906) 56–140, XXX (1906) 169–239, XXXI (1907) 239–81, XXXIII (1908)
145–94, XXXIV (1909) 99–150, XXXV (1910) 1–55. The Spanish *Lancelot*
referred to by Brugger is the *Lanzarote* of MS. 9611 of the Bibl. Nat. in Madrid.
P. Bohigas Balaguer ('El *Lanzarote* español del manuscrito 9611 de la Biblioteca
Nacional', *RFE*, XII (1925) 60–2) has shown, however, that there is no evidence
for assuming that the Spanish *Lancelot* was part of a 'pseudo-Boron' cycle. Its few
departures from the text of the Vulgate *Lancelot*, and its reference to the 'Chevalier
as Deux Espees', could all be attributed to the Spanish translator who clearly knew
other Arthurian romances besides the *Lancelot*.
[2] Sommer, 'The Queste of the Holy Grail', *R*, XXXVI (1907) 369–462 and
543–90; 'Galaad and Perceval', *MPh.*, V (1907–8) 295–322; 'Zur Kritik der
altfranzösischen Artus-Romane in Prosa: Robert und Helie de Borron', *ZRPh.*,
XXXII (1908) 324–37; Introduction to *Die Abenteuer*, xiv–xxvi.
[3] Cf. Brugger's criticisms of Sommer, *ZFSL*, XXXIV, 99–150.
[4] Vettermann, *Die Balen-Dichtungen, Beihefte zur ZRPh.*, LX (1918) 85–192.

she found that the 1535 *Baladro* contained *Brait* episodes[1] and had in parts a more detailed and correct narrative than the Huth MS., which would suggest that the Spanish translator used in addition to the Huth version an older redaction of the *Suite*, the hypothetical *Fassung* A: 'Der inhaltliche Vergleich ergibt, dass der spanische Balen-Text eine ausführlichere, sowie vor allem folgerichtige und fast lückenlose Erzählung bietet, die auf eine ältere Quelle schliessen lässt als das Huth MS., das die Redaktion C oder jüngere Kürzung darstellt.'[2] She discovered also further traces of redaction A in Malory's *Tale of King Arthur*.

It is difficult to reconcile any of these theories with what is known today about the texts in question. Nearly all these theories are based on the assumption that the *Suite du Merlin* is older than the Vulgate. But since the 'Cambridge MS.' contains a remodelled account of a section of the Vulgate *Merlin*, the Vulgate Cycle is clearly the earlier of the two.[3] And as long ago as 1907 Albert Pauphilet established that the 'pseudo-Boron' *Queste* as represented by MS. B.N. fr. 343 was a *remaniement* of the Vulgate.[4] His conclusions were accepted by most subsequent critics, including F. Lot and J. D. Bruce;[5] only Brugger, Sommer and Vettermann continued to maintain that the Vulgate and 'pseudo-Boron' *Questes* derive from a common *Urqueste*,[6] although Sommer admitted that the *Demanda Mort Artu* was based on the Vulgate.[7] But the theory of the three successive redactions was not abandoned. Bruce[8] regarded the 'pseudo-Boron' cycle as having undergone two successive abridgements which involved 'condensation and omissions, but substantially no rewriting of the parts'.[9] He did not think that the cycle was from the outset in the form of a trilogy, but that in the process of shortening some *remanieur* omitted the *Lancelot* and so reduced the cycle to three approximately equal parts, namely

---

[1] Vettermann, *Die Balen-Dichtungen, Beihefte zur ZRPh.*, LX (1918) 127–35, 175–9.   [2] Ibid., 125.

[3] See above, 31–9. Even before then, Vettermann realized that the *Suite du Merlin* depended on the Vulgate *Merlin* continuation for certain details, but this did not prevent her from subscribing to Wechssler's theory in every other respect (see *Die Balen-Dichtungen*, 223–4, 271–5).

[4] Pauphilet, 'La Queste du Saint Graal du ms. Bibl. Nat. fr. 343', *R*, XXXVI (1907) 591–609.

[5] Lot, *Étude*, 281, 284; Bruce, *Evolution*, I, 459, II, 138–9.

[6] Cf. Brugger, *ZSFL*, XXXIV, 148, n. 55.

[7] Sommer, 'The Queste of the Holy Grail', *R*, XXXVI, 585.

[8] Bruce, *Evolution*, I, 458–79.   [9] Ibid., I, 475, n. 57.

(1) the *Estoire del Saint Graal*, (2) the prose *Merlin* followed by the *Suite du Merlin*, (3) the *Queste* and *Mort Artu*. A second redactor (B), who wished to shorten the cycle still further, omitted from the *Suite* the episodes taken over by the *Conte del Brait*.[1] 'It occurred to him also, as it would seem, that by such omissions and, no doubt, by other abbreviations here and there of less significance, he could make the three groups into which . . . the cycle naturally fell, not merely approximately equal in length, but strictly so. Thus, under the influence of a whim, he established an artificial symmetry between the three parts of the cycle.'[2] A third redactor (C) subsequently omitted the *Estoire* and amputated the other branches accordingly, so that this third re- daction, of which the *Suite du Merlin* section is now represented by the Huth MS., would still consist of three equal parts.[3] The theory of the three successively shortened redactions was also accepted by William J. Entwistle.[4]

An examination of the texts shows however that this theory is no more tenable than the view that the 'pseudo-Boron' compilation is older than or derived from the same source as the Vulgate. As far as the *Queste* is concerned, Wechssler and his followers find no extant trace of 'Redaktion C'. Fragments of 'Redaktion A' are, in their view, to be found in the prose *Tristan Queste*, while the Spanish and Portu- guese *Demanda Queste* represents quite simply 'Redaktion B' in foreign dress. As 'Redaktion B' is an abridgment of 'Redaktion A', this amounts to saying that the *Demanda Queste* is an abridgment of an account preserved in part in the prose *Tristan*. But this is emphatically not the case. There are, no doubt, in the *Demanda*, several important omissions, on the strength of which Wechssler built his theory;[5] but no one comparing it closely with the prose *Tristan Queste* would call it a shortened redaction. While the *Demanda* contains fewer Vulgate

[1] Like Wechssler, Brugger and Vettermann, Bruce considered the *Conte del Brait* consisted of excerpts from the original redaction of the *Suite du Merlin* (see *Evolution*, I, 476, 480–2).

[2] Bruce, *Evolution*, I, 477.

[3] Ibid., I, 477–8.

[4] Entwistle, op. cit., 146–64. He believed also that the episodes peculiar to the Spanish version of the *Suite du Merlin* derive from a lost *Conte du Brait* (see op. cit., 151, 153, 157–63).

[5] *Über die verschiedenen Redaktionen*, 60–1. Wechssler here notes that in the episode where Galaad is invested with the *espee as estranges renges*, the *Demanda* omits an account of the sword and its history (the passage that Pauphilet calls the 'Légende de l'Arbre de Vie'), which the prose *Tristan* preserves.

Queste episodes than does the prose *Tristan*, it contains more adventures of the purely marvellous and chivalric type. Moreover, incidents referred to briefly in the prose *Tristan Queste* are related at length; explanations are given for others; the early history of characters is added; Vulgate episodes which have not been omitted have been altered, often with the result that they are much longer than the corresponding scenes in the *Tristan*. This would suggest that the 'pseudo-Boron' *Queste* developed by a process which is the reverse of the one suggested by Wechssler: instead of being continually shortened, it was gradually transformed and expanded by the addition of fresh material which has a definite purpose in the economy of the work as a whole.[1]

A closer study of the texts of the *Suite du Merlin* points to the same conclusion. In a series of illuminating studies, Vinaver has shown that the *Suite du Merlin* is certainly not the result of 'a process of regression and decay, but of consistent evolution from simpler patterns to more coherent and comprehensive ones'.[2] Further, he has indicated that the details peculiar to Malory's *Tale of King Arthur* are not the vestiges of an older, more authentic *Suite du Merlin*, but Malory's own additions.[3] It can similarly be shown that the so-called original passages discovered by Vettermann in the 1535 *Baladro* are in reality the work of a *remanieur* of the *Suite du Merlin* or of the Spanish translator. The fundamental error underlying her argument is the assumption that a more attractive and more cogent reading is necessarily the original. That a scribe may attempt to eradicate discrepancies in his source does not seem to have occurred to her or to any of the other exponents of Wechssler's theory.[4] Yet this is what frequently happened and some of the differences between the *Baladro* and the Huth MS. require no other explanation. One of the 'original' passages discovered by Vettermann occurs in the account of Balain's combat with Pellean. The Huth MS. says that Balain did not use the magic sword, but another;[5]

---

[1] For a discussion of the relationship of these versions of the *Queste*, see Ch. IV.

[2] Vinaver, *Works*, III, 1268. See also idem, in *Le roman de Balain*, ix–xxii; 'La genèse de la *Suite du Merlin*', 295–300.

[3] Vinaver, in *Le roman de Balain*, x, n. 2; *Works*, III, 1267, n. 4, pp. 1306–7, and note to p. 78, ll. 22–7, p. 1317, note to p. 92, ll. 14–21.

[4] How common this peculiar habit of mind was among the scholars of that time was first pointed out by Vinaver (see his 'Flaubert and the Legend of Saint Julian', *BJRL*, XXXVI, no. 1 (1953) 247, n. 3, and 'A la recherche d'une poétique médiévale', 8–16). Cf. above, 14–15.

[5] Huth *Merlin*, II, 27. The Cambridge MS. has the same reading as the Huth MS.

the *Baladro* alone explains why: he had left the magic sword in the room where he had taken his armour off:

… mas no era aquella la que deciñera a la *donʒella, que essa dexaua el en la camara do se vestiera, que no le quisieron consentir que con dos espadas estuuiesse a la mesa.*[1]

But the sentence in italics, which in Vettermann's view makes the narrative more explicit and must, therefore, belong to the original, is in conflict with an earlier passage common to the Huth MS. and the *Baladro*: at the point where Balain removes his armour, neither the Huth MS. nor the *Baladro* mentions the magic sword; they say only that Balain refused to give up *s'espee* (*su espada*).[2] The author of the *Suite du Merlin* obviously chose not to explain what Balain had done with the magic sword, and there is no reason to assume an omission in the Huth MS.

The account of Balain's departure from the Grail castle is supposed to contain another 'original' passage. After the Dolorous Stroke, the *Baladro* relates that Merlin took Balain to the room where he had left his armour, and then led him out of the Grail castle. The Huth MS. does not mention that Balain went to collect his armour, but later, when Balain has left the castle, the author remarks that he had all his weapons except his sword. In Vettermann's view, this latter remark is unintelligible because of the absence of any reference to Balain collecting his armour: 'Im Huth MS. fehlt dieser Gang zur Rüstung, es wird nur berichtet, dass Merlin den Helden aus der Stadt geleitet, *Merlin* II, 29. Dadurch bleibt die folgende Angabe, dass Balen seine Waffen wieder hat, unverständlich.'[3] But the assumption that the Huth MS. lacks part of the narrative, is again unwarranted. The sentence in the Huth MS. which Vettermann considers unintelligible without the passage in the *Baladro*, is in reality the source of the latter. All the Spanish translator or the *remanieur* of his French source did was to invert the order of events in the Huth MS. and to substitute for the remark that Balain had his armour the phrase that he went to collect it. This becomes clear when we put the two texts side by side:

'Voirs est,' fait Merlins.	'Verdad es,' dixo Merlin;
Ensi s'en vont tout	

---

[1] Bonilla, 1535 *Baladro*, Ch. CCLXXXIII, 109b. Lacuna in Bohigas, 1498 *Baladro*.

[2] Huth *Merlin*, II, 24. Bonilla, 1535 *Baladro*, Ch. CCLXXX, 108b. Lacuna in Bohigas, 1498 *Baladro*. See also Vinaver, 'The Dolorous Stroke', *Med. Aev.*, XXV (1956) 179, including n. 14.   [3] *Die Balen-Dichtungen*, 149.

contreval la ville et tant
qu'il vinrent as portes et
passent outre.
Li chevaliers estoit garnis
d'escut et de lanche et de
toutes ses armeures, qu'il
n'avoit riens laissiet fors que
s'espee qu'il avoit perdue, si
comme li contes l'a ja devisé.

y estonce fueron a la
camara do lo desarmaron
e armose de todas sus
armas, fueras de la vna
espada, que se quebro
como oystes.

Merlins li dist: 'Vous avés
pierdu vostre cheval.' [1]

Y desque salio del castillo
con Merlin,
le dixo: 'Vos perdistes
vuestro cauallo?[2]

The other 'original' passages in the *Baladro* could be disposed of in the same way, but one final example should suffice. At the beginning of the narrative, the damsel whom Balain freed of the magic sword, warned him that if he did not return it to her, he would before the year was up have a combat with a knight who would kill him with the sword and whom he would kill.[3] The knight is no other than Balain's brother and the brothers kill each other as predicted. In the fatal combat Balain effectively uses the magic sword, but is himself slain by it only in the *Baladro* where the two brothers, in the heat of the combat, let their swords drop from exhaustion and later, after a short rest, unintentionally pick up each other's weapons. Vettermann considers the additional passage in the *Baladro* essential for the comprehension of the narrative, since it fulfils the prophecy, and assumes that it must have been omitted by *Redaktor* B or C.[4] But this is certainly not the case. The version of the Huth MS. is perfectly intelligible; the fact that the two brothers kill each other in battle is in itself sufficient to justify the

[1] Huth MS., f. 134b; Huth *Merlin*, II, 29.
[2] Bonilla, 1535 *Baladro*, Ch. CCLXXXV, 111b; Lacuna in Bohigas, 1498 *Baladro*.
[3] Huth *Merlin*, I, 217.
[4] 'Dass die ausgelassene Stelle für das Verständniss und die Komposition der Erzählung von grosser Wichtigkeit ist ... ist dem französischen Bearbeiter nicht zum Bewusstsein gekommen. Jedenfalls haben wir hier ... ein interessantes Beispiel für die Art, in der die Kürzung der ursprünglichen *Suite du Merlin* (Redaktion A) erfolgt ist. Die späteren Bearbeiter begnügten sich nicht nur damit, ihnen entbehrlich scheinende Episoden auszulassen oder ganze Abschnitte zu streichen, ... sondern es wurde auch im einzelnen hier und da ein Satz gestrichen', *Die Balen-Dichtungen*, 149–50).

prophecy. Moreover, a close comparison of the two texts shows that the Huth MS. has not omitted anything, but the Spanish compiler —or the French redactor of his immediate source—more literal-minded than the author of the original *Suite*, altered and expanded the sentence in the Huth MS. which says that the two brothers were so weak from fighting that they could hardly hold their weapons:

Mais il n'avoient orendroit tant de pooir que il s'entreblechaissent gramment; *car il avoient si dou tout perdue la forche et le pooir que a painnes se pueent il soustenir, [ne tenir] lor escus et lour espees.*	mas tanto auian pequeña fuerça, que se no podian ferir e que grande afan sofrian, que ya los escudos e las espadas se les reboluian en las manos, y ellos cayeron en tierra, assi que la espada de Balin cayo ante Balan, e la de Balan ante Balin, e pues que holgaron vn poco tomo cada vno la espada que era mas cerca despues, e començaron su batalla, e Balan dio a Balin tal golpe por encima de la cabeça, que le metio la meytad de la espada por el meollo; despues firieronse tanto anbos, que no auian poder destar ni de se dar golpe que cosa fuesse.
Ne che n'estoit pas grans merveilles.[1]	Y esto no era marauilla.[2]

On several occasions the author of the *Suite du Merlin* refers the reader to the *Conte del Brait*[3] for incidents that he does not relate, and explains that the *Conte del Brait*, written by his companion Maistre Helie, forms a 'branch' of his book, but was separated from it so that the book should not become too big.[4] Now the *Baladro* contains some

[1] Huth *Merlin*, II, 52.

[2] Bonilla, 1535 *Baladro*, Ch. CCXCV, 118a; Lacuna in Bohigas, 1498 *Baladro*.

[3] For references to the *Conte del Brait* in other prose romances, see my article in *R*, LXXXII (1962) 383–99.

[4] Thus in Huth *Merlin*, II, 57–8 (Cambridge MS., f. 279c–d) we find: 'Et je prie a mon signeur Helye, qui a esté mes compains a armes et en jovenche et en viellece, que il pour l'amour de moi et pour moi un poi allegier de cele grant painne prenge a translater, ensi comme je le deviserai, une petite branke qui apartient a mon livre, et sera celle branke apielee li *Contes del Brait*, miervilleusement delitable a oïr et

of the incidents to which the *Suite du Merlin* alludes, but this does not necessarily mean, as most critics contend, that the *Suite du Merlin* has omitted anything or that there existed a *Conte del Brait* to which the Spanish compiler had access.[1] As F. Lot has pointed out, it is a common enough procedure in the prose romances for a redactor to refer to an imaginary *branche* for adventures which he does not wish to relate and for a later *remanieur* then to take up some of these allusions: 'Le plus souvent ce renvoi à la *branche* consacrée à tel ou tel héros est un procédé d'auteur, un moyen de se dispenser de donner des aventures épisodiques dont la masse finirait par l'accabler.'[2] This procedure would explain the allusions in the *Suite du Merlin* and account also for some, if not all, the additional *Baladro* episodes. That the Spanish compiler freely developed the indications he had found in his French source is particularly evident from his account of the events following Merlin's entombment.[3] The *Suite du Merlin* does not relate these, but merely refers to them. It says that after Merlin had been entombed no one ever saw him again, dead or alive, until on Tristan's request Niviene returned to the tomb, *coume la droite ystoire de Tristram le devise, et la branke meesmes del Brait en parole, mais che n'est mie gramment.*[4] Baudemagus who visited Merlin four days after his entombment was the last ever to speak to him and attempted to remove the tombstone, but was told by Merlin that this was impossible:

Ne il ne fu puis nus qui Merlin oïst parler, se ne fu Baudemagus, qui i vint quatre jours aprés chou que Merlins i avoit esté mis, et a chelui point vivoit

a raconter. Ne je ne l'en sevraisse ja se je ne doutaisse que li livres fust trop grans, mais pour chou l'en departirai jou et li envoierai. Et je le connois a si sage et a si soutil que je sai bien qu'il l'avera tost translaté, s'i veult metre un poi de painne. Je li pri qu'il l'i meche.' See also Huth *Merlin*, II, 172–3, 197–8 and *Die Abenteuer*, 55, 105, 106.

[1] See above, 42–6. Although Gaston Paris realized that Maistre Helie was a fictitious character (see his 'Note sur les romans relatifs à Tristan', *R*, XV (1886) 600–2), he too believed that there existed a *Conte del Brait* dealing with Merlin's death (see Huth *Merlin*, I, xxviii–xxxvii and lxxiii–lxxix). Pickford, *Évolution du roman arthurien vers la fin du moyen âge d'après le manuscrit 112 du fonds français de la Bibliothèque Nationale* (Paris, 1960) 71–7, while stating that G. Paris was wrong in assuming that the *Baladro* drew for its material on a lost *Conte del Brait*, makes no attempt to explain the genesis of the episodes supposedly derived from the *Conte del Brait*.

[2] Lot, *Étude*, 13, n. 4. Cf. also 259, including n. 8.

[3] For the sake of completeness I repeat here the content of some pages of my article in *R*, LXXXII (1962) 383–99.

[4] Huth *Merlin*, II, 197–8; Cambridge MS., f. 315d.

encore Merlins, qui parla a lui la ou Baudemagus s'assaoit a la lame lever, car il voloit savoir qui c'estoit qui en (*Camb. MS.* dessus) la lame se plaingnoit si durement. Et lors li dist Merlins: 'Baudemagus, ne te travaille a ceste lame lever, car tu ne hom ne la levera devant que celle meismes la lieve qui chi m'a enserré, ne nule forche ne nul engien n'i averoit mestier, car je sui si fort enserrés et par paroles et par conjuremens que nus ne m'en porroit oster fors cele meesmes qui m'i mist.' [1]

Our author adds that he will not relate this adventure because it is dealt with in the *Conte del Brait*:

De ceste aventure que je vous devise chi ne parole pas chis livres, pour chou que li *contes del Brait* le devise apertement.[2]

Nor will he tell of the marvels that accompanied Merlin's last *brait* before he died:

Et del brait dont je vous parole fu la vois oïe par tout le roiaume de Logres si grans et si lons coume il estoit, et en avinrent moult de mierveilles si coume la branke le devise mot a mot. Mais en cest livre n'en parlerons nous pas pour chou qu'il le devise la, ains vous conterai chou qui nous apartient.[3]

Now the Spanish *Baladro*, while omitting all these references, gives a lengthy account based largely on the indications contained in the *Suite du Merlin*.[4] We are told that three days after Niviene had entombed Merlin, Baudemagus and his damsel arrived and found the tents left behind by Niviene. They spent the night there and the following morning Baudemagus, looking for a church, came to the cave where Merlin was entombed. He entered it and found the iron door leading into the room where the tomb of the two lovers was. While looking at the tomb, he heard a loud cry coming out of it and a voice addressing him: it was Merlin who was lamenting his fate. Baudemagus

---

[1] Huth MS., f. 203a–b; Huth *Merlin*, II, 198. The following are the more important variants from the Cambridge MS., f. 315d: 'Ne il ne fut puis qui l'oït parler Merlin fors Baudemagus qui l'oït ne sai quantes foiz, e Meliadus, li amis a la Dame du Lac. Aprés ceo que Merlin i avoit esté mise e a celui point i avoit esté Meliadus qui parla a lui la ou Baudemagus se seoit a la lame pur savoir s'il puet lever, car il voloit saver qui ceo estoit qui desus la lame se plaignoit si durement...'

[2] Huth *Merlin*, II, 198; Cambridge MS., f. 315d.

[3] Huth MS., f. 203b–c; Huth *Merlin*, II, 198; Cambridge MS., ff. 315d–316a (the latter has several scribal errors in this passage).

[4] Pickford (*Évolution du roman arthurien*, 73) states that the '*Baladro* espagnol forme une traduction, peut-être abrégée, du Huth *Merlin*'. This view is not altogether correct, for although the *Baladro* omits some of the *Suite du Merlin* episodes, it has added several others.

E

attempted to comfort him by assuring him that he would remove the tombstone and free him, but Merlin replied, in words almost identical with those in the *Suite* reference, that this could not be, for the tomb was sealed firmly *por encantamento . . . e por fuerça de palabras.* Only Tristan, as yet a baby, would one day be able to open it:

e Merlin dixo: 'En vano vos trabajays ende en este monumento, ca es cerrado por encantamento tan fuerte, e por fuerça de palabras que son de tal natura, que no ha hombre en el mundo que lo pudiesse abrir. E por esto me conuiene de morir aqui, ca en el mundo no ha honbre mortal que me pudiesse dar vida, y esta campana no se mouera, ansi es encantada, por cauallero que ay venga, hasta que Tristan el buen cauallero venga aqui, que me ha de sacar de aqui.'[1]

Then, in reply to Baudemagus' questions, Merlin explained who Tristan is, predicted the fate of the Round Table and advised Baudemagus not to fight against Cliades, but to seek Le Morholt and afterwards return to court and tell Arthur that his nephew Gauvain can only be freed by Gaheriet whom he should knight at once. Merlin revealed also the name of the woman who entombed him, after which he was silent until shortly before noon when, in a devil's voice, he called on his father to come and fetch him. A great darkness set in, and amid a rising storm and the sound of many evil voices, Merlin died uttering one more loud cry. This last cry, the Spanish compiler adds, was heard at a distance of three leagues and accompanied by a great marvel: the candles went out which the thirteen statues representing the thirteen kings conquered by Arthur held in their hands. And on account of this, the book is called *El Baladro de Merlin, que sera de grado oydo de todos caualleros e honbres buenos que del oyeron fablar.*[2] When Baudemagus, who had fainted with fear, came round, he looked for his damsel, but found her dead *por miedo de los baladros.*[3] He then returned to Arthur's court and told him of Merlin's death.

[1] Bonilla, 1535 *Baladro*, Ch. CCCXXXVI, 151b; Bohigas, 1498 *Baladro*, III, 77, l. 497–507.
[2] Bonilla, 1535 *Baladro*, Ch. CCCXXXVIII, 154a. Bohigas, 1498 *Baladro*, III, 83, l. 718–84, l. 723.
[3] Bonilla, 1535 *Baladro*, Ch. CCCXL, 154b. At this point the 1498 edition differs from that of 1535. According to the former, the damsel was not dead, but Baudemagus told her what had happened. Then, together with her, he went to look for Le Morholt as Merlin had advised him. Le Morholt killed Meliadus and then Baudemagus returned to court, where everyone, and in particular Arthur, was grieved to hear of Merlin's death (Bohigas, 1498 *Baladro*, III, 84–5).

Most of the details of the *Baladro* account can clearly be traced to references in the *Suite du Merlin*: Baudemagus' vain attempt to open Merlin's tomb and Merlin's explanation why only Tristan will be able to do so; the reference to the marvels caused by Merlin's last *brait*. Even the explanation of the title *El Baladro de Merlin*, which according to Vettermann and Brugger proves that the Spanish compiler used the *Conte del Brait*, is in reality based on the passage in the *Suite du Merlin* where the author says that the *Conte del Brait* is so called because of Merlin's last *brait* with which the book deals.[1] The statement that Merlin's death was accompanied by great darkness and that the candles held by the statues went out, has its origin in an earlier passage in the *Suite du Merlin*, where Merlin predicts that this is what would happen on his death.[2] Finally, Merlin's request that Baudemagus should tell Arthur that only Gaheriet could free Gauvain can be traced to an incident in the later portion of the *Suite du Merlin*: Tor and Aglant, in search of Merlin, meet Baudemagus who tells them that Merlin, shortly before dying, revealed to him that only Gaheriet would be able to rescue Gauvain and Le Morholt from the *Roche aux Pucelles*.[3]

Not only is there nothing in the *Baladro* account which cannot be explained with reference to the *Suite du Merlin*, but it is clear why the Spanish compiler should have replaced the allusions in the latter by a lengthy narrative: having decided to terminate the *Suite du Merlin* at a point which to him may have appeared its natural conclusion, Merlin's death, he had to round off the narrative in some suitable way, and for this purpose nothing was more fitting than an eye-witness account of Merlin's last moments. But in order to do this, it was necessary to relate how Baudemagus came to the place where Merlin was entombed, and this accounts for the addition of another series of episodes which the *Baladro* has inserted into the middle of the *Balain* story:[4] we are told

---

[1] Et saichiés que li brais dont maistre Helies fait son livre fu li daerrains brais que Mierlins gieta en la fosse ou il estoit, del grant duel qu'il ot quant il aperchut toutes voies que il estoit livrés a mort par engien de feme et que sens de feme a le sien sens contrebatu (Huth MS., f. 203b; Huth *Merlin*, II, 198; Cambridge MS., f. 315d).

[2] Lors fait maintenant son enchantement, et puis dist au roi: 'Rois, saciés que cist chierge n'esteinderont devant que l'ame [me] departira du cors...' (Huth *Merlin*, I, 264).

[3] *Die Abenteuer*, 88.

[4] The adventures are inserted at a point corresponding to Huth *Merlin*, I, 280, end of first paragraph. The second paragraph on 280 (Or laisse li contes... retorne a sa matiere en tel maniere) has been omitted in both the 1498 and 1535 *Baladro*.

that Baudemagus,[1] who has killed Orian,[2] has been imprisoned by the latter's father, but is freed by a damsel, Orian's sister. After leaving the prison, Baudemagus and the damsel spend the night in a hermitage near the forest of Darnantes, where they learn from Nabor de Gaunes that Merlin and Niviene have departed from court and gone to the forest of Darnantes. Baudemagus thereupon decides to go in search of Merlin, and after encounters with various knights, including Le Morholt, comes to the valley where three days previously Niviene entombed Merlin. Then the *Baladro* continues with the rest of Balain's adventures.

Baudemagus' adventures are, of course, out of place at this point, for neither he nor Merlin and Niviene leave Arthur's court until later. But it is probable that they were misplaced in the common source of the two extant editions, and that originally the Spanish compiler inserted them at the point where Baudemagus, grieved that Tor was elected to the Round Table in preference to him, leaves Arthur's court. Baudemagus certainly appears to refer to this incident, for when asked by a knight who he is, he replies:

Sabed que yo soy vn cauallero de la corte del rey Artur, pero no soy de los de la Tabla Redonda, e sali aca nueuamente por buscar aventuras.[3]

---

[1] Bonilla, 1535 *Baladro*, Chs. CCXLI–CCLXI; Bohigas, 1498 *Baladro*, II, 64, l. 68–86, l. 46. Baudemagus' adventures are preceded by another episode not in the French *Suite du Merlin*: after Arthur has beheaded Ebron li felon *porque el dixera de Morgayna su hermana*, his widow comes to him and begs him to let her keep her lands and to knight her son, Breus sans pitié, which Arthur does (Bonilla, 1535 *Baladro*, Chs. CCXXXIX–CCXL; Bohigas, 1498 *Baladro*, II, 62, l. 1–64, l. 67. There can be no doubt that this episode was intended to form a sequel to the incident in the *Suite du Merlin* where, on account of Morgain's accusations, Arthur beheaded one of her lovers (Huth *Merlin*, I, 265–72). There is hence no need to assume that it derives from some other source.

[2] The 1498 and 1535 editions differ here. According to the former Urien was Ebron's father, and it was in Urien's castle that Baudemagus was imprisoned for having killed Urien's son (see Bohigas, 1498 *Baladro*, II, 64, ll. 68–85). But unless Urien had two sons, which the text does not say, there is a contradiction here, for earlier in the narrative, both the 1498 and 1535 editions state that Arthur killed Ebron (see above, 56, n. 1). According to the 1535 edition, on the other hand, Baudemagus killed Orian and was imprisoned in the castle belonging to Orian's father (Bonilla, Ch. CCXLI, 93b).

[3] Bonilla, 1535 *Baladro*, Ch. CCXLVII, 96a; Bohigas, 1498 *Baladro*, II, 71, ll. 312–15. The point where Baudemagus leaves court would be particularly suitable for the interpolation, for the French *Suite du Merlin* says there that it will not relate any of Baudemagus' adventures as 'mes sires Helyes' deals with

The series of episodes which the *Baladro* inserts after Arthur's coronation[1] can be accounted for in a similar way. The purpose of these incidents was to serve as a transition between the end of the prose *Merlin* and the beginning of the *Suite* proper. The story begins with a brief statement that the barons were dissatisfied because they knew nothing about Arthur's origin. Merlin, who was aware of this, told Blaise of his intention to go to Logres to reveal Arthur's parentage to the barons. The night before his departure he had a vision of his death and of the birth of Lancelot. When Blaise heard of this, he was afraid that he might not be able to complete the *Historia del Sancto Grial* before Merlin's death, but Merlin assured him that if he would join him in Logres in eight weeks' time, he would provide him with the rest of the material for his book. All this obviously links up with the prose *Merlin* and looks forward to the *Suite du Merlin*: the reference to the barons' discontent follows on naturally from the mystery surrounding Arthur's birth in the *Merlin* and motivates and prepares for the scenes in the *Suite du Merlin* where Merlin reveals Arthur's parentage; Blaise's discussion with Merlin about the book he is writing forms a sequel to their earlier conversation in the *Merlin*, where Merlin asks Blaise to write the 'History of the Grail' under his dictation.[2] At the same time, the appointment which Merlin makes with Blaise to meet him in Logres prepares for the incident in the *Suite du Merlin* where

---

them in the *Brait*: 'Atant se met Baudemagus a la voie entre lui et son escuier. Mais de chose ne d'aventure qui li avenist en toute la voie ne parole (Camb. MS. *adds* point) mes livres (Camb. MS. *adds* ici), car mes sires Helyes mes compains a empris (Camb. MS. *adds* sue merci) sa matiere a recorder chi et (Camb. MS. *omits* sa matiere .. et) a translater encontre celle partie pour un poi alegier de ma painne, si n'est mie ceste partie dessevree de mon livre pour chou que elle n'en soit, mais pour chou que mes livres en soit mieudres et ma painne un poi allegié (*instead of* partie pour un poi alegier... et ma painne Camb. MS. *reads*: partie deslecee de mon liver, pur ceo que mes livres en soit meudres e ma painne un poi allegié). Et sachent tout cil qui l'ystoire dou Saint Graal voelent oïr et escouter (et escouter *not in* Camb. MS.) qu'il n'avront ja le livre entirement s'il n'ont par dallés les grans contes de ceste branke (Camb. MS. *adds*: qui est apellé le branche du Brait qui est la plus bele branche e) la plus delitable a escouter qui soit en tout le livre...' (Huth MS., f. 192d; Huth *Merlin*, II, 172–3; Camb. MS., f. 309b). The portion of the *Suite du Merlin* where Baudemagus leaves court, has been preserved in Spanish only in the 1498 *Baladro*, and as we should expect, the statement that the author will not relate Baudemagus' adventures has been omitted (see Bohigas, 1498 *Baladro*, III, 44).

[1] Bonilla, 1535 *Baladro*, Chs. CXXXVII–CXLII; Bohigas, 1498 *Baladro*, I, 182, l. 44–187, l. 193.   [2] Huth *Merlin*, I, 46–8.

Merlin sees Blaise and tells him that he has now thought of a possible ending for his book.[1]

Both Brugger and Vettermann have of course noticed that the whole of this addition in the *Baladro* fits its context extremely well, and in particular that Merlin's conversation with Blaise motivates and explains their subsequent meeting in the *Suite du Merlin*. But in their view this means that the section must have figured in the original redaction of the *Suite du Merlin* and was subsequently omitted by redactor B or C: 'Der Umstand, dass die zweite Stelle im Huth MS.—wie in der *Demanda*[2]—auf das früher von Merlin in Northumberland gegebene Versprechen Bezug nimmt, zeigt, dass ursprünglich auch die erste Episode, Merlins Besuch bei Blaise, zu dieser Version gehört hat, später aber weggefallen ist. Die Auslassung fällt entweder dem Redakter B, dem Verfasser der älteren Kürzung, oder dem für die jüngere Kürzung verantwortlichen Redaktor C zur Last.'[3]

Their argument would be of some weight if we did not know that later redactors frequently added episodes in order to elucidate obscure references.[4] Nor is their contention valid that the prediction of Lancelot's birth and future greatness is out of place anywhere except in a cycle which, like *Redaktion* A of the 'pseudo-Boron', included the *Lancelot* proper:[5] the fact that Lancelot is mentioned later on in the *Suite du Merlin* and plays a part in the *Demanda Queste* and *Mort Artu* is sufficient to justify the reference. But what matters most is the fact that the *Suite du Merlin* began originally, as do the Cambridge MS. and Malory's *Tale of King Arthur*, with an account of the barons' rebellion against Arthur. This can only mean that the episodes inserted in the *Baladro* after the end of the *Merlin* proper are not authentic and were added by the Spanish compiler in order to bridge the gap between the *Merlin* and the *Suite* proper created by the omission of the rebellion section.[6]

---

[1] Huth *Merlin*, I, 232–3.

[2] I.e. the *Baladro*.

[3] *Die Balen-Dichtungen*, 177. See also Brugger, *ZFSL*, XXXIV, 123–6.

[4] See above, 15.

[5] *Die Balen-Dichtungen*, 178–9.

[6] In 1925 Bohigas, *Los textos españoles* (40–52) supported the traditional view that the French *Suite du Merlin* omitted the episodes peculiar to the Spanish *Baladros* and that these episodes derive from a lost *Conte del Brait*. More recently (see his 1498 *Baladro*, III, 173–9, 189) he admitted that the so-called *Brait* episodes are simply a development of references in the French *Suite du Merlin*, but argued that it was not the Spanish *translator* who added the *Brait* episodes, but a later *editor*

If, then, we reject, as indeed we must, the theory of the three successively shortened redactions of the so-called 'pseudo-Boron' cycle,[1] the whole problem of development and structure of the compilation to which the *Suite du Merlin* belongs has to be examined afresh in the light of the now available textual evidence.

---

of the Spanish *Baladro* who happened to find a French manuscript to which they had been added by a man anxious to fulfil the forecasts of the *Suite du Merlin*. I agree of course that the episodes peculiar to the Spanish versions need not have been invented by the Spanish translator, but could have been the work of a French *remanieur* of the *Suite du Merlin*. But I see no reason for assuming that the episodes were added to the Spanish *Baladro* only at a later date. The fact that some of the *Brait* episodes are in the wrong place both in the 1498 and 1535 editions (Bohigas, III, 169–70) does not necessarily mean, as Bohigas suggests, that they are the work of a late editor: an editor would probably have taken care to place the episodes in a logical place. The incidents were no doubt misplaced by the common source of the 1498 and 1535 editions and were related in their proper order in the original version of the *Baladro* (see above, 56, including n. 3). It would seem, therefore, that either the Spanish translator found the *Brait* episodes in the French manuscript of the *Suite du Merlin* which he translated, or invented them when he was translating the *Suite du Merlin* into Spanish.

[1] Bohigas also rejects the theory of the three shortened redactions (Bohigas, 1498 *Baladro*, III, 138–43, 162).

CHAPTER III

The Continuation of the 'Suite du Merlin'

IN order to discover the nature of the *Suite* compilation it may be useful to examine first its redactional indications. At several points the author of the *Suite du Merlin* states that his work is part of a *livre* divided into three equal parts. Thus at the point where Balain sets out in quest of the invisible knight who has wounded his companion, we find the following:[1]

Et sacent tuit cil qui l'estoire mon signeur de Borron[2] vauront oïr come il devise son livre en trois parties,[3] l'une partie aussi grant[4] comme l'autre: la premiere aussi grande come la seconde, et la seconde aussi grant coume la tierche. Et la premiere partie[5] fenist il au commenchement de ceste queste, et la seconde el commenchement dou Graal, et la tierche fenist il apriés la mort de Lanscelot, a chelui point meisme qu'il devise de la mort le roi March. Et cest[e]

---

[1] Huth MS., f. 123c–d; Huth *Merlin*, I, 280; *Le roman de Balain*, 47; Cambridge MS., f. 264a. The 1498 and 1535 *Baladros* both omit this passage (see above 55), but it is clear that the ultimate French source of the 1498 and 1535 *Baladros* was a text which, like the Huth and Cambridge MSS., divided the whole compilation into three parts, the second of which began at the same point as in the Huth and Cambridge MSS. For in an earlier passage, which corresponds to the First Part (Huth *Merlin*, I, 253; Cambridge MS., f. 257c; Bonilla, 1535 *Baladro*, Ch. CCXVIII, 85a; Bohigas, 1498 *Baladro*, II, 39), all four texts state alike that Balain and his brother will kill each other in the Second Part of the book (Huth *Merlin*: 'Car de cele espee ne se combati il onques devant le jour que il fu mis ou camp contre Balaan son frere, si qu'il ocist par mesconissance son frere de cele espee, et ses freres le rochist de cele meismes, *si comme Robers de Borron le contera ja avant a la seconde partie de son livre*'; 1535 *Baladro*: 'Ca de aquella nunca firio hasta el dia que entro en canpo con Baalan su hermano e lo mato por desconocimiento. E otrosi fizo Baalan en el con su misma espada, *como adelante os lo contara el Segundo libro del santo Grial*'). Now this announcement is in fact fulfilled in the various texts in what, according to the divisions indicated in the Huth and Cambridge MSS., is the Second Part (Huth *Merlin*, II, 56; Cambridge MS., f. 279b; 1535 *Baladro*, Chs. CCXCVII–CCXCVIII, 119–20. The account is not in the 1498 *Baladro*, for the latter omits everything contained in Huth *Merlin*, II, 1–68).

[2] Cambridge MS.: a mon seignor Robert de Beron.

[3] Cambridge MS.: en. iiii. parties e est l'un ausi.

[4] Cambridge MS.: omits 'grant'.

[5] Cambridge MS.: premiere partie se mist el commencement de la Queste du Graal e la tierce finist il.

chose amentoit en la fin dou[1] premier livre, pour chou que [se][2] l'*Estoire dou Graal* estoit corrompue par auchuns translatours qui aprés lui venissent,[3] tout li sage houme qui meteroient lour entente a oïr et a escouter porroient par ceste parole savoir se elle[4] lour estoit baillie entiere ou corrumpue, et connisteroient bien combien il i faurroit.[5] Puis qu'il a ore ensi devisé l'assenement de son livre, il retorne a sa matiere en tel maniere.

This passage is extremely important not only because it refers to the tripartition of the book and supplies its title—*l'Estoire dou Graal*—but also because it gives some indications of what each part was supposed to contain. The first part, the *Suite du Merlin* says, ends *au commenchement de ceste queste*, that is at the beginning of Balain's quest for the invisible knight. The third part, we are told, begins *el commenchement dou Graal*, that is at the beginning of the *Queste* proper, and ends *apriés la mort de Lanscelot, a chelui point meisme qu'il devise de la mort le roi March*. The fact that it ends after Lancelot's and Mark's death suggests that it included a version of the *Mort Artu*, but not the one familiar from the Vulgate Cycle, for the latter does not relate Mark's death.

As regards the second part, the *Suite du Merlin* indicates that it begins at the point where Balain sets out in quest of the invisible knight and ends at the beginning of the *Queste* proper. But what preceded the *Queste del Saint Graal*? If we were to believe the colophon of the Huth MS., only the remainder of the narrative contained in this MS.:

Si laisse ore a tant li contes a parler et de l[a] dame et del roi et de toute la vie Merlin, et devisera d'une autre matiere qui parole dou Graal, pour chou que c'est li commenchemens de cest livre.[6]

But as Gaston Paris already realized, the Huth scribe has deliberately cut short the triple adventures of Gauvain, Yvain and Le Morholt, and the colophon, which is neither in the 112 fragment nor in the Cambridge MS., must be considered spurious. It is certain that the second part included no work comparable to the *Lancelot* proper, for at several points the author of the *Suite du Merlin* says that the *grant ystoire de Lanscelot* has been excluded from his 'book', not because its subject matter is irrelevant, but because it would make the middle

[1] Cambridge MS.: ceste chose rementoit il en la fine de son premier livre.

[2] Cambridge MS.: pur ceo si l'Estoire du Graal.

[3] Cambridge MS.: venissent e tout.

[4] Cambridge MS.: qui lor entente i mettroient en l'oïr e en l'escouter purroient savoir par ceste parole si l'estoire soit baillie enterine.

[5] Cambridge MS.: e conoistroit combien il lor en faudroit. E puis qu'il.

[6] Huth *Merlin*, II, 254.

portion of the 'book' three times as big as the other two.[1] But it is equally clear that that portion contained some material which bridged the gap between the extant texts of the *Suite* and the *Queste*, and so provided a transition between the two works. There are in the extant *Suite du Merlin* MSS. numerous allusions to the *Queste* and the coming of Galaad who will achieve the adventures of the Grail;[2] but shortly before the *Suite du Merlin* breaks off, we are told that Galaad is not yet *conceu ne engendrés, ne ne sera encore en piece*.[3] Another of the Grail knights, Perceval, is similarly represented as not yet *engenrés ne nés*,[4] and the *Suite du Merlin* announces that it will deal later with *la vie de Perceval*.[5] Lancelot, who is to be Galaad's father, *n'a pas encore deus ans d'aage*,[6] while Baudemagus, who appears in the *Queste* as a venerable king, is towards the end of the *Suite* described as *a bons chevaliers et biaus et de jovene aage*,[7] not yet sufficiently distinguished to merit a seat at the Round Table. Similarly Gauvain, who is represented in the

---

[1] Et cel anelet li avoit douné la Damoisiele del Lac, si coume la *grant hystore de Lanscelot* l[e] devise, cele meisme ystoire qui doit estre departie de mon livre, ne mie pour chou qu'il (*Camb. MS.* qu'ele) n'i apartiegne et que elle n'en soit traite, mais pour chou qu'il covient que les trois parties de mon livre soient ingaus, l'une aussi grant coume l'autre, et se je ajoustaisse cele grant ystore la moi[ene] partie de mon livre fust au tresble plus grant que les autres deus. Pour chou me couvient il laissier celle grant ystoire (*Camb. MS. omits* la moiene ... ystoire) qui devise les oevres de Lanscelot et la naissance, et voel deviser (*Camb. MS.* que devise l'estoire de la naissance trop i averoit a conter, mais a deviser) les neuf lignies des Nascions (*Camb. MS.* Nasciens), tout ensi coume il apartient a la *Haute Escriture* (*Camb. MS. Estoire) del Saint Graal*, ne n'i conterai ja chose que je ne doie, ains dirai mains assés que je ne truis escrit en l'ystoire dou latin (Huth MS., f. 145c; Huth *Merlin*, II, 57; *Le roman de Balain*, 112; Cambridge MS., f. 279c). The 1535 *Baladro* has the same reference to the omission of the *Lancelot*: (Ch. CCXCIX, 120a): 'E aquel anillo le dio la donzella del Lago, assi como la historia de Lançarote lo deuisa; aquella historia deue ser auida e partida de mi libro, no porque le no pertenesca e no sea dende sacada, mas porque todas partes de mi libro sean yguales, la vna tan grande como la otra, e si juntassen aquella tan grande historia que dize de los hechos de Lançarote, e de su nacencia, e de los nueuos linajes de nacion, assi como lo deuisa la alta historia del santo Grial; e no dire cosa que no deua, ante dire menos asas que no es escrito en la grande estoria de latin; y el libro torna en su razon.' (Lacuna in the 1498 *Baladro*.)

[2] See Huth *Merlin*, II, 66.   [3] *Die Abenteuer*, 74.

[4] Huth *Merlin*, I, 160; see also ibid., I, 258.   [5] Ibid., II, 228.

[6] Ibid., II, 66; see also ibid., II, 143.

[7] Ibid., II, 169. At the end of the *Suite du Merlin* Baudemagus can have been little more than about 35. Yvain, who is born at the time when Baudemagus is 17 (Huth *Merlin*, I, 266), is *ja chevaliers nouviaus* (Huth *Merlin*, II, 168) at the point where Baudemagus, grieved that he has not been elected to the Round Table,

Queste as a hardened sinner, is at the end of the *Suite du Merlin* still the *millour jovenchiel* in Arthur's court.[1] Yvain, too, is little more than a *chevaliers nouviaus*[2] when the *Suite du Merlin* breaks off, and Arthur himself is *jovenes durement et sains et haitiés*.[3] Other characters who will appear in the *Queste*, such as Lionel, Hector and Boors, are not mentioned.[4] In fact, although Merlin predicts that Arthur will reign a long time,[5] by the end of the *Suite du Merlin* not more than twenty-four years can have elapsed since his coronation[6] and his kingdom is still, as it were, in its infancy. A considerable stretch of narrative was therefore required to avoid a gap in the sequence of events.

But this is not all. There are also in the *Suite du Merlin* many allusions to future events not to be found in any of its known versions. The final incident in the *Suite du Merlin*, for instance, far from rounding off the narrative, really looks forward to an account of Le Morholt's combat with Tristan, for we are told that Gaheriet, a month after rescuing Gauvain and Le Morholt from the *Roche aux Pucelles*, went to Ireland *devers le Morholt*,[7] where he stayed until Le Morholt went to Cornwall to seek tribute, 'as the story will tell later':

Et n'[y] ot pas demouré huit jours quant Gaheriet vint. Et le Morholt luy fist moult grant joye et le fist demorer avec lui tant qu'il ala en Cornoaille querir

---

leaves Arthur's court (Huth *Merlin*, II, 169–173). This means that only some 16–18 years have so far elapsed since Baudemagus was first mentioned. The rest of the events related in the *Suite du Merlin* occupy about another two years: shortly after Baudemagus' departure from court, Yvain is banished from court, and Gauvain, who accompanies his cousin, comes after several adventures to the *Roche aux Pucelles* where, together with the Morholt, he spends *plus d'un an et demy* (*Die Abenteuer*, 130) in captivity before being rescued by Gaheriet.

[1] Huth *Merlin*, II, 169. Gauvain is 11 shortly before Yvain's birth (Huth *Merlin*, I, 262), and as the events following Yvain's birth occupy some 18–20 years, Gauvain would at the end of the *Suite du Merlin* be about 30.

[2] Huth *Merlin*, II, 168.   [3] Ibid., II, 187.

[4] Hector is mentioned once in an allusion to a later event (Huth *Merlin*, II, 228), which is not related in the extant part of the *Suite*.

[5] See Huth *Merlin*, II, 158.

[6] This can be worked out as follows: at the beginning of the *Suite* proper Gauvain is 10, and shortly before Yvain's birth he is 11; from Yvain's birth until the end of the *Suite du Merlin* another 18–20 years elapse (see above, 62, n. 7). In all therefore the *Suite* proper occupies 19–21 years. The events related in the rebellion section stretch over a period of three years, for Arthur, who was crowned at 15, is 18 shortly after the beginning of the *Suite* proper (Cambridge MS., f. 236d. The Huth *Merlin*, I, 172, which omits the rebellion section, says here that Arthur was 15).   [7] *Die Abenteuer*, 131.

le treu; et se combatit a messire Tristan qui playe mortele lui fist, ainsi que ly comptes devisera.[1]

Now I have recently noticed that one of the manuscripts of the prose *Tristan*, MS. B.N. fr. 12599, compiled in the second half of the thirteenth century by an Italian scribe named Oddo,[2] contains a series of connected episodes which, although they do not join on to the end of the triple adventures of Gauvain, Yvain and Le Morholt, seem to supply a portion of the missing section of the *Suite du Merlin*.[3] The same series of episodes, beginning at a slightly earlier point in the narrative, is found also in a late fifteenth-century manuscript, MS. B.N. fr. 112, where they are inserted into the prose *Lancelot*.[4] In this manuscript the adventures have been somewhat adapted to their new context; in MS. B.N. fr. 12599—the older and more authentic of the two—they have nothing to do with what precedes or follows. But in both fragments the narrative is substantially the same.[5] The 112 fragment begins with an account of Gaheriet's slaying of his mother, the Queen of Orkney.[6] Then both MSS. relate how Gaheriet's brothers attempted to avenge their mother's death.[7] In MS. B.N. fr. 12599 this is followed by a reference to Arthur's conquest of Gaul and of Lancelot's banishment from court,[8] while in MS. B.N. fr. 112 both stories are given in full as in the prose *Lancelot*.[9] After this both manuscripts give identically remodelled accounts of Lancelot's madness, adapted from the prose *Lancelot* and expanded through the addition of fresh incidents, including an account of how Erec in his quest of Lancelot comes to the *Chastel as Dis Chevaliers* where he stays three months until Gauvain arrives and takes his place as *seigneur* of the castle. Hector after searching for Lancelot for four years finds him one day by a fountain, but Lancelot escapes from him and Hector who falls ill out of grief remains in a hermitage for four years, with Erec as his sole companion. Meanwhile five years after being banished from court Lancelot arrives at Corbenic where a year later he is healed at the

---

[1] *Die Abenteuer*, 134. It is at this point that the 112 fragment breaks off.

[2] The name Oddo is found at the bottom of ff. 63r and 71r.

[3] MS. B.N. fr. 12599, ff. 221d–268d.

[4] MS. B.N. fr. 112, *Livre* III, ff. 214c–220b, 240a–272b.

[5] For an edition of the 112–12599 fragments based on MS. 112, see *La Folie Lancelot*, ed. Bogdanow, *Beihefte zur ZRPh.*, no. 109, 1965.

[6] *La Folie Lancelot*, 1–6 (not in 12599).

[7] Ibid., 6–20.

[8] Ibid., 20–21.

[9] MS. B.N. fr. 112, *Livre* III, ff. 220c–240a.

passing of the Grail and then goes to live on the *Isle de Joie*. There follows an account of how Gauvain after being in the *Chastel as Dis Chevaliers* for more than six years is freed by Lamorat the year that Lancelot goes to live on the *Isle de Joie*. Shortly afterwards Gauvain slays Drian and Lamorat. Agloval, after seeking Lancelot for more than six years, comes one day to his mother's castle and takes Perceval to Arthur's court to be knighted. Perceval later leaves the court to go in quest of Lancelot and has a combat with Gaheriet on the island where Perceval's sister has been living since their mother's death in the hope of finding a knight willing to avenge on Gauvain the deaths of her father, Pellinor, and her brothers, Lamorat and Drian. Shortly before Perceval's arrival at Arthur's court, Erec after a number of adventures, including an encounter with the Lait Hardi, meets the Lady of the Lake's messenger who tells him of Lancelot's recovery. On hearing the good news Hector is immediately restored to health and leaves the hermitage. After meeting Lionel, Hector comes to the island where Perceval's sister lives and is forced to stay there until Gauvain arrives, whom he has to face in single combat. Boors, about to be executed by the people of the Chastel d'Agut, is rescued by Erec.[1] Here the 12599 fragment breaks off with the announcement of a tournament to be held at Camalot *devant trois jors la Pentecoste*,[2] but MS. B.N. fr. 112 continues the narrative, relating how Gaheriet after his battle with Perceval on the *isle a la seur Perceval* becomes the prisoner of the damsel who had led Perceval to the island and is taken to the *Isle de Joie* where he has an unsuccessful combat with Lancelot.[3] In the meantime Perceval comes to Beau Repaire and helps the damsel living there to defeat Clamadam and Aguigeron—an adaptation of the Blanchefleur episode in Chrétien's *Perceval*.[4] There follow now in MS. B.N. fr. 112 episodes which are part of the prose *Tristan*: Perceval's arrival at Joieuse Garde and his journey to Cornwall where he frees Tristan from Mark's prison.[5] After Perceval's return to Logres, there are, however, in MS. B.N. fr. 112 two further episodes which may well be part of the *Suite du Merlin*—Perceval's encounter with Sagremor and the Lait Hardi, and Perceval's meeting with Pellean, the Maimed King,

---

[1] *La Folie Lancelot*, 22–135.

[2] The next portion of MS. B.N. fr. 12599 contains among other things a very peculiar version of the *Queste*, which it is impossible at the present moment to identify (see Löseth, *Analyse*, §§ 291a and 299a).

[3] *La Folie Lancelot*, 136–40.   [4] Ibid., pp. 141–7.

[5] Löseth, *Analyse*, §§ 314–18; MS. B.N. fr. 112, *Livre* III, ff. 275c–281c.

who is fishing in a boat.[1] Then follows an account of Perceval's encounter with Hector and Lancelot's return to court, copied without changes from the prose *Lancelot*.[2] As I shall indicate later, the 'second part' of the *Suite du Merlin* compilation was concluded by some such account, but it is probable that the Vulgate account would have been remodelled, for there are many discrepancies between it and the earlier episodes of the 12599–112 fragment.[3] Löseth, who summarized this section of MS. B.N. fr. 12599, did not identify it beyond saying that some of the adventures were taken from the prose *Lancelot*, while others were found in a different form in the prose *Tristan*.[4] Pickford too did not realize the connexion between the 12599–112 fragment and the *Suite du Merlin* and assumed that the episodes involving Erec were part of a *Roman d'Erec* added to the prose *Tristan* at the end of the thirteenth century.[5] There is abundant evidence, however, to show that the whole of the 12599–112 fragment is part of the *Suite du Merlin*.

In the first place, the fragment contains the same redactional indications as the *Suite du Merlin*. Like the latter, it claims (wrongly of course) the authorship of Robert de Boron. At the point where the *damoiselle laide* is described, the redactor says:

Et por ce que l'en ne dout que li contes ne die verité de lui, missire Roberz de Borron aferme que il vit a [O]ssenfort el tresor de l'ablaie de Saint Vincent une figure d'argent que li roi Artus fist faire a sun vivant en la semblance de cele damoiselle et la lessa a [O]ssenefort, por ce que cil qui aprés lui vendroient l'i veissent. Et misire Roberz l'i vit, et encore l'i puet l'en veoir …[6]

The *Suite du Merlin* frequently uses the title *Estoire dou Graal* or *Haute Escriture del Saint Graal* to describe the whole of the com-

---

[1] *La Folie Lancelot*, 148–53. The latter episode is modelled on Tristan and Yseut's meeting with the Maimed King in the prose *Tristan* (see Löseth, *Analyse*, § 331).

[2] MS. B.N. fr. 112, *Livre* III, ff. 282c–285c.

[3] For a list of the discrepancies, see my Introduction to the *Folie Lancelot*, p. xix, n. 32.

[4] Löseth, *Analyse*, 191, n. 2. In fairness to Löseth, it should be pointed out that it was virtually impossible for him to realize that the 12599–112 fragment belongs to the *Suite du Merlin*, for the portion of the *Suite du Merlin* which most links up with this fragment, the triple adventures of Gauvain, Yvain and Le Morholt in MS. B.N. fr. 112, was not published until 1913.

[5] *Erec, roman arthurien en prose*, ed. C. E. Pickford (Geneve: Droz; Paris: Minard; 1959) 16–17. Cf. Pickford, *Évolution*, 30–1, 53–5.

[6] MS. B.N. fr. 12599, f. 268b; cf. *La Folie Lancelot*, 134, ll. 129–35.

pilation, as in the passage quoted at the beginning of this chapter.[1] Now this title occurs also in the 12599 fragment. Lancelot, we are told, performed many marvels during his *desverie*, 'as the story of the Holy Grail tells':

Et quant il fu fors de [Ca]maalot et il comença a regarder la cité et il li souvint des granz joies et de[l] grant bien qu'il i avoit e[u] par tantes foiz, et or estoit a ce menez que celle qu'i[l] amoit plus que soi meemes s'estoit del tout a lui corrocié en tiel maniere qu'il'[n']en cuidoit ja mes recouvrer, il en ot si grant duel qu'il en oissi fors del sens et [del] memoire qu'il ne savoit onques qu'il feisoit ne ou il aloit ne qu'il disoit. *Et la meemes ou il estoit en si grant desverie fist il mainte merveille que li contes del Saint Graal ramentoit.* Mes avant conte une autre chose que nos n'en poem laissier que nostre estoire n'en fust corrumpue.[2]

The *merveille* referred to are Lancelot's defence of his benefactor Bliant against two knights who attack him, and the killing of a giant at Corbenic; both incidents occur in a later portion of the fragment.[3]

Equally significant is the fact that like the *Suite du Merlin* our fragment states clearly that the *Queste del Saint Graal* forms an integral part of the composition. In announcing that Gauvain will slay Erec in the *Queste* and that Hector will later accuse Gauvain of treason for this, 12599 says *si com cist livres le devise apertemant del Saint Graal.*[4] Elsewhere the redactor explains that he cannot give more details about Lancelot's madness because there is too much to say about the Quest of the Grail:

Mes or leisse li contes a parler d'els tout et retorne a Lancelot por conter coment il fu delivrés de cele forsenerie. Et sachiez que misire Roberz de Borron fait savoir por verité a touz cels qui cest conte liront que de ceste forsenerie qui a Lancelot avint par tel maniere com vos avez oï, conte la droite estoire del la[t]in assez greingnors merveiles que li franceis ne devise, quar il ne puet mie tant demorer sor ceste chose com il voxist, *por ce que trop a a conter de la Queste del Saint Graal.*[5]

Finally, as has already been indicated, the author of the *Suite du Merlin* speaks of his 'book' as being divided into three equal parts[6] and refers the reader to the *Conte del Brait* for incidents that he does not

---

[1] See above, p. 61. For similar references, see Huth *Merlin*, II, 57, 61, 137.

[2] *La Folie Lancelot*, 21, ll. 920–30; not in 112.

[3] Ibid., 40–1, 62–3.

[4] *La Folie Lancelot*, 53, ll. 276–7; not in MS. 112. See below, 127.

[5] MS. B.N. fr. 12599, ff. 242c–d; cf. *La Folie Lancelot*, 60, ll. 579–87.

[6] See above, 61.

relate in order to keep the three parts of the book of equal length.[1] The 12599–112 fragment includes a similar reference to the tripartition of the work and the *Conte del Brait*. In referring to Lancelot's madness, the redactor says:

> Mes qui parfitement vodra oïr les merveilles de ceste forsenerie, si voie l'estoire de[l] Brait, quar ilec porra il trover apertement toutes le[s] choses que misire Roberz lesse [a] conter en sun livre por ce que li troi livre soient tuit d'un grant, quar por autre chose ne fu translatee d'autre part l'estoire del Brait, fors por ce que l'en i meist les choses qui en ceste livre seroient obliees a metre.[2]

But perhaps of even greater significance than the redactional indications is the fact that the 12599–112 fragment consists largely of the sort of incidents one would expect to find in the missing part of the *Suite du Merlin*. The episodes related cover some sixteen years of Arthur's reign and include incidents necessary for a smooth transition from the *Suite du Merlin* to the *Queste del Saint Graal*. Some of them, for instance, involve characters who, while playing an important part in the *Queste*, were represented in the *Suite du Merlin* as not yet born or else as children. Thus the *Suite* announces Perceval's birth, but breaks off before dealing with it.[3] Now the 12599–112 fragment includes an account of *la vie de Percheval*. This account, though adapted not directly from the prose *Lancelot*, but from the First Version of the prose *Tristan*,[4] clearly anticipates the *Queste* and Perceval's rôle in it. We are told that Agloval,[5] after seeking Lancelot for six years, comes one day to the tower where his mother lived with Perceval. The latter, who has never before seen a knight, is fascinated by his brother's armour and anxious to become a knight too. One morning while all are still asleep, he sets off for Arthur's court, but his mother, distraught with grief, sends Agloval after him to bring him back. As soon as she sees him again her heart fails for joy, and Perceval, thinking that his mother has only fainted, sets off again. He is soon joined by Agloval and together they go to Carduel, where Perceval is knighted by King Arthur. While Perceval is sitting at the *table des chevaliers moins prisiés*, a miracle takes place: a damsel who has never before spoken, addresses him as *sergent Jhesu Crist, virge chevalier et nect* and bids him to sit at the Round Table to the right of the *Siege Perilleux* for he is

---

[1] See above, 51.
[2] MS. B.N. fr. 12599, f. 242d; cf. *La Folie Lancelot*, 60, ll. 587–93.
[3] See above, 62.   [4] See below, 84.
[5] *La Folie Lancelot*, 82–100.

digne d'estre un des plus souverains chevaliers de la Queste del Saint Graal.[1] She tells him also that the knight who will end the adventures of Logres will sit in the *Siege Perilleux* and that Boors will be to his left:

Perceval, en ceste siege qui est apellez li Sieges Perilleux s'aserra li bonneureux [chevalier] qui metra a fin les aventures del roiaume de Logres et vos seroiz a sa destre, por ce que vos li resemblerés de virginité. Et a senestre sera Boorz. Et bien savront encor cil en cest ostol le senefiance de ceste chose.[2]

Perceval would have stayed at court a long time, but one day at the beginning of winter he learns from a fool that Keu and Mordred have been mocking him because he has not yet struck a single blow. Feeling ashamed, he leaves court secretly, accompanied only by a squire and determined not to return until he has news of Lancelot. Perceval's subsequent adventures are not based on the prose *Tristan* but link up with the rest of the narrative.

Equally important are the incidents centring on Galaad and Lancelot. The *Suite du Merlin* announces the coming of Galaad, but does not deal with his birth. And indeed, it could not have done so, for at the point where it breaks off, Lancelot, who is to be Galaad's father, is a small child.[3] Furthermore, the theme of Lancelot's love for Guenevere, which plays a considerable part in the *Queste* and *Mort Artu*, has only been vaguely referred to in a veiled prophecy made by Merlin shortly before Arthur's marriage.[4] Now the 12599–112 fragment presupposes Galaad's birth and has episodes which bring in the child Galaad and foreshadow Lancelot's failure in the *Queste* by showing how his sinful love for Guenevere could only bring him humiliation. Again, the compiler did not invent these episodes, but adapted them from the prose *Lancelot*, choosing incidents which already in the latter prepare for the *Queste*—the adventures centring upon Lancelot's third madness.[5] When after Arthur's return from Gaul[6] King Pelles' daughter hears of the feast which Arthur is going to hold at Whitsuntide, she decides to take her small son Galaad to court, *por ce que la chose de Galaaȝ fust veraiment seue a cort.*[7] Lancelot, who one night during the feast mistakes King Pelles' daughter for Guenevere, is banished from court and

---

[1] MS. B.N. fr. 12599, f. 253c; cf. *La Folie Lancelot*, 91, ll. 411–12.

[2] MS. B.N. fr. 12599, f. 253d; cf. *La Folie Lancelot*, 91, ll. 429–33.

[3] See above, 62.　　　　　　　[4] See Huth *Merlin*, II, 61.

[5] *Vulgate Version*, V, 378–83, 393–404. Our author has remodelled and expanded the Vulgate account.

[6] *La Folie Lancelot*, 21–4, 36–46, 55–71.

[7] Ibid., 21, ll. 906–7.

F

goes out of his mind with grief. After wandering for several months through the countryside, barefoot and in rags, and completely unrecognizable, Lancelot is welcomed by Bliant with whom he stays.[1] Two years later, hearing the sound of hunters, he leaves to join in the chase of a wild boar and kills it after being wounded by it. Bliant's dwarf, who has been following Lancelot, arrives on the scene shortly afterwards and Lancelot follows him to a nearby hermitage where he is recognized by two former knights. Then, one night after his wounds have been healed, Lancelot leaves the hermitage while all are asleep and wanders through the woods spending much time by a fountain with some shepherds who shear his head and take his clothes from him. In this state he is found asleep by Erec and Hector, but Lancelot, who does not recognize his brother, flees from him and wanders on until he comes to Corbenic five years after the beginning of his madness. No one at first sees in him Galaad's father, but six months later, on Christmas day, he is recognized by Lamorat who tells King Pelles. The latter then has Lancelot bound hand and foot and taken into the *palais aventureux*, where he is healed by the passing of the Grail. After his recovery, Lancelot goes to live on the *Isle de Joie* with King Pelles' daughter and their son Galaad, aged six. In the Vulgate four years later Hector and Perceval find Lancelot and assure him that the Queen desires his return to Camalot. Lancelot takes leave of King Pelles and his daughter and returns to court, taking Galaad with him, who is to be brought up in a convent near Camalot, of which King Pelles' sister is the abbess. The year that Galaad is eighteen, a hermit bids King Arthur to hold a great feast at Whitsuntide, for the knight who is to end the adventures of the Grail will come to court that day and occupy the *Siege Perilleux*. The 12599–112 fragment follows up the account of Lancelot's life on the *Isle de Joie* with adventures which are not in the Vulgate, mostly centring on the theme of the quest of Lancelot, but unfortunately breaks off before dealing with Lancelot's return to court. There can be no doubt, however, that it would have ended with some such account, based on the Vulgate, but remodelled in order to fit in with the revised versions of the earlier episodes. It is essential to bring Lancelot back to court before the beginning of the *Queste*, and, in fact, the 12599–112 fragment says that Lancelot stayed on the island for ten years and four months, implying thereby that after that period one of the knights in quest of Lancelot would find him and take him back to

---

[1] For a close comparison of the Vulgate account with the Post-Vulgate, see *La Folie Lancelot*, notes to Chs. IV and VI.

court, while Galaad would, as in the Vulgate, remain in a convent until he was old enough to begin the quest of the Grail.[1]

The episodes interwoven with the Lancelot adventures are likewise a necessary part of the composition. Most of them are further incidents foreshadowed in the *Suite du Merlin* and without which the latter is incomplete. Thus the *Suite du Merlin* announces adventures involving King Oriant's son, the Lait Hardi, whose name was originally Acanor:

> ... Et estoit li chastiaus et biaus et bien seans, et en estoit sires uns rois qui avoit esté paiiens lonc tans, mais il estoit de nouviel crestiiens, et moult amoit Nostre Signeur et doutoit, et avoit eut de fame siue un fil tout de nouviel, si apieloit l'enfant Acanor, mais puis fu ses nons cangiés en la court le roi Artus, et pour chou qu'il n'estoit mie biaus chevaliers, mais noirs et harlés a la samblance de son pere, et estoit si preus et si hardis que nus plus, ore l'apielerent il par tout le Lait Hardi. *Et de lui parole li contes moult de fies la ou il se traist de la Queste dou Graal et devant.*[2]

Now the 12599–112 fragment includes some adventures of the Lait Hardi.[3] When Erec, in search of the knight whose dwarf has struck him, comes to the forest of Aledon, he sees the Lait Hardi carrying off a damsel who refuses to become his until he has overcome the first three knights he encounters. The Lait Hardi has the worst of the battle, but is delighted when he discovers Erec's name, *car Erec estoit de son lignage*,[4] and gladly sets the damsel free. He tells Erec that the knight whom he pursues is Montenart de l'Isle Reposte, who has wrongfully seized Arthur's castle, Roche Haulte, where in three days' time he is to do battle with Sagremor. On Erec's request, the Lait Hardi goes to Hector who lies ill in a hermitage out of grief for Lancelot's madness, and stays with him until Erec returns with the news of Lancelot's recovery, which restores Hector to health. The Lait Hardi, Erec, Hector and Boors then ride for eight days without finding any adventures; they separate, and when Hector and Erec meet the Lait Hardi again he is being shamefully pursued by the inhabitants of a certain castle. Soon the three companions are joined by Lionel, but they do not remain together long, as four knights may not ride together.[5]

An even more important link is the story of Gaheriet. When in the

---

[1] See above, 70.   [2] Huth *Merlin*, I, 209.

[3] The name Lait Hardi is first found in a list of knights in Chrétien's *Erec* (line 1677). The prose *Tristan* includes the Lait Hardi among the knights who swore to set out on the quest of the Grail, but does not relate any of his adventures.

[4] MS. B.N. fr. 12599, f. 258a; cf. *La Folie Lancelot*, 104, l. 146.

[5] *La Folie Lancelot*, 101–20.

Suite du Merlin Gaheriet is knighted, a damsel from the *Isle aux Fees* sends him a *chapelet de roses* which a fool interprets as signifying that a glorious career lies ahead of Gaheriet and that he would surpass all the knights of the Round Table except two if it were not for his mother's untimely death of which he will be the cause:

'... Sachés [says the fool] que tout ainsi comme la rose est plus prisee que toutes autres flours, aussi sera Gaheriet plus prisiés de chevalerie et de cortoisie que tous ceulx qui huy ont receu l'ordre de chevalerie, et la ou leurs proesses fauldront au grant besoing, la recouvrera Gaheriet et fornira par sa bonté ce qu'il leur conviendra a laisser par leur mauvaistié...' Et lors dist a Gaheriet: 'Tu passasses de bonté et de valeur tous lez compaignons de la Table Ronde fors seulement deus, se ne fust la mort de ta mere que tu hasteras par ton pechié, et ce sera la chose qui plus abaissera ton pris.'[1]

Now the 12599–112 fragment fulfils the prophecy and describes how Gaheriet brought about his mother's death through sin and misfortune (*pechié*).[2] One day, at the beginning of winter, the news is brought to Arthur's court of Lamorat's latest victory at a tournament. Those who are well disposed to Pellinor's lineage are delighted, but Gaheriet is deeply grieved, not out of spite or envy, but because he knows that Lamorat loves *charnellement* his mother, the Queen of Orkney. To avenge this shame he sets out the next day for his mother's castle Rethename, where he expects to find Lamorat. He arrives early in the morning when all are still asleep, and as mischance would have it, no one wakes up as he passes through the *grant sale*. The door leading into his mother's room is open. Daylight has already broken as he enters and he sees Lamorat lying beside her. Overcome with sorrow, he stands and watches them sleeping, and when he beholds Lamorat's beauty and remembers his knightly valour, he cannot bring himself to kill him. But his mother, he reflects, ought to be punished,

pour ce qu'elle a fait honte a ses enfans premierement et aprés a tout son autre lignage.[3]

He then draws his sword, and although his mother wakes up at that very moment, he strikes her down, *si com pechié et mesaventure luy faisoit faire*:

Maiz Gaheriet qui tout estoit desveez de ire et de maltalent, ne luy seufre pas, ains la fiert de l'espee trenchant, si com pechié et mesaventure luy faisoit

[1] MS. B.N. fr. 112, *Livre* II, f. 45c–d; *Die Abenteuer*, 93.
[2] *La Folie Lancelot*, 1–20.   [3] Ibid. 3, ll. 94–5, not in 12599.

faire, si durement qu'il luy fait la teste voler plus d'une lance loing de luy. Et le corps s'estent en my le lit.[1]

As soon as Gaheriet realizes the horror of his crime, he becomes distraught with grief and falls ill, and when his brother Guerrehez finds him at a forester's and asks him how he came to kill their mother, all he can say is:

Frere, ensint m'est mescheu. [Ge] m'en sui honiz en cors et en ame, et tant en ai fet que ge n'arai ja mes honor en leu ou ge viengne*. Et par ce vodroie ge bien que mescheance ou mesaventure m'avenist si grant que l'en feist autant de moi com ge fis de lui, si que mi frere fussent delivré de moi.[2]

The people of the castle of Rethename, afraid that King Arthur might hold them responsible for the Queen's death, sent her body to Camalot. When Gauvain and his brothers see what Gaheriet has done, they promise to take vengeance, and Agravain, who hates Gaheriet, leads the others on. Now in the *Suite du Merlin* there are a number of episodes which show how Agravain began to hate his younger brother Gaheriet. When Tor and Aglant deliver Merlin's message from which it appears that Gaheriet, as yet a squire, is destined to free Gauvain from the *Roche aux Pucelles*, Agravain is full of envy. He asks his uncle to knight him first, but when Arthur is about to gird on his sword, a fool who until that day had not uttered a single word, bids Arthur knight Gaheriet before all his brothers,

car certes il est si digne chose qu'il doit bien ceans tant avoir d'onneur.[3]

Arthur, who sees in this a *miracle et demoustrance de Nostre Seigneur*,[4] obeys the fool despite Agravain's remonstrations, and from now on Agravain hates his brother mortally:

Einsi commença Agravains a penser traïson et desloyauté vers son frere qui estoit bonne chose et simple, ne nul mal ne pensoit vers luy, ne ne pensast en nulle maniere.[5]

When Gaheriet leaves court, Agravain, after changing his armour so that he should not be recognized, follows his brother, ready to attack him at the first opportunity. Twice he is unhorsed by Gaheriet,

[1] *La Folie Lancelot*, 3, ll. 106–10, not in 12599.
[2] MS. B.N. fr. 12599 ,f. 222a; cf. *La Folie Lancelot*, 7, ll. 262–6; *12599 has *viengna*.
[3] *Die Abenteuer*, 91.
[4] Ibid., 91. [5] Ibid., 98–9.

although on the second occasion the latter is *lassé et travaillié et san-glant*[1] from a previous combat. Agravain's hatred now knows no restraint, and as he confided earlier to his squire, he would kill his brother if he could:

'Or me dictes, fait ly escuiers, et s'il vous cheoit ore si bien que vous venissiés au dessus de luy en bataille, qu'en feriés vous?' 'Tous li siecles, fait Agravains, ne le garantiroit que je ne ly couppasse le chief, car je ne poy onques nul home du monde autant haïr comme je fais luy.'[2]

The Vulgate Cycle, of course, has already represented Agravain as the most proud and arrogant of his brothers, but nowhere did it—or for that matter the prose *Tristan*—suggest that he hated Gaheriet. The 12599–112 fragment presents Agravain in the same light as does the *Suite du Merlin*. Whereas Gauvain wishes to avenge his mother's death because he sincerely feels it his duty to do so, Agravain is moved only by feelings of hatred for his brother. When he hears of his mother's death, he is far from displeased, not because he does not care for her, but because he hopes that Gaheriet would have to pay dearly for this:

Mez qui que fust iriés de ceste aventure, Agravains n'en estoit pas moult corrociés, non mie pour ce qu'il n'aymast sa mere de trop grant amour, mez il haioit Gaheriet de si grant haine qu'il vouloit bien qu'il se fust tant mesfait, pour ce qu'il en acuillist la haine du roy et de ses freres, que messire Gauvain et le roy l'en feissent morir a dueil et a vilté. En tel maniere fut liés et doulens Agravains de la mort sa mere...[3]

He constantly urges Gauvain to carry out his design, and when later the brothers find Hector who has taken Gaheriet under his protection, Agravain challenges them and attacks Gaheriet the first:

Et quant il furent remonté et il orent pris lor glaives et lor escuz, il s'adreccent cele part ou il voient Gaheriet. *Et Agrevains tout primers, qui haoit Gaheriet de lonc tens*, li lese corre tant com il puet de cheval treire et le fiert si durement del glaive agu et trenchant qu'il le perce l'escu et le hauberc et li fait en mi le piz plaie grant et merveilleuse...[4]

The remark that Agravain hated his brother *de lonc tens* seems to be a clear reference back to the earlier scenes in the *Suite du Merlin*. Throughout the battle, Agravain and Mordred have the most odious

---

[1] *Die Abenteuer*, 113.
[2] Ibid., 102; MS. B.N. fr. 112, *Livre* II, f. 48b.
[3] *La Folie Lancelot*, 6, ll. 224–30, not in 12599.
[4] MS. B.N. fr. 12599, f. 223b; cf. *La Folie Lancelot*, 10, ll. 409–14.

part and twice Agravain would have beheaded Gaheriet if he had not been prevented first by Hector and then by Lamorat who arrives on the scene just as Gaheriet's fate seems sealed. And whereas Gauvain readily gives up his original intention once Lamorat has reasoned with him, and expresses the hope that his brother will do better another time, Agravain and Mordred forgive Gaheriet only grudgingly and because they have no alternative:

Et quant li autre frere oent que missire Gauvain le velt einsint et il voient qu'il s'i consent, il s'i acordent molt a enviz, quar il voxissent [mieux] la mort Gaheriet que la vie, non mie por ce qu'il se fust de rienz meffet vers els, si de celui meffait n'estoit. Mes il le haoent trop mortelment por le grant biens qu'il veoent en lui et por la grant chevallerie et por ce qu'il veoent que greignor renomee corroit de lui et loing et pres que d'els ne fessoit. Por ceste chose le haoient il plus mortelment que ge ne vos porroie dire. Et neporquant quant il virent que missire Gauvains s'acordoit a la pes, il s'i acorderent molt corroccié et molt doulent de ce qu'il n'avoient Gaheriet occis, quar adonc n'amassent il autant nulle autre mort com la soe.[1]

There can be little doubt that the man who wrote this episode had the *Suite du Merlin* in mind and deliberately made his portrayal of Agravain's character fit in with the earlier scenes. Indeed, it is perhaps not too much to assume that when the author of the *Suite du Merlin* described how first Agravain became hostile to his brother Gaheriet, he already knew that at a later point in the narrative he would give Agravain the same unpleasant rôle.

Perhaps the most striking example of a sequence of episodes fore-shadowed in the *Suite du Merlin* is the motivation of the feud between Gauvain and Pellinor's lineage.[2] After King Arthur had been told that a child born on May-Day will cause his death and destroy Logres, he has all the children born that day assembled at Camalot and put in a rudderless boat. Arthur's brother-in-law, King Lot, sends his child too, and although the infant escapes by a lucky accident, Lot thinks it has perished with the other children and makes war on Arthur. In the battle Pellinor kills Lot. When Lot's sons grow up, they naturally wish to avenge their father's death:

Et il furent desconfi, et [ocist] (MS. li uns) Pellinor le roi Loth d'Orkanie. Et tout si fil, quant il vinrent a chevalerie haute [voudrent vengier la honte de

---

[1] MS. B.N. fr. 12599, f. 226b; cf. *La Folie Lancelot*, 18, ll. 776–87.

[2] The author of the *Suite du Merlin* did not invent the theme, but borrowed it from the First Version of the prose *Tristan*, developing the indications found in the latter (see below, 173).

leur pere] et de tout lour parenté, dont [Gavains] (MS. il) ochist puis [Pellinor et] Meliodiam aisné fil, et Agloval ochist il en la Queste del Saint Graal, si comme [messire] (MS. meismes) Robiers de Borron le devisera apertement en son livre.[1]

At Lot's funeral, Gauvain, then aged eleven, swears to take vengeance. *Et il le fist tout ensi comme il le dist, car puissedi occhist il le roi Pellinor et deus de ses enfans*.[2] Later, when Pellinor is given a seat at the Round Table, Gauvain renews his vow and is spurred on by his younger brother Gaheriet.[3] Finally, the day after one of Balain's companions has been buried, an inscription written by Merlin appears on the tomb announcing that Gauvain will slay Pellinor in this cemetery within ten years of receiving knighthood:

En ceste chimentiere vengera Gavains le roi Loth son pere, car il trenchera le chief au roi Pellinor es premiers dis ans qu'il avra recheu l'ordre de chevalerie.[4]

Despite this elaborate preparation neither the *Suite du Merlin* nor the 12599–112 fragment gives an account of the death of Pellinor.[5] But the fragment *assumes* that it has occurred and refers back to it. At the point where the redactor explains why Perceval's sister went to live on an island, he says:

Vos savez bien, *et li contes l'a devisé*, que missire Gauvain ocist de sa main le roi Pelinor.[6]

---

[1] Huth MS., f. 116c; Huth *Merlin*, I, 261. The Cambridge MS. (f. 259b–c) has an even more corrupt reading than the Huth MS: 'Ensi furent desconfist. E li rois Pelles e tout li filz le roi Loth d'Orquenie s'entrehaierent quant il vindrent a chevalerie. E puis fu Pelles occis pur la vengance dont il fu vengiez; car ses ainez filz l'occist puis en la Queste du Graal, si com misire Robert de Beron devise apertement en son livre.' The readings in the 1498 and 1535 *Baladros* are as follows: 'Desta manera mató el rey Polinor de Galaz al rey Lot de Ortania; porque Galván, su fijo, quando después fué cavallero, desamó mortalmente al rey Polinor, e de aquel linaje mató después sus fijos Lamarate, e Drianes, e Agraval mató en la demanda del Sancto Greal, así como el autor lo dirá adelante' (Bohigas, 1498 *Baladro*, II, 45); 'y en tal guisa mato el rey Pelinor de Galaz al rey Loc de Ortania, por que Galuan su hijo, quando fue cauallero, desamo mortalmente al rey Pelinor. E de aquel linaje mato sus hijos: Lamorante, Dreyanes e Agraual, mas este Agraual mato en la demanda del sancto Grial, como el cuento lo dira despues' (Bonilla, 1535 *Baladro*, Ch. CCXXI, 87b).

[2] Huth *Merlin*, I, 263.   [3] Ibid., II, 75–6.

[4] Huth MS., f. 127d; Huth *Merlin*, II, 11.

[5] An account of Pellinor's death which fits in with the reference in the *Suite du Merlin* is found in one of the manuscripts of the *Palamedes* (Brit. Mus. Add. 36673, ff. 215r–216v). On this text see *Med. Aev.*, xxix (1960) 1–9.

[6] MS. B.N. fr 12599, f. 254d; cf. *La Folie Lancelot*, 95, ll. 573–4.

Other episodes in the 12599–112 fragment also assume the death of Pellinor. After Lamorat has persuaded Gauvain to give up his intention of avenging his mother's death on Gaheriet, he proposes to take Gauvain to a place where his wounds can be attended to. On the way, however, Lamorat reveals to Gauvain who he is and says that his father Pellinor was slain *par ne sai quel chevalier*.[1] Gauvain thereupon feels uncomfortable, for he is afraid that if Lamorat discovered *la verité de la mort son pere*,[2] nothing could save him. In order to be freed of so formidable a companion, Gauvain tells Lamorat outright that he cannot love the man whose father slew King Lot. Lamorat humbly begs Gauvain to forget the past and to remember that

li enfant ne doivent pas comparer les meffait des peres puis qu'il ne sunt present as oevre[s] donc les haines sordent.[3]

But Gauvain remains adamant and assures Lamorat that there will never be peace between them and that at the first opportunity he will do to him *ce que vostre pere fist del mien*:

ne ge ne vodroie mi[e], fait il, que Dex ne home meist ja mes pes ne concorde entre les enfanz le roi Pellinor et les enfanz le roi Loth.[4]

And at a later point in the narrative, Gauvain in fact carries out his threat: after Lamorat and his brothers Agloval, Drian and Tor 'li fils Arés' have left the *Chastel as dis Chevaliers*,[5] they ride on for four days without finding any adventures; then they separate. Drian spends the night at the house of a *vesve dame* and the following day comes to the forest of Lacen where he encounters Gauvain, Mordred and Agravain who attack him. Drian succeeds in unhorsing Agravain and Mordred, but is mortally wounded by Gauvain. Soon Lamorat arrives on the scene and, recognizing his brother, makes great grief over him. Drian begs him to avenge his death, and Lamorat, though severely wounded from a recent combat, goes after Drian's aggressors. He finds them in a valley and challenges Gauvain. The latter is unhorsed, but Agravain and Mordred strike down Lamorat. Gauvain then tears off Lamorat's helmet, and as the latter refuses to declare himself vanquished, beheads him after avowing that he had done the same to his father. A hermit

---

[1] MS. B.N. fr. 12599, f. 226c; cf. *La Folie Lancelot*, 19, l. 808.
[2] Ibid., f. 226d; cf. *La Folie Lancelot*, 19, l. 818.
[3] Ibid., f. 226d; cf. *La Folie Lancelot*, 19, l. 829.
[4] Ibid., cf. *La Folie Lancelot*, 20, ll. 841–3; 12599 has *mia.*
[5] *La Folie Lancelot*, 76–81.

who appears shortly afterwards buries Lamorat's body in the *Abaye de la Petite Aumosne*, but takes his head to King Arthur, who deeply regrets his death.

From this evidence it is clear that there is a close relationship between the *Suite du Merlin* and the 12599–112 fragment: not only do the two dovetail together, but the episodes contained in the 12599–112 fragment are necessary to bridge the chronological gap between the *Suite du Merlin* and the *Queste del Saint Graal*. An examination of their *provenance* shows, moreover, that they were adapted to the general pattern of the *Suite* narrative. Three of these episodes recur, in a somewhat different form, in the prose *Tristan*. The first of these, Gaheriet's slaying of his mother, the Queen of Orkney, is briefly referred to in the First Version of the prose *Tristan*[1] and related in full in the Second Version.[2] The story there is not identical with that given in 12599–112, but the two accounts have enough in common to suggest that they are not based independently on the First Version, but that one is based upon the other. Which, then, is the earlier of the two? One cannot be dogmatic on this point, but the prose *Tristan* account, as compared with the 12599–112 version, is less complete: in both versions Gauvain and his brothers swear to make Gaheriet pay dearly for his crime, but their threat has no sequel in the prose *Tristan*. This would suggest that the 12599–112 fragment—as elsewhere the *Suite du Merlin*—has developed the indications in the First Version of the prose *Tristan*,[3] and that the Second Version in its turn made use of the 12599–112 account.

The other two episodes, the death of Drian and Lamorat, and Perceval's adventures up to the point where he leaves Arthur's court, are found both in the First and Second Version of the prose *Tristan*,[4]

---

[1] See Löseth, *Analyse*, § 302; MS. B.N. fr. 757, f. 54b–c.

[2] Löseth, *Analyse*, §§ 254–7; MSS. B.N. fr. 94, ff. 309c–310c; 97, ff. 260c–261b; 99, ff. 357a–358a; 100, ff. 385b–386c; 103, ff. 279a–280a; 334, ff. 332b–333b; 335, ff. 404a–405b; 349, ff. 100d–102b; 776, ff. 232a–234b; 12599, ff. 175c–178a; Brit. Mus. Royal 20D II, ff. 75d–77b; Add. 5474, ff. 55b–56b; Vienna 2539, ff. 273b–274b; Vienna 2537, ff. 260a–261a. Vienna 2542, ff. 253a–254a; New York, Pierpont Morgan, no. 41, ff. 13a; Aberystwyth, N.L.W., MS. 5667, ff. 90b–91d; Chantilly 648, ff. 268a–269a; Chantilly 646, ff. 175b–176b; Leningrad, State Library MS. fr. f. v. 2, ff. 175c–177c. Also in Vatican Reg. 727.

[3] Cf. below, 84 and Chapter IX, 173, 175, 190–2.

[4] For the account of Lamorat and Drian's death, see Löseth, *Analyse*, §§ 306–7. It is found in the following manuscripts: B.N. fr. 757, ff. 62c–64a; 97, ff. 306e–308a; 99, ff. 531c–533c; 101, ff. 34a–36b; 340, ff. 158f–160e; 349, ff. 178b–180d; 772, ff. 35b–37c; Chantilly 648, ff. 312b–313d; Chantilly 646, ff. 381b–384a. MS. B.N. fr. 103 contains a shortened version only of Lamorat's

but are in our fragment alone closely linked with the adventures of Erec and Gauvain at the *Chastel as Dis Chevaliers*. Löseth thought that the scribe of 12599 and the prose *Tristan* compiler obtained the Lamorat and Perceval incidents independently from a common source, a lost 'geste des quatre filz de Pellinor',[1] while Pickford suggested that the Erec episodes belong to a *Roman d'Erec* which was combined at the end of the thirteenth or the beginning of the fourteenth century with the prose *Tristan*.[2] It can be shown, however, that the assumptions of both Löseth and Pickford are unnecessary. There is nothing in the 12599–112 accounts which cannot be explained as being derived from the prose *Tristan*. The adventures of Erec and Gauvain at the *Chastel as Dis Chevaliers* were added by our author to prepare for Drian and Lamorat's death. In the prose *Tristan* the events leading up to Drian and Lamorat's death are dealt with very summarily. We are told that Gauvain and his brothers who hate Lamorat and Drian seek them in vain for more than five years. During most of this time Gauvain is in the *Chastel as Dis Chevaliers*, which has established a *mauvese costume*, for knights who pass by are forced to joust against ten knights. Eventually Gauvain is freed by Lamorat:

Grant tens dura ceste haine qe por cele achoison come je vous ai dit comença. Bien passa cinq anz et plus qe il ne troverent Lamorat ne Drian. Il ne retornerent pas a cort dedens celui terme, ainz fu veritez qe missire [Gauvain]

---

death. For the account of Perceval's adventures, see Löseth, *Analyse*, §§ 308–312. They are found in the following MSS.: B.N. fr. 757, ff. 64a–67a; 97, ff. 308a–311c; 101, ff. 36b–41c; 340, ff. 160e–166f; 349, ff. 181a–186c; 772, ff. 37d–43b; Chantilly 648, ff. 313d–319a.

[1] 'Cet accord s'explique le plus probablement par la supposition d'une source commune, dans laquelle on pourrait soupçonner quelque chose comme une "geste des quatre fils de Pelinor"... Dans le cas présent, l'histoire des quatre fils Haimon a pu servir de modèle pour cette geste des quatre fils de Pelinor, où tous les mss. du *Tristan* auront pris ce qu'ils racontent des aventures de Lamorat et de ses freres. Cette *geste* doit être postérieure au *Lancelot*, qu'elle utilise' (Löseth, *Analyse*, 213, n. 3).

[2] *Erec*, ed. Pickford, 40: 'Si le roman d'Erec avait formé de très bonne heure une partie du *Tristan en prose*, il eût certainement été mieux connu des copistes. Nous concluons donc que le roman tel qu'il existe aujourd'hui fut composé d'après les indications données par la *Queste* du *Tristan*, à une date impossible de préciser, mais qui se situe selon toute vraisemblance pendant les premières années du quatorzième siècle.' If, as I believe it can be shown, the whole of the 12599–112 fragment, including the Erec episodes, belongs to the *Suite du Merlin*, then Pickford's dating is incorrect; for as I have indicated above, the *Suite du Merlin* was written between 1230 and 1240 (see 13).

demora adoncquez cinq anz et plus qe oncquez n'en issi de celui terme en un chastel qe l'en apeloit le Chastel ax Dis Chevaliers. Et avoit en celui chastel assez mauvese costume, car il convenoit qe chascun chevalier errant qi par illuec trepassoit jostast as [dis] chevaliers. Missire Gauvain, puis qe il i ot demoré si grant terme come je vous ai dit, eschapa toutes voies a quel que paine. Lamorat sanz faille l'en delivra. Mes se ne vous deviserons nous mie coment il le gita de ce chastel, car trop avons a deviser d'autres choses...[1]

After leaving the castle, Gauvain meets his brothers Agravain and Mordred who tell him that the day before Lamorat defeated them. Gauvain thereupon remarks that if Lamorat lives long he will harm them even more, but he feels sure that soon they will be able to take vengeance. They spend the night in a *meson de religion* and the following day come to the forest of La Cenne where, as in 12599–112, they meet Drian, whom they kill.[2]

The 12599–112 fragment, on the other hand, relates these events more fully and involves Erec in some of them. But the account, far from being based on a lost 'geste' as Löseth thought,[3] or on a prose romance of Erec,[4] is in reality a development of the indications in the prose *Tristan*. What the author has endeavoured to do is to answer some of the questions that must occur to any reader of the prose *Tristan* account: what was the origin of the *mauvese costume* of the

---

[1] MS. B.N. fr. 757, f. 62c. Cf. Löseth, *Analyse*, § 306.

[2] See above, 77–8.

[3] 'Cet épisode (i.e. the account of how Lamorat freed Gauvain from the *Chastel as Dis Chevaliers*), que supprime le rédacteur du *Tristan*, est donné par le compilateur de 12599 probablement d'après le roman des fils de Pelinor' (Löseth, *Analyse*, 236, n. 6).

[4] *Erec*, ed. Pickford, 40. Pickford seems to imply that the theme of the *Chastel as Dis Chevaliers* was derived by the *Tristan* from the hypothetical *Roman d'Erec*: 'Les cinq premiers chapitres du roman (i.e. of Pickford's *Erec*) ne sont qu'une suite d'aventures courues par un nouveau chevalier. Elles ressemblent à celles du *Tristan en prose*, auquel elles sont liées par l'épisode du Château des Dix Chevaliers. Ce n'est que dans les mss. B.N. fr. 112 et 12599 que les aventures de ce château sont racontées tout au long. Cependant, on relève dans le *Tristan* en prose des allusions aux exploits de Gauvain. Il est curieux que ces épisodes, qui constituent une sorte de roman biographique d'Erec, n'aient pas laissé plus de traces dans les romans en prose. Notre texte était peu connu; *tout au plus s'est-on rappelé les circonstances de la mort du héros et l'incident du Château des Dix Chevaliers. Cela s'explique sans doute par sa date plutôt tardive*' (*Erec*, ed. Pickford, 39–40; the italics are mine). It is clear, however, that the reverse of what Pickford assumes is the case. As I shall indicate (see pp. 81–4) the Erec episodes were invented by the author of the 12599–112 fragment to elucidate the theme of the *Chastel as Dis Chevaliers* borrowed from the First Version of the prose *Tristan*.

Chastel as Dis Chevaliers? How did Gauvain come to the castle? Why did he have to stay there for more than five years? How did Lamorat free him? And he did so in a way characteristic of the *Suite du Merlin*—by means of a coherent sequence of events stretching far into the past and carefully linked with the main theme of the narrative, the quest of Lancelot.[1] When Lancelot has been banished from court,[2] some forty knights set out in quest of him, but three months later Mordred asks twenty of them to return to court. Erec, alone of the *refusés*, is unwilling to do so, and soon comes to a valley where he sees a magnificent tower and ten pavillons. A damsel tells him that unless he places himself in her *conduit* he will have to joust with ten knights. Erec defeats all ten, but as he is about to go another knight appears who vanquishes him and then rides off. The people of the castle welcome Erec. A damsel explains to him that the castle is called *li Chastel as Dis Chevaliers*, because any knight who comes to it must do battle with ten knights; if he is successful, he must do battle with the *seigneur* of the castle; if he is again victorious, he becomes *seigneur* in his turn; if he is defeated, he can still be made *seigneur* if the former lord does not wish to remain, but he has to swear that he will stay until he has vanquished a knight and left him in his place. The damsel explains also the origin of this custom: long ago the father of the damsel who is mistress of the castle decreed that no one was to marry her whose valour did not equal her beauty. Now a poor knight once offered to prove his valour by fighting first against the ten best knights of the country and then against the *seigneur* himself. He was successful and married the daughter, but on his wedding day he was killed by his enemy while unarmed. The damsel's father, as he lay on his death bed, made the people of the castle promise that his daughter should only marry a knight who would overcome the ten best knights; if the victor did not wish to marry the daughter, he would have to remain as *seigneur* of the castle

dusqu'a tant q'uns autres i reveigne qui les dis puist oltrer. Et en ceste maniere avroiz vos tot dis avec* vos um proudome qui sera sire en leu de moi dusqu'a tant que Dex vos amaint acum ou ma fille soit bien, quar se elle ne

---

[1] On the narrative technique of the *Suite du Merlin*, see Vinaver, in *Le Roman de Balain*, xi–xxii; *Works*, III, 1265–73; 'La genèse de la *Suite du Merlin*', *Mélanges... Hoepffner*, 296–8; 'The Dolorous Stroke', *Med. Aev.*, XXV (1956) 175–80; 'King Arthur's Sword or the Making of a Medieval Romance', *BJRL*, XL (1958) 513–26. See also below, Ch. IX.

[2] *La Folie Lancelot*, 22–35.

recouvroit mari par chevalier errant ausint com elle le perdi par chevalier errant, donc li seroit il trop mal avenu.[1]

When Erec's wounds have been healed he has to promise in his turn that he will remain in the castle

dusqu'a tant q'uns autres i reviendroit qui la seignorie conquerroit.[2]

This narrative already explains some of the puzzling features of the prose *Tristan*, and Gauvain's adventure can now be fitted into the pattern.[3] We are told that after Erec had been in the castle for three months, Gauvain came and defeated the ten knights, but was unhorsed by Erec. Erec was now free to go, and Gauvain had to take his place as *seigneur* and make the same promise. When, after a further digression, the author returns to the theme of the *Chastel as Dis Chevaliers*, the scene is set for the final episode.[4] For six years no one passed who was able to defeat the ten knights, but after Lancelot's recovery, Lamorat leaves Corbenic to go to court and on the way comes to the *Chastel as Dis Chevaliers*, vanquishing both the ten knights and Gauvain. The latter thereupon departs and the people retain Lamorat in his place, but put him in prison until he agrees to become their *seigneur* and marry the damsel. Lamorat finally complies with their wishes and the custom of the castle is thus ended. On his wedding day, Lamorat's brothers, Agloval, Drian and Tor 'li fils Ares' arrive and ten days later set out for Arthur's court to see if there is any news of Lancelot. Lamorat, who has permission to absent himself temporarily from the castle, accompanies them, but after riding on for four days without finding any adventures, the brothers separate. The following day Drian comes to the forest of La Cenne where he meets with his death at the hands of Gauvain and his brothers whom he encounters there.

It is clear that the 12599–112 account of the events leading up to Lamorat and Drian's death is not derived from a lost 'geste des quatre fils de Pelinor' or a '*Roman d'Erec*', but was invented by our author who here as elsewhere provides 'motive and circumstance'[5] where his sources fail to do so. The other differences between the prose *Tristan* and the 12599–112 accounts can likewise be explained as an attempt by the compiler of the latter to adapt the prose *Tristan* material to its new

---

[1] MS. B.N. fr. 12599, f. 233a; cf. *La Folie Lancelot*, 34, ll. 401–6; *12599 has *avez*.

[2] MS. B.N. fr. 12599, f. 233b–c; cf. *La Folie Lancelot*, 35, ll. 459–60.

[3] *La Folie Lancelot*, 47–9.

[4] Ibid., 72–81.   [5] See Vinaver, *Works*, III, 1271.

context. For instance, when in the prose *Tristan* Gauvain and his brothers find Drian, Mordred remarks:

Veez ci venir Drian, le frere Lamorat. Or poons venger grant partie de nostre courrouz. Ce est tout le meillor des freres, fors Lamorat. Ce cestui ocions, ja mes Lamorat ne devrons riens douter. Et ocirre le poons nous bien, a ce qe il est seul et nous somes trois.[1]

In the 12599–112 fragment, on the other hand, Mordred says that they can now avenge their mother whom Gaheriet slew on account of Lamorat:

Sire, veez ci venir uns des freres Lamorat. Or poom auches venchier la mort de nostre mere, la reine d'Orcanie, quar en despit et en desdeing de Lamorat l'occist Gaheriet, nostre frere.[2]

And Gauvain, 'qui trop haoit Lamorat com cil qui ja avoit bien apris que ce estoit il qui abatu l'avoit devant le *Chastel as Dis Chevaliers*', replies:

Or a lui Agravain. Or i parra se vos vencheroiz* la mort de vostre pere et de vostre mere. Li suens peres ocist le nostre, et li suens freres fist nostre mere morir.[3]

Mordred's and Gauvain's remarks serve here, of course, to link the account with two earlier incidents: the episodes where Pellinor killed Lot, and Gaheriet slew his mother, the Queen of Orkney.

Similarly, at the point where Agloval and Perceval arrive at Arthur's court, the 12599–112 fragment has a long passage which is not in the prose *Tristan*. The author remarks that the whole court was grieved for there was no news yet of Lancelot, although most of the knights had already returned from the quest of Lancelot. Erec, however, *qui n'estoit de cels qui avoient esté esleuʒ en la queste*, had not yet come back, for he stayed a long time with Hector in the hermitage; but shortly before Perceval's arrival at court, Hector recovered his health and he and Erec set off in search of adventures:

Et se aucuns me demandoit ou il (i.e. Erec) demoroit si long tens qu'il n'estoit venuz a cort, ge li respondroie qu'il demoroit avec Hestor chiez l'ermite. Mes un pou devant Perceval venist a cort, estoit Hestor gueriz et

---

[1] MS. B.N. fr. 757, f. 62d.
[2] MS. B.N. fr. 12599, f. 248c; cf. *La Folie Lancelot*, 77, ll. 214–16.
[3] MS. B.N. fr. 12599, f. 248c–d; cf. *La Folie Lancelot*, 77, ll. 223–5; *12599 has *vencheroit*.

s'estoient de l'ermite partiz entre lui et Erec por querre aventures. Et avoit alors Erec tant fait en un pou de terme que l'en ne paroloit se de lui non.[1]

This links up with the story of how Hector became ill as a result of his grief over Lancelot's madness and how he recovered when he learned that Lancelot had been healed.

There is no reason, therefore, why the 12599–112 accounts could not be based on the prose *Tristan*. But from which version of the prose *Tristan*, the First or the Second, did the 12599–112 fragment derive its prose *Tristan* material? From a comparison of verbal variants it is clear that the Second Version cannot represent the source of 12599–112, for there are several instances where the reading of the latter agrees with that of the First Version against the Second.[2] On the other hand, none of the extant MSS. of the First Version of the prose *Tristan* can be regarded as the immediate source of the 12599–112 fragment, for in the account of Perceval's arrival at Arthur's court, 12599–112 has preserved certain details from the Vulgate *Lancelot*—the ultimate source of the account—which have been omitted in the prose *Tristan*.[3] This means that the compiler of our fragment had access to a manuscript of the prose *Tristan* nearer the original than any of the manuscripts that have survived.

E. Brugger, who saw that the 12599–112 fragment[4] included material related to the *Suite* compilation, thought that the whole of it, as well as the prose *Tristan* accounts of Drian and Lamorat's death and of Perceval's arrival at Arthur's court, were part of a 'pseudo-Robert de Boron *Lancelot*', which was originally supposed to have followed the *Suite du Merlin*.[5] The references in the *Suite du Merlin* to the omission

---

[1] MS. B.N. fr. 12599, f. 252d; cf. *La Folie Lancelot*, 89, ll. 326–31.

[2] For examples see *La Folie Lancelot*, notes to 78, ll. 300–79, l. 302; 77, ll. 233–5; 88, ll. 288–9.

[3] For an example see *La Folie Lancelot*, notes to 92, ll. 439–44. On the other hand, the prose *Tristan* MSS. also preserve details from the *Lancelot* omitted in 12599–112, which indicates that the latter cannot be the source of the extant prose *Tristan* MSS. See *La Folie Lancelot*, note to 91, ll. 407–8.

[4] Brugger was not aware of the 112 fragment and knew the 12599 fragment only at second hand—from Löseth's *Analyse*.

[5] See Brugger, 'L'Enserrement Merlin', *ZFSL*, XXIX, 130 n. 109 and *ZFSL*, XXXIV, 109 n. 13. Brugger states wrongly that the greater part of the 12599 fragment is found also in MS. Brit. Mus. Add. 5474 and other prose *Tristan* MSS. In his 'El *Lanzarote* español del manuscrito 9611 de la Biblioteca Nacional' (*REF*, XI, 1924, 288–90) P. Bohigas agreed with Brugger's suggestion that the 12599 fragment is part of a 'pseudo-Boron' *Lancelot*, but in his study attached to

of the *Lancelot*[1] were interpreted by Wechssler and his followers, including Brugger, as additions by a later redactor (B), who omitted the *Lancelot* from the original *Suite* cycle and then divided the rest into three equal parts. But since the extant texts of the *Suite du Merlin* do not support the theory of the three successively shortened redactions,[2] there is no reason why we should not accept the references to the exclusion of the *Lancelot* as authentic.[3] It is true, of course, that the 12599–112 fragment contains remodelled *Lancelot* episodes; but while reproducing these in order to fill in the background, the auther refers us to the *grant estoire de Lancelot*. So for instance when mentioning Arthur's expedition to Gaul:

Et sachient tuit cil qui cest conte escoutent que droitement après ceste venue envoie li rois Artus en Gaulle, por deseriter lo roi Claudas, munseingnor Gauvain et Boort et Hestor [et] les compeingnons de la Table Reonde, et assidrent a celui termine la cité. Et neporquant ja ne l'eussent prise, ne le roi Claudes destruit, si li rois Artus n'i fust venuz atout son host. Et par sa venue fu la terre des deus roiaumes conquise, de celui de Benoic et de celui de Gaunes, *si com la grant estoire de Lancelot [l]e doit deviser*.[4]

In describing how Guenevere banished Lancelot from court, the redactor again adds 'as the story of Lancelot tells':

A cele grant feste sanz faille, ainceis que elle fust del tout departie *si com la grant estoire de Lancelot le doit deviser apertement*, prist la reine Lancelot la ou il s'estoit couchiez el lit de la damoiselle et il cuidoit veiraiment gesir avez la reine, et li vea la cort, et il s'en fuï tout nu fors de la sale et se mist el jardin le roi en tiel maniere qu'il n'avoit vestu fors sa chemise et ses braies.[5]

It is very probable, therefore, that the 12599–112 fragment was not preceded by the rest of the *Lancelot* proper, but by the *Suite du Merlin* and a few episodes, now lost, necessary to bridge the gap between it and the end of the triple adventures. These would almost certainly

---

his edition of the 1498 *Baladro*, Bohigas accepts the theory that the 12599–112 fragment is part of the *Suite du Merlin* (see 1498 *Baladro*, III, 139).

[1] See above, 62, n. 1.

[2] See above, Ch. II.

[3] Furthermore there are in the 12599–112 fragment references to the *Conte du Brait* and the tripartition of the work which, on Brugger's own admission, do not fit the 'pseudo-Boron' *Lancelot* which was supposed to belong to the first unshortened redaction of the cycle (see Brugger, *ZFSL*, XXXIV, 109 n. 13).

[4] *La Folie Lancelot*, 20–1, ll. 880–7.

[5] Ibid., 21, ll. 915–20.

have included incidents foreshadowed in the *Suite du Merlin* but not related in the 12599–112 fragment, as for instance Tristan's combat with Le Morholt,[1] Gauvain's slaying of Pellinor,[2] Gauvain's combat with Naborn the enchanter,[3] Gaheriet's adventures on the *Isle Merlin*,[4] and Lancelot's encounter with Hector and Gauvain whom he almost killed while they were looking at the tomb in Morgain's castle Tugan where she had placed the *escrit* relating Arthur's death.[5] Interwoven with these incidents there may also have been summaries of certain *Lancelot* episodes.

The significance of the 12599–112 fragment lies, then, not in that it preserves part of a hypothetical 'pseudo-Boron *Lancelot*', but in that it enables us to see how the compiler of the *Suite du Merlin* succeeded in doing without a *Lancelot* branch. It is not surprising that critics have attempted to explain the references to the exclusion of the *Lancelot* as late additions, for naturally they could not see how a work which, like the *Suite du Merlin* compilation, included a Lancelot *Queste* and *Mort Artu*, could do without an account of some of Lancelot's earlier adventures. If, however, the 12599–112 fragment with its mixture of *Lancelot* episodes and other material is, as seems certain, part of the *Suite du Merlin*, it becomes clear what the compiler tried to do. His intention was to provide a transition to the third part of his book, the *Queste-Mort Artu*, by including not the whole of the *grant estoire de Lancelot* which, in his own words, would have made the middle portion of his book three times as big as the other two parts, but by selecting from it

---

[1] See above, 63–4. It is quite probable that the *Suite du Merlin* account would have been based on the First Version of the prose *Tristan* (Löseth, *Analyse*, § 28).

[2] See above, 75–6.

[3] At the point where Morgain casts Arthur's scabbard into a lake, the *Suite du Merlin* says that no one ever benefited again from the scabbard except Gauvain when he did battle with Naborn; but after the battle, the scabbard vanished *si coume cis contes meismes le devisera apertement quant lius et tans en sera* (Huth *Merlin*, II, 222). See below, 174–6.

[4] See Huth *Merlin*, II, 58–9 and *Die Abenteuer*, 55.

[5] '... De cele tombe avinrent puis maint mal, *ensi coume li contes le devisera apertement*, et maint boin chevalier en morurent puis, qui voloient savoir des deus preudommes la verité et comment il fineroient. Et puis fu il tel heure que Gavains et Hestor de Mares furent a la tombe por garder la, et lors i sorvint Lanscelos qui andeus les euust occhis, a che que il estoient navré et de che k'il s'estoient combatu ensemble, mais il avint qu'il les connut ansdeus et il connurent lui. *Et ceste aventure devise ceste ystoire anchois que on kieche a conter la vie de Percheval.*' (Huth MS., ff. 215d–216a; Huth *Merlin*, II, 228.)

only a few relevant episodes which he was able to combine with material borrowed from the First Version of the prose *Tristan* and with his own inventions.[1]

---

[1] Although Malory's *Tale of King Arthur* ends with the triple adventures of Gauvain, Yvain and Le Morholt, it is possible that the French manuscript of the *Suite du Merlin* used by Malory continued beyond the triple adventures and ended with Lancelot's return to court after his stay on the *Isle de Joie*. For in the *explicit* at the end of the *Tale of King Arthur*, Malory says: 'Here endyth this tale, as the Freynshe Booke seyth, fro the maryage of kynge Uther unto Kyng Arthure that regned aftir hym and ded many batayles.

'*And this booke endyth whereas Sir Launcelot and Sir Trystrams com to courte.* Who that woll make ony more lette hym seke other bookis of kynge Arthure or of Sir Launcelot or Sir Trystrams; for this was drawyn by a knyght presoner, Sir Thomas Malleorré, that God sende hym good Recover. Amen' (Vinaver, *Works*, I, 180).

But Lancelot and Tristan do not come to court in the portion of the *Suite du Merlin* ending with the triple adventures of Gauvain, Yvain and Le Morholt, and the italicized sentence in the *explicit* can therefore only refer, as Vinaver has suggested, to Malory's source.

CHAPTER IV

An Attempt to establish the Existence
of the Post-Vulgate 'Queste'

THE third part of the *Suite du Merlin* compilation includes, as we
have seen according to the redactional indications, a version of the
Queste del Saint Graal.[1] References in the *Suite du Merlin* to incidents
contained in the latter bear this out. The *Suite* predicts, for instance,
that Gauvain will slay Agloval and Baudemagus,[2] and announces that
the leprous lady whom Balain's companion was unable to heal will not
recover until the coming of Perceval's sister,

qui acompli l'aventure dou chastiel; car de son sanc fu la dame de laiens garie,
si tost coume elle en fu ointe, *si coume li contes le devise en la grant Queste dou
Graal.*[3]

Many of the allusions in the *Suite*, however, do not fit the Vulgate
version of the *Queste del Saint Graal* and can only be explained with
the aid of the *Queste* incorporated into the Second Version of the
prose *Tristan*,[4] and of the Spanish and Portuguese *Demandas*[5] which

---

[1] See above, 61.

[2] Huth *Merlin*, I, 261, 273.   [3] Ibid., II, 19.

[4] There exist today two redactions of the prose *Tristan*, the 'First Version'
and the 'Second Version'. The former, as Vinaver has pointed out (*Études*, 27–31),
refers only briefly to the opening events of the *Queste* and then goes on to deal
with the adventures of Tristan. The Second Version, on the other hand, incorporates the story of the *Queste* in full, remodelling, however, many of the Vulgate
episodes and adding much fresh material, including incidents taken over from
the First Version. The prose *Tristan* MSS. which contain the complete *Queste* are:
MSS. B.N. fr. 97 (*H*), 99 (*A*), 101 (*C*), 336 (*B*), 349 (*L*), 758 (*F*), 772 (*T*),
24400 (*I*), Brit. Mus. Add. 5474 (*K*), Egerton 989 (*E*), Royal 20 D II (*G*),
Dijon 527 (*J*), Aberystwyth, N.L.W. 5667 (*W*), Chantilly 647 (*M*), Brussels
9086 (*Q*), Vienna 2537 (*P*), Vienna 2540 (*V*), Vienna 2542 (*R*), New York,
Pierpont Morgan Library, no. 41 (*U*).

[5] From a critical point of view the Portuguese *Demanda* is of greater value
than the Spanish in which numerous episodes are missing, while others are
shortened. All references will therefore be to the Portuguese *Demanda* (Magne,
P. *D.*, or *D*). For a comparison of the two *Demandas*, see Sommer, 'The Queste
of the Holy Grail', *R*, XXXVI (1907) 542–90, and Bohigas, *Los textos españoles*,
52–67.

go back ultimately, though not independently, to the same French original. The latter half of their prototype must have been identical with the corresponding part of the 343 *Queste*;[1] other fragments of it are found in MS. B.N. fr. 112.[2] But before we can profitably discuss the connexion between them and the *Suite du Merlin*, it is necessary to determine the relationship of the various versions of the *Queste*.[3]

The prose *Tristan Queste* and the Portuguese *Demanda*, both ultimately based on the Vulgate, follow the same general outline and reproduce, in the same order, a large number of identical episodes. They are, in fact, so similar that if we set aside all preconceived ideas, it is obvious at the outset that they can only be related to one another in one of the following three ways:

(1) The *Queste* incorporated in the prose *Tristan* may be the source of the Portuguese *Demanda Queste* ($T > Z$).

(2) Since the Portuguese *Demanda* is a literal translation of a French work (Z), some fragments of which are still extant, this work may be the source of the *Tristan Queste* ($Z > T$).

(3) The prose *Tristan Queste* and the Portuguese *Demanda* (that is its French original Z) may both be independent *remaniements* of a common original $\left(Y \diagdown{\stackrel{\textstyle T}{Z}} \right)$.

Although there exists no comprehensive study of the relationship between the Portuguese *Demanda* and the prose *Tristan Queste*, the view that the prose *Tristan Queste* is the source of Z and the view that Z is the source of the prose *Tristan Queste* have both been held at various times.

---

[1] The first 60 folios of MS. B.N. fr. 343 correspond to 1–246 l. 6 of Pauphilet's edition of the Vulgate *Queste*; ff. 61r–104v, on the other hand, are identical with the latter portion of Magne, P. *D.*

[2] MS. B.N. fr. 112 contains a fifteenth-century compilation of Arthurian prose romances, including a version of the *Queste del Saint Graal* made up of episodes taken from the Vulgate *Queste* (112, *Livre* IV, ff. 1c–6a, 6b–28b, 128b–138c, 152c–160a, 163b–179d, 180c–182a), the prose *Tristan* (112, *Livre* IV, ff. 6a–b, 28b–84d, 138d–146d), the *Palamède* (112, *Livre* IV, ff. 160a–163a) and the French original of the *Demandas* (*Livre* IV, ff. 84d–128b, 146d–152c, 179d–180c). It should be added that one of the MSS. of the Vulgate Cycle, B.N. fr. 116, inserts between the end of the *Queste* and the beginning of the *Mort Artu* a shortened version of one of the *Demanda* episodes (MS. 116, ff. 676v–677v = *D*, §§ 201, 206), while MSS. B.N. fr. 340, 355 and 1463 have a remodelled version of another *Demanda* episode (Löseth, *Analyse*, § 625 = *D*, §§ 74–80).

[3] I am preparing a critical edition of the Post-Vulgate *Queste* (*SATF*).

Thus, in his *Études*, Pauphilet suggested that the 343 fragment is a combination of Vulgate *Queste* and prose *Tristan* episodes,[1] a view which was accepted by Pickford:

> Cette partie du MS. 343 n'est donc rien de plus qu'un morceau du *Tristan* cyclique et n'a de sens que dans le cadre du *Tristan*... Dans sa plus grande partie la *Queste* du MS. B.N. fr. 343 est une simple copie de plusieurs épisodes du *Tristan* en prose, d'après un groupe particulier de manuscrits...[2]

As regards the Portuguese *Demanda*, Pickford holds that it too is made up of sections of the prose *Tristan* intermingled with other material:

> Les *Demandas* se composent donc d'une combinaison de la *Queste del Saint Graal* du *Tristan* en prose avec des éléments nouveaux, comme le roman d'Erec, les aventures de Palamède pendant la chasse de la Bête Glatissante, l'épisode d'Arthur le Petit, etc., qui n'ont pas une grande signification religieuse, mais qui servent plutôt à enjoliver le récit et à compléter des situations et des données provenant d'autres romans, notamment du *Tristan* en prose.[3]

On the other hand, Wechssler suggested that the prose *Tristan* contained a mixture of material, some of which came from the Vulgate *Queste*. The position is complicated in Wechssler's case because of his belief in the three 'Redaktionen',[4] but Sommer, who simplified

---

[1] Pauphilet, *Études*, xi–xii: 'Le ms. B.N. fr. 343... c'est une contamination obtenue en intercalant entre les épisodes de la fin de la *Queste* de Map, *exactement reproduits*, des récits relatifs à Tristan, Palamède, Sagremor etc. Ces récits, à part ceux des 7 ou 8 derniers feuillets, qui relatent des aventures de Palamède qu'on ne retrouve pas ailleurs, figurent tous dans le *Tristan* en prose, à l'ordre près. Et de même que les fragments de la *Queste* de Map figurant dans ce ms. s'apparentent au texte d'une certaine famille de mss. de cette *Queste*..., de même ces fragments du *Tristan*, de leur côté, reproduisent la version d'un des groupes de mss. déterminés par Löseth: (mss. 772 etc.) C'est donc un mélange d'éléments connus par ailleurs et qu'il y a tout lieu de considérer comme antérieurs à ce mélange même.'

[2] Pickford, *Évolution*, 98.

[3] Ibid., 105. Pauphilet does not mention the *Demanda*, but in his Introduction to the Vulgate *Queste* (p. xiii) he put forward the view that the original 'pseudo-Boron *Queste*' was identical with the prose *Tristan Queste*: 'Ce livre subtil et artiste (i.e. the Vulgate *Queste*) participa à la célébrité du *Lancelot*, auquel il était lié. Néanmoins il paraît avoir été très vite mal compris. Remanié, encombré de nouveaux personnages dont les aventures n'avaient rien de commun avec l'intention morale du premier auteur, il fut mis sous le nom de Robert de Borron, et, en cet état, incorporé à la vaste compilation qu'est le *Tristan* en prose.'

[4] See above, 42–4.

Wechssler's view, regarded the original 'pseudo-Boron' *Queste* as to all intents and purposes identical with the Portuguese *Demanda* and explained the prose *Tristan Queste* as a combination of episodes from 'pseudo-Boron' with episodes from the Vulgate.[1] This is also the view expressed by Löseth, Bohigas Balaguer and Bruce.[2]

Nobody, as far as I am aware, has envisaged the third possibility— namely that the prose *Tristan Queste* and the Portuguese *Demanda* (or rather its source *Z*) are independent *remaniements* of the same lost original. This is the possibility I wish to explore.

*   *   *

It will be convenient at this point to compare the prose *Tristan Queste* and the Portuguese *Demanda* in detail.[3]

Both versions begin with the initial episode of the Vulgate, the knighting of Galaad and Arthur's return from church, but whereas the prose *Tristan* reproduces it without changes, the *Demanda* gives it in a modified form.[4] Then in both follow incidents not in the Vulgate— in the prose *Tristan* a second account of Arthur's visit to church and return, taken over from the First Version of the prose *Tristan*,[5] in the *Demanda* the episode of the Irish knight.[6] They rejoin the Vulgate,

---

[1] H. O. Sommer, 'Galaad and Perceval', *MPh*, V (1908) 317–22; 'The Queste of the Holy Grail', *R*, XXXVI (1908) 378, 380, 395; 'Zur Kritik der altfranzösischen Artus-Romane', *ZRPh*, XXXII (1908) 328.

[2] Löseth, *Analyse*, § XI, p. xvi; Bohigas, *Los textos españoles*, 59, n. 1: 'Desde aqui en adelante (i.e. from Löseth, *Analyse*, § 505 onwards), el *Tristan* en prosa reproduce la *Demanda*, conforme a la version del seudo Robert de Borron'; Bruce, *Evolution*, I, 485 remarks that the Second Version of the prose *Tristan* incorporates 'the greater part of the *Queste* branch, in a mixture of its Vulgate and Pseudo-Robert forms'.

[3] References are to the 1944 Magne, P. *D*. (§ references introduced by *D*); to the Bonilla 1535 Sp. *D*.; to Löseth's *Analyse* of the prose *Tristan*. Page references for the Vulgate *Queste* are to Pauphilet's edition. All the prose *Tristan* MSS. have been consulted, but except for certain episodes, I give here references to only two: MS. B.N. fr. 772 (*T*) and B.N. fr. 97 (*H*). For folio references to the other MSS., see my Ph.D. thesis, Manchester, 1957, 119–31.

[4] Vulgate *Queste*, 1–5, l. 10; *D*, I, §§ 1–8; Sp. *D*, Chs. I–VI; Löseth, § 392a; MSS. *T*, ff. 191b–192b; *H*, ff. 416d–417e.

[5] Löseth, *Analyse*, § 392a; MSS. *T*. ff. 192b–192c; *H*, ff. 417e–f. The episode has many points in common with the *Demandas'* remodelled version of the Vulgate account of King Arthur's visit to church and return (see *D*, I, § 8; Sp. *D*., Ch. VI).

[6] *D*, I, § 9; Sp. *D*, Ch. VII.

however, with the account of the arrival of the *épée du perron*, but the prose *Tristan* alone reproduces it word for word.[1]

After this the *Tristan Queste* inserts from the First Version of the prose *Tristan* the incident of the Weeping Knight,[2] while the *Demanda* relates how Erec and Elain are made knights of the Round Table.[3] Then the story of the Vulgate reappears in both with the account of the coming of Galaad, the *Demanda* giving it in a somewhat revised form.[4] The *Tristan Queste* follows up the account with material taken over from the First Version of the prose *Tristan*.[5] One of the additions, the remark that King Arthur reproached Yseut for seemingly keeping Tristan from court, is also in the *Demanda*.[6]

After this both versions return to the Vulgate with the account of the tournament before Camalot, the prose *Tristan* reproducing the narrative verbally, the *Demanda* remodelling it.[7] Then the prose *Tristan* adds further material from the First Version, including the account in which Tristan appears in the field where the tournament is being held.[8] The *Demanda* likewise gives an account of Tristan's arrival in the field.[9]

After this both *Questes* take the story of the Vulgate up again. The prose *Tristan* reproduces the contents of 14 l. 16–55 l. 32 of Pauphilet's edition; the *Demanda* gives in a remodelled form those of 15 l. 7– 41 l. 17.[10] At points corresponding to 23 l. 7 and 25 l. 3 of Pauphilet's

[1] Vulgate *Queste*, 5, l. 11–7, l. 11; *D, I*, §§ 10–13; Sp. *D*, Ch. VIII–XI; Löseth, § 393a; MSS. *T*, ff. 192d–193a; *H*, ff. 417f–418a.

[2] Löseth, *Analyse*, § 393a; MSS. *T*, ff. 193a–194a; *H*, ff. 418a–e.

[3] *D, I*, §§ 14–15; Sp. *D*, Chs. XII–XIII.

[4] Vulgate *Queste*, 7, l. 12–9, l. 3; *D, I*, §§ 16–17; Sp. *D*, Chs. XIV–XV; Löseth, § 393a; MSS. *T*, ff. 194a–c; *H*, ff. 418e–f.

[5] Löseth, Analyse, § 393a; MSS. *T*, ff. 194c–195a; *H*, ff. 418f–419b.

[6] The remark is found in *D* at the end of § 17, in Sp. *D*, at the end of Ch. XV.

[7] Vulgate *Queste*, 9, l. 4–14, l. 15; *D, I*, §§ 18–22; Sp. *D*, Chs. XVI–XX; Löseth, *Analyse*, § 394a; MSS. *T*, ff. 195a–196c; *H*, ff. 419b–420a.

[8] Löseth, *Analyse*, § 394a; MSS. *T*, ff. 196c–197a; *H*, ff. 420a–b; *A*, ff. 567c–d; *C*, ff. 204a–c; *B*, ff. 101c–d; *L*, ff. 387a–d; *F*, ff. 149c–d; *K*, f. 169a; *G*, ff. 181d– 182a; *J*, ff. 5c–6a; *W*, ff. 248c–d; *M*, ff. 9b–c; *P*, f. 335c–d; *V*, f. 80b; *R*, ff. 357d–358c; *U*, ff. 154d–155d.

In MSS. *ABFGKMPRUVW* the account of Tristan's arrival in the field is identical with that of the MSS. of the First Version of the prose *Tristan*, but in MSS. *THJLC* many of the details have been changed.

[9] *D, I*, §§ 23–4; Sp. *D*, Chs. XXI–XXII. The details in the *Demandas'* account are the same as those in MSS. *THJLC* (see Appendix I).

[10] *D, I*, §§ 25–69; Sp. *D*, Chs. XXIII–XXXI = *D*, §§ 25–33; Sp. *D*, Chs. XXXII–XLIX = *D*, §§ 37–51; Sp. *D*, Chs. L–LII beginning = *D*, §§ 56–9; Sp.

text, both versions add an expanded list of the Grail knights and the incident of Gauvain and the bleeding sword.[1]

There follow in the *Tristan Queste* a long series of adventures taken over from the First Version of the prose *Tristan*,[2] while the *Demanda* relates a different series of adventures, some of which have their starting point in the Vulgate.[3]

After these additions the prose *Tristan* gives all the Vulgate episodes contained in 55 l. 33–146 l. 33 and 163 l. 3–195 l. 17 of Pauphilet's edition.[4] The *Demanda*, on the other hand, reproduces in a modified form those contained in 147 l. 1–165 l. 1 and 187 l. 32–195 l. 17.[5] That is, the *Demanda* here has some Vulgate episodes not in the prose *Tristan*[6] and, as elsewhere, has omitted or remodelled others which are in the corresponding part of the prose *Tristan*.[7]

These incidents are followed in the prose *Tristan* by accounts in which Galaad ends the marvel of the Boiling Fountain and meets Helain li blanc;[8] in the *Demanda* they are followed by a different series

---

D, Chs. LII–LX = *D*, §§ 63–9; Löseth, *Analyse*, §§ 394a–8a; MSS. *T*, ff. 197b–209c; *H*, ff. 420b–426f. That is, the *Demandas* give a remodelled account of Melyant's adventures, and omit the accounts of the 'Château des Pucelles' and Gauvain's early adventures.

[1] The *Demandas* insert the list of Grail knights at the same point as the prose *Tristan*, but the incident of Gauvain and the bleeding sword is inserted at the point corresponding to 18, l. 13 of the Vulgate *Queste*, and differs somewhat from the prose *Tristan* account.

[2] Löseth, *Analyse*, §§ 399–495; MSS. *T*, ff. 209d–311b; *H*, ff. 426f–485e.

[3] *D, I*, §§ 70–152; Sp. *D*, Chs. LXI–CXXVI. The episode corresponding to *D*, §§ 74–80 (Dalides' death) is related in a somewhat briefer form in MSS. B.N. fr. 340, ff. 17f–18d; 355, ff. 16a–16e; 1463, ff. 25d–27a. The incidents corresponding to *D*, §§ 81–123 and 129–44 (from the end of the Dalides episode up to Hector's combat with Palamedes) are found in MS. B.N. fr. 112, *Livre* IV, ff. 84d–97c. The adventures contained in *D, I*, §§ 145–52 are not extant in French.

[4] Löseth, §§ 496–501; MSS. *T*, ff. 311b–342d; *H*, ff. 485f–505e.

[5] *D, I*, §§ 153–81 (omitted in Sp. *D*).

[6] That is, Gauvain and Hector's vision. Only five of the prose *Tristan* MSS. (*BEPQV*) relate this adventure (Löseth, *Analyse*, 351, n. 1; MSS. *B*, ff. 252d–256d; *E*, ff. 276v–283v; *Q*, ff. 206c–211a; *P*, ff. 430a–432b; *V*, ff. 177b–179d. All these five MSS., which are closely related, have used a manuscript of the Vulgate *Queste* in conjunction with a prose *Tristan* manuscript and give composite versions of the *Queste*. [7] See below, 97–8.

[8] Löseth, *Analyse*, § 502; MSS. *T*, ff. 343a–344c; *H*, ff. 505e–506f. The incident of the Boiling Fountain occurs in the Vulgate in a different form towards the end of the *Queste* (Pauphilet, 263, l. 27–264, l. 2). The *Demanda* (*D, II* §§ 578–580; Sp. *D*, Ch. CCCLIV–CCCLV) has the adventure in still another

of adventures, some of which are Vulgate episodes (those corresponding to 56 l. 1–146 l. 33 of Pauphilet's edition), remodelled almost
beyond recognition.[1] Then both versions relate the Vulgate incident of
the *tornoiement merveilleux*, but the prose *Tristan* gives the account
with slightly less remodelling than the *Demanda*.[2]

The *Demanda* follows up the tournament account by more adventures which occur neither in the Vulgate nor in the prose *Tristan*,[3]
after which it rejoins the latter. Both versions relate the series of
episodes beginning with Tristan's pursuit of Galaad and ending with
Galaad and Eliezer's combat.[4] Then both rejoin the Vulgate, giving
identically remodelled and expanded accounts of Galaad's visit to the
hermitage from which Perceval's sister leads him to the sea where they
join Perceval and Boors in the holy boat. After this the *Demanda* and
the prose *Tristan* continue together, giving the same remodelled accounts of the Vulgate description of the holy boat and the *espee as
estranges renges*; but whereas the prose *Tristan* follows the Vulgate
right through, giving even the long account of the 'Légende de l'Arbre
de Vie', the *Demanda* abridges the text, omitting everything that falls
between MS. *T*, ff. 358d (middle) and 364b.[5]

After this omission the *Demanda* rejoins the prose *Tristan* and both

---

form, also towards the end of the *Queste*. MS. B.N. fr. 343, ff. 100c–101a, has
the episode in the same place as the *Demanda* and agrees verbally with the latter.

[1] *D*, §§ 182–250 (omitted in Sp. *D*). The adventures corresponding to *D*,
§§ 201–7 (Lancelot's vision and 'L'Olivier vermeil') are found in MS. B.N. fr.
112, *Livre* IV, ff. 97d–100b while *D*, §§ 201, 206 correspond to MS. B.N. fr. 116,
ff. 676c–677d.

[2] Vulgate *Queste*, 195, l. 18–197, l. 30. *D*, §§ 251–4 (omitted in Sp. *D*); Löseth,
Analyse, § 503; MSS. *T*, ff. 344c–345b; *H*, ff. 506f–507b.

[3] *D*, I–II, §§ 255–363; Sp. *D*, Chs. CXXVII–CXCIV = *D*, §§ 280–363. The
adventures corresponding to *D*, §§ 263–363 (from Baudemagus' death to the
account of Artus le Petit's and Meraugis' visit to Arthur's court) are found in
MS. B.N. fr. 112, *Livre* IV, ff. 97c–d and 100c–117b.

[4] *D*, II, §§ 364–93; Sp. *D*, Chs. CXCV–CCX = *D*, §§ 377–93; Löseth,
§§ 504–10; MSS. *T*, ff. 345b–354a; *H*, ff. 507c–512c. These adventures are also
in MS. B.N. fr. 112, *Livre* IV, ff. 117b–124c; and in MS. B.N. fr. 343, ff. 82b–90c.

[5] Vulgate *Queste*, 197, l. 31–226, l. 7; *D*, II, §§ 394–413; Sp. *D*, Chs. CCXI–
CCXXV = *D*, §§ 394–408; Löseth, *Analyse*, §§ 511–12; MSS. *T*, ff. 354a–364a;
H, ff. 512c–519b; *A*, ff. 732a–738d; *C*, ff. 343a–352b; *B*, ff. 277b–288d; *L*, ff. 558b–
570a; *F*, ff. 310b–321d; *I*, ff. 124d–134d; *K*, ff. 265a–266d (lacuna for most of
the incidents); *E*, ff. 322r–335r; *G*, ff. 261c–270c; *J*, ff. 112b–120a; *W*, ff. 434d–
448b; *M*, ff. 228a–237a; *Q*, ff. 234d–247c; *P*, ff. 444b–451b; *V*, ff. 192d–200d;
R, ff. 458e–465b; *U*, ff. 257a–263b.

MS. B.N. fr. 112, *Livre* IV, ff. 125c–128b contains the adventures correspond-

give exactly the same revised versions of all the Vulgate incidents contained in 226 l. 8–246 l. 6 of Pauphilet's edition.[1] Then both leave the
Vulgate account and relate Mark's invasion of Logres,[2] his defeat and
return to Cornwall, Galaad's meeting with Frolle's son and the episode
of the *Chastel Felon*. They both rejoin the Vulgate, however, with a
remodelled account of Lancelot's arrival at the *rive de Marcoise*.[3] Then
leaving the Vulgate account, both relate Galaad's encounter with
Tristan who lies ill in an abbey.[4]

At this point the *Tristan Queste* leaves the *Demanda* version, insert-
ing as it does from the First Version of the prose *Tristan* an account of
Mark's return to Cornwall and of the death of Tristan and Yseut.[5] It
rejoins the *Demanda*, however, with the remodelled Vulgate account of
Galaad and Lancelot's sea voyage,[6] but, at a point during the voyage
where the *Demanda* (and MS. 343) follow the Vulgate faithfully, the
various prose *Tristan* MSS. insert accounts of the healing of Mordrain
and the delivery of Moïs.[7]

---

ing to *D*, §§ 394–408 (that is from Galaad's visit to the hermitage up to his
arrival at the sea).

At the point where Galaad, Perceval, Boors and the damsel find the inscription
on the holy boat (MS. *T*, f. 358a), MSS. *BQEPV* leave the account of the other
prose *Tristan* MSS., and give from here up to Mark's invasion of Logres an
account identical with that of the Vulgate *Queste*.

[1] *D*, II, §§ 414–44; Sp. *D*, Chs. CCXXVI–CCXXIX = *D*, §§ 418–21;
Löseth, *Analyse*, §§ 513–15; MSS. *T*, ff. 364a–371b; *H*, ff. 519b–523e.

[2] MS. B.N. fr. 343 joins the *Demanda* at this point.

[3] Vulgate *Queste*, 246, l. 7–250, l. 6.

[4] *D*, II, §§ 445–515; Sp. *D*, Chs. CCXXX–CCXL = *D*, §§ 445–7; Sp. *D*,
Chs. CCXLI–CCLV = *D*, §§ 464–79; Sp. *D*, Chs. CCLVI–CCLXXXIV =
D, §§ 481–509; Sp. *D*, Chs. CCLXXV–CCLXXXVIII not in *D* owing to lacuna;
Sp. *D*, Chs. CCLXXXIX–CCXCI = *D*, §§ 513–15; Löseth, *Analyse*, §§ 516–
533; MSS. *T*, ff. 371b–390c; *H*, ff. 523e–535d. MS. B.N. fr. 343 omits the
episode of the *Chastel Felon*, but has Mark's invasion, Lancelot at the *rive de
Marcoise*, and Galaad's meeting with Tristan (ff. 61a–74c).

[5] Löseth, *Analyse*, §§ 534–51; MSS. *T*, ff. 390d–402d (lacuna at end); *H*,
ff. 535d–543c.

[6] Vulgate *Queste*, 250, l. 6–252, l. 30; *D*, II, §§ 516–19 (lacuna at end of *D*;
Sp. *D* omits *D*, §§ 516–18, but Sp. *D*, Ch. CCXCII = *D*, § 519); Löseth,
Analyse, 392, n. 2; MSS. *H*, ff. 543c–f; *C*. ff. 386d–388a; *B*, ff. 331a–332c; *L*,
ff. 611a–612c; *F*, ff. 363b–365a; *I*, ff. 170d–172c; *J*, ff. 147c–150a; *E*, ff. 425r–
427v; *G*, ff. 302a–303c; *K*, ff. 293b–295a; *W*, ff. 500a–502c; *M*. ff. 263d–265c;
Q, ff. 301a–302c; *R*, ff. 490c–491d; *U*, ff. 278a–279b; *P*, ff. 477b–478a; *V*,
ff. 228c–229c; (lacuna in *TA*); MS. B.N. fr. 343, ff. 74c–75c.

[7] See below, 101–4.

After the sea voyage, the prose *Tristan* and the *Demanda* both have identical accounts of Galaad's war with the Conte de Bedoin, of Samaliel's adventures, of Lancelot, Hector, Gauvain and Gaheriet's visit to Corbenic,[1] and of Palamedes' combat with Lancelot.[2] Then, however, the agreement between the two texts ends for the time being; each now gives varying versions of Palamedes' conversion and of the final scene at Corbenic; in addition, the *Demanda* (and MS. 343) has after the conversion and before the final scene at Corbenic a number of minor adventures, including the death of the *beste glatissant*, references to the healing of Mordrain and the delivery of Moïs, Palamedes' combat with Athanas, and the adventure of the Boiling Fountain.[3]

After the final scene at Corbenic, the prose *Tristan* and the *Demanda* come together again, both giving identical accounts of the adventures leading up to the death of Palamedes and Esclabor.[4] This is followed in the *Demanda* alone by Galaad, Perceval and Boors' visit to King Pellean's hermitage and the history of the three marvels of Logres.[5] Then both the *Demanda* and the prose *Tristan* give a somewhat re-modelled version of the Vulgate account of the three chosen knights' voyage to Sarraz and of the death of Galaad and Perceval;[6] but,

---

[1] The account of Lancelot's and Hector's visit is based on the Vulgate *Queste* (252, l. 31–262, l. 19 of Pauphilet's edition), but has been considerably remodelled.

[2] *D*, II, §§ 520–51; Sp. *D*, Chs. CCXCI–CCCXXVII (lacuna in *D* for the beginning of the episode, corresponding to Sp. *D*, Chs. CCXCIII–CCXCVI); Löseth, *Analyse*, §§ 552–9; MSS. *T*, ff. 405a–408d (lacuna at the beginning); *H*, ff. 543f–550b. MS. B.N. fr. 343, ff. 75c–82b and 90c–94a.

[3] *D*, II, §§ 552–94; Sp. *D*, Chs. CCCXXVIII–CCCLVIII, 297a = *D*, §§ 552–84 (Sp. *D* relates the final scene at Corbenic at a later point; the version which it gives is found in a particular group of Vulgate *Queste* MSS. and differs from that of *D* and MS. 343); Löseth, *Analyse*, §§ 560–62; MSS. *T*, ff. 408d–411a; *H*, ff. 550c–552a; *A*, ff. 768d–770d; *C*, ff. 394b–395d; *B*, ff. 344a–347b; *L*, ff. 620b–622b; *F*, ff. 374b–377a; *I*, ff. 181b–183d; *K*, ff. 301b–303a; *E*, ff. 444r–453v; *G*, ff. 310d–313a; *J*, ff. 156d–158c; *W*, ff. 513c–516d; *M*, ff. 271d–276b; *Q*, ff. 315b–323b; *R*, ff. 495b–496c; *P*, ff. 484a–487d; *V*, ff. 236d–239a; MS. 343, ff. 94a–104c (same account as *D*). The account of the final scene at Corbenic is ultimately based on the Vulgate, 266, l. 9–273, l. 5).

[4] *D*, II, §§ 595–602; Sp. *D*, Chs. CCCLVIII (297, col. 2)–CCCLXI; Löseth, *Analyse*, §§ 563–66; MSS. *T*, ff. 411b–415a; *H*, ff. 552a–554a.

[5] *D*, II, §§ 603–13; Sp. *D*, Chs. CCCLXII–CCCLXXII. MS. B.N. fr. 112, *Livre* IV, ff. 150c–152b contains the story of one of the three marvels, that of the birth of the *beste glatissant*; MS. B.N. fr. 24400, ff. 239a–241d has the story of the origin of the healing fountain and that of the *beste glatissant*.

[6] Vulgate *Queste*, 273, l. 11–279, l. 20; *D*, II, §§ 614–24 middle (Sp. *D* as in certain Vulgate *Queste* MSS.); Löseth, *Analyse*, § 567; MSS. *T*, ff. 415a–416b; *H*,

whereas the *Demanda* begins the account of the voyage at a point corresponding to Vulgate 273 l. 11, the prose *Tristan* omits a portion of it, taking up the narrative at a point corresponding to Vulgate, 275 l. 5.[1]

After Galaad and Perceval's death, the prose *Tristan Queste* takes over from the First Version of the prose *Tristan* the account of Sagremor's return to Arthur's court with Tristan's shield.[2] Then it rejoins the *Demanda*, both terminating the *Queste* with a revised and expanded account of the final Vulgate episode—Boors' return to Camalot.[3]

From this comparison it is clear that the Portuguese *Demanda* and the prose *Tristan* are very much alike: for the most part they contain the same episodes arranged in the same order and differ mainly in the episodes that come from the Vulgate *Queste*. Many of these have been taken over *tel quel* by the prose *Tristan* and remodelled or omitted by the Portuguese *Demanda*. At the same time, the Portuguese *Demanda* contains a number of incidents not found in the prose *Tristan*.

Typical of the Vulgate episodes remodelled by the *Demanda* but preserved in its original form in the prose *Tristan*, is the incident of 'Bohors appelé de deux côtés'.[4] In the Vulgate as in the prose *Tristan*, Boors had a vision after which he saw two knights carry off his brother Lionel. At the same moment he noticed another ill-treat a damsel who cried out to him for help. Boors was in a dilemma, but after imploring

ff. 554a–f; *A*, ff. 773b–774b; *C*, ff. 397d–398d; *B*, ff. 350d–352b; *L*, ff. 624d–626a; *F*, ff. 380b–381d; *I*, ff. 186d–187d; *K*, ff. 305a–c; *G*, ff. 313a–314c; *E*, ff. 459r–462r; *J*, ff. 165a–166a; *W*, ff. 520c–521d; *M*, ff. 277b–278c; *Q*, ff. 328b–331a; *R*, ff. 498f–499e; *P*, ff. 489d–490d; *V*, ff. 241b–242b. (MSS. *PQEG* differ from the other Prose *Tristan MSS.*, all having used a manuscript of the Vulgate in conjunction with a Prose *Tristan* manuscript; Sp. *D* also uses here a Vulgate manuscript in conjunction with its main source.)

[1] In other words, the prose *Tristan* omits the contents of *D*, §§ 614–17.

[2] Löseth, *Analyse*, §§ 568–70; MSS. *T*, ff. 416b–417b; *H*, ff. 554f–555c.

[3] Vulgate *Queste*, 279, l. 20–280, l. 5; *D*, §§ 624 middle –626 (Sp. *D* as in certain Vulgate *Queste* MSS.); Löseth, *Analyse*, § 571; MSS. *T*, ff. 417b–418b; *H*, ff. 555c–f. (Not in MSS. *AM*; in MS. *G* the account is the same as in the Vulgate and precedes the account of Sagremor's return to Arthur's court; in MS. *F* the account of Boors' return to Arthur's court is the same as found at the beginning of the Vulgate *Mort Artu*.)

[4] Vulgate *Queste*, 170–94; MS. *T*, ff. 336b–342c; *D*, I, §§ 168–81 (not in Sp. *D*).

God to help his brother, he went to rescue the damsel. Shortly afterwards a 'faux religieux' reproached Boors with having neglected his brother, but 'white monks' subsequently told Boors the true significance of his vision and of his adventure with Lionel: as the latter was in a state of sin, it was right that Boors helped the damsel who was 'vierge'. Moreover, He in whose service Boors was, had aided Lionel by means of a miracle: the two knights who had carried off Lionel had suddenly fallen down dead. After leaving the monks, Boors met Lionel who reproached him for having abandoned him in time of need. Now the *Demanda* keeps the incident of how Boors helped the damsel, but omits the account of Boors' vision and his encounter with the 'faux religieux' as well as the explanation of the significance of the adventure. Instead it relates what the Vulgate and the prose *Tristan* do not—namely how Lionel came to be in the plight in which he was and how he regained his freedom. We are told that one day Lionel saw some tents in a meadow, and as he was tired and wished to rest, he went into one of the tents where he found a damsel. Soon the latter's father and husband arrived, and believing that she had been unfaithful, the husband killed her. Lionel struck down one of the aggressors and then fled, but the husband and the damsel's two brothers pursued him. Lionel killed the husband, but the brothers took him prisoner and prepared to drag him to their father. Then a miracle happened in answer to Boors' prayer: the brothers fell down dead as they approached the tents. After being freed, Lionel was determined to avenge himself on Boors and, as in the Vulgate and the prose *Tristan*, almost killed him.

Most of the incidents not found in the prose *Tristan* also seem late additions. A number of them are obviously based on hints elsewhere in the story; some supply the early history of characters; others are explanations of certain events; others again establish a link with another part of the romance to which the Post-Vulgate *Queste* belongs. Thus for instance while the prose *Tristan* frequently refers to the combats in which Gauvain killed Erec and Baudemagus, it is only in the *Demanda* that we find a complete account of the death of these two characters.[1] Similarly, only the *Demanda* relates the story of the birth of Artus le Petit and of Meraugis de Porlesguez.[2] It gives likewise the early life of

---

[1] *D*, II, §§ 336–52 (= Sp. *D*, Chs. CLXIX–CLXXXIV) and *D*, I, 263–71 (not in Sp. *D*); MS. B.N. fr. 112, *Livre* IV, ff. 110a–113d and ff. 97c–d.

[2] *D*, I, §§ 357–61 (= Sp. *D*, Chs. CLXXXIX–CXCIII) and *D*, I, §§ 277–8 (not in Sp. *D*); MS. B.N. fr. 112, *Livre* IV, ff. 115b–116d and 101a–b.

Esclabor and his eleven children, supplying at the same time a reason why Palamedes pursues the *beste glatissant*.[1] The long account in which we are told how Gauvain forsook Yvain de Cenel at the moment when he most needed his aid, was obviously added in order to explain the hostility of Yvain's sister to Gauvain when the latter arrived at Corbenic.[2] But perhaps the most characteristic of these additions, and the one which explains best the process by which the Vulgate *Queste* was remodelled, is that connected with the white stag. In the Vulgate *Queste*, Galaad, Perceval and Boors witness the transformation of the white stag;

Et quant il i furent entré, si regarderent devant els et virent venir le Blanc Cerf que li quatre lyon conduisoient, celui que Perceval avoit veu autrefoiz. 'Galaad, fet Perceval, ore poez vos veoir merveilles: car par mon chief onques mes ne vi ge aventure plus merveilleuse.'[3]

In the prose *Tristan* and the corresponding part of the *Demanda*, Galaad remarks that the white stag is the creature for which he formerly toiled:

Prose *Tristan*	*Demanda*
Quant il furent entré dedenz, il n'orent pas granment alé qu'il virent par devant eus passer un blanc cerf, celui que li quatre lyon con- duisoient, et s'en ala par devant eus le travers de la forest. 'Or voi ge, fet Galaad, une aventure que je ai autre foiz veue et pour coi me traveilloie je autre foiz.'[5]	E depois que forom dentro, nom andarom muito que virom passar perante si uũ cervo branco que aguarda- vom quatro leoões. E foi-se perante êles atravessando a froresta. 'Ora vejo, disse Galaaz, ua aventura que já outra vez vi, por que me trabalhei uũ pouco.'[4]

But neither the prose *Tristan* nor the Vulgate *Queste* explains Galaad's

---

[1] *D*, I, §§ 124–8; Sp. *D*, Chs. CII–CV. Cf. MS. B.N. fr. 112, *Livre* II, f. 175b–c. Palamedes pursues the *beste glatissant* in order to avenge the death of his ten brothers whom this animal killed.

[2] *D*, I, §§ 129–37; Sp. *D*, Chs. CVI–CXIII. For the scene in which Yvain's sister reproaches Gauvain, see *D*, II, §§ 548–9, Sp. *D*, Chs. CCCXXIV– CCCXXV, and MS. B.N. fr. 343, f. 93a–b.

[3] Vulgate *Queste*, 234, ll. 13–17.

[4] *D*, II, § 431 (not in Sp. *D*).

[5] MS. *T*, f. 368a.

or Perceval's familiarity with the stag: it was left to the author of the *Demanda* (or rather of his immediate French source) to invent a whole episode in the early part of the *Queste* (*D*, §§ 84–6)[1] in which Galaad is shown in pursuit of the creature.

One thing is certain, therefore: the prose *Tristan Queste* cannot be based on the immediate source of the *Demanda*, since it contains many Vulgate *Queste* episodes that have either been remodelled or omitted in the *Demanda*. Nor is it, as Wechssler, Sommer, Löseth, Bohigas Balaguer and Bruce have assumed, a combination of the two. The differences between the prose *Tristan* and the *Demanda* are due to omissions in the French source of the *Demanda*, not to direct borrowings by the author of the prose *Tristan* from the Vulgate. In the story of Galaad's investiture with the *espee as estranges renges*, the prose *Tristan* gives us the whole of the Vulgate account in a somewhat remodelled form.[2] The *Demanda*, on the other hand, agrees with the prose *Tristan* version up to the point where Galaad, Boors and Perceval enter Solomon's ship and find the sword and the crown lying on the bed,[3] omits the remainder of the description of the sword as well as the *Légende de l'Arbre de Vie*,[4] and then continues to agree word for word with the prose *Tristan* version. The omission is clearly deliberate, and in order to conceal it the *Demanda* adds a small transition passage summarizing the missing material.[5] The fact that the portion of the Vulgate episode preserved in the *Demanda* is identical with the remodelled *Tristan* account, suggests that the omitted portion was similar to the version found in the prose *Tristan*.

On the other hand, it looks as though the *Demanda Queste* might be based on the prose *Tristan Queste*. We need only suppose that some late redactor copied a considerable number of episodes from the Vulgate *Queste* and added to them a number of incidents of his own invention. The work would then have been incorporated into the prose *Tristan* 'en cet état', if indeed it ever existed apart from this latter work. At a later date, a second *remanieur* would have revised the prose *Tristan* account, modifying or dropping the Vulgate *Queste* episodes and adding more material of his own invention in the earlier part of

---

[1] Also in MS. B.N. fr. 112, *Livre* IV, ff. 85b–c.

[2] MS. *T*, ff. 357d–365a; Vulgate *Queste*, 199–228.

[3] *D*, II, § 413, p. 97 (not in Sp. *D*).

[4] That is, the *Demanda* omits the equivalent of MS. *T*, ff. 358d–364b, which corresponds to Vulgate *Queste*, 202, l. 15–226, l. 22.

[5] See *D*, II, § 413.

the work. This elaboration of the prose *Tristan*, translated into Portuguese, would be the *Demanda do Santo Graal*.

Unfortunately, if we look more deeply into the facts, such an explanation is seen to be inadequate. The theory that the *Tristan Queste* is the source of the *Demanda* requires us to suppose that wherever the same episode occurs in variant forms in the prose *Tristan* and the *Demanda*, the form in the prose *Tristan* is the original and the form in the *Demanda* is a modification. There are several incidents where this is clearly not the case. One of these is the delivery of Mordrain and Moïs. The *Demanda* and the 343 fragment[1] briefly refer to these events after Palamedes' conversion.[2] The prose *Tristan* MSS., on the other hand, interpolate lengthy accounts of them into Galaad and Lancelot's voyage at a point where *D*-343 follows the Vulgate faithfully. After stating (as in the Vulgate and *D*-343) that Galaad and Lancelot came to many strange islands where they ended many adventures 'que par lour prouesce que par la grasce du Saint Esperit qui en tous leus lour aidoit', the prose *Tristan* MSS. conveniently omit the sentence (in *D*-343 and the Vulgate):

Et de celes aventures qu'il trouverent adonc ne fait pas mencion l'estoire del Saint Grahaal, pour ce que trop i couvenist a demorer qui tout voxist conter quant qu'il lor avenoit,[3]

and go on as follows:

... en tous leus lour aidoit. La vraie estoire dist que tant gaucrerent par la mer qu'il vindrent au pié d'une montaigne.[4]

A voice bids Galaad leave the boat. He finds a white horse tied to a tree, mounts it and rides on until he comes to the abbey where Mordrain lies. Mordrain is healed and Galaad departs, riding on all day until in the evening he finds Moïs in his burning tomb. After relieving the latter's ordeal, Galaad continues on his way 'tant qu'il vint a la nef ou Lancelot estoit qui la atendoit Galaad'.[5] Galaad dismounts and joins Lancelot in the boat. 'Ensi furent lonc tans en la mer [et] virent maintes merveilles.'[6]

---

[1] Henceforth the Portuguese *Demanda* and 343 are referred to as *D*-343.

[2] The healing of Mordrain is in MS. 343 on f. 98b, the delivery of Moïs on f. 100c. *D* omits the Mordrain episode, but it is in Sp. *D*, Ch. CCCXLVI, 291b. The Moïs incident is in *D*, II, § 577 and in Sp. *D*, Ch. CCCLIII.

[3] MS. B.N. fr. 343, f. 75b; Vulgate *Queste*, 251, ll. 28–30; *D*, II, § 517 (not in Sp. *D*).

[4] MS. *F*, f. 363d.   [5] MS. *F*, f. 364d.   [6] Loc. cit.

H

The text of the Vulgate and D-343 reappears in the prose *Tristan* with the description of Spring, and from this point there is complete agreement between the prose *Tristan* and the other versions: Galaad leaves the boat, comes to a hermitage and goes from there 'chiés une veve dame gentil fame et de bone vie', whom he helps to win her lands back from the Conte de Bedoin.[1]

The version of the prose *Tristan* is obviously late and cannot be the source of D-343: it breaks up the text of the Vulgate, omits a sentence in D-343 and the Vulgate, and has an awkward repetition: Galaad enters and leaves the boat twice over. An examination of the content of the Moïs episode reinforces this conclusion. Whereas D-343 only alludes to the incident, saying that Galaad delivered Moïs in the same way as he had done Simeu,[2] the prose *Tristan* MSS. relate the adventure in full,[3] giving exactly the same details as they and D-343 gave earlier of Simeu's delivery.[4] Not only is such a duplication suspect, but there is also textual evidence which suggests that the detailed account of the prose *Tristan* MSS. is a later addition. As we should expect, there are certain verbal differences in the prose *Tristan* accounts of Simeu and Moïs' delivery. Parallel readings are not always identical. Now the curious thing is that often when there are verbal differences, the reading of the Moïs account agrees with the corresponding one of the Simeu account in D-343. In other words, the Moïs account in the prose *Tristan* agrees with the Simeu account in D-343 against the Simeu

[1] MSS. *HIGJWMRUK* are identical with MS. *F*. MSS. *TA* have a lacuna here. MSS. *CL* omit the account of the healing of Mordrain: after leaving the boat for the first time, Galaad passes immediately on to the abbey where Moïs lies. MSS. *BEPQV* agree with MS. *F* etc. up to the point where the boat arrives 'au pié d'une montaigne'. But then the account jumps to the point where Galaad leaves the boat in order to help the widow oppressed by the Conte de Bedoin: ('au pié d'une montaigne, qui estoit aucques pres d'une forest. Et lors virent yssir de la forest un chevalier armé d'unes armes blanches'—MSS. *B*, f. 331d, *V*, f. 229a, *Q*, f. 302b, *E*, f. 426v, *P*, f. 477c). Instead of going straight to the house of the widow, however, he calls first at the abbey where Mordrain lies.

[2] Leienz trouva il la tombe Moïs, le filz Simeu, qui toute voies ardoit, si [com li] contes a ja devisé ça en arrieres. Et tout ausint com Simeu avoit esté delivrez de l'ardoir del feu qui tant avoit duré, en la venue de monseignor Galahaz, tout ausint fu Moïs delivrez, et par celle meemes maniere (MS. B.N. fr. 343, f. 100c; *D*, II, § 577; Sp. *D*, Ch. CCCLIII).

[3] Cf. above, 95.

[4] In both the prose *Tristan* and D-343, Galaad delivers Simeu on his way to Camalot where he is to help Arthur against the Saxons (Löseth, *Analyse*, § 522; MS. 343, ff. 65b–66a; *D*, II, §§ 460–3); not in Sp. *D* which omits *D*, §§ 458–63.

account in the prose *Tristan*.[1] And for such a distribution of variants there is only one reasonable explanation: *D*-343 and the Archetype of the extant MSS. of the prose *Tristan Queste* are derived from a version

[1] The following is a complete list of the readings in question. The quotations are taken from MS. 343, *D* and MS. *G*. The readings of the latter have been compared with those of all the other prose *Tristan* MSS., and all variants are noted.

Moïs	*Simeu*	*Simeu*
MS. *G*, f. 303a	M.S. *G*, 280a	MS. B.N. fr. 343, ff. 65d–66a
(i) verais chevaliers *et* *preudom*	verais chevaliers [*EBQUM* Galaad, chevaliers (*BMPV* sergent, *U* servant) Jhesu Crist]	verai chevalier *et preudome* [*D* verdadeiro cavaleiro *e* verdadeiramente *homem boõ*]
(ii) m'a delivré de *ceste* grant doleur ou j'ai *demoré* [*W* ou je estoie et ai demouré; ou ... demoré *not in UM*]	m'a hui delivré de *la* grant dolor ou j'ai *esté* [*QBPV* m'a aujourd'ui delivré de la grant douleur et martire ou j'ay esté; hui *not in F*; m'a... esté *not in UM*]	m'a delivré de *ceste* grant doulor ou je ai *demoré* [*D* me livrou da grã coita u eu *vivi*]
(iii) tu fus mis a tel *dolor* et a tel martire [et a ... martire *not in UM*]	tu fus mis a si grant martire [*UM* en si]	tu fus mis a si grant *dolor* et a si grant martire [*D* em tam grã coita e em tam grande marteiro]
(iv) l'oscurté estoit ja *del tot* faillie [*UM* et la fumee si estoit]	l'oscurté estoit ja faillie [*Q* et la fumee obscure faillit; *VBMP* et la fumee et l'oscurté]	l'oscurté estoit ja si *del tout* faillie [*D* o fumo se partiu assi]
(v) Venez avant *si leveron ceste lame* et verrons *q'il a desoʒ* [*JHLP* levons; *KM* il i a]	Venez avant et verrons *s'il a riens* sos ceste lame [*KI* desous; *U*, verrez; *M*, si verrons s'il y a ame dessoubz...]	Venez avant *si leverrom ceste lame* et verrom *qu'il a desoʒ* [*D* viinde e *ergamos esta* pedra e veremos *que ha sob ela*]
		[contd. overleaf]

which gave only Simeu's delivery in full; the prose *Tristan* compiler,
wishing to relate in detail also Moïs' adventure, turned back to the
account of Simeu's delivery in the MS. he was copying and transcribed
it again, making certain minor changes necessitated by the fact that he
was transferring the incident from the father to the son, but otherwise
keeping on this occasion more closely to his source than he did when
he copied the episode the first time.

The story of how Palamedes was converted, made a knight of the
Round Table and entered the Quest of the Grail is equally instructive.[1]
Both versions deal with the incident after Lancelot's departure from
Corbenic and the latter's combat with Palamedes, but their treatment
of it is totally different. The *D*-343 account is well prepared and has a

Moïs	*Simeu*	*Simeu*
MS. *G*	MS. *G*	MS. B.N. fr. 343
(vi) Quel que	Que qu'il ait	Quel que *dolor*
dolor q'il ait	soufert, fet	qu'il ait souferte,
souferte, fet	Galaz, *a l'ame*	dit Galahaz,
Galaz, *il li est*	*en est bien*	la merci Deu,
bien avenu	*avenu*	*il li est bien avenu*
[*KFI* quel dolour	[*KI* quel cose que;	
que; quel ...	*VLPEBQP* quoy qu'il	[*D*, Qual quer
avenu *not in*	ait s.; *Q* il lui	*marteiro*,
UM]	en est bien	disse Galaaz,
	advenu; *BPV* a l'ame	que sofresse,
	de lui en est;	muito *lhe*
	not in M]	*aveo bem*]
(vii) por veoir	*FKJWTIBLPV*	pour veoir *se*
se ce estoit	pour veoir *la*	*ce estoit*
verité	verité	veritez
[*M* chascun	[*GUM* l'aventure;	[*D se era*
ala veoir	*Q* has completely	*verdade*]
l'aventure quant	altered the passage:	
il en oïrent	et quant la nouvelle	
parler]	fut espandu par	
	leans que l'aventure	
	estoit affinee, chascun	
	l'ala veoir. Adont	
	monta Galaad ...]	

[1] MS. 343, ff. 94a–98b; *D*, II, §§ 552–68; Sp. *D*, Chs. CCCXXVIII–
CCCXLV; Löseth, *Analyse*, § 560; MSS. *T*, ff. 409a–b, *H*, ff. 550c–d, *A*, ff.
768d–769a, *C*, ff. 394b–c, *B*, ff. 344a–c, *L*, ff. 620b–d, *F*, ff. 374b–d, *I*, ff. 181b–c,
K, ff. 301b–c, *E*, ff. 444r–v, *G*, ff. 310d–311a, *J*, ff. 156d–157a, *W*, ff. 513c–514a,
M, ff. 271d–272a, *Q*, ff. 315b–316a, *R*, ff. 495b–d, *P*, ff. 484a–b, *V*, ff. 236d–237a.

sens and direction. The conversion follows the pattern of Evelac's in the *Estoire*[1] and is the outcome of a certain necessity. After leaving Lancelot, Palamedes encounters Gauvain whom he overcomes in a joust and the latter, thirsting for vengeance, tells Galaad that Palamedes has killed a knight of the Round Table. Galaad forces Palamedes to meet him in single combat, but agrees to put off the battle for twenty days until his wounds are healed. Palamedes returns home, but the knowledge of the impending battle makes him 'mat et pensif oltre ce qu'il n'avoit onques mes esté'.[2] When Esclabor discovers the cause of his son's worry, he speaks to him much in the same strain as Josephés did to Evelac before the battle with Tolomer. He reminds him that 'Jesu Crist li debonaires Sire et li piteux' has been his friend until now, but will abandon him in his greatest need unless he changes his faith. Thereupon Palamedes, like Evelac, promises to receive baptism if he returns safely from his combat. The vow is, moreover, by no means mere expediency, as the redactor makes evident by tracing carefully Palamedes' spiritual evolution between the two terms of the action. A gradual change is seen in Palamedes. At the beginning of the scene he is still a staunch pagan. On his father's admonition, it is true, he promises to accept Christianity eventually; when, however, his father wishes him to do so at once, he refuses. Yet some days later, as he is about to set out for the battle, a difference is visible in him. When those around him remark that he will not lose 'par defaute d'armeures' he retorts:

Cil a cui je ai fait le veu de droite creance tenir, me vaille a cestui point, car je cuit que si secors me porra plus valoir au grant besoing que totes mes armeures.[3]

and the redactor adds:

Tex paroles dist Palamedes com cil qui ja avoit tornee sa creance a la droit foi.[4]

During the battle the change in Palamedes is even more marked, as is evident from his spontaneous utterances;[5] and when finally he accepts Galaad's offer to relinquish the battle on condition that he becomes a

[1] *Vulgate Version*, I, 21-9, 41-59, 73-5.
[2] MS. B.N. fr. 343, f. 95b.
[3] MS. B.N. fr. 343, f. 96a.
[4] MS. B.N. fr. 343, f. 96a.
[5] When for instance he sees Galaad coming towards him 'l'espee el poing', he utters a spontaneous prayer to 'Jhesu Crist' declaring that his faith is already in Him (MS. B.N. fr. 343, f. 97a).

Christian, his words suggest clearly that he does so because he is already converted:

Et sachiez que je onques n'oi greignor volenté de riens avoir que je ai de crestienté recevoir, primierement por ce que je l'avoie voé a Jhesu Crist, et puis por vostre priere.[1]

The rest of the episode continues in the same strain and is the necessary sequel: it is intended to show that the baptism has a real meaning for Palamedes and constitutes a turning point in his life. After leaving the 'sainte onte' where a miracle has cured all his wounds,[2] Palamedes, in his own words, feels himself a 'nouvel home', and as such wishes to enter Christ's service, the Quest of the Holy Grail.[3] As only knights of the Round Table may do so, however, he sets out for Camalot on Galaad's advice. On the way, there is no hermit that he meets to whom he does not confess, no 'home de religion' from whom he does not ask advice, and on his arrival God does a second miracle for him: his name is found inscribed on one of the seats of the Round Table.

It is evident that the whole episode in D-343 has been so constructed as to illustrate the power of 'la loi crestiane'. On the other hand, what strikes one most in the prose *Tristan* account is its extreme abruptness and lack of coherence and motivation. It is barely more than an outline of the main facts, and these are presented in a rather strange light. After leaving Lancelot, Palamedes arrives one day by chance at Camalot where the King, the Queen and all the barons beg him to become a Christian and a knight of the Round Table. The following day, when all are assembled in Church, King Arthur asks him if he wishes to receive baptism and he replies, without hesitation: 'Sire, oïl.'[4] On their return to court the saints are brought out and Palamedes is made a knight of the Round Table. Then, when they have dined, Palamedes asks the King for 'un don': he desires to have leave to go on the Quest of the Grail.

Nor do the minor details which vary in the different prose *Tristan* manuscripts add anything to the significance of the account. Some

[1] MS. B.N. fr. 343, f. 97c.

[2] Cf. the *Estoire del Saint Graal* where Nascien's wounds are similarly healed after his baptism (*Vulgate Version*, I, 75).

[3] 'Sire, de nouvel home, nouvelles œvres. Je sui nouvel serjant Jhesu Crist, si me metrai en sun [service], ce est en la Queste del Saint Grahal, se vos [le me loez]' (MS. B.N. fr. 343, f. 98a).

[4] MS. *T*, f. 409a.

manuscripts, for instance, expand a little Palamedes' reply[1] or the King's question;[2] others suggest that before going to Church, Palamedes already consented to become a Christian[3]—or refused to commit himself.[4] None, however, attempt to give a reasonable explanation for Palamedes' sudden change of heart, unless it is the persuasive power of Arthur's court;[5] and in all the baptism is treated as a social affair, on the same level as the institution of the Round Table: Palamedes accepts the one as he does the other, and for all moral preparation the king has, in some manuscripts, the court,[6] in others Palamedes himself,[7] dressed in rich garments of gold and silk. Nor do any of the manuscripts underline the possible significance which the baptism could have for Palamedes; on the contrary, in all he enters the Quest clearly in his capacity as a knight of the Round Table and not as a 'nouvel serjant Jesu Crist'.[8]

The D-343 account is obviously more cogent than the prose *Tristan* version, which might suggest that the former filled in the outline suggested by the prose *Tristan*. It is equally probable, however, that the

[1] In MSS. *MA* Palamedes replies: 'Sire, je feray vostre plaisir. Nostre Seigneur me vueille octroier s'amour et sa grace' (*M*, f. 272a, *A*, f. 768d); in MS. *BP* we have: 'Et Palamedes respondi que il le demandoit com vray filz de Sainte Eglise' (*B*, f. 344b, *P*, f. 484a).

[2] In MSS. *MA* the King says: 'Palamedes, je vous prie avant que plus parle a vous que vous deveignés crestien et vueillés estre baptisé' (MS. *M*, f. 272a, MS. *A*, f. 768d).

[3] MS. *B*, f. 344a, MS. *I*, f. 181b, MS. *K*, f. 301b.

[4] MS. *M*, f. 272a, MS. *A*, f. 768d.

[5] In all MSS. the whole court beg Palamedes to accept baptism, but certain MSS. underline this fact more heavily. Thus MSS. *KI* (ff. 301b and 181b respectively) write: 'Or dist li contes que quant Palamedes se fu partis de Lancelot a qui il avoit jousté, il chevaucha tant par ses journees qu'il vint a la court le roi Artu et tant i demoura que li rois et la roine et tout li baron de la court li proierent que il devenist crestiens et conpains de la Table Reonde, *tant qu'il lor otroia.*' The words in italics are not in any of the other MSS. except MSS. *B*, f. 344b, *P*, f. 484a, *V*, f. 236d, which have: '... tuit li baron de la court lui prierent *moult doulcement* qu'il devenist crestien et conpaignon de la Table Ronde, *et tant firent qu'il leur ottroia.*' MSS. *M* (f. 272a) and *A* (f. 768d) add after *Table Ronde*: 'Le roy fist apparaillier chevaliers, barons, dames *et leur pria qu'ilz priassent Palamedes qu'il devint crestien, car Palamedes ne vouloit encore octroier ne dire qu'il n'en feroit riens.*'

[6] As e.g. in MSS. *ABFHKMPV*.

[7] As e.g. in MSS. *GJTW*.

[8] In all the prose *Tristan* MSS. Palamedes asks for leave to go on the Quest 'puis qu'il est ainsi que je sui compainz de la Table Roonde par la grace de Dieu' (quoted from MS. *T*, f. 409a).

prose *Tristan* redactor deliberately remodelled an account similar to the *D*-343 version so as to give it a more purely 'adventurous'[1] atmosphere and make Palamedes' admittance to the Round Table parallel to Tristan's. Moreover, the fact which above all suggests that the *D*-343 version represents the original redaction is that the adventures of Palamedes after his conversion continue in the same strain as before and complete the picture of the 'nouvel home', and that some of these adventures are in the prose *Tristan* as well as in *D*-343. Thus, the scene of Palamedes' death is found in both versions and the accounts are identical except for minor variants.[2] After leaving Corbenic, Palamedes fights a battle with Lancelot, in which he is seriously wounded. In this state, he meets his mortal enemy, Gauvain, who forces him to give combat despite his condition.[3] Palamedes knows well that he cannot escape; with the serenity of one, however, whose faith is firm, he prepares to defend himself, knowing that whatever happens to his 'cors', his soul will be in safety:

Et nepourquant, puis que deffendre me couvient, je deffendrai ma vie. Et se je muir a tort, que qu'il aviengne de mon cors, Nostres Sires ait merci de m'ame, se Lui plest.[4]

And when he is mortally wounded, he utters 'un cri mout angoisseus' and begs Christ for mercy; 'Ha! Jhesu Crist, aiez merci de moi.'[5] Equally revealing are his words to Lancelot and Hector who come his way. When asked who has caused his death, he asserts that it was Gauvain, but expresses the hope that Gauvain will be forgiven as he has forgiven him:

Ce fist, fet il, [Gauvain] li niés le roy Artus, qui m'a ocis sans reson. Dieus li pardoint, et je si faz.[6]

Most significant of all, however, are Palamedes' last words before passing from this world. The passage is worth quoting in full:

Aprés ceste parole coumence a batre sa courpe et a pleurer trop durement. Et quant il parole a chief de piece, il dist: 'Jhesu Crist, fontainne de pitié et de misericorde, aiez merci de moi. Et si con je t'ai loiaument servi et de bone volenté puis que je reçui bautesme, si aiez merci de m'ame a cestui terme ou je

---

[1] See Vinaver, *Works*, I, lxxi.
[2] For references see above, 96, n. 4. Also in MS. 112, *Livre* IV, ff. 147d–150c.
[3] MS. 343 breaks off before reaching this point.
[4] MS. *T*, f. 413a.
[5] MS. *T*, f. 413b.   [6] MS. *T*, f. 413d.

vois que je n'ai mestier fors de la teue misericorde.' Lors se test une grant piece et aprés redist: 'Hé! morz, pour coi m'es tu si tost seurvenue? Se tu demourasses et atendisses aucun pou, encor cuidasse je estre preudoume et a Dieu et au monde.' Aprés redist: 'Ha! Jhesu Crist, pere de pitié, en tes mains comant je mon esperit.' Et lors met ses mains en croiz seur son piz. Et maintenant li part l'ame du cors, si que li dui compagnon le virent trespasser en tieus paroles.[1]

There are perhaps few death scenes in the prose romances more moving in their dignity. The redactor does not dwell on Palamedes' agony, but emphasizes the strength that his new faith is giving him. His last thoughts are directed to God, and if he regrets his untimely death, it is only because he had hoped yet awhile to be of service 'et a Dieu et au monde'. He asks for mercy, knowing that he has served Him loyally since his baptism, and passes away calmly, 'ses mains en croiz seur son piz'.

The similarity in inspiration between this scene and the account of Palamedes' conversion in D-343 is only too apparent, and this would suggest that both are due to the same redactor. On the other hand, it is difficult to believe that the author who composed this last act of Palamedes' life would not have made more of his conversion than does the prose Tristan. There is, moreover, a peculiar parallelism in D-343 between the events that lead to Palamedes' spiritual rebirth and those that bring about his death. Gauvain is the cause of both. It is Gauvain's characteristic lust for vengeance that brings about the battle between Galaad and Palamedes which leads to the latter's conversion.[2] Similarly, it is Gauvain who, finding Palamedes wounded after a second en- counter with Lancelot, forces him once more to fight a battle with him which this time causes his death. The effect of this symmetry is too studied to be accidental and suggests that the whole series of episodes —some of which are in the prose Tristan and some of which are not— were invented 'd'un seul jet' by a single author.[3]

Another important episode which differs in the prose Tristan and

[1] MS. T, ff. 413d–414a.

[2] See above, 105.

[3] There is also some external evidence to support the view that the D-343 version represents the original. When Palamedes is about to die, he tells Lancelot that he is the man he loved most 'fors seulement Galaad' (MS. I, f. 413b). Now this remark is unintelligible unless it is a veiled reference to the part which Galaad played in Palamedes' life; for nowhere except at the time of his conversion, did Galaad do anything for Palamedes which could cause such a strong bond of friendship between them.

D-343 is the final scene at Corbenic.[1] While the ultimate source of the
episode is, of course, the Vulgate, the prose *Tristan* and D-343 accounts are not derived independently from it; in certain details they
agree with one another and together differ from the Vulgate, suggesting that there is a definite relationship between them. Thus, for instance, they describe in a similar way how Galaad is taken to the
Maimed King: in D-343 an old man, after asking 'Li quex de vos est
Galahaz?' fetches him while he is engaged in conversation with his
companions in the 'paleis aventureux' shortly after their arrival; in the
prose *Tristan* MSS. two knights who also ask 'Li quieus de vous est
monseigneur Galaad?'[2] take him from his companions while he is talking to them just outside Corbenic. Similarly, whereas in the Vulgate
Galaad heals the Maimed King towards the end of his stay in Corbenic,
in D-343 and the prose *Tristan* MSS. he does so immediately after his
arrival.[3] Again, unlike the Vulgate, D-343 and the prose *Tristan* MSS.
bring in Palamedes and distinguish the 'palais aventureux' from the
Grail chamber.

Apart from these points of contact, however, the two accounts are
wholly different. Which of them is the original? There can be no doubt
that the D-343 version is not derived from the prose *Tristan*: it is much
closer to the Vulgate, their ultimate source. It is true that there are
considerable differences between D-343 and the Vulgate; this is almost
inevitable when we realize that the latter, although a *roman de chevalerie*, is essentially a work of religious inspiration. Material reality
meant nothing to the author of the Vulgate; hence many of his episodes
leave the impression of a mystical vision rather than of incidents
occurring in space and time.[4] Thus in the Vulgate, the communion of

---

[1] MS. B.N. fr. 343, fr. 102a–104c; D, II, §§ 585–94; Löseth, *Analyse*,
§§ 561–2; MSS. T, ff. 409b–411c, H, ff. 550d–552a, A, ff. 769a–770d, C, ff. 394c–
395d, B, ff. 344c–347a, L, ff. 620d–622b, F, ff. 374d–377a, I, ff. 181c–183d, K,
ff. 301c–303a, E, ff. 444v–453v, J, ff. 157b–158c, W, ff. 514a–516d, M, ff. 272a–
276b, Q, ff. 316a–323b, R, ff. 495d–496c, P, ff. 484b–487d, V, ff. 237a–238d.
For a transcription of the final scene at Corbenic in 343, see Appendix, 250–61.

[2] MS. T, f. 409d.

[3] MS. B.N. fr. 343, ff. 102c–103c; MS. T, ff. 409d–410a. *Infra*, 253–5.

[4] Pauphilet (*Études*, 174) sums up the position as follows: 'La réalité matérielle
est absente de ce livre; les personnages y flottent dans un décor étrange, impossible, et qui ne parle guère à la sensibilité; les formes et les couleurs s'y dis-
solvent en abstractions; à peine si, de temps en temps, quelqu'une, un peu
plus consistante, donne un instant l'illusion de la réalité: ... C'est peut-être
le charme le plus singulier de la *Queste* que l'esprit y soit continuellement sus-
pendu entre l'invraisemblable et l'abstrait.'

the chosen knights at Corbenic is not a fantastic adventure taking place in a feudal castle, but the record of a spiritual experience in which the material setting of the narrative fulfils merely a symbolic function. The later prose writers, however, thought of their stories—however improbable they might be—as real happenings, records of fact. They were after all relating 'the adventures of the kingdom of Logres'. It is the matter of the narrative that is of paramount interest rather than the ideas for which the narrative is only a vehicle.[1] It is therefore not surprising that the D-343 redactor did not appreciate the extreme mysticism of the Vulgate and attempted to bring the narrative down to a concrete plane. He gives the healing of the Maimed King its full episodic significance by relating it in much greater detail and linking it with the scene of the maiming of King Pellean in the *Suite du Merlin* of the Huth and Cambridge MSS.,[2] but he omits most of the supernatural features[3] and adds many small details intended to give the account a concrete and realistic character.[4] None the less, he keeps what forms the central part of the scene in the Vulgate *Queste*: the spiritual experience of the Grail knights. In order to make it acceptable, he has replaced Josephés and Christ by a 'clers', 'un home vestu tout de blanc'. The 'clers' is, however, much more than he seems; the words he uses are similar to those used by Christ and are clearly inspired by the Vulgate *Queste*. 'Venez avant, chevaliers plains de foi, filz de Sainte

[1] On the habits of the later prose writers, see Vinaver's illuminating account in his *Études*, 11–17. In particular note the following statement on 13: 'Leur intérêt n'est plus dans les idées qu'ils illustrent; il réside dans les intrigues et les événements qu'ils racontent. Ce que le lecteur reclame et ce que l'auteur lui fournit, ce n'est plus le 'sens', mais la matière pure et simple, la matière autonome, seule raison d'être de la narration.' See also Vinaver, *Le Roman de Tristan et Iseut*, 101–9.

[2] See below, 129–37.

[3] He omits, for instance, the hot wind which rises at 'hore de vespres'; the successive voices bidding first the one then the other to depart until only the twelve knights and the Maimed King remain; the mysterious appearance of Josephés borne in by four angels; the procession of the angels; the miraculous Mass celebrated by Josephés; the appearance of Christ who, taking Josephés' place, gives the knights communion (see Vulgate *Queste*, 267, l. 8–270, l. 25).

[4] Galaad, for instance, recognizes Corbenic when he arrives there and explains to his companions that it is impossible to enter the 'paleis aventureux' if they are not 'chevalier del Sainte Grahal' (MS. 343, f. 102a–b). Again when Galaad, Perceval and Palamedes are joined by the other nine Grail knights, they all tell each other their experiences in the Quest, and the redactor adds 'Et se vos adonc i fuissiez la, adonc peussiez oïr conter maintes belles merveilles et maintes belles aventures' (MS. 343, f. 102c).

Eglise, si [s]eroiz repeu de la viande que vos avez tant desirré. Et tu Galahaz, filz que je ai trouvé plus loial serjant et meillor que nul autre chevalier, vien avant,'[1] is what he says as he offers each 'une oblee'. And all as they partake 'de la dolce viande et de la glorieuse del Saint Grahal' have the same mystical experience as in the Vulgate *Queste*: each one realizes that he has received 'joie et grace esperitex'.[2]

Moreover, the end of the scene in *D*-343 consists almost entirely of passages taken over from the Vulgate, with changes in order, minor differences in expression, and a 'voice' speaking the words attributed to Christ in the Vulgate.[3] At the beginning, too, certain features recall the Vulgate: when Galaad, Perceval and Palamedes have entered the 'paleis aventureux' they take off their armour,[4] and are eventually joined by the other nine Grail knights.[5] Finally, the Maimed King, after his healing, retires to a hermitage as in the Vulgate.[6]

But while the Vulgate is still clearly visible beneath the text of *D*-343, practically nothing of it remains in the prose *Tristan*:[7] the prose *Tristan* compiler, even more a man of his time than the *D*-343 redactor, has carried the process of remodelling a stage further. One would look in vain in his account for anything that resembles the com-

---

[1] MS. B.N. fr. 343, f. 103d. *Infra*, 257.

[2] MS. B.N. fr. 343, f. 104a. *Infra*, 258.

[3] See Appendix, 255–61.

[4] MS. B.N. fr. 343, f. 102b; Vulgate *Queste*, 266, l. 16. *Infra*, 252.

[5] MS. B.N. fr. 343, f. 102b–c; Vulgate *Queste*, 267, ll. 22–31. *Infra*, 252.

[6] MS. B.N. fr. 343, f. 103b–c; Vulgate *Queste*, 272, ll. 3–7. *Infra*, 255–6.

[7] What I say about the prose *Tristan* applies to all MSS. except *GEQP*. MS. *G* agrees with MS. *T* up to the point where Palamedes meets Galaad, Perceval and eight other knights 'a deus lieus de Corbenic', and explains to them that he has become a Christian (MS. *T*, f. 409c, MS. *G*, f. 311b). Here MS. *G* takes up the account of the Vulgate *Queste* at a point corresponding to 262, l. 20 of Pauphilet's edition, continuing with it right to the end of the *Queste*. MSS. *QEP* likewise agree with MS. *T* up to the point where Palamedes tells the other knights of his conversion (MSS. *Q*, f. 316c, *P*, f. 484c, *E*, f. 445r), but then Galaad and Perceval leave Palamedes and the other eight knights and go alone to Corbenic. They find a boat in the stream as in MS. *T* and from here up to the point where Galaad leaves the castle to join Perceval and Boors, MSS. *QE* agree with MS. *T* (MSS. *T*, f. 411b–c, *Q*, f. 320a, *E*, f. 450v, *P*, f. 486b). After this MSS. *PQE* take up the text of the Vulgate *Queste*, at a point corresponding to 266, l. 15 of Pauphilet's edition, and continue with it up to 273, l. 28 (MSS. *Q*, f. 323b, *P*, f. 487d, *E*, f. 453v). Then follows the account of Esclabor's and Palamedes' death, after which MSS. *QEP* continue with the Vulgate account up to the point of Galaad's and Perceval's death. From there up to the end of the story, they agree with the other prose *Tristan* MSS.

munion of the Grail knights in *D*-343 and the Vulgate. The only knight who has anything approaching a mystical experience is Galaad, but he does not receive communion: it is merely a sensation that he has on entering the Grail Chamber for the second or third time, and there is nothing to recall the text of the Vulgate.[1] As regards the other eleven knights, nine of them never enter Corbenic at all, but remain patiently outside until Galaad has performed his duties within;[2] the remaining two (Perceval and Boors) only go in at the end in order to help Galaad carry out the silver table with the Grail on it.

All the other features which *D*-343 shares with the Vulgate are also again absent from the prose *Tristan* account. Nor, on the other hand, does the prose *Tristan* have any important details which are in the Vulgate and not in *D*-343.[3] Instead, we find a series of incidents more in accordance with the " 'adventurous' spirit"[4] of the prose *Tristan*. When the prose *Tristan* redactor incorporated the *Queste* into his compilation he took over a number of adventures from the prose *Lancelot* which serve as an introduction to the *Queste*. They include the stories of Galaad's birth, of Lancelot's madness, of Perceval's arrival at Arthur's court and of Boors' first visit to Corbenic.[5] In this latter episode, Boors spends the night in the 'paleis aventureux', but is powerless

[1] MS. *T*, f. 410b.

[2] When all the Grail knights except Boors have arrived outside Corbenic (Boors arrives only later), two knights from the castle invite Galaad to enter, and the latter asks his companions to wait for him: 'Et Galaad prie Perceval et les autres chevaliers qu'il l'atendent, car il revendra tost' (MS. *T*, f. 409d).

[3] The only exception is the reference to Galaad joining together the pieces of the sword that broke in Joseph de Barimacie's thigh, found in the prose *Tristan* and Vulgate accounts, but not in *D*-343. There are no verbal similarities, however, between the prose *Tristan* and Vulgate accounts. All the former says is: 'Et li rois le mainne en une chambre et li moustre l'espee qui ert brisiee, qui se brisa en la cuisse de Joseph de Barimacie. Galaad la prent et la joint ensemble, et ele se solde, ainsint coume ele fu onques mieuz' (MS. *T*, f. 410a). In the Vulgate, on the other hand, Elyezer brings the Broken Sword into the room and the author refers to it as the one with which Joseph had been struck in the thigh. Then Boors and Perceval make an unsuccessful attempt to join the pieces of the sword before Galaad eventually succeeds in doing so (Vulgate *Queste*, 266, ll. 16–33).

[4] Vinaver, *Works*, I, lxxi.

[5] These adventures, taken over from the prose *Lancelot*, are found in the following prose *Tristan* MSS.: *HACLFRUK* and Chantilly 646, Chantilly 648. Sommer has transcribed them from MS. *K* and published them under the title of 'Galaad and Perceval' in *MPh.*, V (1907–8) 55–84, 181–200, 291–341. Löseth summarizes them, *Analyse*, § 388a. On the origin of these episodes, see

to achieve the adventures which present themselves as they are reserved for 'li boins chevaliers qui les aventures du Saint Graal metra
a fin'.[1] From this the author of the prose *Tristan* got the idea of making
Galaad accomplish all these adventures during the last visit to Corbenic. Boors sees a man with snakes round his neck who tells him that
he will not be delivered until the coming of 'li boins Chevaliers'.[2]
Consequently in the final scene at Corbenic Galaad sees this man and
frees him of the snakes.[3] Similarly, Boors is unable to deliver the twelve
poorly clad damsels,[4] but Galaad frees them by leading them out of the
palace.[5] Finally, Boors sees the Bleeding Lance, but is told that he will
never know the truth about it until the coming of Galaad who will
tell him.[6] Galaad does not in fact tell him, but in the final scene at
Corbenic the Maimed King gives Galaad a full account of its history.[7]
In addition, the Maimed King relates the history of the man with the
snakes, of the twelve poorly clad damsels, and of Moïs and Simeu.[8]

The author of the Vulgate *Queste*, who presumably knew the prose
Lancelot, did not think it necessary to fulfil its predictions, the Grail
communion serving as a fitting close for the story. For the compiler of
the prose *Tristan*, on the other hand, nothing less concrete than the
accomplishment of the adventures witnessed by the first knight to enter
Corbenic could indicate that the *Queste* was drawing to its end. But
this is not all. The whole account of the final scene at Corbenic is given
a concrete aim. Neither the Vulgate *Queste* nor *D*-343 relates how the
Grail left Corbenic, but both say that Galaad, Boors and Perceval find
the Grail and the silver table in the boat by the sea which takes them to
Sarraz. The account is in line with their general concept of the Grail,
which can displace itself without the intervention of a human agent.[9]
The compiler of the prose *Tristan*, however, could no more appreciate
this than the fact that 'un boivre'[10] could cause the love of Tristan and

Sommer, *Studies on the sources of 'Le Morte Darthur'*, London, 1890, vol. III,
272–8, and *art. cit.*; also, Wechssler, 19–21, and Brugger, 'Der Schöne Feigling',
ZRPh., LXV (1945) 359, n. 2.

[1] MS. *K*, f. 148d.   [2] MS. *K*, f. 148d.
[3] MS. *T*, f. 410a.   [4] MS. *K*, f. 149a–b.
[5] MS. *T*, f. 410a.   [6] MS. *K*, f. 149a.
[7] MS. *T*, f. 410b–d.   [8] MS. *T*, ff. 410d–411b.

[9] See Pauphilet, *Études*, 24 and MS. B.N. fr. 343, f. 88b: 'car li Sainz Vaxiaux n'estoit nulle foiz porté de Corbenic par main d'ome mortel.'

[10] See Vinaver, *Études*, 11–20; *Le Roman de Tristan et Iseut*, 107–9; and *Works*,
I, lxxi.

Yseut. He replanned accordingly the whole scene, making the trans-portation of the Holy Vessel its real and only *raison d'être*. Galaad, Perceval and Boors are sent for to Corbenic simply in order to fetch the Grail and take it to Sarraz. In the other versions they come to Cor-benic by accident; in the prose *Tristan* a voice tells them to go there 'pour le Saint Graal' and the redactor asserts very naïvely that if it had not been for this voice they would not have gone, 'car autrement nel seust il'.[1] A 'brief' in the boat outside Corbenic reminds them of their duty.[2] Galaad in particular is very aware of the nature of his task. When, for instance, the Maimed King takes him to see his mother, Galaad does not allow her to embrace him, explaining that it is his duty to bear the Holy Grail.[3] And he remains with her only until he is in a position to carry out his task: as soon as Perceval sends a message to tell him of the arrival of Boors, he leaves her, joins his companions outside the castle and returns with them to the 'sainte chambre' in order to carry the silver table with the Grail onto the boat:

Lors se prennent li troi compagnon main a main et s'en vont droit au palés aventureus. Et quant il sont dedenz, si vont en la sainte chambre et trouverent la table d'argent ou il avoit desus le Saint Vessel couvert d'un drap de soie. Et Boort et Perceval prennent la table par devant, et Galaad par derrieres, si l'emportent jusqu'a la nef. Et quant il sont venu a la nef, si la meitent dedenz. Et quant il furent dedenz, le vent se fiert en la nef, si la mainne si grant oirre coume ele puet plus.[4]

The final scene at Corbenic is perhaps the most striking case where *D*-343 is closer to the Vulgate than is the prose *Tristan*. The view that the similarity is due to the fact that the author of *D*-343 knew both the Vulgate and the prose *Tristan* and combined the two accounts can easily be dismissed. The remarkable thing about the episode in the

---

[1] MS. *T*, f. 409b.

[2] The *brief* explains that when Galaad, Perceval and Boors are all three together, but not before, they are to take the Grail onto the boat: '... Et bien vous gardez que vous dedenz moi n'enterez, se vous n'estes touz trois ensemble. Et puis vous en alez en la sainte chambre qui est u palés aventureus et prenez la table d'argent ou ele est desus le Saint Vessel, et si l'aportez dedenz ceste nef, et enterrez dedenz, et puis vous en irez la ou ele vous voudra mener' (MS. *T*, f. 409c–d).

[3] Et quant la mere le voit, si saut sus et le volt acoler et beisier. Mes il nel sueffre mie, ainz dist: 'Dame, pour Dieu merci, ne me touchiez mie, que je ne voudroie en nule maniere que fame me touchast, pour ce que je doi porter le Saint Vessel' (MS. *T*, f. 411b).

[4] MS. *T*, f. 411c.

prose *Tristan* is that it differs in style and treatment not only from the Vulgate *Queste*, but also from the parts of the prose *Tristan*'s narrative that recur in *D*-343. A vague religious atmosphere hangs about many of the episodes common to *D*-343 and the prose *Tristan*.[1] The prose *Tristan*'s account of the last scene at Corbenic is, on the other hand, confused, repetitive and wholly secular in tone. For instance, the King and Galaad walk to and from the Grail Chamber as though it was an ordinary room.[2] Only a writer interested in 'adventures' pure and simple rather than ideas could so change the *sens* of the episode.

There are, in addition, one or two minor contradictions in the prose *Tristan* which suggest that this version is a remodelled account of *D*-343. Thus according to *D*-343, when Galaad is about to heal King Pellean, the Lance is taken up to Heaven as soon as he has removed the 'vessel' beneath it.[3] This detail, which is neither in the prose *Tristan* nor in the Vulgate *Queste*,[4] serves to explain a feature common to the prose *Tristan* and *D*-343. Whereas in the Vulgate *Queste* Lance and Grail are both taken up to Heaven after Galaad's death,[5] in the prose

---

[1] We may for example mention one of King Pelles' conversations with Lancelot (MS. 343, f. 91d), the punishment of the magician from Barbarie (MS. 343, f. 88b), Galaad's vision (MS. 343, f. 71c), Palamedes' death (MS, *T*, ff. 413d–414a. See also below, 204–8).

[2] When Galaad is first taken to the Maimed King, the latter bids him go in to the 'sainte chambre' to fetch the Bleeding Lance (MS. *T*, f. 409d). When the Maimed King is healed, he tells Galaad to go with him to the 'sainte chambre' to take the Lance back (MS. *T*, f. 410a). Later, when Galaad has ended various adventures, the King repeats once more the phrase 'Fuiz Galaad, alons en la sainte chambre', and both go in to the room again (MS. *T*, f. 410a–b). Finally, accompanied by Boors and Perceval, Galaad goes a fourth time into the 'sainte chambre' to carry out the Grail (MS. *T*, f. 411c).

[3] *D*, II, § 589; MS. B.N. fr. 343, f. 102d (see Appendix, 254).

[4] In the prose *Tristan*, Galaad takes the Lance back to the Grail Chamber after the healing of Pellean: 'Et li rois, quant il le vit, dit: "Bien soies tu venuz et beneoit soit Dieus quant il ceste part t'a amené." Lors li dist: "Fuiz Galaad, alez en cele sainte chambre et si prenez la [l]ance que vous i trouveroiz et si la m'aportez." Et Galaad dist: "Mout volentiers". Lors vet en la chambre. Et quant il fu dedenz, si li fu avis que tout le basme et toute l'odeur du monde i fussent. Il regarde et voit la lance dont Nostre Sires fu feruz u flanc en la sainte croiz et la prent, si s'en ist hors et vient au Roi Mahegnié. Et quant il est venuz la, si li dist li rois: "Fuiz Galaad, prenez de cest sanc qui est seur la pointe de cele lance et m'en oindrez ces jambes et ces cuisses." Et Galaad prent du sanc o grant devocion et o grant pitié et li oint ses jambes et ses cuisses. Et quant il en est oint, si en est touz guieriz. Et lors li dist li rois: "Fuiz, alons en la sainte chambre et aportez la lance"' (MS. *T*, ff. 409d–10a).

[5] Vulgate *Queste*, 279, ll. 2–7: 'Qar li dui compaignon virent apertement que

Tristan and the *Demanda*[1] only the Grail is removed, the Lance not being mentioned.[2] The inference is clear. The source of the prose *Tristan* and *D*-343 made the lance disappear after the healing of Pellean, but kept the Grail until after Galaad's death. Only *D*-343 keep this feature; the prose *Tristan* has, as we have seen, altered the narrative by making Galaad put the lance back in its place after he used it.

Again after leaving Corbenic, Palamedes meets Lancelot who asks him if he has any news of Galaad. The reply is as follows:

> Et lors li coumence a conter la ou il avoient esté jusqu'a douze compagons [chiés] le Riche Roi Pescheeur, et l'aventure belle qui a Boort avint, et coument il se departirent.[3]

This reading is common to the great majority of prose *Tristan* MSS.[4] and is similar to that in the *Demanda* and MS. B.N. fr. 112.[5] The first part of the remark is surprising since in the prose *Tristan* only three, not twelve knights enter the Grail castle. Moreover, the reading 'l'aventure belle qui a Boort avint' is a plain attempt to cover up the deficiencies of the narrative. The right reading is 'belle aventure

---

une mein vint devers le ciel; mes il ne virent pas le cors dont la mein estoit. Et elle vint droit au seint Vessel et le prist, *et la Lance ausi*, et l'enporta tot amont vers le ciel, a telle eure qu'il ne fu puis hons si hardiz qu'il osast dire qu'il eust veu le Seint Graal.'

[1] MS. 343 breaks off before reaching this point.

[2] MS. *T*, f. 416a: 'Car les deus compagnons virent tout apertement que une main vint devers le ciel, mes il ne veoient pas le cors dont la main estoit; et ele vint droit au Saint Vessel et le prist et l'en porta amont vers le ciel a si grant chant et a si grant gloire que c'estoit merveille d'oïr et la plus douce chose du monde. Ne il ne fu puis nus hons si hardiz qu'i osast dire que li Sainz Graal fust puis veuz en terre.' *D*, II, § 623: '... e filhou o Santo Vaso e levou-o contra o céu com tam grã canto e com tam grã ledice, que nunca homem viu mais saborosa cousa de ouvir, assi que nunca houve homem na terra que pois podesse dizer com verdade que nunca o i er virom.'

[3] MS. *T*, f. 412c.

[4] MSS. *B*, f. 348b, *P*, f. 488b, *V*, f. 239c have: 'l'aventure qui avint a Galaad et a Bohort et a Perceval, et coment ...'; MSS. *QE* (f. 324d and 455r respectively) read: 'Lors lui comença a compter coment il l'avoit veu ou chasteau de Corbenic et lui compta toute l'aventure come vous l'avez oÿ cy devant.' The scribes of these MSS. evidently realized that the reading of the other prose *Tristan* MSS. is inappropriate.

[5] Et lors ly commence a compter comment ilz avoient esté douze compaignons chés le Riche Pescheur, et la belle aventure qui leur advint, et comment ilz se deppartirent. (MS. B.N. fr. 112, *Livre* IV, f. 148d; also in *D*, II, § 597; MS. 343 breaks off before reaching this point.)

I

qui leur advint' as in *D*-112 and the allusion is to the Grail communion. Realizing that 'leur' was not appropriate in his version, the prose *Tristan* replaced it by 'Boors'. In so doing he betrayed himself absolutely, for it would require great imagination for anyone to refer to the fact that Boors arrived at Corbenic after the other knights as an 'aventure belle'.

The evidence derived from the episodes that have been examined, thus seems quite unambiguous: the prose *Tristan Queste* cannot be the source of the *Demanda* any more than the *Demanda* is the source of the prose *Tristan Queste*. To explain, therefore, that the two works reproduce the same incidents in the same order and have the same general framework, we must assume that they both go back to a common source.

This source, no longer extant, was a *remaniement* of the Vulgate *Queste* to which, for want of a better name, we may refer as the Post-Vulgate *Queste* (*Y*). It contained all the episodes common to the prose *Tristan Queste* and the *Demanda*, was identical with the Vulgate *Queste* for all those incidents which either in the prose *Tristan* or in the *Demanda* have been reproduced from the Vulgate without alteration, and was closer to the *Demanda* in those cases where an episode occurs in variant forms in the *Demanda* and the prose *Tristan*. In other words, the Post-Vulgate *Queste* would have agreed with *D*-343 for Palamedes' conversion and the final scene at Corbenic, and would have included the whole complex of adventures found in *D*-343 between Palamedes' conversion and the final scene at Corbenic—namely Galaad's delivery of Mordrain and Moïs, the adventure of the Boiling Fountain, Palamedes' combat with Athanas and the death of the *beste glatissant*. In addition, there can be no doubt that it would have contained also the *Demanda* account of how Galaad, Perceval and Boors, on their way to the sea, came to King Pellean's hermitage, learned the history of the three marvels of Logres, and then, reaching the sea, set sail for Sarraz in Solomon's boat in which they found the silver table with the Holy Grail on it.[1] On the other hand, as there are in the

[1] The omission in the prose *Tristan* of the above account can be readily explained: according to the prose *Tristan* MSS., Galaad, Boors and Perceval carry the Grail on the silver table into a boat which is waiting in the stream outside Corbenic, and set sail at once. It was not necessary to relate, therefore, how the knights arrived at the sea shore, and the easiest point at which the story could be picked up again was in the middle of the voyage, where the *Demanda* and the Vulgate *Queste* alike say: 'Grant tens, ce dit li contes, demourerent les trois compagnons en la mer' (quoted from MS. *T*, f. 415a; also in *D*, II, § 618

Post-Vulgate *Queste* a large number of prose *Tristan* characters and situations, we must assume that its redactor, like the author of the *Suite du Merlin*, knew and used the First Version of the prose *Tristan*.[1]

The Post-Vulgate *Queste* (*Y*) was not the immediate source of the *Demanda*. If the present state of the latter is partly due to the Portuguese translator, it is certain that most of the differences between the Post-Vulgate *Queste* (*Y*) and the *Demanda* are due to a French *remanieur*. Large sections of the episodes peculiar to the *Demanda* are, in fact, extant in French in a number of manuscripts. Thus MS. B.N. fr. 112 contains all the adventures found in *D*, §§ 81–123, 129–44, 201–7, 277–363; MS. B.N. fr. 116 has the adventures contained in *D*, §§ 201, 206 and Turin L-I-9 has those in *D*, §§ 125–6, while MS. B.N. fr. 340, 355, 1463 contains in a modified form those found in *D*, §§ 74–80. Moreover, in MS. B.N. fr. 112 the episodes peculiar to the *Demanda* are found together with some of the episodes that the *Demanda* shares with the prose *Tristan Queste*, in exactly the same order in which they occur in the *Demanda*. Thus, for instance, the series of episodes beginning with Tristan's pursuit of Galaad, related in all three texts, follow in the prose *Tristan* immediately after the *tornoiement merveilleux*;[2] in the *Demanda* and MS. B.N. fr. 112, however, they are preceded first by a long series of other episodes: Artus le Petit's adventures, Meraugis' adventures, the incidents leading up to Erec's death, Baudemagus' death and Gauvain and his brothers' visit to Morgain.[3] This suggests clearly that the Post-Vulgate *Queste* (*Y*) underwent further remodelling and that there existed at one time a second French version of it (*Z*) in all respects identical with the Portuguese *Demanda*.[4]

---

and Vulgate *Queste*, 275, l. 5). The result is the omission of much material, including not only the contents of 273, l. 11–275, l. 4 of the Vulgate *Queste*, but also the history of the three marvels of Logres.

[1] E.g., the Post-Vulgate *Queste* knows that Tristan and Yseut found refuge in Lancelot's castle, Joieuse Garde (Löseth, *Analyse*, §§ 343–4), that Mark invaded Logres during the *Queste* (Löseth, *Analyse*, 350, n. 1, 372, n. 5), that Palamedes accidentally killed Hebés (Löseth, *Analyse*, § 27) and is Tristan's rival for Yseut's love (Löseth, *Analyse*, § 31 ff.). Again, like the prose *Tristan*, the Post-Vulgate *Queste* blackens the characters of Mark and Gauvain (see below, 122–3).

[2] See above, 94.

[3] *D*, §§ 263–363; MS. B.N. fr. 112, *Livre* IV, ff. 100c–117a.

[4] It is very probable that this second redaction of the Post-Vulgate *Queste* (*Z*) is later in date than the prose *Tristan Queste* (see Appendix I).

The foregoing conclusions may be expressed by the following table of filiation:

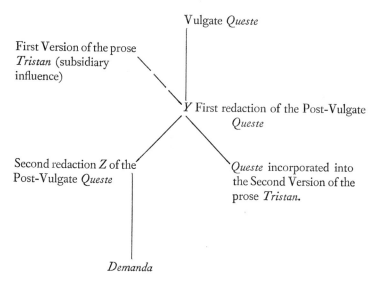

Vulgate *Queste*

First Version of the prose *Tristan* (subsidiary influence)

Y First redaction of the Post-Vulgate *Queste*

Second redaction *Z* of the Post-Vulgate *Queste*

Queste incorporated into the Second Version of the prose *Tristan.*

Demanda

CHAPTER V

The Post-Vulgate 'Queste' and the 'Suite du Merlin'

IT has long been assumed by critics that the *Suite du Merlin* fore-shadows a version of the *Queste del Saint Graal* differing from the Vulgate *Queste* and similar to the Portuguese and Spanish *Demandas*, but its exact nature has never been established.[1] There is ample evidence, however, that the *Queste* which formed the bulk of the 'third part' of the *Suite* compilation was no other than the Post-Vulgate *Queste*, the common source of the *Demanda* and the *Tristan Queste*.

In the first place, the Post-Vulgate *Queste* contains the same redactional indications as the *Suite du Merlin*. Like the latter it assumes (wrongly) the authorship of Robert de Boron, refers the reader to the *Conte del Brait* for incidents that it does not relate, and not only speaks of the tripartition of the work, but actually contains a statement to the

[1] Pickford (*Évolution*, 94-6, 104-5) accepts the traditional view that the 343-*Demanda Queste* represents the third part of the *Suite* compilation, but later (119-21) suggests that the *Demanda Queste* may have been written to form the third part of the prose romance of *Palamède*: 'Un remanieur du *Palamède* eut l'idée d'en faire un roman cyclique qui contiendrait une *Queste del Saint Graal* et une *Mort Artu*... A la fin du roman le rédacteur parle d'une division tripartite de l'œuvre: la seconde Partie devrait se terminer après la mort du roi Arthur... Se peut-il que les épisodes où figurent Palamède, Esclabor et d'autres personnages du roman de *Palamède*, qui forment une si grande partie de la *Queste del Saint Graal* du faux Robert de Borron, aient été composés pour ce troisième livre du *Palamède* qui n'existe plus? Cette version de la *Queste* nous présente Palamède qui tue la Bête Glatissante, assiste à la Messe du Graal après s'être fait baptiser, et enfin meurt assassiné par Gauvain. Il est bien possible qu'un remanieur voulant combler la lacune du troisième livre du *Palamède* ait composé ces aventures qui furent recopiées par Micheau Gonnot. Nous ne saurons sans doute jamais la vraie provenance de ces histoires à moins qu'on ne découvre un exemplaire du *Palamède* complet avec ce troisième livre.' While it is true that the various *Palamèdes* MSS. announce that their third part begins with the *Queste del Saint Graal*, there is no evidence to suggest that this *Queste* would have been the *Demanda Queste*. All the characters which the Post-Vulgate *Queste* shares with the *Palamède* figure already in the prose *Tristan*, and there is no reason to suppose that the Post-Vulgate obtained these characters from any other source.

effect that it *is* the third part of the *livre de cil de Boron*:

Et Galahaz, quant il se fu partiz del chevalier, chevaucha puis mainte jornee
et maintes aventures mist a fin, dont cil de Beron ne parole mie, car trop eust
a faire se il voxist a cestui point raconter toutes les merveilles del Grahal, et
la darraine partie de son livre fust trop grant avers les autres deus premieres. Mes
ce, sanz faille, qu'i lesse a devisser en ceste partie devisse e[l] contes del Brait,
car li conte del Brait sanz doute trait d'une part por faire les [trois] parties del
livre egalles a nostre pooir.[1]

Further, like the *Suite du Merlin*, the Post-Vulgate *Queste* refers to
incidents related in the *Lancelot* to fill in the background. Thus in
speaking of Lancelot's fight with the two lions that guarded King
Lancelot's tomb, the redactor adds 'si come la grant estoire de Lancelot
le doit deviser'.[2]

In the second place, many of the allusions in the *Suite du Merlin*
which do not fit the Vulgate *Queste* are intelligible in the context of the
Post-Vulgate. Thus according to the *Suite du Merlin* one of the Grail
winners, Perceval li Galois, is Pellinor's son.[3] Now while in the Vulgate *Queste* Pellehen, not Pellinor, is Perceval's father, the Post-
Vulgate agrees with the *Suite du Merlin*: in the Vulgate Perceval's sister
says to him:

Sachiez, fet ele, que je sui vostre suer et fille au roi Pellehen.[4]

But in the Post-Vulgate she remarks:

Sachiez que li rois Pelinors fu mes peres, et Perceval qui ci est, si est
mes freres de pere et de mere.[5]

Moreover, the Post-Vulgate *Queste* assumes, like the *Suite du Merlin*,
that Perceval's father was slain by Gauvain: as the latter is about to
leave Corbenic, Yvain de Cenel's sister reproaches him for this in no
uncertain terms:

Gauvain! Gauvain! Or aperent vos males oevres. Assez avez mal fait en ceste
Queste et maint bon chevalier ocis en desloiauté et en traïson... Et sachiez

---

[1] MS. B.N. fr. 343, f. 101a; *D*, II, § 581; Sp. *D*, Ch. CCCLV, 295b.
[2] MS. B.N. fr. 343, f. 100c.
[3] Huth *Merlin*, I, 160.
[4] Vulgate *Queste*, 201 l. 24.
[5] MS. B.N. fr. 772, f. 365a. Cf. *D*, II, § 416: 'Sabede que rei Pelinor foi meu
padre, e dom Persival, que aqui é, é meu irmão de padre e de madre' (not
in Sp. *D*).

que Perceval, li loiaux chevaliers, qui pere vos oceistes en felenie et en traïson, istra de leienz a mult greignor honor que vos [n]e faites.[1]

At the point where Balain kills in self-defence the Chevalier d'Irlande, King Mark, then newly crowned, appears on the scene and the redactor of the *Suite* explains that he later married Yseut 'as the story will tell', and refers to an incident in the *Graaus*:

Endementiers que li dui chevalier parloient ensi au nain, issi fors de la forest li roi Mars, qui puis ot a feme Yseut la blonde, *si comme chis contes meismes devisera apertement, pour chou que conter i couvint pour une aventure dont li Graaus parole.* Li rois Mars avoit adonc esté couronnés nouvielement, ne n'avoit pas d'aage plus de dis et set ans, et aloit au roi Artus pour lui aidier de sa guerre, car toute sa terre estoit sougite au roiame de Logres.[2]

The *Graaus* is, of course, the *Queste del Saint Graal,* but the Vulgate *Queste,* as is well known, relates no adventure involving either King Mark or Yseut. The Post-Vulgate *Queste,* on the other hand, has a long episode where, as the *Suite du Merlin* announces, Mark's marriage with Yseut is of great importance. It relates how King Mark has heard that Tristan and Yseut have gone to Logres and live in Joieuse Garde; but Mark loves Yseut so much that he cannot forget her, 'ainz en estoit tant a mal aise que nus plus'.[3] He would many a time have asked King Arthur to send her back, but does not dare to do so, for he knows that King Arthur cares too much for Tristan to distress him in any way. Consequently Mark remains for more than two years 'en tel angoisse et en tel destrece' and conceives deep hatred for Arthur. Not long after the beginning of the Quest, however, a rumour spreads that all the companions of the Round Table have been killed, and on Andret's advice Mark invites Arthur's mortal enemies, the Saxons, to join forces with him and invade Logres. The two armies land at Ossenedoc and after marching stealthily by night for six days reach Joieuse Garde one Saturday evening. The people of the castle, unaware of any danger, have left the doors open and with five hundred men Mark enters, makes his way straight to the room where Yseut is and takes her by force. Then he sets fire to Joieuse Garde and his men seize all the booty they can, but he desires none of it, 'puis qu'il avoit Yseut'.[4] From here Mark leads the men to Camalot, Arthur's residence, and after wounding

---

[1] MS. B.N. fr. 343, f. 93a–b; *D,* II, § 548, p. 236; Sp. *D,* Ch. CCCXXIV, 283b.

[2] Huth MS., f. 104b–c; Huth *Merlin,* I, 230; *Le roman de Balain,* 23.

[3] MS. B.N. fr. 343, f. 61a.   [4] Ibid., f. 61d.

Arthur in battle, lays siege to the town, but is finally defeated by
Galaad and three of his companions who, having heard of Arthur's
distress, go to his aid.[1] What more likely than that the allusion of the
Suite du Merlin is to this episode?

Another reference in the *Suite du Merlin* can likewise be explained
in relation to the Post-Vulgate *Queste*. The *Suite du Merlin* relates how
the day after his vision Arthur goes out hunting, loses all his men and
his horse which collapses under him, and while resting by a fountain
deep in thought hears

uns grans glas de chiens qui faisoient aussi grant noise que se il fuissent trente
ou quarante, et venoient viers lui, che li samble, si cuide que che soient si
levrier.[2]

He lifts up his head, looks in the direction from which the noise is
coming and shortly after sees running towards him

une beste mult grant que estoit la plus divers que onques fust veu de sa
figure, car tant estoit divers, laide e orible e estraunge e granz a desmesure. E
plus se merveille lui rois d'une chose, car la beste que prainz estoit s'en
venoit grant oire a la fontaigne e aloient abaiant e glatissant dedenz son
ventre si faon.[3]

While the *beste* is drinking from the fountain, the whelps within it
cease barking, but as soon as it has left the fountain, 'si recommen-
cierent a glatir autressi comme il faisoient devant. Et fisent autretel
noise comme fesissent vint braket apriés une beste sauvage.'[4] Arthur
is completely taken aback, but soon Pellinor appears, asks him if he has
seen *la diverse beste*, and explains that he hunts it because he has been
told that it is destined to be killed by the best knight of his lineage.
'Et pour chou que je voloie counoistre se j'estoie li mieudres de
nostre lignage, pour chou l'ai jou si longement sivie et [sui] alés aprés
lui, si ne l'ai mie dit pour vantance de moi, mais pour savoir la verité
de moi meesmes.'[5] Later Arthur asks Merlin about the *beste* and is told

---

[1] MS. B.N. fr. 343, ff. 61a–72d; *D*, II, §§ 445–74; Sp. *D*, Chs. CCXXX–
CCLI.   [2] Huth *Merlin*, I, 149.
[3] Cambridge MS., f. 230d. The Huth *Merlin* has abridged the passage: 'une
beste moult grans, ki estoit la plus diverse qui onques fust veue de sa figure qui
tant estoit estraingne de cors et de faiture, et non mie tant defors comme dedens
son cors' (Huth MS., f. 75a; Huth *Merlin*, I, 149).
[4] Huth MS., f. 75b; Huth *Merlin*, I, 150.
[5] Huth MS., f. 75c; Huth *Merlin*, I, 151.

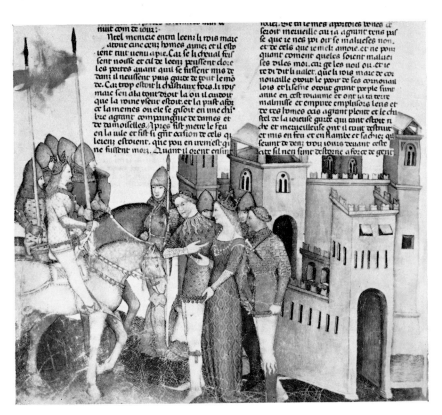

PLATE I

King Mark abducts Yseut from Joieuse Garde
from MS. B.N. fr. 343, f. 61v

PLATE 2

Hypomenes' son being torn up by dogs utters a curse on his sister; the birth of the *beste glatissant* from MS. B.N. fr. 112, *Livre* IV, f. 152r

that it is 'une des aventures dou Graal' and that he will not know the truth about it until Perceval li Galois, Pellinor's son, will tell him.[1]

Needless to say, the Vulgate *Queste* does not know of the *beste diverse*, but the Post-Vulgate *Queste* contains several adventures connected with it. Pellinor is, of course, already dead at the beginning of the *Queste*, and the chase of the *beste diverse*, here usually referred to as the *beste glatissant*, is assigned to Palamedes.[2] And although, contrary to Pellinor's prediction, it is not a knight of his lineage who ends the adventure, one of Pellinor's sons, Perceval, is present when the *beste glatissant* is killed. After Palamedes has hunted the monster for more than fourteen years, he joins company one day with Perceval and Galaad, and together they track it down in a valley by a lake, whither it has gone to quench its thirst, 'lasse et travaille[e] par scemblant mult durement'.[3] Palamedes goes after it into the lake and strikes it with his lance 'par andeus les costés', whereupon the *beste* utters a loud and horrible cry and disappears under the water. A great storm then rises over the lake as if all the devils were there and the water begins to burn and flame 'si merveilleusement que c'estoit la greignor daiaublé del monde a veoir'.[4] The three companions wait a while, and when they see that the *beste* does not reappear, they thank God that the adventure has been ended and leave the lake, which is henceforth called 'le lac de la beste'.[5] At a later point in the narrative, the Post-Vulgate deals also with the origin of the *beste glatissant*. When Galaad, Perceval and Boors visit King Pellean in his hermitage, the latter reveals it to them in accordance with what 'Nostre Seigneur' told him while he was in the 'sainte chambre' in Corbenic. There was once, Pellean relates, a king named Hypomenes who had a beautiful daughter well versed in the seven arts, but in particular in *nigromance*, who fell in love with her brother. The latter repulsed her, and as the damsel was about to kill herself in despair, the devil appeared to her in the form of a handsome

---

[1] Huth *Merlin*, 160. The Sp. *Baladros*, after stating (as does the French version) that Arthur will know the truth about the *beste* from Perceval, adds a brief account of its birth, which is a summary of the account in the Post-Vulgate *Queste* (see Bonilla, 1535 *Baladro*, Ch. CLII, 57; Bohigas, 1498 *Baladro*, I, 200–1). Cf. above, 27, n. 3.

[2] In the First Version of the prose *Tristan*, Palamedes is the 'chevalier a la beste glatissant', which explains why of all knights the chase of the monster should have been assigned to him in the Post-Vulgate *Queste*.

[3] MS. B.N. fr. 343, f. 101c.   [4] Ibid., f. 101d.

[5] Ibid., ff. 101b–102a; *D*, II, §§ 581–4; Sp. *D*, Chs. CCCLVI–CCCLVIII, 297a; MS. 112, *Livre* IV, ff. 146d–147d.

man and promised to help if she would do his will. She did so, and then on the devil's advice accused her brother of having done violence to her. Hypomenes had his son imprisoned, and after the barons had condemned him to death, the damsel urged that he be given alive to dogs 'en jeusnes de set jours'.[1] But before his death the brother warned his sister that God would take vengeance and that she would be delivered of a devil in the form of 'une beste la plus diverse qui oncques fu[s]t veue'. 'Et pour ce que tu a chiens a[s] livree ma char, avra ceste beste dedens son ventre chiens qui toutes voiez yront glatissant en memoire et en reproche des bestes a qui tu me faiz livrer.'[2] All happened as the brother predicted, and as soon as the *beste* was born it ran away 'qu'il n'eust homme au chastel ne au palaiz qui retenir la peust, mais toutes voiez entendoient il bien le glatissement qu'elle demenoit'.[3] Hypomenes forced a confession out of his daughter, and then had her put to death.[4] Perceval, it is true, never returns to court to tell Arthur the truth about the *beste* as Merlin had told him he would,[5] but despite this discrepancy it is evident that the *beste glatissant* episodes in the Post-Vulgate *Queste* are a continuation of the incidents in the *Suite du Merlin*.[6]

There is another allusion to the Post-Vulgate *Queste* at the point

[1] MS. B.N. fr. 112, *Livre* IV, f. 151d. MS. B.N. fr. 24400, f. 241a has 'effamez de set jour'.

[2] MS. B.N. fr. 112, *Livre* IV, f. 152b; MS. B.N. fr. 24400, f. 241c.

[3] loc. cit.

[4] MS. B.N. fr. 112, *Livre* IV, ff. 150b–152b; MS. B.N. fr. 24400, ff. 240c–241bis d; *D*, II, §§ 603–9; Sp. *D*, Chs. CCCLXII–CCCLXVII. Löseth, *Analyse*, § 615.

[5] See above, 125.

[6] The second redaction of the Post-Vulgate *Queste* moreover adds two allusions to the *beste glatissant* incidents in the *Suite du Merlin*. At the point where Galaad, Yvain and Dodinel see the *beste glatissant* for the first time, the redactor remarks that it is the same monster as Pellinor hunted and which Arthur saw while he was sitting by the fountain: 'Et ainsi qu'ilz parloient de leur departement, ilz se regardent et voyent sourdre des brosses la beste diverse que le roy Pellinor avoit ja chassee si long temps, celle que le roy Artus avoit veue quant il pensoit a la fontaine, celle mesmes qui dedans son ventre avoit les faons qui glatissoient' (MS. B.N. fr. 112, *Livre* IV, f. 85a; also *D*, I, § 82; Sp. *D*, Ch. LXXII). And later, when Perceval decides to hunt the *beste glatissant* for a while, he explains that he does so because his father before him had also chased it: 'Eu foi após ela, disse Persival, porque meu padre, rei Pelinor, a seguiu grã tempo e nom lhe pôde dar cima, e era tam boõ cavaleiro, que ainda hoje per todo o mundo falam dêle. E eu, que nom soom de tam grã nomeada, querria veer de graado se poderia dar cima a aquêlo u êle faleceu' (*D*, I, § 194, p. 250; not in Sp. *D*).

where Erec swears never to tell a lie. The redactor of the *Suite du Merlin* here remarks that on account of this vow Erec later beheaded his sister and was himself slain by Gauvain during the Quest of the Grail; for after Erec had killed Yvain as blanches mains *par mesconoissance*, Gauvain followed him in the hope of taking vengeance, but when he recognized Erec, he could not believe that he had done it and asked him the truth. Erec who had never told a lie then explained what had happened, whereupon Gauvain attacked him although he was in no fit condition to undertake a combat. Later Hector accused Gauvain of treason for this in Arthur's court, 'as the story of the Grail will tell':

Et lors tient ses mains vers le ciel et creante a Deu com chevalier loial que ja mes de couvenant ne mentira s'il i devoit lessier la vie, si s'en repenti puis si chierement qu'il fu puis cele ore qu'il voxist melz avoir la teste pardue qu'il eust fait icestui veu, quar il en colpa puis le chief a sa seror qui estoit une des plus belles puceles del munde. Et dit la ver[a]ie estoire qu'il reconut puis a sa mort quant misire Gauvain l'ocist en la Queste del Sa[i]nt Graal qu'il unques n'avoit menti de parole qu'il dist puis le couvenant qu'il avoit fet a Damdeu. Einsint ot Erec une grace molt merveilleuse que li autre chevalier de la Table Reonde n'avoient pas, quar il ne voloit nulle foiz mentir, si li en mesavint si durement qu'il en reçut mort. Quar le jor que il avoit navré a mort par mesconoisance Yvain as blanches mains et misire Gauvain le sivoit por venchier Yvain, non mie por ce qu'il cuidast, quant il le conut, qu'il l'eust occis. Quant il l[i] demande la verité, Erec qui nule foiz ne mentoit de chose qu'il seust, li dist que voirement l'avoit il navré, mes ce estoit par mesconoisance. Et misire Gauvain qui trop amoit Yvain as blanches mains, quant il ot la verité, il deffie maintenant Erec et l'asailli la ou Erec estoit navrez de plus de set plaies et l'ocist en tel maniere, dunt il fist blasmer molt durement, quar puis que Erec estoit compeinz de la Table Reonde, ausint com misire Gauvain estoit, missire Gauvains ne deust en nulle maniere metre main en lui. *Et de cele chose qu'il en fist fu il puis clameℨ desloiaul et parjuré de la boche Hestor de Mares, veiant le cors le roi Artus, si com cist livres le devise apertemant del Saint Graal.*[1]

Now Erec plays no part in the Vulgate, but the Post-Vulgate has several references to him. Moreover while the First Version of the Post-Vulgate *Queste* (*Y*) does not actually relate the circumstances in which Erec was killed,[2] it assumes that Gauvain slew him during the

---

[1] MS. B.N. fr. 12599, f. 240a–b. The first portion of the passage, up to *reçut mort*, is also in MS. B.N. fr. 112, *Livre* III, f. 249a. Cf. *La Folie Lancelot*, 52, l. 253–53, l. 277.

[2] The Second Version of the Post-Vulgate *Queste* (*Z*) furthermore not only

Queste and represents Hector and Meraugis as anxious to avenge Erec's death. Thus when shortly after Mark's invasion of Logres Hector and Meraugis meet Gauvain, Hector immediately challenges the latter:

[Gauvain], gardez vous de moi. Vous oceistes en traïson Erec le filz Lac, le plus loial chevalier du monde que je mout amoie. Vous l'oceistes en traïson, et je vous ocirrai en apert.[1]

Gauvain does not refute the accusation, but as he is still suffering from the wounds received in a previous combat, he does not wish to meet Hector in combat. He therefore tries to avoid the battle by telling Hector that two knights of the Round Table cannot fight each other without committing perjury, adding however that he would be willing to defend himself if Hector accused him of treason in Arthur's court. Hector finally agrees to postpone the combat, but assures Gauvain that he will yet avenge Erec's death:

Et sachiez se Dieus me mainne en l'ostel le roi Artu et je vous i truisse, je vous ferai honte voiant tout vostre lignage. Ne vous n'oceistes onques houme de qui la mort fust si bien venchiee coume sera la mort Erec, se je vif. Si vous les en tel point jusqu'a tant que Dieus me remaint a court.[2]

Henceforth Gauvain tries to avoid Hector. Hearing one day that Hector is in a certain castle, Gauvain refuses to go there, for, as he explains to Gaheriet, Hector hates him 'por la mort Erec, dont je ne fui onques, se Dex m'aït, si colpa[b]le com il me met sus'.[3] Gaheriet promises Gauvain to make his peace with Hector, but the next day Hector and Gaheriet part without the latter having dared to broach the subject. Consequently when at the end of the *Queste* Hector returns to court, he accuses Gauvain of having slain Erec in treason, just as is announced in the *Suite du Merlin*:

Quant il furent reperié de la Queste du Saint Graal adont l' (i.e. Gauvain) apela Hector de traïson pour la mort Herec...[4]

---

gives an account of how Erec beheaded his sister on account of the vow he had made never to tell a lie (*D*, I, §§ 292–6; Sp. *D*, Chs. CXXVIII–CXLII; MS. B.N. fr. 112, *Livre* IV, ff. 101b–104d), but relates also *in extenso* Erec's death, giving exactly the same details as those found in the *Suite du Merlin* passage quoted above (*D*, II, §§ 330–52; Sp. *D*, Chs. CLXIII–CLXXXIV; MS. B.N. fr. 112, *Livre* IV, ff. 110a–113d).

[1] MS. B.N. fr. 772, f. 384c; *D*, II, § 493; Sp. *D*, Ch. CCLXVIII, 264b.

[2] MS. B.N. fr. 772, f. 385a–b; *D*, II, § 495; Sp. *D*, Ch. CCLXX, 265a.

[3] MS. B.N. fr. 343, f. 93b; *D*, II, § 549, p. 236; Sp. *D*, Ch. CCCXXV, 283b.

[4] MS. B.N. fr. 772, f. 417c; *D*, II, § 625. Not in Sp. *D*. Cf. below, 146.

Finally, the account which the *Suite du Merlin* gives of the in-
auguration of the marvels of Logres and of the maiming of King
Pellean foreshadows the account which the Post-Vulgate *Queste* gives
of the healing of King Pellean. Until Vinaver identified the Cambridge
MS. of the *Suite du Merlin*, we had for this incident only the fragmentary account of the Huth MS., which just at that point is wanting
some two folios,[1] and the 1535 edition of the Spanish translation[2]
together with Malory's extremely condensed adaptation.[3] It was not
possible therefore to realize how much better the Post-Vulgate *Queste*
fits in with the *Suite du Merlin* than does the Vulgate *Queste*. The *Suite
du Merlin* relates the incident in question as follows:[4]

Balain or the 'Chevalier as Deus Espees', the unhappy knight who
attracts misfortune wherever he goes, has accidentally offended King
Arthur and seeks to win back his favour by carrying out all his wishes.
And so, one day, on Arthur's request, he follows a certain knight who
is soon slain by an invisible hand while riding under his protection.
Led by the dead knight's damsel, Balain goes in search of the murderer
and learns from Merlin that he is King Pellean's brother, Garlan, the
knight who rides invisible, but he is warned that if he continues with
his quest he will strike the Dolorous Stroke, the effects of which will
last 'jusques a tant qu'il verra avant qui metra a fin les aventures de la
Grant Bretaigne'.[5] Balain does not heed the warning and soon another
companion of his is struck down. But Balain still refuses to turn back, and
discovering at length that Garlan will be serving at table in Pellean's
castle, the *Pallés Perilleus*, on the next feast, he goes to seek him out
there. During the meal Garlan insults Balain, who forthwith kills him.
The people clamour for revenge and King Pellean, 'the most worthy
prince alive and the king most beloved of our Lord', challenges Balain
to a single combat. In the ensuing fight Balain's sword breaks and he
runs from room to room in search of another weapon until finally
he comes to the Grail Chamber. As he is about to enter, a voice tells
him not to do so: 'Mar i entrez, car tu n'es mie dignez d'entrer en si
haut lieu.'[6] None the less he goes in and sees the Holy Lance without

---

[1] The lacuna occurs Huth *Merlin*, II, 27 (*Le roman de Balain*, 78). It corresponds to the Cambridge MS., ff. 270c–271d. Cf. Appendix II, 241–9.

[2] Bonilla, 1535 *Baladro*, Chs. CCLXXXIII–CCLXXXIV, 109b–111a. Lacuna
in Bohigas, 1498 *Baladro*.

[3] Vinaver, *Works*, I, 84–6.

[4] Huth *Merlin*, I, 212–33, 275–80, II, 1–32; *Le roman de Balain*, 1–28, 41–83.

[5] Huth MS., f. 126c; Huth *Merlin*, II, 8; *Le roman de Balain*, 55.

[6] Cambridge MS., f. 270d. *Infra*, 245.

knowing what it is,[1] seizes it in spite of another voice which tells him not to touch it ('ne la touchie, pechierez')[2] and strikes King Pellean with it who is already hard behind him:

Mais il ne laisse onques por ceste parole qu'il ne preigne la lance as ·ii· mains et fiert le roie Pelleham, qui ja estoit deriere lui si durement qu'il li trenche ambdeuz lez quissez. E il chiet a tere, qu'il se sent navrez trop durement.[3]

This 'dolerouz colp' has far-reaching consequences: not only is Pellean maimed and unable to be healed until the coming of the Good Knight, but it inaugurates also the perilous adventures of Logres and two kingdoms are laid waste. As soon as the fatal blow has been struck, the walls of the castle fall down and a loud voice proclaims that the marvels of Logres will now begin and that 'li Haus Maistrez' will take vengeance on those who have not deserved it for Balain's sin in touching the Holy Lance and wounding so worthy a man as Pellean:

E lors vint entr'ex une voiz ausi grosse que un bosine qui dist apertment: 'Ore comenchent lez aventurez et lez mervaillez du roialme aventurus, qui ne remandero[n]t devant que chierement sera achaté che que la Seintim Lanche ont atouchez les mains ordes et cunchiés et ont navré lez plus preudhome dez princez; si en prendra li Haus Maistres sa venjanche sor cheus qui ne l'ont pas deservi.' [4]

Later when Merlin comes to the palace and stands before the Grail Chamber and sees the Holy Lance, he too remarks, weeping 'et del quer et dez oex', that those who have not merited it will have to suffer for the 'grante utragez' of the Chevalier as Deus Espees:

A! Diex, tant fist fole hardement li chaitifs pechierz maleaventur[u]z, qui de sez mainz ordeez et vilainz, cunchiees de vileté et de l'ort venim de luxure, atoucha si haut fust et si prechieus cum jeo voie la, et en mehaigna si preudhom cum li roiz Pellehans estoit. Ha! Diex, tant sera chier vendus cil grante utragez et cil granz forfais et tant l'acateront chier cil qui ne l'avoient pas deservi et tant en sofferont encore painez et travax lui preudhome et lui bon chevalier del roialme de Logrez et tantez mervaillez et tantez aventurez perilleusez en avendront encore pour cest Doleroux Colp qui a est[é] fais.[5]

The *Suite du Merlin* also describes in a vivid manner some of the immediately visible effects of the *doleroux colp*. When the voice re-

---

[1] 'Lui Chevalier as Deus Espeez [r]egarde le lanche, mais il ne [la] conoist pas trez bien'. Cambridge MS., f. 270d. *Infra*, 245.

[2] Cambridge MS., f. 270d. *Infra*, 245.   [3] loc. cit. *Infra*, 245.

[4] Cambridge MS., f. 271a. *Infra*, 246.   [5] Ibid., f. 271c–d. *Infra*, 248.

sounds throughout the castle announcing the beginning of the 'aventurez', a great fear seizes the people and more than a hundred fall down dead. Others are wounded or maimed by falling debris:

E de chele grant paour en morut ele palais plus de c.; dez autrez qui ele chastel estoient et non pas ele palais, en morust assez de paour. Et lui auter [furent] mahaigné et quassé, car plusurs dez maisonz de la ville caïrent et grant partie dez murez versa au croille que lui chasteaux fist, si out par laeinz de chevaliers et de villains assez bleschiez.[1]

For two days no one has the courage to enter the palace, but Merlin at last comes to the castle 'pour veoir la grant dolour qui i estoit avenu et de povrez et de richez, car il savoit bien que sanz grant mervaile avenir ne serrot pas fais le cols de la Lanche Vengeresse'.[2] As he passes from room to room, he finds nothing but fear-stricken people: the father cannot help the son and the son cannot help the father:

Quant il vint el chastell, si lez trova si malades et si disconfortez que li pieres ne puet aidier au fil, ne le fiex au pier.[3]

On the threshold of the palace the porter and two squires lie dead; in the court yard two hundred knights and squires are stretched out, the rest unconscious; and in the 'grant palais' there are more than seven hundred knights, ladies and squires, some dead, some as if they were dead:

... Et Merlin s'en vait el grant palais. E quant il fu venuz amount, il trove en mi la sale gisant plus de .vii.ᶜ. que chevaliers que damoisels que esquierz, si en i avoit plusurs mors, ne li plus fors n'avoit tant de pooir qu'il se puet dreschier en seant, ainz estoient ainsi cum tuit mort.[4]

But this is not all: the whole country suffers. When the Chevaliers as Deus Espees at last leaves the castle and comes out into the open, he sees the countryside blighted and half the inhabitants slain:

Et ensi comme il chevauchoit par la terre, il trouva les arbres a travers et les blés destruis, et toutes les choses si desgastés comme se effoudres fust courus en chascun lieu... Il trouvoit, par mi les viles, la moitiet des gens mort et des bourgois et des chevaliers, et par mi les chans trouvoit il les labourans mors. Que vous dirioe jou? Il trova si dou tout destruit le roiame de Listinois qu'il fu puis de tous apielés li Roiames de Terre Gastee et li Roiames de Terre

---

[1] Ibid., f. 271a. *Infra*, 246.   [2] Ibid., f. 271a–b. *Infra*, 246.
[3] Ibid., f. 271b. *Infra*, 246.   [4] Ibid., f. 271c. *Infra*, 247.

Forainne, pour chou que si estraigne et si agastie estoit devenue trestoute la terre.[1]

Everywhere in fact King Arthur's people are tormented by the wrath of Heaven which the 'utragez' of the Chevalier as Deus Espees has unleashed. Knights can no longer sleep by the 'Perron du Cerf' without being wounded or killed.[2] Le Morholt who spends the night there with his squire and a damsel is wounded and his companions are killed.[3] Yvain and his companions, also a squire and a damsel, suffer the same fate. But as Keu and Giflet explain to the unhappy Yvain, he must submit to his loss, for this is one of the marvels of Logres, of the adventures of the Grail which the Lord has sent to punish the just and the unjust:

Et ilz ly dient: 'Vous avez tort que tel duel en accuilliés sur vous. De ceste chose ne devés vous faire tel duel, car certes se vous fussiés le meilleur chevalier qui onques fust, si fust il ainsi avenu comme il est ou encore pis, *car les merveilles de ceste terre, mesmement celles du Saint Graal, ne laisseront pas a avenir ne pour vous ne pour chevalier tant comme a Nostre Seigneur plaira qu'elles aviengnent; car ainsi espant Nostre Seigneur ses vengences sur les justes et sur les pecheurs tout a sa volenté'*.[4]

The ideas which underlie the theme of the maiming of Pellean recur in the Post-Vulgate *Queste* but not in the Vulgate. Pellean, the Maimed King, is described not only as an innocent man, but as a very worthy one. In the Vulgate, on the other hand, the *Rois Mehaignié* suffers for his own rashness and presumption in going on board Solomon's ship and touching the sword reserved for Galaad.[5] The theme of the just being punished for the sins of others in fact plays no significant part in this version. The marvels of Logres are never at any time represented as a divine retribution.

If, however, we compare the account of Galaad's visit to Corbenic in the Post-Vulgate with that in the Vulgate, we shall at once see that the former is in outlook very close to the *Suite*. As in the *Suite du Merlin*, Pellean is a good man who is expiating the sin of another:

Entrés i por la guerisson del roi Maahigné qui leienz a longuement travaillié non mie por sa deserte, mes por le pechié d'autrui.[6]

[1] Huth MS., f. 134d; Huth *Merlin*, II, 30; *Le roman de Balain*, 81–2; Cambridge MS., f. 272b.   [2] *Die Abenteuer*, 48–54, 66—71.
[3] Ibid., 52.   [4] Ibid., 71. See below, 188–90.
[5] Vulgate *Queste*, 209, l. 9–210, l. 4.
[6] MS. B.N. fr. 343, f. 102c; *D*, § 588. *Infra*, 253.

says the *preudom* to Galaad as he shows him into the Grail Chamber. And when King Pellean uncovers his wounded thighs, he explains that it was the Chevalier as Deus Espees who maimed him:

Et cil joint les mains encontre le Saint Vessel et descouvre ses cuisses et dit: 'Veez ci li doloreux cop que li Chevaliers as Deus Espees fist. Par cestui cop sunt maint mal avenu. Ce me poise.' Et les plaies estoient encor ausint fresches com le jor memes qu'il avoit esté feruz.[1]

The 'maint mal' in question seem obviously to include both the calamity which befell the castle after the striking of the *Doloreux Cop* and the 'aventures du Saint Graal' which this same stroke inaugurated.[2]

Not only is the outlook of the two works similar, but their description of the Grail and its surroundings is in essentials the same. In the *Suite du Merlin* the room where the Grail is kept is very large, square, beautiful and richly decorated and sweetly scented as if all the spices in the world were there. The silver table stands on 'trois pilerez d'argent', and the vessel beneath the lance is made of gold and silver. These details, some of which have been borrowed from the account of Gauvain's visit to the Grail castle in the First Continuation of Chrétien de Troyes' *Perceval*,[3] are not found in the Vulgate *Queste* and are in fact

---

[1] MS. B.N. fr. 343, f. 103a; *D*, § 590, p. 279. *Infra*, 254.

[2] The idea of a vengeful God which is so strong in both the *Suite du Merlin* and the Post-Vulgate *Queste*, but is comparatively absent from the Vulgate *Queste*, is found also in the *Estoire del Saint Graal*. In fact, as M. Lot-Borodine has shown, it is one of the dominant themes of the *Estoire del Saint Graal*: 'L'atmosphère qui nous enveloppe dans l'*Estoire* est en général une atmosphère lourde et orageuse; le Dieu qui envoie Joseph et Josephé évangéliser le monde et, plus spécialement, la Grande-Bretagne, reste un maître jaloux et redoutable qui n'a rien de l'infinie mansuétude du Crucifié. La moindre infraction à une loi, parfois ignorée de celui qui la transgresse, entraîne de terribles représailles, même pour le juste' (*De l'Amour profane à l'Amour sacré*, Paris, 1961, 162–3). It was undoubtedly under the influence of the *Estoire* that this idea of an implacable God came into the *Suite du Merlin* and Post-Vulgate *Queste*. As we shall see later (Ch. VII) the author of the *Suite du Merlin* and Post-Vulgate *Queste* took over from the *Estoire* many themes and endeavoured to bring his composition into line with the spirit and outlook of the *Estoire*.

[3] The First Continuation of Chrétien's *Perceval* has been preserved in three redactions: one long (MSS. *EMQU*), one mixed (MSS. *TVD*) and one short (MSS. *ALPRS*). All three have been edited by William Roach (*The Continuations of the Old French Perceval of Chrétien de Troyes*, I, *The First Continuation, redaction of MSS. TVD*, Philadelphia, 1949; II, *The First Continuation, redaction of MSS. EMQU*, Philadelphia, 1950; III, part 1, *The First Continuation, redaction of MSS. ALPRS*, Philadelphia, 1952). The similarities between the events leading up to Gauvain's visit to the Grail castle and Balain's have been pointed out

K

out of keeping with its severe ascetic tone. But in the Post-Vulgate *Queste* as in the *Suite du Merlin*, the Grail Chamber is large, square, beautiful and richly decorated:

Cambridge MS., f. 270d; *infra*, 245.	MS. B.N. fr. 343, f. 102d.
Il entent bien la voice, mais	*Infra*, 254.
pur ceo ne laisse il pas sa	
voie, ainz se fiert en la	La chambre ou il estoit
chamber et troeve que *ele est*	*estoit granz a merveilles*
si bele et si riche qu'il ne	*et faites esquarie et si*
quidast mie qu'en toute le	*richement qu'en tout le*
monde eust sa paraille de biauté.	*mont ne peust l'en pas*
La chamber estoit quarré et grans	*trouver chambre de*
a mervaille et soefflerant ainsi	*greignor biauté.*
cum se toutez lez espicez du	
monde i fussent aporteez.	

The descriptions include the same details, and the one is obviously based on the other.[1] The same remark applies to the description of the table on which the Grail stands, of the vessel beneath the Lance and of the Lance itself:

Cambridge MS., f. 270d. *Infra*, 245.	MS B.N. fr. 343, f. 102d. *Infra*, 253.
	Et il se siegne maintenant et
	comande mult a Nostre Seignor
	et entre leienz et voit maintenant
En un lieu de la	*en mi leu de la chambre, qui mult*
chamber avoit un tabel	*estoit granz et riche, la table*
d'argent mult grante [*et*]	*d'argent et le Santime Vessel si*

by Vinaver in (*Le Roman de Balain*, xxvi–xxvii). See also, Heinzel, *Über die Französischen Gralromane*, 31, and Vettermann, *Die Balen-Dichtungen*, 255–61.

[1] The First Continuation of Chrétien's *Perceval* also stresses that the Grail Chamber was large, rich and sweetly scented. Note for instance the following passages: 'Mais la chaucié erra et tint / Tant qu'en une grant sale vint / Qui molt ert haute, longue et lee; / Bien duroit une arbaleste[e]' (MSS. *TVD*, lines 13141–44); '... Et autresi quatre encensiers / De fin or et riches et chiers / As quatre candeliers pendoient / Et tot plain d'especes estoient / Qui flairoient molt dolcement' (MSS. *TVD*, lines 13193–97); '... Com li Graals fait le servise / Que il avoit le soir veu / En la riche sale ou il fu' (MSS. *TVD*, lines 13552–54). It is clear, however, that there are no verbal similarities between the First Continuation and the accounts in the *Suite du Merlin* and the Post-Vulgate *Queste*, and some of the details common to the latter two are not in the former. This means that the *Suite du Merlin* and the Post-Vulgate *Queste* are not based independently on the First Continuation, but that there is a direct relationship between them.

haute par raison, et
seoit sor·iii· pilere$z$
d'argent.

E desus la tabel, droit
en mi lieu, avoit un
orçuel d'argent et d'or
et deden$z$ *cele orçuel*
estoit une lance drescie,
la point
deso$z$ *et le haut desu*z*.*
E qui regardast a mult
la lanche, il
merveillaist coment ele
tenist droite, car ele
n'estoit apoié ne d'un
part ne d'autre.

hautement et si bel aorné com
nostre estoire a ja autre foi$z$
devisé. Il ne s'ose pas aprouchier
del Saint Vessel, car il ne li est
pas avis qu'il en soit digne; mes
i l'encline et aore de cuer parfont,
a lermes et a plors, *et il voit tres*
desus la table d'argent celle
meemes lance dont la santime car
Jhesu Crist avoit esté navree.
Et ele estoit mise en l'air, la
pointe desou$z$ *et li fust desus,*
et pendoit si merveilleussement
que mortex hom ne peust pas
veoir qui la sostenoit.

Et sachiez que ele rendoit par
la pointe gotes de sanc qui
cheioient en un mult riche vessel
d'argent assez espessement; mes
aprés ce que eles estoient venues
el vesel, ne pooit nus savoir que
li sanz devenoit.

The Post-Vulgate *Queste* seems to contain here a clear reference
back to the *Suite du Merlin*, for instead of describing 'la table d'argent'
and 'le Santime Vessel', it says that they were 'si hautement et si bel
aorné com nostre estoire a ja autre foiz devisé'. Like the *Suite du Merlin*,
the Post-Vulgate *Queste* mentions also that the lance stood unsup-
ported, 'point downwards and handle upwards', a detail not found elsewhere, though suggested by the First Continuation of Chrétien's
Perceval, where the lance

> En un molt riche orçuel d'argent
> Ert enfichié droitement.[1]

---

[1] Ed. Roach, MSS. *VTD*, lines 13325–6. The readings of the other MSS. are
similar, all mentioning the *orçuel d'argent* except MSS. *ASP* (lines 7277–81)
which have: 'La sale vuide an tel meniere / Qu'il n'i vit rien fors que la biere, /
Et d'autre part *an un lancier. /* Une lance molt fort sainnier / Dedanz une cope
d'argent.' The full description of the Lance according to MSS. *TVD* is as
follows: 'Atant a veü une lance / Dont li fers ert blans come nois, / Dalez le
chief del maistre dois. / *En un molt riche orçuel d'argent / Ert enfichié droitement. /*
Et dui chierge devant ardoient, / Qui grant clarté laiens jectoient. / *De la pointe*

On the other hand, the only important difference between the accounts is that the Lance does not bleed in the *Suite du Merlin*, whereas in the Post-Vulgate *Queste* 'ele rendoit par la pointe gotes de sanc'. The significance of this will be discussed later.[1]

The general location of the Grail Chamber is also the same in both versions: it can only be reached from the main palace after many rooms have been crossed. Compare for instance Galaad's approach to the Grail Chamber:

Et Galahaz s'en vait toute voies aprés lui, si vont tant de chambre en chambre en tel maniere qu'il vindrent dusqu'a la ou li rois Mahaigniez gisoit. Et ce estoit en la chambre meemes ou estoit li Sainz Graaux.[2]

and Lancelot's:

Et il s'en vait oltre de chambre en chambre et tant qu'il vint a l'entree de la chambre ou li Sainz Grahal estoit.[3]

with Merlin's in the *Suite du Merlin*:

E Merlin s'en vait toutez lez voiez avant de chambre en chambre et tant qu'il vint pres de la chamber ou la Sainte Lanche estoit et li Sainz Vasseax que ome apeloit Grale.[4]

But not only does the account in the Post-Vulgate *Queste* corre-spond to that in the *Suite du Merlin*, it also completes it. The 'cols de la Lanche Vencheresse' caused not only King Pellean's wound, but also 'lez aventurez et lez mervaillez' of Logres; the healing of King Pellean by the blood of this same Lance signifies by this same token also the end of the marvels of the 'roialme aventurus'. The symmetry of the situation demands therefore that when the last of the marvels caused by the Lance is about to end, the Lance should disappear. In the Vulgate

---

del fer issoit / Uns rais de sanc qui descendoit / Aval la lance el riche orçuel. / Tot entor dusqu'a l'arestuel / Paroient les traches des goutes / Qui el vaissel chaoient toutes / Et si n'en i set tant venir / Que li orçuels en puisse emplir. / Par un tüel molt riche et grant, / D'une esmeraude verdoiant, / En un canel d'or s'en chaoit, / Qui fors de la sale coroit / Par grant engien, par grant esgart, / Mais il ne vit mie quel part. / Mesire Gavains, quant ce vit, / A lui meisme pense et dit / C'ainc mais ne vit si grant merveille. / De la lance trop se merveille / Qui est de fust et si saignoit' (MSS. *TVD*, lines 13322–47).

  [1] See below, 163–4.
  [2] MS. B.N. fr. 343, f. 102c; *D*, § 588, p. 278. *Infra*, 253.
  [3] MS. B.N. fr. 343, f. 91a; *D*, II, § 541; Sp. *D*, Ch. CCCXVII.
  [4] Cambridge MS., f. 271c. *Infra*, 248.

Queste it is taken up to Heaven only on the death of Galaad.[1] In the Post-Vulgate *Queste*, on the other hand, the Lance disappears as soon as Galaad takes the Vessel beneath it in order to heal King Pellean:

Mes quant il ot pris le vessel, il vit que la lance s'en ala sus vers le ciel et s'esvanoï en tel meniere qu'il n'ot puis si hardi en toute la Grant Bertaingne qu'i osast dire qu'il veist la Lanche Vencheresse.[2]

There can be no doubt that the Post-Vulgate *Queste* introduced this alteration with the scene of the *Suite du Merlin* in mind.

It would seem, then, that the Dolorous Stroke theme occupies the key position both in the *Suite du Merlin* and the Post-Vulgate *Queste*. The maiming of Pellean is the beginning of the adventures of Logres; the healing of Pellean is the end. The episodes that precede the maiming deal with the youth of Arthur and the early years of his kingdom; those that follow the healing treat of its decay and end. The Lance begins to bleed only after the Dolorous Stroke; once the marvels are ended and Pellean healed it is appropriate that the Lance should disappear into Heaven. The healing of the Maimed King becomes Galaad's principal function; whereas in the Vulgate he is the New Lancelot, freed from the burden of sin that clogs his predecessor, and thus able to achieve the *visio Dei*, in the Post-Vulgate *Queste* he is the counterpart of Balain, the Renewer who restores what the 'chevalier mescheans' had destroyed.

[1] *Vulgate Queste*, 279, l. 5.
[2] MS. B.N. fr. 343, f. 102d; *D*, II, § 589, p. 279. *Infra*, 254.

CHAPTER VI

The 'Suite du Merlin' and the Post-Vulgate 'Mort Artu'

THE last words of the chosen knights as they leave Corbenic in the Post-Vulgate *Queste* have a strange, foreboding ring: 'A si haute joie ne si haute viande ne seront ja mes chevaliers apellez com nos [avom] esté. Iceste est la deriene feste del roiaume de Logres.'[1] It seems as if they sensed an impending tragedy. Elsewhere, too, in the Post-Vulgate *Queste* there are veiled references to the end of the Round Table,[2] but it is in the *Suite du Merlin* that we find the first dark hints of the coming destruction of Logres. The theme of Arthur's death runs like a *leitmotiv* throughout, and the end of various characters is announced: Giflet, we are told, will be the last man to see Arthur alive;[3] Gaheriet will be slain unintentionally by Lancelot, the knight he loves most, and with him will be killed his brothers Agravain and Guerrehes;[4] Gauvain will suffer for his pride and receive his mortal wound from Lancelot after Gaheriet's death,[5] while Sagremor and Yvain are to be slain by Mordred in the same battle as the father of the Round Table[6] who is to die

par la main de son filz. Et lors devendra orphelins de son bon pere le royaume de Logres, ne ja puis ne sera en si grant honneur comme il est orendroit, ne

---

[1] MS. B.N. fr. 343, f. 104b. *Infra*, 260.

[2] Thus shortly before his death the Count Hernoul confesses to a hermit that he feels guilty for not having revealed to Arthur Lancelot's love affair with Guenevere, for this would have been of benefit to the kingdom: 'Sire, je me sent durement courpables vers le roi Artu qui hom liges je sui, et sai l'afere de sa fame et de Lancelot du Lac qu'ele aime de si fole amour qu'il a a li geu charnelment. Et sachiez que cele folie et cele traïson qu'il a feite vers son seigneur le roy Artu, je sanz faille qui estoie houme le roy Artu, ne m'en deusse pas estre teuz que je ne l'eusse acointié de cele vilennie. Si vous en acointe et vous requier que vous au roi le diez; et se vous l'en acointiez je croi qu'il fera si la reyne garder que ja mes en cest pechié n'en charra, si seroit granz biens a tout le roiaume de Logres' (MS. B.N. fr. 772, f. 367c–d; cf. *D*, II, § 429).

[3] Huth *Merlin*, I, 177.   [4] *Die Abenteuer*, 125.

[5] Huth *Merlin*, II, 59; *Die Abenteuer*, 63.

[6] Huth *Merlin*, II, 139; *Die Abenteuer*, 78.

en si grant pouoir, car adont commenceront a voler les deus filz du dragon et pourprendront le plus de ceste terre et mectront dessous leurs esles; mes aprés viendra ça le liepars qui les devorera et transglotira. Et quant il les avra devorés, il s'en yra la queue entre les jambes et se repondra en une roche tout son eage que ja puis n'en savra l'en nouvelles. Et aprés cellui temps regneront les mauvaiz hoirs de pis en pis si que le royaume de la Grant Bretaigne, que Dieu a orendroit si essaulcee, plorera et regretera les preudomes qui a cestui temps regneront. Car alors seront en ceste terre toutes proesces tournees a neant.[1]

The 'deus fils du dragon' are, of course, Mordred's two sons who after the dolorous battle on Salisbury Plain seize Logres, but are defeated by Lancelot ('le liepars') in the battle of Winchester.

All this suggests—as did already the redactional indications—that the *Suite* compilation was to include a version of the Death of Arthur story. But this version cannot have been the *Mort Artu* which forms the last branch of the Vulgate Cycle, for, as I have pointed out, the *Suite du Merlin* compiler states clearly that the third part of his book is to end with Lancelot's death, *a chelui point meisme qu'il devise de la mort le roi March*.[2] The only extant version of the *Mort Artu* which fulfils the announcement in the *Suite du Merlin* is the shortened redaction which follows the *Queste* of the Spanish and Portuguese *Demandas*.[3] The particular account, moreover, which the *Demanda Mort Artu* gives of Mark's death is obviously intended to link up with one of the episodes of the Post-Vulgate *Queste*, Mark's first invasion of Logres and defeat by Galaad.[4] When Mark hears that Lancelot, the last powerful man in Logres, has passed away, he invades the country again. His first words on landing are a clear reference to his earlier shame and losses:

Or sui je venuz en la terre ou j'ay plus receu honte et dommage que je ne fis oncques en lieu du monde. Or ne vueil je que ja maiz soye tenuz a roy, se je ne m'en venge a cestui point.[5]

He orders his men to lay waste the whole country, sparing neither

[1] MS. B.N. fr. 112, *Livre* II, f. 36a–b; *Die Abenteuer*, 63.

[2] Huth *Merlin*, I, 280. Cf. above, 61.

[3] The Spanish *Demanda Mort Artu* is contained in Sp. *D.*, Chs. CCCXC–CCCCLV; the Portuguese version is contained in *D*, II, §§ 626–706. Only two small fragments of the Post-Vulgate *Mort Artu* have been preserved in French in MS. B.N. fr. 340 (see Appendix II, 261–70).

[4] For details of this incident, see above, 123-4.

[5] MS. B.N. fr. 340, f. 206c; cf. *D*, II, § 701; Sp. *D*, Ch. CCCCLII, 336b.

man, woman nor church. 'Et je faiz ceste destrucion faire, pour ce que
je ne vueil mie que aprés ma mort n'apere mie riens que li roys Artus
ait fait en son vivant.'[1] One night he enters Joieuse Garde 'en emblee',
and finding Lancelot's rich and beautiful tomb there, he has it broken
open and Lancelot's body burnt together with Galehaut's bones. Then
he moves on to Camalot, razes the city to the ground and destroys the
Round Table, Galaad's seat first of all, for it was the latter who defeated him and the Saxons:

Et quant il vint devant la Table Reonde et il vit le lieu Galehas, il dist:
'Ce fut le lieu de cellui qui destruit en un seul jour et moy et le royaume de
Saxoigne. Je destruiray pour l'amour de li la Table Reonde, son lieu premierement et tous les autres aprés.' Tout ainsi comme il le dist le fist il faire, car il
fist adonc la Table Reonde destruire si merveilleusement qu'il n'y remest
siege entier; et cellui siege que l'en appelloit le Siege Perilleux et dont tant de
merveilles estoient avenues, fist il premierement destruire.[2]

At this point Mark learns that four of the companions of the Round
Table, Boors, Blioberis, the Archbishop of Canterbury and Meraugis
de Porlesguez, are still alive. He seeks them out in their hermitage with
the intention of killing them, but after slaying the Archbishop, he is
himself beheaded by Paulars, a knight of Ban's lineage, who has come
to visit the hermits.[3]

---

[1] Loc. cit.; *infra*, 267.

[2] MS. B.N. fr. 340, f. 206e; cf. *D*, II, § 703; Sp. *D*, Ch. CCCCLIII, 337a.

[3] None of the extant manuscripts of the prose *Tristan* contains an account of
Mark's death (cf. Löseth, *Analyse*, xviii–xix). MS. B.N. fr. 112 (*Livre* IV, ff. 162d–
163a) relates how Mark was torn up by a bear in a forest. Sir Thomas Malory
in his *Tale of the Healing of Sir Urry* states, on the other hand, that Sir Bellynger
slew King Mark: 'And thys sir Bellynger revenged the deth of hys fadir, sir Alys-
aundir, and sir Trystram, for he slewe kynge Marke' (Vinaver, *Works*, III, 1150).
The Italian *Vita di Merlino*, written in the fourteenth century, contains a reference
to Mark's death obviously based on the Post-Vulgate account as E. G. Gardner in
The Arthurian Legend in Italian Literature (London, 1930, 205–7, 210) pointed
out. I quote below Gardner's translation of Merlin's prophecy referring to Mark's
death: ' "My lady," said Merlin, "I would have thee set in writing that the false
King Mark of Cornwall will pass the sea, and come into Great Britain after the
death of the adventurous king, where that evil King Mark will devastate all that
country, and then he will come to Joyous Gard, and will have the tomb opened
in which he will find the bodies of Galehaut le Brun and Lancelot of the Lake,
and he will have them burnt to ashes. And, having done this, he will wish to be
crowned King of Logres; but this will not be suffered him, for King Bors will
come out of a hermitage, and take arms, and assemble the folk of that country,
and set himself against that evil king and take him, and then he will put him to

Only two small fragments of the *Demanda Mort Artu* have survived in French in one of the manuscripts of Rusticien de Pise, MS. B.N. fr. 340. The first fragment contains a remodelled account of Guenevere's death;[1] the other one deals with the episode I have just considered, Mark's second invasion of Logres and his death.[2] Both fragments, however, agree closely with the corresponding passages in the Portuguese *Demanda* and we may assume, therefore, that the latter is a reasonably faithful rendering of its ultimate French source.[3]

According to Sommer and Bruce, the *Demanda* or Post-Vulgate *Mort Artu* is a mere abridgement of the Vulgate, with a few uninspired additions here and there.[4] But this view, unchallenged until now, does less than justice to the Post-Vulgate *Mort Artu*. A close comparison of it with its ultimate source, the Vulgate *Mort Artu*, reveals that it is a work of marked originality: its excisions, minor additions and other alterations reflect a new conception of the Death of Arthur story and are the result of an attempt to link it up with the preceding parts of the romance, the Post-Vulgate *Queste* and the *Suite du Merlin*. In the

---

death for the outrage done upon the bones of that cousin of his and those of Galehaut le Brun" ' (Gardner, 205). The Italian *Vita* either deliberately substituted Boors in place of Paulars as the man who slew Mark, or else one of the French MSS. of the Post-Vulgate *Mort Artu* (now lost) contained a variant version of Mark's death. The French *Prophecies de Merlin* from which the Italian *Vita* is translated does not contain the prophecy relating to Mark's death. A number of other Italian texts contain different accounts of Mark's end: in the *Tavola Ritonda*—a fourteenth-century adaptation of the prose *Tristan*—Mark is put in a cage on the top of a tower to watch over Tristan's tomb, where he remains until he dies through forced overeating (see Gardner, *The Arthurian Legend*, 185–7). In a fourteenth-century poem, *La Vendetta di Tristano*, Mark is slain in battle by Lancelot, but in a sixteenth-century prose romance, the *Due Tristani*, which is translated from the Spanish *Coronica... del buen cauallero don Tristan de Leonis y del rey don Tristan de Leonis el Joven, su hijo*, Sevilla, 1534, Mark dies a natural death after ceding his kingdom to Tristan's son (see Gardner, *The Arthurian Legend*, 263–5 and 300–2).

[1] MS. B.N. fr. 340, f. 205a–e corresponds to *D*, II, §§ 687–9, and to Sp. *D*, Ch. CCCCXLI–CCCCXLIII, 331–2. *Infra*, 261–4.

[2] Löseth, *Analyse*, 575a. MS. B.N. fr. 340, ff. 205e–207c corresponds to *D*, II, 701–6, and to Sp. *D*, Ch. CCCCLII–CCCCLV, 336–8. *Infra*, 264–70.

[3] The Sp. *D* is on the whole less close to the French than is the Portuguese.

[4] Sommer, 'The Queste of the Holy Grail', *R*, XXXVI (1907) 584–90; Bruce, *Evolution*, I, 473; Bruce, 'The Development of the Mort Arthur theme in medieval romance', *RR*, IV (1913) 429–34. Sommer and Bruce refer, of course, to the *Demanda Mort Artu* not as the Post-Vulgate *Mort Artu* but as the 'pseudo-Boron *Mort Artu*'.

earliest stories dealing with Arthur's death, the verse chronicles of Geoffrey of Monmouth and of Wace,[1] Arthur's downfall is represented as a mere accident of warfare. Arthur, having subdued many peoples and vanquished the Emperor of Rome, was preparing to march into Italy when news reached him that his nephew Mordred had seized his crown and married the Queen. He returned to Britain and defeated Mordred at Richborough and at Winchester, but in the final battle on the river Camel in Cornwall he was fatally wounded and Mordred killed. The *Mort Artu* of the Vulgate Cycle combines the original narrative with the story of Lancelot and Guenevere's adultery, and gives it an elaborate spiritual background by linking up Arthur's downfall with the doctrine of the Wheel of Fortune and that of the Grail: the Grail leaves Logres because the people were not worthy of it,[2] and the destruction of the kingdom is interpreted partly as a retribution for the sin of Arthur's knights, and partly as a sequel to their rise to fortune: 'Mes tel sont li orgueil terrien qu'il n'i a nul si haut assiz qu'il ne le coviegne cheoir de la poesté del monde'.[3] At first Mordred appears simply as Arthur's nephew, as in the chronicles, but towards the end the author represents him also as Arthur's son. On hearing of Mordred's treason, Arthur exclaims that never did father do to his son what he will do, for he will kill him with his own hands:

Ha! Mordret, or me fez tu connoistre que tu ies li serpenz que ge vi jadis eissir de mon ventre, qui ma terre ardoit et se prenoit a moi. Mes onques peres ne fist autretant de fill comme ge ferai de toi, car ge t'ocirrai a mes deus meins, ce sache touz li siecles, ne ja Dex ne vueille que tu muires d'autrui meins que des moies.[4]

Later on, after the fatal battle, the author remarks: 'Einsi ocist li peres le fill, et li filz navra le pere a mort.'[5]

---

[1] In Geoffrey of Monmouth's *Historia Regum Britanniae* Arthur's death is found in Book X, Ch. XIII and Book XI, Chs. I–II; in Wace's *Brut* it is in ll. 13010-298 of Ivor Arnold's edition (Paris, 1938–40). For a very lucid and illuminating account of the development of the Death of Arthur theme from Geoffrey down to Malory's adaptation, see Vinaver, *The Tale of the Death of King Arthur by Sir Thomas Malory* (Oxford, 1955), vii ff.

[2] See *Vulgate Queste*, 274, l. 28–275, l. 4.

[3] *La Mort le Roi Artu*, 201, ll. 2–3. For an account of the treatment of the 'Wheel of Fortune' motif in the Vulgate *Mort Artu*, see Frappier, *Étude*, 258–288.

[4] *La Mort le Roi Artu*, 185, ll. 12–17.

[5] Ibid., 220, l. 11.

The theme of Mordred's incestuous birth seems to serve mainly to heighten the horror of the final tragedy.[1] The circumstances in which Arthur committed incest are not explained, and he is not reproached for his sin. There is a vague suggestion, however, that if Arthur dies by the hand of Mordred, it is because of his sin of incest. Arthur himself leads us to believe this. When he comes to Salisbury Plain and realizes that a battle between him and Mordred is inevitable, he remarks that if he is vanquished it will be on account of his sin:

Mes or soit Jhesucrist en nostre aide, car ge n'en partirai jamés jusques a tant que Nostre Sires en ait donee enneur a moi ou a Mordret; et se il m'en meschiet, ce sera par mon pechié et par mon outrage, a ce que ge ai greigneur plenté de bons chevaliers que Mordres n'a.[2]

The *pechié* and *outrage* to which Arthur refers is certainly his incest. The reading of MSS. *DVO*, which is still more explicit, justifies this assumption:

... ne je me dout de riens tant ki honor me toille comme je fac de mon pechié, car mon pechié sai je bien et connois et croi ke por lui me mescara s'il me meschiet en ceste bataille.[3]

But the theme of retribution for Arthur's guilt remains a mere suggestion and is never developed in the Vulgate Cycle.[4] In the last part of the *Lancelot* proper, the *Agravain*, we learn that Mordred is the son of Arthur and his sister, King Lot's wife, but the hermit who tells Mordred of his future rôle, explaining that he is the serpent whom Arthur saw in a vision the night that he begot him, is clearly reprimanding Mordred, not Arthur: the latter's sin is not even mentioned:

'Mordret, fet il, dont ne sez tu pour coi je di que tu es li plus maleureus chevaliers del monde? Je le te dirai. Pour chou que tu feras encore plus de mal que tous lez hommes du monde; quar par toi sera mis a destruction la grant hautesce de la Table Roonde. Et par toi morra li plus preudoms que on

---

[1] In this connexion it should be noted that in neither Geoffrey nor Wace does Mordred himself slay Arthur; the theme of a personal combat between Arthur and Mordred was first introduced by the Vulgate Cycle.

[2] *La Mort le Roi Artu*, 203, ll. 6–10.

[3] Ibid., 203, n. 21.

[4] John E. Housman, in his review of Vinaver, *Works*, *Erasmus*, I, nos. 21–22 (Dec. 1947) 921–6, suggests that 'Mordred's rebellion . . . is . . . intelligible only if considered as the result of Arthur's guilt which, only when the mission of his court has been fulfilled, can emerge from the potential to the actual' (924). But this is surely going further than the texts of the Vulgate Cycle justify.

sache qui tes peres est. Et tu morras par sa main. Ensi sera mors li peres par
le fil et li fils par le pere. Et lors tournera tout a noient tes parentés qui ore est
li plus soverains du monde, si te pues moult haïr quant tant de prodomme
morront par tes mains...' [1]

Similarly, in one of the later additions to the Cycle, the *Estoire de
Merlin*, the circumstances in which Arthur committed incest are twice
mentioned,[2] but on neither occasion does the author establish any
connexion between Arthur's initial offence and his death: on the contrary, the one purpose of the incest theme appears to be to explain why
Lot's wife favoured Arthur and attempted to make peace between him
and Lot:

Quant ce vint al terme que li enfés (i.e. Mordred) fu nés et la novele fu
partout le païs que cil seroit rois qui fu fiex Uterpandragon, si l'ama miex la
dame en son cuer que nus ne poroit dire, mais ele n'en osa faire samblant por
le roy Loth son seigneur, et moult li pesa de la guerre qui fu levee entre lui et
cels du païs.[3]

Now the *Suite du Merlin* and the Post-Vulgate *Mort Artu* elaborate
the theme and make Arthur's downfall a direct consequence of his sin
of incest. The *Suite du Merlin* relates how shortly after Arthur's
coronation Lot's wife, the Queen of Orkney, comes to court with her
four sons and how Arthur, not knowing that she is really his sister,

[1] *Vulgate Version*, V, 284, ll. 12–18. See also the rest of the passage (284,
l. 19–285, l. 15). According to Bruce the theme of Mordred's incestuous birth
was invented by the author of the *Mort Artu* and the passage in the *Agravain*
was interpolated by the latter (see 'The composition of the Old French prose
Lancelot', *RR*, IX (1918) 382–5; *RR*, X (1919) 108–9; 'Mordred's incestuous
birth' in *Medieval Studies in memory of Gertrude Schoepperle Loomis*, 197–208).
Frappier originally supported Bruce's theory, but in the Introduction to his
second edition of the *Mort Artu* he suggests, rightly in my view, that it was
probably the *Agravain* which first introduced the theme (see his *Étude*, 32–6;
La Mort le Roi Artu, Paris, 1954, xvi–xvii and xxiii, n. 1). According to Micha,
the source of the motif of Mordred's incestuous birth may have been the legend
about Charlemagne's incestuous begetting of Roland preserved in the *Karlamagnus saga* and the Provençal *Ronsasvals* (see 'Deux sources de la *Mort Artu*',
ZRPh., LXVI [1950] 371–2 and Roques, *R*, LXVI [1941] 458–60). But Frappier
thinks that the theme belongs to an almost universal tradition of heroes born in
incest (see Frappier, in *ALMA*, 310 and O. Rank, *Inzest-Motiv in Dichtung und
Sage*, Leipzig, Vienna, 1912).
[2] *Vulgate Version*, II, 96 and 128–9.
[3] Ibid., II, 129, ll. 34–8. The *Estoire del Saint Graal* (*Vulgate Version*, I, 280–1)
also mentions briefly that Mordred was the son of Arthur and Lot's wife.

falls in love with her and begets the boy Mordred who is subsequently to destroy him and his kingdom:

Adont [conut] li freres carneument sa serour et porta la dame chelui qui puissedi le traist a mort et mist a destruction et a martyre la terre, dont vous porrés oïr viers la fin dou livre.[1]

When Lot's wife has returned to her country, Arthur has a terrifying vision in which he sees a serpent devastating Logres; he succeeds in killing the serpent, but is himself wounded by it. Merlin tells Arthur the significance of his dream and informs him of his 'grant desloiauté' without sparing his feelings. He calls him 'dyables et anemis Jhesucrist et le plus desloial chevalier de ceste contree',[2] and henceforth the knowledge of his sin pursues Arthur: whenever he is hard-pressed he sees the hand of God punishing him for his offence. Thus when he hears that King Lot has invaded his land, he exclaims:

Ha! Dieus,… tant a chi grant pestilence! Ceste painne m'envoiiés vous pour mon pechié. Ore cuide que li preudomme comparront chou que je me sui mesfais viers vous.[3]

At the beginning all that Arthur knows is that a child already conceived but not yet born will cause his death and destroy Logres. He attempts to find the child, but his efforts are all in vain, for God himself has decreed that it shall be so. As he is about to destroy all the children born on the day that the 'evil child' was born, he has a divine vision which tells him that this action will be fruitless;

Che n'est pas venjance que tu feras, car il ne mesfirent onques riens ne a toi ne a autrui, mais chou est pour ta volenté acomplir, et pour chou que tu cuides par ceste chose destorner la destruction del roiame de Logres; mais non feras, car elle averra tout ensi comme li fieus a l'anemi le t'a devisé.[4]

We know, therefore, from the beginning of the *Suite du Merlin* that Arthur will be punished for his sin the day that he does battle with Mordred on Salisbury Plain. And this is what happens in the Post-Vulgate *Mort Artu*. In the Vulgate the real cause of the final disaster is neither Arthur's sin nor Mordred's rebellion, but Lancelot and Guenevere's sinful love: Mordred's revolt only succeeds because of the dissensions that weakened the kingdom, and these dissensions are the direct result of Lancelot's adultery and its discovery by Agravain. Now while preserving the original structure of the *Mort Artu* and leading up

---

[1] Huth *Merlin*, I, 147–8.   [2] Huth MS., f. 76d; Huth *Merlin*, I, 154.
[3] Huth *Merlin*, I, 258.   [4] Ibid., I, 208.

to the final catastrophe by the same *péripéties* as the latter, the Post-Vulgate reduces as much as possible the part played by Lancelot and Guenevere, omitting most of the episodes which concern the two of them alone. It begins at a point corresponding to 85 l. 22 of Frappier's first edition of the *Mort Artu*; subsequently the accounts of Arthur's siege of Joieuse Garde and of the battles before Gaunes are considerably shortened, and such details as Lancelot's grief when Arthur refuses his offer for peace, Arthur's combat with Lancelot and the latter's moving farewell speech as he leaves Logres have been suppressed.[1] On the other hand, in explaining the enmity between Arthur's and Ban's people, the Post-Vulgate strengthens the vendetta motif. Whereas in the Vulgate Agravain denounces Lancelot for purely personal reasons,[2] and Gauvain's affection for Lancelot does not turn to hatred until after the death of his beloved brothers, in the Post-Vulgate there is discord between the knights of Ban's lineage and the other knights of the Round Table long before on account of Gauvain and Hector's quarrel.[3] Indeed, the denunciation of Lancelot's adultery is represented as the consequence of this quarrel, as is clear from the episode which the Post-Vulgate inserts between the end of the *Queste* and the beginning of the *Mort Artu*. In the Vulgate Boors goes to Camalot immediately on reaching Logres,[4] but in the Post-Vulgate he spends first a night at a forester's house[5] where, on enquiring about his lineage, he learns that Hector on his return from the *Queste* accused Gauvain of treason for having slain Erec and Palamedes. Only Arthur's[6] and Lancelot's inter-

---

[1] The first 85 pages of the Vulgate *Mort Artu* deal almost exclusively with Lancelot and Guenevere.

[2] When in the Vulgate Agravain becomes aware of Lancelot's love for the Queen, he is delighted for he had little affection for Lancelot: '... Agravains, li freres monseigneur Gauvain, qui onques ne l'avoit amé clerement et plus se prenoit garde de ses erremens que nus des autres...' (*La Mort le Roi Artu*, 5, ll. 18–20). Cf. also, ibid., 5, ll. 28–30: 'Quant Agravains se fu aperceüz de la reïne et de Lancelot, il en fu liez durement et plus por le domage que il cuida que Lancelos en eüst que por le roi vengier de sa honte.'

[3] See above, 127–8.

[4] Vulgate *Queste*, 279, ll. 25–6.

[5] The Post-Vulgate account is preserved wholly in *D*, II, §§ 624–6 (not in Sp. *D*) and partly in the prose *Tristan Queste* (MSS. B.N. fr. 772, ff. 417b–d; 97, ff. 555c–f; 101, ff. 399c–400a; 336, ff. 353c–354c; 349, ff. 627b–628a; 758, ff. 382d–383b; 24400, f. 188d; Dijon 527, ff. 166d–167b; Brit. Mus. Egerton 989, ff. 463v–65r; Aberystwyth, N.L.W. 5667, ff. 523a–d; Brussels, 9086, ff. 332d–334a; Vienna 2537, ff. 491b–d; Vienna 2540, ff. 243a–d; Vienna 2542, ff. 500c–f.).

[6] In the prose *Tristan* MSS. it is Arthur who intervened, but in *D* (II, § 625) it is the Queen.

vention prevented a combat between Hector and Gauvain, and ever
after there was little love lost between them. In order to avenge themselves on Ban's people, Arthur's relatives began to denounce Lancelot,
saying 'par derrieres. . . que messire Lancelot tient la reyne Guenievre
par dejouste le roi Artus et qu'il gist a lui. Et doivent ceste chose fere
entendre au roi pour meitre mortel haine entre le roy Artus et le
parenté le roi Ban.'[1] When Boors reached Camalot he attempted to make
peace between Hector and Gauvain, but without success, 'for Hector
was very angry and could not agree that there was any good in Gauvain; for he considered him disloyal and loved Erec so much that he
could not forget his death, and said that it would yet be avenged'.[2] The
rumours about Lancelot and Guenevere's love continue therefore to
spread, and only fear of retaliation from Ban's lineage stops Arthur's
relatives from telling the king directly.[3]

In the actual episodes dealing with the revelation of Lancelot's love,
the Post-Vulgate also stresses the feud motif. As in the Vulgate Gauvain advises his brothers not to reveal Lancelot's disloyalty to Arthur
for fear of the consequences,[4] but in the Post-Vulgate alone Gauvain
points out that this does not mean that he has any affection for Ban's
lineage:

Be silent, for it is of no avail, for if we told the king such war could result that
more than sixty thousand men would die in it, and with all this our shame
would not be avenged, for the power of Ban's lineage is very great, and God
has given them such honour that I do not think that they can be defeated by
any one. And for this reason let us leave this matter, for great misfortune
could arise from it. *And I do not say this because I do not wish Ban's lineage
more harm than you can think, and if I had the opportunity I would show them.*[5]

---

[1] MS. B.N. fr. 772, f. 418a–b; *D*, II, § 625.

[2] *D*, II, § 626: 'E Boorz se tremeteu de meter paz entre Estor e Galvam, mas
nom podia seer, que Estor era de mui grã coraçom e nom se podia outorgar em
cousa que prol fôsse de Galvam, ca o tiĩa por desleal e amava tam muito Erec,
que lhi nom podia escaecer sa morte, e dizia que ainda seeria vingado' (not in
Sp. *D*).

[3] *D*, II, § 626: 'e nom no encobrem al-rei senom com pavor que ham da
linhagem de rei Bam, ca sabem que o nom dira tal que morte nom prenda'
(not in Sp. *D*).

[4] *La Mort le Roi Artu*, 85, l. 23–86, l. 21; *D*, II, §§ 627–629; Sp. *D*, Chs.
CCCXCI–CCCXCIII.

[5] *D*, II, § 627: 'Calade-vos, ca nom há mester, ca se o al-rei dissermos, tal
guerra poderá i nacer per que mais de LX mil homens poderiam i morrer, e com
todo êsto nom poderia seer nossa desonra vingada, ca sobejamente é grande o

Later when Arthur has been informed of Lancelot's adultery, Gauvain
and Gaheriet refuse as in the Vulgate to have anything to do with
Agravain's plot, but whereas in the Vulgate Gaheriet's reason for not
becoming involved was that he did not wish to accuse Lancelot of such
shame, in the Post-Vulgate Gaheriet's argument is simply that it would
be unwise to come into conflict with Ban's people.[1] Gauvain fully
agrees, but significantly adds that he is willing to bide his time only
until he is in a position to harm Ban's people:

By God, said Gauvain, there are no people in the world whom I hate so
much. But there are so many of them and they are so strong that my hatred
does them but little harm. And for this reason I leave them alone until I
see my opportunity.[2]

But it is particularly towards the end of the Post-Vulgate that a
difference in conception between the two versions becomes apparent.
When Arthur suffers his first great loss, the death of his nephews
Gaheriet, Guerrehes and Agravain, he blames, as in the Vulgate,
Lancelot alone and refuses to admit the possibility of divine vengeance;[3] but after the last battle Arthur finally realizes that the real cause
of the tragedy is his own sin. He recognizes that the misfortune that
has overtaken him is a just retribution for the wrong he has done:

Giflet [he says], I am no longer the King Arthur that they used to call the
rois aventureux on account of the good fortune he had. He who would now

---

poder da linhagem de rei Bam e Deus os pôs em tal honra e em tal poder, que
nom cuido que podessem seer dirribados per homem, e por êsto leixemos-nos
em, ca mui grã malaventura sobejo poderia em nacer. *E nom digo êsto que eu
nom queira peor aa linhagem de rei Bam ca vós nom poderiades cuidar, e se eu visse
meu poder, vós veeriades o que eu mostraria*' (cf. Sp. *D*, Ch. CCCXCI). The
Vulgate *Mort Artu* (85, l. 26) has only: 'Tesiez.'

[1] *La Mort le Roi Artu*, 89, ll. 20–22: 'Or l'en couviengne bien, fet Gaheriet,
que ja ne m'en entremetrai; *ja si preudom comme Lancelos est ne sera par moi
encusez de ceste vilennie*.' *D*, II, § 631: 'Ora, como quer que venha bem, disse
Gaeriet, al-rei e a vós, meu irmão, jamais, nom me trabaharei dêste preito, *ca sei
verdadeiramento que nunca se homem tomara com a linhagem de rei Bam, que a
bõa cima em possa viir*' (cf. Sp. *D*, Ch. CCCXCIII, 314a). It is the words in
italics which differ in the two versions.

[2] *D*, II, § 631: 'Par Deus! disse Galvam, nom há homens no mundo que eu
tanto desame. Mas som tantos e tam boõs, que lhis nuz mui pouco meu desamor.
E porém os leixo atá que veja meu poder' (cf. Sp. *D*, Ch. CCCXCIII, 314a–b).
There is no trace of Gauvain's reply to Gaheriet in the Vulgate.

[3] *La Mort le Roi Artu*, 109, ll. 14–20; *D*, II, § 645; Sp. *D*, Ch. CCCCIX,
321a.

call me by my right name should call me unfortunate and wretched. Fortune did this to me; she has turned into my stepmother and enemy. And Our Lord whom it pleases that I should spend in grief and sadness what little of my life is left makes me realize that just as He once desired and had the power to raise me through many beautiful adventures without my meriting it, so He now has the power to lower me again through ill adventures that I deserve on account of my sin.[1]

Not that Arthur's sin of incest was a deliberate outrage. Linked closely with it is a theme which plays but little part in the Vulgate—that of *aventure et mescheance*. From the beginning Arthur and his knights are destined to mischance; they are not just the victims of a universal law, Fortune, as they are in the Vulgate. An atmosphere of gloom hangs over the kingdom of Logres.[2] The first adventure to take place at Arthur's court after his accession to the throne is interpreted by Merlin as a sign of worse to come:

Rois, es tu esbahis de ceste nouviele? Onques n'i pense, car trop averoies a faire se tu te voloies courechier toutes les fois que tu verras a court tes nouvielles avenir. *Che est la premiere aventure qui est a ta court avenue, si me poise moult que li commenchemens en est teuls, car li signes en est malvais et anieus.* Fai ceste metre en escrit et les autres aprés ensi coume elles avenront ou roiaume de Logres. Et saces que anchois que tu trespasses de cest siecle en seront tantes avenues que li escris qui en sera fais porra faire un grant livre. Ceste parole t'ai jou dite pour chou que je ne voel pas que tu t'esbahisses de teus aventures, ains voel que tu te mantiengnes vighereusement quant tu les verras avenir.[3]

---

[1] 'Giflet, eu nom soõ rei Artur, o que soíam chamar rei aventuroso polas bõas-andanças que havia. Mas quem me agora chamar per meu direito nome, chamar-me-á mal-aventurado e mizquinho. Êsto me fêz ventura, que xi me tornou madrasta e enmiga. E Nosso Senhor, a que praz que viva em doo e em tristeza êste pouco que hei-de viver, bem mo mostra: que assi como el quis e foi poderoso de me erguer per mui fremosas aventuras e sem meu merecimento, bem assi é poderoso de me derribar per aventuras feas e más, per meu pecado'; (*D*, II, § 672; cf. Sp. *D*, Ch. CCCCXXVII, 326b). Arthur speaks these words when in the Noire Chapelle he accidentally killed Lucan by falling on him. In the corresponding passage in the Vulgate, Arthur simply blames Fortune: 'Girflet, Fortune qui m'a esté mere jusque ci, et or m'est devenue marrastre, me fet user le remenant de ma vie en douleur et en corrouz et en tristesce' (*La Mort le Roi Artu*, 222, l. 20–223, l. 1). See also below, 152–3.

[2] See also below, 215–20.

[3] Huth MS., f. 84c–d; Huth *Merlin*, I, 174–5. Merlin speaks thus to Arthur when the news is brought to court that in a neighbouring forest the knight of the pavillon, Pellinor, forces all passers-by to joust with him and has just wounded unto death a certain knight.

L

Pure accidents unleash catastrophes: as Vinaver has shown, Balain's Dolorous Stroke which inaugurated the fearsome adventures of Logres and destroyed three kingdoms, though described as a 'sin which renews that of Eve our first mother',[1] was not a deliberate outrage, but an unintentional fault, the culmination of a series of mischances which befell the unhappy knight.[2] Now Arthur's incest was likewise an accident, another example of the *mescheance* which overshadows Logres. And this idea of *mescheance* which dominates the *Suite du Merlin* recurs also in the Post-Vulgate *Mort Artu*: it justifies the Arthurian tragedy and makes it emotionally convincing.[3] Practically all the references to Fortune have been omitted: the account of Arthur's journey from Dover to Salisbury Plain during which he has a vision of the relentless turning of the Wheel of Fortune and finds letters engraved on a rock by Merlin warning him of his destiny, has no place in the Post-Vulgate.[4] Instead the *remanieur* brings out the pathetic element in the situation. In the final battle King Arthur does not blame Fortune or God for the calamity that has befallen him.[5] He fights bravely and inspires courage. Lucan seeing him valiantly face the enemy feels convinced that they will return triumphant from this mortal battle: 'Giflet,' he says, 'we can be sure of winning this battle; look at King Arthur who is of good courage. He has learnt well how to confound and kill his enemies. He is rightly called king who thus knows how to help his people.'[6] When in the Vulgate Arthur sees Mordred strike down Sagremor, he utters a cry of self-pity:

Ha! Dex, por quoi me lessiez vos tant abessier de proesce terriene? por amour de cest coup veu ge a Dieu qu'il couvient ici morir moi ou Mordret.[7]

---

[1] Huth *Merlin*, I, 231–2.   [2] See Vinaver, *Le roman de Balain*, xxii–xxx.

[3] In the Vulgate *Mort Artu* there are only a very few references to mischance (see 4, l. 20, 92, l. 25, 109, l. 8, 118, l. 12, 201, l. 7), and it was left to the Post-Vulgate to develop the theme.

[4] Frappier (in *ALMA*, 311) states wrongly that 'the vision of Fortune and her wheel which precedes the battle of Salisbury and presages Arthur's downfall is a conventional motif, adopted also by the *Suite du Merlin* (*Huth Merlin*)'. Neither in the *Suite du Merlin* nor in the Post-Vulgate *Mort Artu* is the Wheel of Fortune mentioned.

[5] Frappier characterizes the Arthur of the Vulgate *Mort Artu* as a 'vieillard larmoyant' (see his *Étude*, 279–83).

[6] 'Dom Giflet, sejamos seguros que venceremos esta batalha; vêdes aqui rei Artur, que bõo sembrante nos mostra. Bem aprês a cofonder e a matar seus enmigos. Bem deve seer chamado rei quem assi sabe ajudar sa gente' (*D*, II, § 665, cf. Sp. *D*, Ch. CCCCXXIV, 326a).

[7] *La Mort le Roi Artu*, 219, ll. 22–4.

In the Post-Vulgate *Mort Artu*, Arthur's remark stresses the pathos of the death of so many good knights caused by the machinations of one bad man: 'Ah! God, what mischance that a traitor should kill so many good and loyal knights.'[1] Whereas the Vulgate describes in detail the numerous battles waged by the separate divisions, the Post-Vulgate concentrates upon the conflict between Arthur and Mordred. Arthur does not as in the Vulgate watch the approach of Mordred with fear, but bravely seeks out the traitor, gives him the first blow[2] and warns him that his treachery has done him no good: 'Mordred,' he says, 'you have done me much harm, but it has been of no avail to you.'[3] When Arthur has killed Mordred and Mordred has wounded Arthur unto death, Blioberis remarks that the prediction that Arthur shall die by the hand of his son has now come true: 'Ah! God, now I see the prophecy fulfilled which the wise men of this country used to utter many a time that King Arthur would die by the hand of his son. Ah! God, what harm and what loss!'[4] And as Arthur sees Mordred lying dead before him, he curses the hour that Mordred was born and that he knighted him, for he regards him as the instrument of his death and of the destruction of Logres: 'Mordret,' he says, 'in an evil hour did I knight you. You have confounded me and the kingdom of Logres, and yet you are dead. Cursed be the hour that you were born.'[5]

Equally significant are the constant references to the *champ douloureux* and the *bataille douloureuse* which are not in the Vulgate version. When the last survivors of the battle, the King, the Archbishop of Canterbury, Blioberis, Lucan and Giflet,[6] see that none are left to fight

---

[1] 'Ai, Deus, camanha má-andança do traedor, matar os boõs cavaleiros e os leaes!' *D*, II, § 666 (not in Sp. *D*).

[2] In the Vulgate, Mordred strikes Arthur first (*La Mort le Roi Artu*, 216, ll. 6–7).

[3] 'Morderet, muito mal me hás feito, mas nom se te tornou a prol' (*D*, II, § 665 (not in Sp. *D*). In the Vulgate when Arthur sees Mordred's division approaching, he regrets the absence of Lancelot and Gauvain and his men have to tell him to put his fear aside, for no good can come from fear (*La Mort le Roi Artu*, 215, ll. 16–19).

[4] 'Ai, Deus! Ora vejo a profecia comprida que os homens sisudos desta terra disserom per muitas vezes, que rei Artur morreria per mão de seu filho. Ai, Deus! Que dano e que perda!' (*D*, II, § 667; not in Sp. *D*). In the Vulgate, the people once more reproach Heaven when they see Arthur smitten by Mordred (*La Mort le Roi Artu*, 220, ll. 12–14).

[5] 'Morderet, [em] mau-ponto [te] eu fiz [cavaleiro]. Tu confundiste-mi e o reino de Logres, e tu és porém morto. Maldita seja a hora em que tu naceste!' (*D*, II, § 667; not in Sp. *D*). This remark is not in the Vulgate.

[6] The Vulgate does not mention the Archbishop or Blioberis.

and that Salisbury Plain is covered with their dead, they do not as in the Vulgate indulge in a long discourse on their misfortune.[1] They utter but a few words which reveal their deep realization of the tragedy: 'Ah! God, how great is this harm and this loss. Ah! God, what more ill could you do to us, for we see lying here the whole world dead in anguish and in sorrow.'[2] But it is Arthur himself who realizes the full extent of the mischance which has befallen them. He leaves the *champ douloureux* making great grief, and when the Archbishop attempts to comfort him, telling him that he has had good fortune in that he has remained alive and won this mortal battle, he can but say: 'Ah! if I am alive, what good does it do? For my life is nothing; I can see that I am wounded unto death. Ah! God, what mischance has befallen a great country through the treason of one bad man.'[3] The first sentence may have its origin in Arthur's remark in the Vulgate *Mort Artu* that he feels his end approaching,[4] but the second belongs to the Post-Vulgate. Yet greater sorrow, however, awaits the King. When that same evening after the battle, he, Giflet and Lucan come to the Noire Chapelle, Arthur who is kneeling before the altar accidentally falls backwards on to Lucan and crushes him to death.[5] Now whereas in the

[1] The passage in question is the following: Quant cist qui estoient remés virent que einsint estoit avenu de la bataille, si commencierent a plorer trop durement et distrent: 'Ha! Dex, fu onques nus hom mortex qui veïst ausi grant douleur? Ha! bataille, tant avez fet en cest païs et en autres d'orfelins et de veves fames! Ha! jor, pour quoi ajornas tu onques por metre a si grant povreté le roiaume de la Grant Bretaigne, dont li oir estoient molt renomé de proesce qui ci gisent mort et destruit a si grant douleur? Ha! Dex, que nos poez vos plus tolir? nos veons ci morz touz noz amis.' (*La Mort le Roi Artu*, 220, l. 17–221, l. 7.)

[2] 'Quando êles virom que nom ficou i homem com que se combater podessem e virom o campo de Salaber coberto de tôdas partes de cavaleiros mortos, disserom antre si chorando: 'Ai, Deus! Como há grã dano e grã perda! Ai, Deus! que nom nos poderiades chus mal fazer, ca nós veemos aqui todo o mundo jazer morto a marteiro e a door.' (*D*, II, § 667; not in Sp. *D*.)

[3] 'Ai! disse el-rei, se eu escapei vivo, que prol me vem? Ca mĩa vida nom e nada, ca eu bem vejo que soõ chagado aa morte. Ai, Deus! que foi fatal vĩir tam maa-andança a ũa grã terra, per traiçom de uũ mau homem.' (*D*, II, § 668; not in Sp. *D*.)

[4] When the survivors ask Arthur how he feels, he replies: 'Il n'i a fors del monter et d'eslongnier ceste place; car ge voi bien que ma fins aprouche, ne entre mes ennemis ne vueill ge pas finer.' (*La Mort le Roi Artu*, 221, ll. 9–11.)

[5] In the Vulgate *Mort Artu* Arthur spends the night in prayer and kills Lucan only the following morning. According to most MSS. Lucan dies because Arthur embraces him too tightly (*La Mort le Roi Artu*, 222, ll. 9–13), but MSS. *DV* give the same version of Lucan's death as the Post-Vulgate (see *La Mort le Roi Artu*, 222, n. 8).

Vulgate *Mort Artu* Arthur blames once more Fortune, in the Post-Vulgate he sees in it another example of the *male aventure* which is pursuing him.[1] He spends the night in grief for he knows that his end is near and the next morning he has only one desire, to leave the land where he has had such great mischance: 'Let us ride on and go straight to the sea, for such great mischance has befallen me on this occasion in Logres that I do not wish to die here . . .'[2]

If there is any explanation for King Arthur's mischance, it is simply his own destiny: he is, as Merlin remarks in the *Suite du Merlin*, the *roi aventureux*, the king of chance and mischance, and his kingdom is the *roiaume aventureux*, and just as *aventure* gave him his crown, so *aventure* will take it:

Rois Artus, qui es rois par aventure e fus conceus par aventure, e fus norris par aventure tele que cil qui te norissoient ne savoient qe tu estoies, et quant tu venis jovens enfés entre les homes le quele que ne te conoissoient e Nostre Sires [te] reconoie bien e t'aleva par sa grace desor toz e te fist seignur si com tu le devoies estre, e si fus engendrés par aventure e par aventure receus tu la corune, car ensi plaisoit il a Nostre Seignor. E sachez que tanz aventures ne si merveilluses ne t'est pas avenues pur nient, ainz estoient signefiancez e commencemenz de ceo qu'il devoit avenir en ton ostel e en ta subjection e en mainte autre lieu; e pur ceo te di jeo que tu dois estre apellez rois aventurus e li teons realmes [li realmes] as aventures. E sachiez que tut einsi com aventure te dona le realme, si le te toudra aventure.[3]

In the Post-Vulgate *Mort Artu*, Arthur explains his destiny to Giflet in very similar terms: when Giflet has at last thrown Escalibor into the lake and the hand has seized it and Arthur consequently knows that his end is fast approaching, he tells Giflet that as he came, so he will pass: 'Ah! Giflet, you served me well and kept me company for a long time. But now the term approaches that you must leave me. You may well boast that you are the knight of the Round Table who kept me company the longest. But now I tell you to go, for my end is

---

[1] See above, 149, including n. 1.

[2] 'Cavalguemos e vaamos-nos direitamente ao mar, ca tanta maa-andança me veo desta vez em Logres, que nom querria i morrer . . .' (*D*, II, § 672; Sp. *D*, Ch. CCCCXXVII, 327a).

[3] Cambridge MS., f. 289 c–d; Huth *Merlin*, II, 97. Merlin speaks thus to Arthur when Gauvain returns from his quest of the white stag. He adds that he has told him all this because many more adventures will befall his knights, and he wants him, in order to be able to distinguish 'les bons des mauvais', to establish the custom that each knight before setting out on a quest should swear to relate his adventures on returning.

approaching and it is not right that any one should know the truth about my end, for just as I was king here *par aventure*, thus shall I pass from this kingdom *par aventure*, for no one shall from now on be able to vaunt that he knows for certain what has happened to me. And this is why I want you to go; and when you have left me, if any one should ask for news of me, tell them that King Arthur came *par aventure* and went *par aventure*, and he alone was the *rois aventureux*.'[1] Finally, when Giflet explores Arthur's tomb, he finds nothing there but the helmet that Arthur wore in the dolorous battle and he echoes Arthur's last words: 'So?' said Giflet. 'In vain shall I ask how Arthur died. Indeed he is the *rois aventureux* about whose end no one will know; and indeed he spoke the truth, for just as he came to the kingdom of Logres *par aventure*, so he went from it *par aventure*.'[2]

There can be no doubt that the *Suite du Merlin* and the Post-Vulgate *Mort Artu* go together. Not only do they have the same conception of Mordred's part in the destruction of Logres, but the theme of 'aventure' and 'mescheance' which links the *Suite du Merlin* and Post-Vulgate *Queste–Mort Artu* requires the downfall of the 'roialme

---

[1] 'Ai, Giflet! Longo tempo me servistes e me tevestes companha. Mas ora chegou já o têrmo em que vos convém já de mi partir. E bem vos podedes louvar que vós sodes o companheiro da Távola Redonda que mais longamente me teve companha. Mas ora vos digo que vos vaades, ca dês hoje-a-mais, nom quero que fiquedes comigo, ca mia fim se achega; e nom é cousa posta que në uũ saiba verdade de mia fim, ca bem como eu aqui per ventura fui rei, assi passarei dêste reino per ventura, ca nenguũ nom se poderá louvar, dês aqui adiante, que certamente saiba que será de mim. E por êsto quero que vos vaades; e pois fordes de mim partido, se vos preguntarem novas de mim, respondede-lhis que rei Artur veo per ventura e per ventura se partiu, e ele soo foi rei aventuroso.' (*D*, II, § 679; Sp. *D*, Ch. CCCCXXXIII, 329b.) In the Vulgate, Arthur tells Giflet to go without any further explanation: 'Et quant il a esté grant piece en ce pensé, si dist a Girflet: "Il vos en couvient aler de ci et partir de moi a tel eür que, jamés que vos vivoiz, ne me verroiz.—Par tel couvent, fet Girflet, ne partirai ge de vos en nule maniere.—Si feroiz, fet li rois, ou autrement vos harrai ge bien de mortel haine.—Sire, fet Girflet, comment porroit ce estre que ge vos lessasse ici trestout seul et m'en iroie, et encore me dites vos que ge ne vos verrai jamés. —Il couvient, fet li rois, que vos le façoiz einsi com ge vos di. Alez vos en de ci vistement, que del demorer n'i a il point; et gel vos pri par cele amor qui a esté entre moi et vos." ' (*La Mort le Roi Artu*, 224, l. 31–225, l. 9.)

[2] 'Assi? disse Giflet; em vão me trabalharei de preguntar como rei Artur morreu. Verdadeiramente êste é o rei aventuroso, cuja morte në uũ homem nom saberá; e bem disse el verdade, que assi como el veo ao reino de Logres per ventura, assi se foi em per ventura.' (*D*, II, § 683; Sp. *D*, Ch. CCCCXXXVII.) In the Vulgate, Giflet does not open Arthur's tomb, but accepts the hermit's

aventureus' to be the consequence of an 'adventure': Arthur, no more than the Chevalier as Deus Espees, realized fully the wrong he was doing when he committed his 'utragrez'. 'Tout se tient': the first tragedy to befall Arthur's kingdom, the beginning of the 'aventurez e mervaillez', was due to an unwitting transgression which the whole of Logres had to expiate; the final tragedy repeats the pattern.

---

statement that he saw twelve damsels bring hither Arthur's body and bury him (see *La Mort le Roi Artu*, 226-7).

The author of the Post-Vulgate account may have been influenced by the passage in Wace's *Brut* which describes Arthur's death as *dutuse*:

> Merlin dist d'Arthur, si ot dreit,
> Que sa mort dutuse serreit.
> Li prophetes dist verité;
> Tus tens en ad l'um puis duté,
> E dutera, ço crei, tut dis,
> Se il est morz u il est vis.
>
> (*Brut*, ed. I. Arnold, ll. 13285-90.)

CHAPTER VII

The 'Estoire del Saint Graal' and the 'Suite du Merlin'

WE have so far considered the second and third parts of the *Suite du Merlin* compilation. It is necessary now to turn to the first part. According to the redactional indications, this section ends at the beginning of Balain's quest for the invisible knight.[1] It consisted, therefore, at least of the early portion of the *Suite du Merlin* and the prose *Merlin* which precedes the latter. If there is any truth in the constant assertions of the author that the three parts of his 'book' are equal in size, the first part must have contained something else, for the *Merlin* together with part of the *Suite du Merlin* is considerably shorter than the second or third part. As the Huth MS. begins with the prose rendering of Robert de Boron's *Joseph*, Gaston Paris thought that this belonged to the first part.[2] Apart from the fact, however, that the Cambridge MS. of the *Suite du Merlin* begins with the *Estoire del Saint Graal* and that the Portuguese *Josep Abaramatia* bears the sub-title '*A primeira parte da Demanda do Santo Grial*',[3] there is in the Post-Vulgate *Queste* a reference which indicates clearly that the *Estoire del Saint Graal*, not the *Joseph*, belonged to the 'first part'. When Galaad heals Mordrain, the redactor remarks that Mordrain has been in the abbey since the time of Joseph of Arimathea, 'as the first part of our book relates':

Dedenz cellui an avint il que aventure l'aporta a l'abeie ou li rois Mordrains avoit demoré des le tens Josep d'Arimathie dusqu'a la venue de Galahaz, *si plaié et si navré com li contes l'a devisé en la premiere partie de nostre livre*.[4]

Now it is only the *Estoire del Saint Graal* which relates how Mordrain, having gone too near the ark containing the Holy Vessel, lost the sight of his eyes and the use of his body, and was told that he would remain in this condition until the coming of Galaad, 'li buens chevaliers noevismes del lingnage Nascien, cil qui doit les merveilles del Saint Graal veoir apertement'.[5]

---

[1] See above, 61.   [2] See above, 40.   [3] Cf. above, 44, including n. 8.
[4] MS. B.N. fr. 343, f. 98b. This reference is not in the Vulgate *Queste*.
[5] MS. Rennes 255, f. 80e; *Vulgate Version*, I, 241.

It is unlikely that the *Estoire del Saint Graal* preceding the *Suite du Merlin* differed substantially from the *Estoire* forming the first branch of the Vulgate Cycle. There exist today some fifty manuscripts of the Vulgate *Estoire*, which can be divided into two broad groups—a shorter redaction represented by Sommer's edition[1] and a lengthier one which frequently differs verbally from the shorter version and includes more descriptive details, but no additional episodes.[2] The version of the *Estoire* contained in the Cambridge MS. is to all intents and purposes identical with the longer version and contains nothing to indicate that the scribe intended to go on with the *Suite du Merlin* rather than with the rest of the Vulgate Cycle.

The Portuguese *Josep Abarimatia* of MS. 643 of the Torre do Tombo, copied in the sixteenth century by Manuel Alvarez,[3] but derived from a version executed in 1313 by Joam Bivas on the order of a certain João Samchez, *mestre escolla* at Astorga,[4] is textually of considerable interest. It begins with the incipit of the shorter version and

---

[1] *Vulgate Version*, I.

[2] Two MSS. of the long version have been published, one by Hucher and Furnivall, see above, 6, n. 1. The short version begins with the following incipit: '*Cil qui se tient et juge au plus petit et au plus pecheor de toꝛ, mande saluꝛ el commencement de ceste estoire a touꝛ ceuls qui lor cuers ont et lor creance en la sainte trinité*' (quoted from MS. Brit. Mus. Royal 19 C XII). The long version, on the other hand, begins as follows: '*Chil ki la hauteche et la signourie de si haute estoire comme est chele du Graal, met en escrit par le commandemement du grant maistre, mande tout premierement salus a tous cheus et a toutes cheles ki ont lor creanche en la sainte glorieuse trinité*' (quoted from Furnivall's edition, vol. I, 1). For a comprehensive list of *Estoire* MSS., see Woledge, *Bibliographie des romans...*, 72–6.

[3] On ff. 1r–2r of MS. 643 is a dedication by Manuel Alvarez to King John III of Portugal (1521–57). In it he explains that his book is a translation or transcription of an illuminated parchment manuscript two hundred years old found by him at Riba d'Ancora in the possession of a very old lady at the time when his father was the king's *corregidor* in Entre Douro e Minho. For a transcription of the dedication, see Bohigas, *Los textos españoles*, 105–7.

[4] The name of the translator is found in MS. 643 on ff. 123v and 199r. The same name is also in the fragmentary Spanish *Josep*, as well as in Sp. *D* (see Bohigas, *Los textos españoles*, 72–4, 81–4, and Bohigas, *1498 Baladro*, III, 186–93). From this scholars have rightly inferred that the Spanish and Portuguese texts go back to a common original (O). The reference to João Samchez, as well as the date, are found in the final colophon of MS. 643: '*Este livro mamdou fazer João Samchez mestre escolla d'Astorga no quimto ano que o estado (read estudo) de Coimbra foy feito e no tempo do papa Clemente que destroio a ordem del temple e fez o comçilio geral em Biana e pos ho emtredito em Castela, e nesto ano se finou a rainha dona Costamça em São Fagumdo e casou o ymfamte*

subsequently alternates between the two redactions, sometimes combining the readings of both.[1] The only extant French MS. which does the same is Rennes 255 (R).[2] In substance, however, the Portuguese version does not differ markedly from the Vulgate *Estoire*. Only two or three allusions have been modified to link up with the *Suite du Merlin* and the Post-Vulgate *Queste*. Thus according to all the extant MSS. of the *Estoire*, 'le coup d'une seule espee' will inaugurate, in King Arthur's time marvels and adventures:

En ceste terre qui est apelee Bretaigne la Grant avra un roi qui ert apelez Artus, si ert si aspre et de si buene chevalerie que ce sera merveilles. Et a celui tens avendra en ceste terre *par le coup d'une seule espee* aventures et si granz merveilles que maintes genz qui puis en orront parler le tendront a fantosme.[3]

The Portuguese *Josep*, obviously with Balain's Dolorous Stroke in mind, has altered the reference to the effect that the marvels would be caused 'por golpe de lamça':

... Naquele tempo avera nesta terra *por golpe de lamça* tão gramdes avemturas e tão maravylhosas que has gemtes que depois o ouvirom falar o terão por maravilha.[4]

Elsewhere the MSS. of the *Estoire* remark that Pellean, the Maimed King, received his wound in a battle in Rome:

Dom Felipe com a filha de Dom A[ffonso] ano de 13XII[I] anos' (f. 311v). The last stroke of XIII is hardly visible, but from the events mentioned in the passage the correct date would appear to be 1313. (Cf. Entwistle, *The Arthurian Legend*, 136–41; Bohigas, *Los textos españoles*, 76–80 and Bohigas, *1498 Baladro*, III, 192.)

[1] The view hitherto taken was that the Portuguese *Josep* follows the longer redaction (see Bohigas, *Los textos españoles*, 31, 112–17). The Spanish *Libro de Josep Abarimatia* contained in MS. 2-G-5 of the Madrid National Library (ff. 252r–282r) is incomplete at the beginning and the end, but agrees with the Portuguese *Josep* as far as it goes.

[2] MSS. Tours 951, Bourg 55, Chantilly 476 (formerly 644) and the early printed editions also combine the two versions, but do *not* agree with Rennes and the Portuguese *Josep*. For details, see my article on the 'Relationship of the Portuguese *Josep Abarimatia* to the extant French MSS. of the *Estoire del Saint Graal*', *ZRPh.*, 76 (1960) 343–75. (In this article, p. 343, n. 4, I included in error MS. Chantilly 644 among the MSS. beginning *Cil qui se tient*, and on p. 344, n. 5 I referred in error to Chantilly 476 [formerly 644] as 644.)

[3] MS. Rennes 255, f. 75a–b; *Vulgate Version*, I, 226.

[4] Portuguese *Josep*, f. 232v. The Spanish *Josep* breaks off before reaching this point.

Aprés lo roi Lambor regna Pellehan ses filz qui fu mehaigniés des dous cuisses en une bataille de Rome. Et por celui mehaing qu'il prist en cele bataille, l'apelerent puis tuit cil qui le conoissoient comunalment lo roi Mehaignié. Et por ce l'apelerent lo roi Mehaignié qu'il ne pout onques garir de cele plaie jusq'a tant que Galaaz li fiz Lancelot le vint visiter. Et lors sanz faille gari il.[1]

The Portuguese version, on the other hand, explains that the Chevaliers as Deus Espees wounded Pellean, 'as the story will relate'. The reference could not be more precise:

Depos el-rey Lambor reinou depos ele seu filho que foi tolheito de ambas as coxas de hũa lamçada que lhe deu o Cavaleiro das duas espadas com a Lamça, Vimgador, por omde as avemturas vierão em Lomdres asy como depois esta estorea vos comtara. E por aquele tolhimemto foy depois chamado tolheito e chamaromno tolheito porque depois numqua pode sairar daquella chaga ata que o muy bom cavaleiro Galaz, o filho de Lamçarote, o veio ver, mas em tão sem falta gareçeo.[2]

Finally, at the point where the *Estoire* speaks of Bron's twelve sons,[3] the Portuguese *Josep* adds Tristan's genealogy and the remark that it will not deal with Tristan's early life as this would make the book too big:

Depois fez aos outros jrmãos o que lhes prometeo, que os casou todos tão altamemte que foi maravilha e omde eles quiserão a fora somemte dous, que huũ chamabão Perõ que depois por sy casou e outro chamabão Sador que se nom quis casar senão a sua vomtade. Deste Sador saio Apollo, ho bem avemturado de Chelida, filho del rey de Babilonia, que achou prenhada e casou com ela, e deste Apollo por linagem de herdeiro em herdeiro saio el-rey Felix, e deste Felix saio el-rey Metilamdes, e de Metilamdes e de Elliabel, yrmã de ell-rey Mares, saio Tristão o namorado e fermoso e bom cavaleiro, asy como a gram estorea o devisara, que se aquela istorea for a esta ajumtada sera noso llivro muy gramde, e quamdo for llugar falaremos nele que depois foi companheiro da Tavola Redomda.[4]

No extant French MS. of the *Estoire* contains these references to Tristan or the Chevaliers as Deus Espees, and it is not possible to say

---

[1] MS. Rennes 255, f. 98v col. 1; *Vulgate Version*, I, 290. Some MSS. have simply 'en une bataille', and do not mention Rome.
[2] Portuguese *Josep*, f. 304v. The Spanish *Josep* breaks off before reaching this point.   [3] *Vulgate Version*, I, 250.
[4] Portuguese *Josep*, f. 263r–v; the Spanish *Josep* breaks off before reaching this point. All these allusions were first noted by Bohigas, *Los textos españoles*, 31–3, 107–10.

whether they were added by the Portuguese translator or were already in a French manuscript now lost.[1]

But if, as it seems, the Vulgate *Estoire* was adapted only slightly, if at all, for the *Suite du Merlin* compilation, this does not mean that it does not form an integral part of it. On the contrary, the connexion between the *Estoire* and the *Suite du Merlin* and Post-Vulgate *Queste* is in many ways much closer than that between the *Estoire* and the rest of the Vulgate cycle. It frequently happens that when the redactor of the Post-Vulgate *Queste* takes over material from the Vulgate *Queste* which is in some way connected with a prediction in the *Estoire*, he brings of his own accord the connexion forcibly before the reader. For instance both *Questes* relate the healing of Simeu, which is foretold in the *Estoire*. But whereas the Vulgate *Queste* merely says that Simeu has lain 'en ceste grant chalor' for three hundred and fifty-four years to expiate a sin committed 'jadis envers Joseph d'Arymacie',[2] the Post-Vulgate lays the greatest stress on the antecedents of the episode. Simeu, we are told, is 'li pere Moïs' and has lain in his burning tomb

des le tens Josep d'Arimacie dusqu'a celui, si com l'estoire en a ja devisé la droite verité.[3]

After the healing, Simeu relates his and Moïs' adventures 'as the story has already told it':

Et la voiz li comence tot maintenant a conter l'aventuire de Simeu et de Moïs ensint com l'estoire l'a ja devisé.[4]

---

[1] The *explicit* of the Portuguese *Josep* is as follows: 'E agora se cala a estorea de todas estas linagens que de Celidones sairão e torna aos outros ramos que chama Estorea de Merlim, que comvem por toda maneyra jumtar com a Estorea do Greal, porque he dos ramos e lhe pertemçe, *e saibão todos aqueles que esta estorea ouvyrem que esta estorea era jumtada com a de Merlim, na qual he comemça-memto da Mesa Redomda e a naçemça de Artur e comemçamemto das avemturas, mas por nosó livro nom ser muy gramde repartimolo cada huũ em sua parte, porque cada huũ por sy serão milhores de traʒer. Aquy se acaba este livro, o nome de Deus seja louvado para sempre jamais, e deixe Deus bem (bem) viver e bem obrar aquele que o mamdou faʒer'* (f. 311r–v). The first part of the *explicit* up to *pertemce* can be traced to the French MSS. of the *Estoire*, but the passage in italics which explains that the Merlin has been separated from the *Estoire* so that 'noso liuro nom ser muy gramde' must be attributed to the Portuguese translator; for, as we have seen above, according to the redactional indications in the *Suite du Merlin*, the first part does not end with the *Estoire*, but includes a portion of the *Suite du Merlin*.

[2] Vulgate *Queste*, 264–5.

[3] MS. B.N. fr. 343, f. 65c.   [4] Ibid., f. 65d.

The double reference to the account of Simeu's adventure in the *Estoire*[1] makes it clear that the author regards the latter as part of his romance. It is noteworthy that the relationship between Simeu and Moïs is not mentioned in the Vulgate *Queste*;[2] the fact that the *Estoire* and the Post-Vulgate *Queste* both make Moïs the son of Simeu is thus proof that the Post-Vulgate *Queste* knew and exploited the *Estoire* independently.

There is a similar case in the episode of Lancelot's visit to Corbenic. Whereas the Vulgate *Queste* says:

Si resgarde dedenz la chambre et voit sor une table d'argent le Saint Vessel covert d'un vermeil samit,[3]

the Post-Vulgate *Queste* has

Et il regarde la chambre, si la voit tant belle et tant riche qu'il ne vit onques nulle chose qui tant le pleust. Et en mi leu de la chambre estoit la table d'argent et li Sainz Vaxiaus desus, *couvert si richement com il estoit a celui point que Josephés li primiers evesques i chanta.*[4]

There can be no doubt that the phrase in italics would recall to a medieval reader the scene in the *Estoire* in which Josephés was consecrated bishop and celebrated his first Mass before the people in Sarraz.[5]

A number of incidents peculiar to the Post-Vulgate *Queste* are quite obviously intended to provide a sequel to the account in the *Estoire*. Thus the *Estoire* relates that the Bishop of Jerusalem, Cayphas, was the only one of Christ's persecutors whose life Vespasian spared: he was put in a rudderless boat on the open sea to go where 'aventure' would lead him:

Lors fist maintenant apareillier un batel, puis i fist metre Cayfas et puis le fist bien elloignier en la mer et ala la ou aventure le mena.[6]

---

[1] *Vulgate Version*, I, 262–5, 282–4.

[2] The *Lancelot* proper mentions, however, that Simeu was Moïs' father (see *Le Roman en prose de Lancelot du Lac*, ed. G. Hutchings, 43, 50).

[3] Vulgate *Queste*, 255, ll. 14–15.   [4] MS. B.N. fr. 343, f. 91a.

[5] *Vulgate Version*, I, 31–41. The description of the Holy Vessel is as follows: '... Et el mi leu de l'autel avoit un molt riche vaissel d'or en semblance d'un henap, et desus avoit un corvecle qui estoit d'or autresi, mes le corvecle ne pot il pas veoir a delivre ne ce qu'il avoit desoz, car il estoit coverz d'un blanc drap, si que l'en nel pooit veoir fors par devant' (MS. Rennes, f. 13a; *Vulgate Version*, I, 33).

[6] MS. Rennes 255, f. 7c–d; *Vulgate Version*, I, 18.

Now while no one hears anything of Cayphas in the Vulgate *Queste*, the Post-Vulgate *Queste* contains an account in which he is discovered on an island by Galaad, Perceval and Boors.[1] He tells them that he has been living there for more than two hundred years to expiate the wrong he did Christ at the time when Titus was emperor of Rome:

Jadis fui evesques de Jherusalem au tens que Tytus fu empereres de Roume. Mes par un forfet que li Juyf firent du prophete qui estoit apelez Jhesu, fumes tuit dampné et destruit. De moi, voirement, qui ne l'avoie pas tant deservi con li autres, ot Vaspasiens greigneur merci (de moi) que des autres, car il ne me volt pas ocirre coume il fesoit les autres, ainz me fist meitre en une barge sanz compagnie de gent et sanz aviron, et me fist enpeindre en la mer pour recevoir tel mort con Dieus me voudroit envoier.[2]

The *Estoire*, it is true, does not announce that Galaad would one day meet this sinner, but some of the other additions serve to fulfil predictions of the *Estoire* which are not accomplished in the Vulgate *Queste*. The *Estoire*, for instance, relates that Moïs, who did not heed Josephés' warning that no one should sit in the 'siege vide' unless he felt himself such as he ought to be, was punished for his presumption: flaming hands carried him off to the forest of Darnantes where he was to remain 'en feu ardant' until 'li buens chevaliers, cil qui menra a fin les aventures de la Grant Bretaigne, le vendra visiter por savoir la merveille de ceste chose'.[3] Now while the Vulgate *Queste* knows about Moïs, its account of his punishment differs from that of the *Estoire*, and there is no reference to his deliverance.[4] The details which the Post-Vulgate *Queste* gives of Moïs' punishment are in accordance with the facts of the *Estoire*: when Simeu has been delivered, he tells Galaad that he will find his son Moïs in great pain 'en la salle perilleuse en la forest de Darimantes'.[5] Later Galaad in effect finds Moïs there and brings him relief as the *Estoire* said he would:

Quant il se furent departi, Galahaz chevaucha toz sels cerchant les aventures del roiaume de Logres en touz les leux ou il en oït parler et tant que aventure l'aporta en la forest [de] Darnantes, el palleis perilleux. Leienz trouva il la

---

[1] MS. B.N. fr. 772, f. 365b–d; *D*, II, 417–21; Sp. *D*, Chs. CCXXVI–CCXXIX.

[2] MS. B.N. fr. 772, f. 365c.

[3] MS. Rennes 255, f. 87d; *Vulgate Version*, I, 261.

[4] The Vulgate *Queste* (75, l. 29–76, l. 23) does not mention Moïs by name and relates his punishment according to the account of Robert de Borron's *Estoire dou Graal*. For explanations of this contradiction between the Vulgate *Queste* and the *Estoire*, see Lot, *Étude*, 253–6; Frappier, *Étude*, 57; Pauphilet, review of Lot's *Étude*, *R*, XLV (1918) 522.   [5] MS. B.N. fr. 343, f. 65d.

tombe Moïs, le filz Simeu, qui toute voies ardoit, si [com li] contes a ja devisé ça en arieres. Et tout ausint com Simeu avoit esté delivrez de l'ardoir del feu qui tant avoit duré, en la venue de monseignor Galahaz, tout ausint fu Moïs delivrez, et par celle meemes maniere.[1]

This is not the only instance of its kind. Many other references in the *Estoire* which are in contradiction with the Vulgate *Queste* alone or with all the other branches of the Vulgate Cycle have been taken up and developed by the *Suite du Merlin* and the Post-Vulgate *Queste*. When in the *Estoire* the angel withdraws from Josephés' thigh the spear head of the Lance with which he has been smitten, he tells him that the Lance will not bleed again till the marvels of Logres begin:

Et il (i.e. the angel) revint a Josephés, si li demanda se il savoit que la lance senefioit. Et il dist que nenin. Et il li dist qu'ele senefioit les granz merveilles qui avendroient en la terre ou Dex les menroit. Iluec seront les granz proeces veues et mostrees, et la seront les veraies chevaleries [Jhesu Crist] descovertes, car les choses terrienes devendront celestiaus, ne ja nus ne sera certains del termine ou eles avendront, mais avant qu'eles doivent comencier rendra ceste lance sanc einsi come tu l'as veu. Ne ja mes des ore en avant n'en charra nule gote devant a icele ore que les aventures devront avenir, einsi come tu as oï. Et lors comenceront a avenir les merveilles par totes les terres ou ceste lance sera. Et seront si epoentables que totes les genz en seront esbahies, si n'avendront ne mes por la conoissance del Graal et de la lance. Lors seront abandonees les merveilles et establies, a cui li verai hardi abandoneront lor cors, et par ce seront coneu cil qui les granz proeces avront faites. Ne ja mes les merveilles, ce saches tu bien, ne seront descovertes ne veues del Saint Graal par nul home mortel que par un sol. Et cil sera pleins de totes les bontez que cors d'ome doie avoir, car il sera buens a Deu et tres buens au siecle, come cil qui sera pleins de totes proeces et de totes bontez et de toz hardemenz.[2]

The Vulgate Cycle does not seem to fulfil this prediction; nor does it in any way associate the Lance with the beginning of the 'merveilles'. Hence Lot writes in a puzzled manner:

Comment résoudre l'antinomie de la présence simultanée (à Corbenic) du graal, fontaine de bénédictions et de prospérités, et de la lance qui, lorsqu'elle recommence à saigner est cause,—on ne sait pourquoi ni comment—de merveilles 'épouvantables'?[3]

and:

Il existe un rapport mystérieux, avons-nous vu, entre la lance, et aussi le

[1] Ibid., f. 100c.   [2] MS. Rennes 255, f. 28b; *Vulgate Version*, I, 80.
[3] Lot, *Étude*, 228.

graal, et les 'merveilles' ou 'aventures' de Logres, autrement dit de Grande-Bretagne.[1]

Now the *Suite du Merlin* and the Post-Vulgate *Queste* elucidate these references in the *Estoire*. We have already noted that the description of the Lance is identical in the *Suite du Merlin* and the Post-Vulgate *Queste* except in one respect: in the *Suite du Merlin* it is not represented as bleeding and in the Post-Vulgate *Queste* it is.[2] Now the *Suite du Merlin* describes the Lance before the Chevaliers as Deus Espees struck the Dolorous Stroke with it which inaugurated the adventures of Logres, and the fact that the Lance is not described as bleeding could, therefore, be interpreted as implying that it had ceased to bleed previously, as the *Estoire* says. After the Dolorous Stroke has been struck we should expect the Lance to begin bleeding again, but there is no specific mention of this. When the Chevalier as Deus Espees puts the Lance back, the *Suite du Merlin* merely remarks:

E lui chevaliers retrait a lui la Lanche et la remette ariere en l'orchuel ou il l'avoit prise. Et si tost come ele i refu, ele se tint ausi droit cum ele faisoit devant.[3]

It may well be, however, that the absence of this feature is due to some deficiency in the Cambridge manuscript. As Vinaver has pointed out, the corresponding scene in Malory contains certain details which are not in any of the extant French MSS. of the *Suite du Merlin* and which he is unlikely to have invented himself. This suggests that some French manuscript of the *Suite du Merlin* existed 'which had more to say about the whole episode of the Dolorous Stroke than either the Huth or the Cambridge MS.'[4] Such a manuscript may well have described the Lance as bleeding after the 'doleroux cop'. But although we cannot point to such a manuscript, it is not without significance that the Lance which is traditionally represented as bleeding does not do so before the Dolorous Stroke, and is said to be bleeding in the final scene at Corbenic.

In the *Estoire*, the duration of the marvels of Logres is limited: in the passage referred to, the angel says that they are to last as many years as

---

[1] Lot, *Étude*, 230–1.   [2] See above, 136.

[3] Cambridge MS., f. 270d. *Infra*, 245.

[4] Vinaver, *Works*, III, 1312. Malory does not mention that the Lance began to bleed again, but this is not surprising, for he does not even reproduce the description contained in the Cambridge MS. and omits the statement that Balain put the Lance back.

the number of days that Josephés bore the spear head in his thigh. In some MSS. this is twelve, but in others, including the Portuguese *Josep*, it is twenty-two:

'Et si saches tu bien, Josephez, que autretanz jorz come tu as porté le fer, autretanz anz dureront les merveilles en la terre ou Dex te voudra mener...' Et Josephés comença a conter combien il avoit porté le fer en sa cuisse. Lors si trova par droit nombre que il avoit vint et deus jorz.[1]

In another passage the *Estoire* says that the marvels which will be inaugurated in King Arthur's time 'par le coup d'une seule espee'[2] will last twenty-four years (fourteen according to some MSS. and twenty-two according to the Portuguese *Josep*):

Et dureront cez merveilles et cez aventures qatorze anz, ne ja ne faudront fors par le desreain chevalier del lingnage Nascien.[3]

Now neither the Vulgate *Queste* nor any of the other branches of the Vulgate Cycle place any limit on the duration of the marvels of Logres: the 'aventures' have already begun at the beginning of the *Lancelot* proper,[4] and although they come to an end when the *Queste* is over, no indications are given of how long they lasted.[5] The *Suite du Merlin*, on the other hand, brings its account into line with that of the *Estoire* and says on several occasions that the marvels continued for twenty-two years:

Or laisse li contes a parler dou roi et de Merlin et parole del Chevalier as Deus Espees, et pour conter comment il vient de la queste a chief, et comment il fist le cop par coi les aventures avinrent el roiame de Logres qui durerent vint et deus ans...[6]

The Post-Vulgate *Queste* has only one reference to time: when Galaad comes to Corbenic, we are told that King Pellean has lain for more than four years in the Holy Chamber:

Et li rois Pellians, por cui Dex avoit fait maint bel miracle et qui avoit ja

---

[1] MS. Rennes 255, f. 28c–d; *Vulgate Version*, I, 80; Portuguese *Josep*, f. 79v.
[2] See above, 158.
[3] MS. Rennes 255, f. 75b; Portuguese *Josep*, f. 232v: 'E estos havemturas durarão *vimte dous anos*, que nom averam fim se naão por o derradeiro cavaleiro da linhagem de Nascião.' *Vulgate Version*, I, 226, ll. 13–16.
[4] *Vulgate Version*, III, 13, 29, 107; IV, 217.
[5] At the beginning of the Vulgate *Queste* (38, ll. 21–29) is a statement that the hermits announced the delivery of Logres by Galaad for more than twenty years; but this does not indicate how long the 'merveilles' lasted (see also Lot, *Étude*, 232–4).   [6] Huth *Merlin*, I, 280; see also ibid., I, 264.

M

demoré en la chambre, qu'il ne s'en estoit oissuz, plus avoit de quatre anz, ne n'i avoit eu sostenence, se ce n'estoit de la grace de Nostre Seignor ou del Saint Vessel.[1]

Although the Portuguese *Demanda* has also 'bem havia quatro anos',[2] this number is very possibly a corruption of some bigger number, perhaps twenty-two. What is important, however, is not the numerical discrepancy, but the fact that the *Estoire*, *Suite* and Post-Vulgate *Queste* all limit the duration of the adventures.

Both the *Estoire* and the Vulgate *Queste* explain the theme of the Waste Land by means of the Lambor-Varlan story: Varlan, a newly converted Saracen, having been defeated by Lambor, comes to the sea where he finds a sacred ship, enters it and discovers the sword reserved for Galaad. He takes it, and finding Lambor 'en mi sa voie' as he is about to leave the boat, strikes him down with it. As a result of this 'cop' the country is blighted. When Varlan returns to the boat to fetch the scabbard, he falls dead before the bed on which it lies.[3] There are, however, some minor discrepancies between the *Queste* and the *Estoire* versions, and the two narratives appear inconsistent.[4]

Now the *Suite du Merlin* attributes the blighting of the land to Balain's Dolorous Stroke which maimed King Pellean. The account is clearly based on the Lambor-Varlan story in the *Estoire*. The parallelism between them is very close. There are verbal similarities in the description of the characters of Pellean and Lambor:

Cil Lambors fu chevaliers molt buens et tant ama Deu qe l'en ne cuidoit pas que en tote la Grant Bretaigne ne en region ne en autre leu eust plus preudome de lui.[5]

and

Li rois (i.e. Pellean) sans faille estoit moult boins chevaliers et moult preudom

---

[1] MS. B.N. fr. 343, ff. 102d–103a. *Infra*, 254.

[2] *D*, II, § 590, p. 279.

[3] *Vulgate Version*, I, 290; Vulgate *Queste*, 204.

[4] Pauphilet (review of Lot's *Étude*, *R*, XLV, 1918, 524–7) suggests that the redactor of the *Estoire* copied the account of the Lambor-Varlan battle from the *Queste* without quite understanding it: 'L'*Estoire*, selon nous, contient un passage au moins que l'auteur a copié dans la *Queste*, en le modifiant juste assez pour montrer qu'il ne l'avait pas exactement compris. C'est le combat du roi Lambar et du roi, Varlan' (524). The first redaction of the Post-Vulgate *Queste* also includes the Lambor-Varlan story, but the second redaction of the Post-Vulgate *Queste* omits it (see *D*, II, § 413).

[5] MS. Rennes 255, f. 98b; *Vulgate Version* I, 290, ll. 1–2.

vers Dieu, ne on ne savoit a chelui tans en toute la Grant Bretaigne nul prinche qui autant fust amés de Nostre Signour.[1]

The Vulgate *Queste*, it is true, also represents Lambor as a deeply religious king: he is described as 'l'ome del monde de crestiens ou il avoit greignor foi et greignor creance et ou Nostre Sires avoit greignor part'.[2] There is no suggestion, however, that the land is blighted because Varlan killed him: the country suffers solely on account of Varlan's sacrilege in touching the sword reserved for Galaad. In the *Estoire*, on the other hand, the blight befalls Arthur's kingdom not only for this reason, but also because 'Deus' desires to avenge King Lambor:

Itex fu li premiers cox de l'espee qui fu faiz en la Grant Bretaigne, si en avint si grant persecucion a ambedous les roiaumes, el roiaume de terre foreine et el roiaume de Gales *por le vengement del roi Lambor qe Dex amoit tant*, qe de grant tens les terres as laboreors ne furent gaaigniees, ne ne croissoit ne blé ne autre chose, ne li arbre n'i portoient fruit, ne es eves ne trovoit l'en poisson, se molt petit non. Et par ce fu puis apelee la terre des dous roiaumes la Terre Gaste.[3]

Similarly, in the *Suite du Merlin* the country is blighted partly because Balain had desecrated the Holy Lance, and partly because 'li Haus Mestrez' wishes to avenge Balain's 'utrage' in wounding King Pellean:

Ore comenchent lez aventurez et lez mervaillez du roialme aventurus, qui ne remandero[n]t devant que chierement sera achaté che que la Seintim Lanche ont atouchez lez mainz ordes et cumchies *et ont navré lez plus preudhome dez princez; si en prendra li Haus Maistrez sa venjanche* sor cheus qui ne l'ont pas deservi.[4]

In the Vulgate *Queste*, the 'cop de l'espee' blights the land for all time:

Itiex fu li premiers cox de ceste espee, qui fu fet ou roiaume de Logres. Si en avint si grant pestilence et si grant persecucion es deus roiaumes, que *onques puis* les terres ne rendirent as labourers lor travaus, car puis n'i crut ne blé ne autre chose, ne li arbre ne porterent fruit, ne en l'eve ne furent trové poisson, se petit non. Et por ce a l'en apelee la terre des deus roiaumes la Terre Gaste, *por ce que par cel doulereus cop avoit esté agastié*.[5]

---

[1] Huth *Merlin*, II, 27; *Le roman de Balain*, 78.
[2] Vulgate *Queste*, 204, ll. 17–19.
[3] MS. Rennes 255, f. 98c; *Vulgate Version*, I, 290, ll. 15–20.
[4] Cambridge MS., f. 271a. Cf. above, 133, n. 2. *Infra*, 246.
[5] Vulgate *Queste* 204, ll. 21–28.

In the *Estoire*, on the other hand, the effects of the 'cop de l'espee' are
clearly intended to be temporary: in addition to omitting the phrase
'por ce que par cel douloureus cop avoit esté agastié', it replaces the
words 'onques puis' by 'de grant tens'.[1] Now when Merlin warns
Balain against undertaking his quest, he tells him that if he achieves it
he will strike 'un caup' which will be more terrible and presumably
more lasting in its effects than was Varlan's 'cop de l'espee':

'Je vous loc, fait Merlins, en droit conseil que vous retornés et que vous
laissiés ceste queste. Car certes se vous a chief le menés, *vous ferrés un caup
dont [averra] si grans duels el roiaume de Logres et si grans maleurtés que onques
gringnor dolour n'avint ne gringnour pestilence par le cop de l'espee qui fu n'a
gaires fais entre le roi Lambor et le roi Urlan que averra par le cop de la Lanche
Vencheresse*. Ne de chelui mesfait n'avras tu pooir de l'amender, ne tu ne
hom qui ore soit, ains en sera chis roiames tornés a dolour et destruction, et
avoec che maint autre. Et durra chis essieus jusques a tant qu'il verra avant
qui metra a fin les aventures de la Grant Bretaigne. Et tu meismes qui feras si
grant dolour avenir, se tu vais cele part ou tu bees [a] aler, en morras a grant
dolour.'[2]

The *Suite du Merlin* thus establishes a comparison between the 'cop
de l'espee' and the 'cop de la Lanche Vencheresse', but distinguishes
between the two. The result is not tiresome reduplication, but an account in which the Varlan-Lambor episode in the *Estoire* serves to outline the theme that will be taken up again in the *Suite du Merlin*. The
unhappy Varlan, looking about for means of self-defence, lights on a
weapon not meant for him and strikes a hasty blow unmindful of the
consequences, just as Balain will do later. We have as a result just one
more example of the technique of repeating a theme with climatic
intention that is used so happily in the *Suite du Merlin*.[3]

A favourite theme of the *Estoire* is that of the Evangelization of the
pagans. The theme does not appear in the *Suite du Merlin*, but the
Post-Vulgate *Queste* makes some use of it, and treats it quite in the
spirit of the *Estoire*. Thus the account of Palamedes' conversion is
evidently modelled on that of Evelac.[4] The 'Chastel Felon' episode
shows a similar influence of the *Estoire*. The inhabitants of this castle,
it tells us, were the only people in Britain whom the successive efforts

[1] See above, 167.
[2] Huth MS., f. 126b–c; Huth *Merlin*, II, 7–8; *Le roman de Balain*, 55.
[3] See Vinaver in *Le roman de Balain*, xxii–xxx.
[4] See above, 105.

of Mordrain and Nascien, Joseph and Josephés and even Saint Augustine failed to convert:

Quant cil lignages, ainsi con il descendoient, orent tenu cel chastel et la terre d'entour jusqu'a la venue de la crestienté et jusqu'au roi Mordrain et Nascien, quant il furent en la Grant Bretaingne venu, il ne leur porent nul mal fere; n[e] Joseph de Barimacie, n[e] Josephé ses filz ne nel porent tourner a la foi crestienne. Sainz Augustins qui a celui tens estoit venuz en cele terre ne les pot tourner de leur erreur ne de leur mescreance, ainz leur firent toute leidure. Dont il avint que pour ce qu'il trouverent les genz les plus cruieus qu'il onques eussent trouvees, il apela le chastel 'le Chastel Felon' que onques puis [li] nons ne li fu changiez.[1]

Utherpendragon and Arthur were no more successful, each in turn besieging the castle in vain.[2] There is nothing in the *Estoire* about the 'Chastel Felon', but the appearance of the episode in the Post-Vulgate *Queste* at least proves that the latter was familiar with the fact that Mordrain and his people, and Joseph and Josephés with their people, came to Britain and undertook the task of converting the pagan inhabitants. Both the Palamedes and the 'Chastel Felon' narratives show a desire on the part of the author of the Post-Vulgate *Queste* to prolong the proselytizing activities of the early Christians into King Arthur's time, and thus establish a certain continuity between the *Estoire* and the latter parts of the story.

There is thus a close similarity of spirit and outlook between the *Estoire*, the *Suite du Merlin* and the Post-Vulgate *Queste*. The *Suite* and the Post-Vulgate *Queste* have been described as a collection of trivial adventures without any unifying theme.[3] They have been compared—very much to their disadvantage—with the Vulgate *Queste* and their romanticism has been unfavourably contrasted with the deep mysticism of the latter work. Such a view, although not wholly false, is less than just. The idea of the Grail as a source of calamities that will be repaired when the Grail quest is achieved is as old as Chrétien de Troyes. The theme of the Maimed King and the related theme of the Waste Land are both prominent in the *Estoire* where they are treated of course in a purely religious spirit. Moreover, the *Estoire* regards Galaad as the *chevalier desirré* whose coming long foretold will end an old dispensation and begin a new. Hence the accumulation in the

---

[1] MS. B.N. fr. 772, f. 385d. Cf. *D*, II, § 497; Sp. *D*, Ch. CCLXXII.

[2] MS. B.N. fr. 772, f. 385d.

[3] See Pauphilet, '*La Queste du Saint Graal* du MS. Bibl. Nat. fr. 343', *R*, XXXVI (1907) 591–609; Lot, *Étude*, 281, 284; Bruce, *Evolution*, I, 463–72.

Estoire of victims to be healed, spells to be broken, and marvels to be brought to an end when the appointed knight appears. It looks very much as though the *Suite du Merlin* and the Post-Vulgate *Queste* have taken over this conception from the *Estoire* and developed it along the lines indicated in the latter.

CHAPTER VIII

The Elaboration of the Material

IN the foregoing chapters an attempt has been made to reassemble the *disjecta membra* of the *Suite du Merlin* compilation. It is certain that the *Estoire del Saint Graal*, the prose rendering of Robert de Boron's *Merlin* followed by the *Suite du Merlin*, the continuation of the *Suite du Merlin* and the Post-Vulgate *Queste-Mort Artu* belong together. It now remains to be seen how this romance, which we have entitled the *Roman du Graal* or Post-Vulgate Grail Romance,[1] grew up. Most critics have hitherto not only failed to realize of what the *Roman du Graal* consisted, but misunderstood its nature and place among the other Arthurian prose romances. G. Paris and J. D. Bruce referred to the then known sections of the *Roman du Graal* as a mere agglomeration of disconnected episodes, a 'labyrinth of fantastic adventures' put together without design or purpose.[2] More recently, Alexandre Micha described the *Suite du Merlin* as a 'collection d'aventures plus ou moins merveilleuses, où la haine de Morgue pour son frère est peut-être le trait dominant'.[3] Albert Pauphilet regarded the Post-Vulgate *Queste* as the work of a 'barbare maladroit' whose sole contribution was the addition of a number of ill-assorted incidents —'des aventures sans suite'.[4] Similarly Pickford called 'le roman du pseudo-Robert' 'une mer morte où se jettent comme affluents les autres romans arthuriens'.[5] But the view that the prose romances are formless productions has been made quite untenable by Vinaver's studies of the 'shaping spirit of medieval narrative art'.[6] He indicated that the 'voluminous prose romances of the thirteenth century were

---

[1] See Introduction, 10–11.

[2] Bruce, *Evolution*, I, 464; Huth *Merlin*, I, xlviii–xlix.

[3] *MA*, VII, 305, n. 6.

[4] Pauphilet, '*La Queste du Saint Graal* du MS. Bibl. Nat. fr. 343', *R*, XXXVI (1907) 606.   [5] Pickford, *Évolution*, 107.

[6] Vinaver, 'The Dolorous Stroke', *Med. Aev.*, XXV (1956) 175–80; *Works*, III, 1265–68; *Le roman de Balain*, ix–xxx; 'La genèse de la *Suite du Merlin*', *Mélanges de Philologie romane... offerts à E. Hoepffner*, Paris (1949) 295–300; 'King Arthur's Sword or the Making of a Medieval Romance', *BJRL*, XL, no. 2 (March, 1958) 513–26; 'A la recherche d'une poétique médiévale', *Cahiers de Civilisation Médiévale, Université de Poitiers*, IIᵉ Année (1959) 1–16.

not mere compilations of unco-ordinated fragments of narrative', but 'reflections of a steadily growing tendency to convey more convincingly and more coherently what earlier writers were content to state as fact'.[1] The *Roman du Graal* is no exception. The process by which it grew up was 'not one of indiscriminate accumulation or gradual "decomposition", but of continuous development from simple and incomplete patterns to more elaborate and consistent designs'.[2] It was conceived as an organic whole and is remarkable for its inner cohesion. The author drew for his themes on a large body of Arthuriana—the Vulgate Cycle, the First Version of the prose *Tristan* and the early verse romances—but he never borrowed passively or haphazardly. Throughout he endeavoured to reshape and reinterpret his material, for he was no mere story-teller content with a chronicle of loosely connected adventures: his approach was rather that of a novelist anxious to fit events into a scheme and to explain how and why they came about.[3] His aim was to produce a unified and well-balanced Arthurian epic in which the various *péripéties* of the great king's reign were more adequately prepared for than in the versions at his disposal. And to achieve this result he consistently used methods characteristic of thirteenth-century writers: he elucidated events not by consistent motivation through character, but structurally, by supplying their antecedents.[4] Hence the coherent expansion of the themes derived from the earlier texts and the closely-knit composition of the *Roman du Graal*: long sequences of events begun in one part find their complement only in another; no section is complete in itself: they are all linked up with another. Any portion of the narrative that we may choose to examine will reveal this, but it should suffice to analyse a few of the more interesting incidents.

Arthur's incest

The story of Arthur's incest,[5] with which the *Suite* proper begins, provides perhaps one of the most obvious examples of our author's method of treating his material. Whereas in the Vulgate *Merlin* continuation the incident is referred to casually and lost in the midst of the account of Arthur's war against the rebel kings,[6] in the *Roman*

---

[1] Vinaver, 'Flaubert and the Legend of Saint Julian', *BJRL*, XXXVI, no. 1 (Sept. 1953) 236.   [2] Vinaver, in *Le roman de Balain*, xvii.

[3] See Vinaver in *Le roman de Balain*, xiii.

[4] For references, see above, 15, n. 3.   [5] Huth *Merlin*, I, 147–8.

[6] *Vulgate Version*, II, 129, ll. 34–8. See also above, 34.

du Graal it is placed in a prominent position and so developed as to prepare for the final portion of the romance, Arthur's death and the destruction of Logres. A deliberate link is established between Arthur's offence and his downfall as a result of which the whole story acquires a new meaning and a sense of unity such as the Vulgate Cycle where the two events are unconnected does not possess.[1] To give the romance still greater cohesion, Mordred's incestuous birth is used further to motivate and integrate a theme found previously only in the prose *Tristan*, the feud between Gauvain and Pellinor's lineage.[2] The prose *Tristan* (both the First and the Second Versions) mentions that one of the reasons for the feud was that Pellinor had slain Lot, the father of Gauvain and his brothers:

Monseigneur Gauvain et tuit si autre frere fors seulement Gaheriet haoient de mortel haine les quatre filz au roi Pellinor. Et estoit cele haine venue de plusieurs achoisons. Ele estoit premierement venue du roi Pellynor qui avoit ocis le roi Loth d'Orcanie, qui estoit pere Gauvain et aux autres freres. Mes tele vanjance en avoit ja esté prise que monseigneur Gauvain avoit ocis de ces mains le roy Pellynor. De ceste chose ne savoient riens li enfans le roy Pellynor, car se il eussent seu, il eussent vengié la mort de leur pere que il ne lessassent ne por le roi Artus ne por autre chose.[3]

Neither version of the prose *Tristan* explains, however, in what circumstances Pellinor slew Lot, and it was left to the author of the *Roman du Graal* not only to relate in detail the fatal battle in which Lot was killed, but to link the theme with the rest of the Arthur story by making the birth of Mordred the initial cause of the feud: Arthur, having heard that a child born on May-day will cause his death, has all the children born that day exposed on the sea; Lot, thinking that his son Mordred has perished too, makes war on Arthur and is slain by Pellinor.[4] Gauvain swears vengeance and eventually kills Pellinor and three of his sons—Lamorat, Drian[5] and Agloval. Perceval's sister in her turn attempts to avenge her father and her brothers, and this sets in motion a further series of adventures in the later portion of the *Suite*

---

[1] Cf. Vinaver in *Le roman de Balain*, xiv.

[2] The First Version of the prose *Tristan* invented the feud theme to explain how Perceval's father and brothers were killed (see above, 21).

[3] MS. B.N. fr. 757, f. 54b; Löseth, *Analyse*, § 302.

[4] Huth *Merlin*, I, 158-9, 203-12, 247-9, 254-63. For further details, see above, 75-6.

[5] For our author's skill in adapting from the First Version of the prose *Tristan* the accounts of Gauvain's slaying of Lamorat and Drian, see above, 78-82.

du Merlin.[1] Finally when Gauvain comes to Corbenic, Yvain de Cenel's sister reproaches him with having slain Pellinor. And so a theme begun at the beginning of the *Suite du Merlin* has repercussions throughout the romance and binds together its various parts.

The story of Escalibor

The treatment of the theme of Arthur's sword Escalibor reveals, as Vinaver has shown, the same principle of composition.[2] In the Vulgate Cycle Arthur obtained the sword by drawing it from a magic anvil, but disposed of it by having it cast into a lake where a hand came out of the water, caught the sword, 'brandished it thrice or four times' and then disappeared with it into the water.[3] No reason is suggested, however, why Arthur should wish to get rid of the sword in this way. Now the author of the *Roman du Graal*, having taken over from the Vulgate the final Escalibor episode,[4] endeavoured to elucidate and complete it by inventing a new series of incidents in the earlier portion of his romance. After Arthur broke the sword he drew from the anvil in a combat with Pellinor, Merlin took him to a lake behind a mountain where they saw rising out of the water a hand holding a sword which a damsel fetched for Arthur on condition that he should grant her the first gift she will ask of him.[5] As Arthur thus obtained the sword from a hand in a lake, it is only right that when his last hour comes he should return the sword to this same hand. The desire to produce a coherent whole accounts also for the other Escalibor incidents. When Arthur receives the good sword, Merlin tells him that no one who bears the scabbard shall lose a drop of blood.[6] This means that as long as Arthur possesses the scabbard he cannot receive a mortal wound in battle, and yet he is destined to receive one. For this reason the author invents another sequence of episodes which serves not only to dispose of the

[1] See above, 65. The author's desire to link up the different sections of his romance occasionally led him into difficulties: he allows Perceval's sister to die at the beginning of the *Suite* (Huth *Merlin*, II, 125), but brings her back to life in a later portion to enable her to avenge her brother's death; subsequently she dies again during the *Queste* after giving of her blood to heal a leprous damsel.

[2] Vinaver, 'King Arthur's Sword or the Making of a Medieval Romance', *BJRL*, XL, no. 2 (March 1958) 513–26; *Le roman de Balain*, xiv–xvii; *Works*, III, 1269–70.

[3] *La Mort le Roi Artu*, 223–4. For possible sources of the theme of the casting of Escalibor into a lake, see Frappier, ed., *La Mort Artu*, 1954 edition, xvii–xviii, including notes.

[4] *D*, II, §§ 677–9; Sp. *D*, Chs. CCCCXXXII–CCCCXXXIII.

[5] Huth *Merlin*, I, 188–98.   [6] Ibid., I, 199.

scabbard, but to motivate Arthur's and Morgain's enmity, a theme not properly accounted for in any of the earlier romances.[1] In the *Lancelot* proper and the Vulgate *Merlin* continuation Morgain hates Guenevere rather than Arthur,[2] but the First Version of the prose *Tristan* suggests that all was not well between Arthur and his sister. We are told in a very brief reference that Arthur banished Morgain from court on account of her disloyalty and would have killed her if he had been able to get hold of her, but this was not possible as she had many secret dwellings in Logres and was moreover able to make herself invisible 'par la force de ces enchantemenz':

Cele Morgain sanz faille estoit seur le roi Artus et avoit par le roialme de Logrez plusors herbergiages merveilleusement estorez, car, quant ele vouloit, ses mesons estoient si celeez par les enchantemenz qu'elle savoit que se vos feussiez tres devant, si n'en puissiez riens savoir... Et sachiez que li rois Artus l'avoit gitee de sa cort por ce que il avoit en lui trové plus de desloiauté que en fame que il eust veue. Et se il la peust tenir en aucune maniere, touz li monz ne la peust garantir que il ne la feist de male mort morir. Por ce s'aloit ele reponnant de forest en forest et deffendoit bien par la force de ces enchantemenz, car sanz faille, se elle bien vouxist, james por home ne feust veue, et si la garanti de mort par moult de foiz.[3]

Now in the *Roman du Graal*, as in the prose *Tristan* passage quoted above, the real conflict is between Morgain and Arthur, but whereas the prose *Tristan* does not mention the circumstances under which Arthur banished Morgain, our romance leads up to this episode by means of a coherent sequence of events linked intimately with the rest of the narrative. Arthur, who at the beginning was very fond of his sister, entrusted the scabbard to her care, and she had a duplicate made of it,

[1] See Vinaver in *Le roman de Balain*, xvi–xvii.

[2] In the *Lancelot* the discord between Morgain and Guenevere dates from their earliest acquaintance. When Morgain was living at Arthur's court, she fell in love with Guenevere's cousin, Guiomar, but Guenevere did not approve and banished the knight from court. Out of anger Morgain left the court too and went to find Merlin who taught her magic. 'Et de la mut la grant hayne que elle ot tout jors envers la royne' (*Vulgate Version*, IV, 124). In the Vulgate *Merlin* continuation Morgain hates Guenevere for the same reasons (*Vulgate Version*, II, 338–9), and here too nothing is said of her feelings towards her brother. The theme of Morgain's love for Guiomar is itself, of course, a development of the reference in *Erec* (ll. 1904–8) where Chrétien states that Guingamars was Morgain's *ami*: 'Et Guingamars ses freres i vint, / de l'isle d'Avalons fu sire: / de cestui avons oï dire / qu'il fu amis Morgant la fee, / et ce fu veritez provee.'

[3] MS. B.N. fr. 757, f. 15b–c; Löseth, *Analyse*, § 190.

intending to give the real thing to one of her *amis*, but she made a mistake and her lover, thinking she wished to deceive him, told Arthur all he knew. Merlin, however, who loved Morgain greatly,[1] warned her, and to save herself she accused the knight of having stolen the scabbard, whereupon Arthur had him beheaded. From then on Morgain hated her brother and sought to bring about his death, but Arthur, unaware of his sister's feelings towards him, continued to entrust the scabbard to her.[2] And so, some fifteen years later,[3] when the opportunity arose, Morgain gave both the scabbard and Escalibor to another of her lovers, Accalon de Gaule, whom she contrived to pitch in battle against Arthur, hoping to make Accalon king after Arthur's death. But Niviene's timely arrival saved Arthur, and as Accalon was about to die, he revealed Morgain's treachery.[4] Arthur now banished his sister from court, but she succeeded in stealing the scabbard once more, and when pursued by Arthur, she cast it into a deep lake before changing herself and her people temporarily into statues. Hereafter, the author says, the scabbard was not seen again until Gauvain received it from Marsique la fee the day that he did battle against Naborn the enchanter. After the combat, however, the scabbard disappeared again so that no one ever knew what became of it.[5] Thus not only is the scabbard removed, but the theme of Morgain's hatred of Arthur becomes an integral part of the romance, for it is through her treachery that the weapon which alone could have protected Arthur in his last battle is lost for ever.

Arthur's war against Rion and the Balain story

Another example of constructive borrowing is the story of Arthur's war against Rion provoked by the latter's request that Arthur should send him his beard and become his vassal.[6] In the Vulgate *Merlin*

---

[1] The *Roman du Graal* tells us earlier in the story that when Morgain saw the marvels which Merlin performed to celebrate Arthur's victory against Rion, she decided to make Merlin's acquaintance. Merlin fell in love with her and taught her all she wanted to know of the art of *nigromanchie* (Huth *Merlin*, I, 266).

[2] Huth *Merlin* I, 267–72.

[3] This can be worked out as follows: at the time when Arthur first entrusted the scabbard to Morgain she had just given birth to her son Yvain (Huth *Merlin*, I, 266–7), but when Morgain gave the scabbard to Accalon, her son Yvain was already newly knighted (Huth *Merlin*, II, 168).

[4] For further details, see Vinaver in *Le roman de Balain*, xvi–xvii.

[5] Huth *Merlin*, II, 168–91, 199–228. See also above, 86.

[6] Huth *Merlin*, I, 202.

continuation the incident is just one of a series of military campaigns: Arthur, angered by Rion's insolence, joins forces with Leodogan whom Rion was besieging before Carohaise and slays Rion in single combat.[1] The *Roman du Graal*, on the other hand, has interwoven the incident with the Balain story and given it a fresh purpose: to explain how Balain won back Arthur's favour after he had incurred his displeasure by killing a damsel in his presence.[2] After Arthur's refusal to do homage, Rion invades Logres, and Balain and his brother capture him with Merlin's aid and send him to Arthur as prisoner.[3]

That the author did not tell adventures for their own sake, but subordinated them to the overall design of his romance, is equally clear from the Balain story itself. It not only introduces in the form of a coherent narrative the main motifs of the Grail Quest—the marvels of Logres, the Blighted Land and the Maimed King[4]—but links up with the Death-of-Arthur section: the tragic combat between Balain and his brother[5] foreshadows the last great battle of Arthur's knights, in particular the combat of Lancelot and Gauvain: in the one case two blood brothers kill each other by mischance, in the other two knightly brothers. The parallel is made evident largely through the skilful use of a reference in the *Lancelot* proper. According to the latter, Gauvain on his return from one of his quests describes the marvels he found on the *Isle de Merveilles*—the *lit Merlin* in which no one can lie without losing one's memory and the 'espee aventureuse cui nus hom ne poet enpoingner par le heut tant eit la main grant' with which, a hermit told

---

[1] *Vulgate Version*, II, 410–19.

[2] This lady was no other than the damsel who had fetched Escalibor from the middle of the lake. She came to Arthur's court to claim her *don* the same day as did the damsel who had the *espee as estranges renges* girded round her. After Balain had succeeded in untying the sword, the lady who had fetched Escalibor demanded that Arthur should give her Balain's head or the head of the other damsel. Balain did not give Arthur a chance to make a choice, but beheaded the damsel who had asked for his head (Huth *Merlin*, I, 197–8, 218–20). By identifying the lady whom Balain killed as the one who fetched Escalibor for Arthur, our author succeeded in linking the Balain story firmly to the preceding part of his narrative. [3] Huth *Merlin*, I, 212–44.

[4] The various branches of the Vulgate Cycle had previously endeavoured to explain some of these themes, but, as Vinaver has shown, it was left to the author of the *Roman du Graal* to combine the different strands of the narrative into a coherent whole (see *Le roman de Balain*, xvii–xxii and *Med. Aev.*, XXV, 175–80). The Balain story occupies in the G. Paris edition, I, 212–45, 275–80, II, 1–59.

[5] Huth *Merlin*, II, 46–56. The combat is modelled on an episode in *Meraugis de Portlesgues* (see *Le roman de Balain*, xxviii–xxix). For the other sources of the Balain story see *Le roman de Balain*, xxv–xxviii.

him, his best friend is to slay him.[1] All these details reappear in the
Roman du Graal, but they have been made part of a new sequence of
events which serves to link the fate of Balain and his brother with that
of Lancelot and Gauvain. After the burial of the two brothers, Merlin
performed many enchantments on the island: he erected a magic bed
beside their tomb[2] and replaced the pommel of Balain's sword by one
which no one could hold except Lancelot who would kill with it his
best friend, Gauvain. On account of these marvels, the island was
henceforth called the *Isle Merlin ou Isle de Merveilles*.[3] The *espee
aventureuse* being thus identified as Balain's former sword, the fratri-
cidal struggle no longer appears an isolated event, but symbolizes
and foreshadows the civil strife of the Round Table.

The triple adventures of Gauvain, Tor and Pellinor

Even seemingly trivial incidents such as the triple adventures of
Gauvain, Tor and Pellinor,[4] to which Gaston Paris referred as 'des
spécimens des productions ordinaires de la pauvre imagination des
auteurs de romans en prose',[5] in reality have a purpose in the economy
of the romance as a whole. The episode echoes the story of the staghead in the Second Continuation of Chrétien's *Perceval*,[6] but whereas
in the latter it is the title-hero who has to undertake a complicated
series of adventures before being able to hand over the staghead and
the hound to the damsel of the chess-board, in the *Roman du Graal*
the adventures are divided among three knights. Shortly after Arthur's

---

[1] *Vulgate Version*, V, 332–3.

[2] Huth *Merlin*, II, 57. The wording in the *Lancelot* and the *Roman du Graal* is
very similar:

Vulgate Version, V, 332, ll. 34–37	Huth MS., f. 145b
En cel isle, fet misire Gawain, trovai jo lo lit Merlin. En celui lit ne se couche nus tant soit bons chevalers ne poissanz qu'il ne perde lo sen et tou[t] son memoire et tant qu'il i gise; et si tost cum il en est hors, si revent en son sen et en sa vertu cum devant.	Et dalés la tombe estora on un lit si estrange que nus n'i puet puis dormir qu'il n'i perdist le sens et le memoire en tel maniere qu'il ne li souvenist ja de chose qu'il eust devant fait tant comme il demourast en l'ille.

[3] Huth *Merlin*, II, 57–60.

[4] Huth *Merlin*, II, 76–136.   [5] Huth *Merlin*, I, xlviii.

[6] *Perceval*, ed. Potvin, ll. 22392 ff. For further details see Vinaver, *Works*, III,
1268.

wedding a white stag leaps into the hall, followed by a *braket* and by Niviene, the *damoisele caceresse*, together with *trente muetes de chiens*. The stag, wounded by the *braket*, disappears almost immediately in the nearby forest, while one of the knights jumps up from the table and rides off with the *braket*. As Niviene is about to complain, another knight mounts on a white steed, enters the hall and carries her off. Merlin assigns the quest of the stag to Gauvain and that of the *braket* to Tor, while Pellinor is to rescue the damsel. Now while some of the adventures encountered by the three knights recall the Second Continuation of *Perceval*, they have been so modified as to acquire a new significance within the context of the *Roman du Graal*. Gauvain's exploits are intended to show how already as a young knight he was merciless and vindictive. Coming to a ford he slays outright the knight guarding it; later on, angered because one of his dogs has been killed,[1] he refuses to show mercy to a vanquished knight and beheads the damsel who interposes herself between him and his opponent. On his return to court Gauvain is told by Merlin to be in future more merciful to defeated knights, but he soon ignores this advice and treacherously slays one knight after another.

Tor's adventures, on the other hand, serve as a contrast to Gauvain's: during his quest Tor brings two knights to the point of defeat, but spares them both. Eventually he finds the *braket* in the lap of a damsel sitting in a tent and, like Perceval, has to fight with the damsel's *ami*, Abelin l'Orgueilleux.[2] But whereas Perceval's opponent, Garsalas, cries for mercy, Abelin refuses to admit defeat. Nevertheless Tor does not wish to kill Abelin, and when a damsel asks him to grant her the knight's head he is displeased: 'Che me poise, fait il, car il estoit bons chevaliers.'[3] He attempts to persuade the damsel to pardon Abelin any wrong he has done her, but she refuses, and against his will Tor has to behead the knight.

As for Pellinor's adventures in quest of Niviene, these link up with the theme of his death. Like Perceval, Pellinor meets a sorrowful damsel sitting by a fountain, but whereas Perceval stops to speak to the damsel,[4] Pellinor takes no heed of her cries for help and passes on.

---

[1] Gauvain was angered as Merlin had told him to bring back all the dogs (Huth *Merlin*, II, 79). This detail has been adapted from the *Perceval* continuation (Potvin, ll. 22569–574) where the damsel of the chess-board tells Perceval not to lose the *braket*.

[2] *Perceval*, ed. Potvin, ll. 27047–27317. Perceval finds the *braket* in the possession of a damsel sitting outside a tent.

[3] Huth *Merlin*, II, 111.   [4] *Perceval*, ed. Potvin, ll. 23779 ff.

The damsel thereupon prays that Pellinor may one day receive no more help than he has given her.[1] After completing his quest Pellinor returns by the same road and finds that the damsel has been devoured by wild beasts. He blames himself greatly, and at court Merlin reveals that the damsel was Pellinor's own daughter and that the curse she uttered must one day take effect. The prophecy Pellinor heard on his coronation day will then have been fulfilled, for when he begged God to protect him all his life and not to let him die through mischance, a voice had replied that just as he will fail his kin, so will his kin fail him. 'Et che sera pour coi tu morras plus tost.'[2] Thus as a result of the damsel's curse, which Pellinor unwittingly brought upon himself, his death becomes part of his tragic destiny and forms a curious parallel to Arthur's: just as the one dies through mischance, expiating an unintentional sin, so does the other.

Merlin's entombment

The skill with which the *Roman du Graal* elaborates and integrates borrowed material is equally apparent in the story of Merlin's entombment.[3] The *Lancelot* proper, which first mentions the incident, disposes of it briefly. All it says is that Merlin fell in love with Niviene who promised to do his will if he taught her 'partie de son grant sens', but when she had learnt all she wished to know she entombed him in the forest of Darnantes.[4] The Vulgate *Merlin* continuation elaborates the theme, adding a new motif, Merlin's premonition of his death, but fails to make the episode an integral part of the whole. The narrative is inserted quite artificially into the account of Arthur's wars.[5] Before setting out for Benoic to aid Ban and Boors, Merlin prophesies that he will lose his freedom in that country. In the forest of Briosque he meets Niviene who is willing to return his love when he has taught her his magic arts. Merlin leaves Arthur periodically to visit Niviene and as he sets out to rejoin her for the last time he knows that he will never return. But his love for her is so great that despite this foreknowledge he cannot resist going[6] and is eventually enclosed by her inside a magic wall of air.

[1] Huth *Merlin*, II, 116.   [2] Ibid., II, 131.

[3] Huth *Merlin*, II, 139–59, 191–8. Cf. Vinaver, *Works*, III, 1271–2.

[4] *Vulgate Version*, III, 21.

[5] Ibid., II, 208–12, 280–81, 376, 421, 451–3, 461–2.

[6] 'Aler m'i couvient, fait Merlins, quar jou li ai en convent et jou sui si souspris de s'amour que jou ne m'en porroie partir' (*Vulgate Version*, II, 451).

The *Roman du Graal* reproduces details from both these versions,[1] but makes them part of a more coherent and more convincingly motivated narrative closely linked with the rest of the romance. Thus Merlin and Niviene are not allowed to meet by chance as in the Vulgate: Niviene is the *damoisele caceresse* rescued by Pellinor. After she has returned to court, Arthur invites her to stay at Camalot and it is here that Merlin falls in love with her and teaches her his magic arts.[2] Subsequently Niviene entombs Merlin as in the *Lancelot*, but whereas the latter does not explain how Niviene conceived the idea, the *Roman du Graal* elucidates her action, as has been shown,[3] by means of a new series of events. After Niviene has spent four months at Arthur's court, her father, the Duke of Northumberland, summons her to return. Although she hates Merlin she allows him to accompany her, for she is afraid to let him know her real feelings. Their adventures on the journey not only explain the origin of Niviene's underwater manor and how she first became interested in Lancelot,[4] but have a direct bearing on Merlin's fate.[5] After passing through Benoic where they see the small child Lancelot in the castle of Trebe, Merlin and Niviene come to the lake of Diana in the forest of En-Val.[6] As Niviene does not know how the lake acquired its name, Merlin tells her: Felix, one of Diana's lovers, having learned how Diana had killed Faunus, another of her lovers, by pouring boiling lead over him after she had persuaded him to lie down in the tomb by the lake on the pretext that she would heal his wounds by covering him with medicinal herbs, cut off Diana's head and threw it into the lake which henceforth bore her name. This story so impressed Niviene that from now on she deliberated constantly on how to kill Merlin, and instead of returning home, asked him to build her an invisible manor near the lake.[7]

For the last phase of Merlin's life the *Roman du Merlin* adapts from

[1] G. Paris and Brugger assumed wrongly that the *Suite* account was independent of the Vulgate *Merlin* (Huth *Merlin*, I, xlv, lxiv–lxvii; *ZFSL*, XXXV, 12 ff.)

[2] Huth *Merlin*, II, 139.

[3] See Vinaver, *Works*, III, 1271–2.

[4] Neither of these themes has been explained in any of the earlier romances.

[5] See Vinaver, *Works*, III, 1271–2.

[6] The *Roman du Graal* borrowed from the *Lancelot* the detail that the lake of Diana was in the forest of En-Val (*Vulgate Version*, III, 8, ll. 12–14), but added an explanation of why the forest was so called: 'Et l'apieloit on, cel bois, En Val, pour chou que en valee estoit la gringnour partie de cel bois' (Huth *Merlin*, II, 145). The *Lancelot* (III, 8, ll. 10–11) mentions like the *Roman du Graal* Diana's love of hunting, but does not explain how the lake of Diana acquired its name.

[7] Huth *Merlin*, II, 150–1.

N

the Vulgate *Merlin* continuation the theme of Merlin's premonition of his impending end. In the Vulgate the motif simply underlines Merlin's foolishness; in the *Roman du Graal* it is used to link up Merlin's death with his rôle as Arthur's protector. One day, during their stay by the lake, Merlin tells Niviene that Arthur has just been in great danger as he had to repel the attack of five kings. Niviene reproaches Merlin for not having gone to Arthur's aid, and he admits that he had refrained from doing so because he knows that he will meet with his end in Great Britain. Shortly afterwards Merlin announces that Arthur is being forced to do battle with Accalon whom Morgain has armed with Escalibor and the magic scabbard. Niviene urges Merlin to protect Arthur, and although he fears that he himself will die 'par traïson',[1] he agrees to go with her to Logres. On the way they encounter two wicked enchanters and Merlin, knowing that he has not much longer to live, performs one more great marvel by which he hopes to be remembered after his death.[2] His end finally comes when they reach the *forest perilleuse* where in a small chamber cut among the rocks they find the tomb of the two lovers. Remembering Diana's stratagem, Niviene persuades Merlin to remove the lid from the tomb, and then, after he has fallen asleep, she casts a spell over him and has him thrown into the tomb which she seals firmly 'par conjuremens et par force de paroles'.[3]

Merlin dies, then, in the Post-Vulgate not so much on account of his foolish love as in an attempt to save his king, and his death becomes

---

[1] Huth *Merlin*, II, 153.

[2] Merlin places the two enchanters in a tomb where they will burn until the passing of Arthur (Huth *Merlin*, II, 154–8). The whole episode is a development of the reference in the *Lancelot* to Merlin's killing of two enchanters: '... si vienent a une piere qui a a non li perons Merlins, la ou Merlins ochist les ·ii· encanteors' (*Vulgate Version*, III, 275, ll. 37–8).

[3] Huth *Merlin*, II, 197. Paton (*Studies in the Fairy Mythology of Arthurian Romance*, 213) and W. A. Nitze ('The Esplumoir Merlin', *Spec.*, XVIII [1943] 75) both consider the *Lancelot* account to be 'a condensation of some more complete narrative'. Similarly, Zumthor assumes that the version of Merlin's entombment found in the Vulgate *Merlin* and the *Suite du Merlin* are closer to the original than the *Lancelot* reference: 'Il se peut que VM et HM représentent, bien que postérieurs à L, une version plus proche de la source; L semble ne l'avoir que résumée et utilisée pour ses propres besoins sans égard au sens ni à la valeur de l'épisode' ('La délivrance de Merlin', *ZRPh.*, LXII [1942] 378). There can be no doubt, however, that here as elsewhere the most complete version represents the *last* and not the first redaction, and that what we find in the *Suite du Merlin* is a development of the details found in the *Lancelot* and the Vulgate *Merlin*.

an integral part of the new Arthuriad. When Arthur eventually hears
of the passing of Merlin, he knows that Logres has lost its best
friend: 'Or puet bien dire le royaume de Logres, quant Merlin le sage
est mors, qu'il est moult abaissiés, car tant comme il vesquist il ne
feist s'amender non, et en povoir et en honneur. Jamais ne sera homs
qui l'amast de si bonne amour comme il l'a tous jours amé...' [1] Finally,
to give the whole still greater cohesion, Niviene is henceforth made to
use the magic she learnt from Merlin to help Arthur: it is she who
rescues him in his combat against Accalon[2] and warns him about the
poisoned cloak sent by Morgain.[3]

Arthur's war against the five kings

A further example of how the author of the *Roman du Graal* reshaped
his borrowings and gave them a function in their new context is the
episode of Arthur's war against the five kings[4] interwoven with the
Merlin–Niviene story. This incident, for which no source has hitherto
been found, is a development of a short passage in the *Lancelot*
proper.[5] At the point where Lancelot comes to the Queen's ford, the
Lancelot explains how the ford acquired its name. Shortly after his
marriage Arthur was attacked by seven kings near the Humber. The
Queen found a way through the river before anyone else, and for this
reason the ford was named after her. Urien suggested they should all
make for the other side of the river, but on Keu's advice they first
made a stand against the enemy kings. Keu himself slew two of them,
while Arthur, Gauvain, Urien, Lot and Yvain each killed one. Now
although this was 'la plus honeree aventure qui onques avenist au roi
Artu',[6] the *Lancelot* adds nothing to this short statement. It is not
surprising, therefore, that two later writers, our author and the
redactor of the *Livre d'Artus*,[7] were tempted to elaborate the account.
What is interesting is the difference in their approach. The *Livre
d'Artus* inserts the story into the account of Arthur's wars against
the Saxons, thereby merely adding one more incident to an already
bulky series of adventures. The *Roman du Graal*, on the other hand,

---

[1] *Die Abenteur*, 89; MS. B.N. fr. 112, *Livre* II, f. 44b.
[2] Cf. above, 176.   [3] Huth *Merlin*, II, 198–212, 249–54.
[4] Huth *Merlin*, II, 159–73.
[5] *Vulgate Version*, III, 142.   [6] Ibid., loc. cit.
[7] *Vulgate Version*, VII, 121, l. 4–123, l. 37. Bruce (*RR*, IX, 1918, 263–4)
wrongly assumes that the reference in the *Lancelot* is based on the *Livre d'Artus*
and was inserted by a later redactor. Bruce did not know that the incident is also
in the *Suite du Merlin*.

assumes that the war took place in a later period of Arthur's reign. In this way the episode not only acquires a structural significance by forming a parallel to Arthur's earlier victories, but could be used to introduce the theme of Merlin's premonition of his death[1] as well as to underline Arthur's central position in the romance. Shortly after Merlin's and Niviene's departure for Northumberland, five hostile kings invade Logres and raze to the ground all the towns and villages they pass through. Arthur, anxious to help his people, refuses to wait for reinforcements and sets out at once accompanied by the Queen. When he approaches Norgales, the enemy, afraid to meet him in the open field, decide to make a surprise attack. Early in the morning they rush down upon Arthur's camp and slaughter many of his unarmed men. Arthur, Keu, Gauvain and Giflet try to lead the Queen to safety, but find the river too swollen to cross. While they are deliberating what to do, the five kings appear in person. Giflet considers the position hopeless and suggests they should try to reach the other side of the river, but as in the *Lancelot* Keu urges them to make a stand. Arthur, Gauvain and Giflet each kill one of the kings, while Keu slays two of them as he said he would.[2] Meanwhile the Queen having found a way through the river tells the others where to cross. Those of the enemy who try to follow are drowned. When Arthur learns that it was the Queen who discovered the ford, he decides to name it 'li gués

[1] See above, 180–2.
[2] The wording in the *Lancelot* and the *Roman du Graal* is similar.

Vulgate Version, III, 142, ll. 13–19	Huth MS., ff. 188d–189a; Huth *Merlin*, II, 163
Et lors dist Keus que dehais ait qui passera l'aigue quex qu'il soit devant qu'il eust josté a roi. 'Ja sont il,' dist il, 'autretant com nous.' Et li rois Uriens dist: 'Keu, il sont set et nous sommes six.' 'Moi ne caut,' dist Keu, 'car jou en ochirai deux a par moi. Bien se gart chascuns de vous qu'il fera.'	'Je ne sai', fait Kex, 'que vous ferés, mais je vous di que je ne passerai hui eve devant que jou aie jousté a roi.' 'Mesires Kex,' che dist Gavains, 'se nous jousterons a eus che sera a meschief, car il sont cinc et nous ne soumes que quatre.' 'Ne vous caille,' che dist Kex, 'ne ne vous esmaiiés. Je tous seus en ochirrai bien deus, et chascun de vous en occhie le sien.' 'Dehait ait il,' che dist li rois, 'en qui il remanra qu'i[l] ne joustera'.

de la roine'. The death of the five kings so demoralized the enemy that
Arthur and his people now had no difficulty in defeating them. And
so what would have been a major defeat is turned into one of Arthur's
greatest victories, comparable to his earlier successes.

The sequel to the episode explains why Baudemagus was not made
a knight of the Round Table until comparatively late in life—another
theme borrowed from the *Lancelot*, but not adequately motivated there.[1]
In the war against the five kings more than five hundred of Arthur's
men were killed, including eight knights of the Round Table. To
replace them Arthur requested Pellinor to elect four knights from the
younger generation and four from the older. Gauvain, Keu and Giflet
were chosen without hesitation, but it was difficult to decide between
Tor and Baudemagus. The former was eventually elected and Baudemagus, deeply grieved, left the court determined not to return until
he had proved his worth. His adventures on his way through Logres
are a series of mishaps and form a parallel to the final tragedy awaiting
him, his untimely death at the hands of his childhood friend, Gauvain.[2]

The Roche aux Pucelles

How even material originally quite unrelated to the Arthur story is
made an integral part of the romance is well illustrated by the episode
of the *Roche aux Pucelles*.[3] The initial *donnée* of the story, the theme of
the twelve prophetic maidens, is derived from Raoul de Houdenc's
Meraugis de Portlesgues:[4] the hero in search of Gauvain comes to a
very high rock 'tote d'une pierre' and sees sitting on the top twelve
maidens who spend their time speaking of things to come. Anxious
to ascend the rock, he walks round it, but finds neither 'huis ne fenestre
ne degré'. Then he shouts, asking the way up, but is told 'que ça en
haut ne monte nus'. In reply to his question where he might find

---

[1] In the Vulgate Cycle Baudemagus is not made a knight of the Round Table
until towards the end of the *Lancelot* proper (*Vulgate Version*, V, 194–5). When
the death of Ganor left a vacancy at the Round Table, Lancelot urged that
Baudemagus be given the seat, saying that he deserves it not only because he is a
very good knight, but 'il est encore en son meillour eage, comme cil qui n'a mie
encore plus de .xlvi. ans'. No reason is suggested, however, why Baudemagus
had to wait until now before receiving this honour.

[2] At one point Baudemagus speaks of himself in the following terms: 'Je suis,
fait il, Baudemagus, le plus maleureux chevalier et le plus mescheans qui oncques
fust, car il ne me puet faire se mescheoir non en lieu ou je viengne' (*Die Abenteuer*,
104).   [3] *Die Abenteuer*, 61–6, 75, 78–81, 125–9.

[4] *Meraugis von Portlesguez*, ed. M. Friedwagner (Halle, 1897), ll. 2633–2723.

Gauvain, he is advised to go to the cross near the chapel on the other side of the wood. Not satisfied with this answer, Meraugis asks the way to the *esplumeor Merlin*, to which the damsel replies:

> Esgarde moi,
> Vez ci l'esplumeor, j'i sui.
> Assez porras muser mes hui,
> Que ja plus riens ne t'en diron,
> Ne ce ne quoi, ne o ne non (ll. 2702–6).[1]

Now the *Roman du Graal* has not only elaborated the theme, explaining how the damsels came to be on the rock and their connexion with Merlin, but has built round it a coherent narrative in which the prophetic gifts of the damsels are used to keep in the foreground one of the basic themes of the romance, the future destruction of Logres. When Arthur expelled Morgain's son Yvain from court, Gauvain decided to accompany his cousin and soon they were joined by Le Morholt. They find by a fountain three damsels aged fifteen, thirty and seventy respectively who offer to show them the adventures of the country.[2] The knights, each accompanied by one of the damsels, now separate, but promise to return to the fountain in a year's time. After several adventures, Gauvain and Le Morholt meet again and together they come to the *Roche aux Pucelles*, which, like the rock in *Meraugis*, is very high and polished, without 'degré ne voye par ou l'en peust aler lassus'.[3] On its summit they see twelve beautifully clad damsels who pass the time talking of things to come: 'Et sachés qu'elles ne paroloient pas des choses trespassees ne de celles qui estoient faictes, ains tenoient illec leur plait et leur conseil des choses qui

---

[1] Various attempts have been made by critics to explain what the *Esplumeor Merlin* was (for full bibliographical references see W. A. Nitze, 'The Esplumoir Merlin', *Spec.*, XXVIII (1943) 69–79 and R. S. Loomis, 'The Esplumeor Merlin again', *BBSIA*, 9 (1957) 79–83). Although the *Roman du Graal* knew and used the *Meraugis* episode, it does not use the term 'Esplumeor Merlin'. Nitze's statement (*art. cit.*, 72) that the author of the *Suite du Merlin* thought of the *Esplumeor Merlin* as an island is based on a mistaken reference: the *Isle Merlin* mentioned in the *Suite* (*Die Abenteuer*, 55) has no connexion whatsoever with the *Meraugis* episode.

[2] This detail may be modelled on the incident in the *Lancelot* (*Vulgate Version*, V, 15) where Guerrehes meets by a fountain three ladies aged twenty, forty and sixty respectively.

[3] *Die Abenteuer*, 61. See also ibid., 78: '... qu'il n'a leans ne huys ne fenestre ne degré' which is copied from *Meraugis*, ll. 2658–9, '... qu'il n'i avoit / Huis ne fenestre ne degré'.

estoient a advenir . . .; ne elles ne servoient nulle saison d'autre mestier que de parler des choses qui estoient a avenir.'[1] In reply to Gauvain's questions Le Morholt relates the history of these damsels: they are twelve sisters, the eldest of whom knows a great deal of magic. She once quarrelled with Merlin and attempted to kill him, 'pour ce qu'il luy nuysoit souvent a maintes choses qu'elle vouloit faire'.[2] But Merlin, who fortunately knew more than she did, had her and her sisters carried onto the rock 'par force d'enchantement'. He thought that they would soon die there, 'mez ce ne peust pas estre, car cele y est qui tant scet d'anchantemens que s'il n'avoit que ung pain ou monde et il estoit cent journees loing, si le feroit elle a soi venir en une heure de jour'.[3] When Le Morholt has finished his tale, the companions hear the damsels speaking of Gauvain's death and the end of Arthur's kingdom. Le Morholt, anxious to know his fate too, addresses the damsels who tell him he will die 'pour une faulce querele', and then bid him go. But both he and Gauvain wish to see more of the damsels and ask to be transported onto the rock. Once they are there they are kept captive in a state of oblivion, and fail to recognize Yvain when he comes to join them. Meanwhile the damsels predict that Yvain will die in battle the same day as the father of the Round Table.

The conclusion links the episode with Merlin's death and Baudemagus' departure from court. Arthur, on hearing of Gauvain's imprisonment, is convinced that Merlin alone will be able to help and sends knights in quest of him. Two of the questers, Tor and Aglant, encounter Baudemagus who, after jousting with them to prove that he had been wrongfully deprived of a seat at the Round Table, tells them that Merlin's last words before dying were that only Gaheriet would be able to rescue Gauvain.[4] The message is delivered at court and Gaheriet, after various adventures which in their turn link up with later incidents,[5] finds the *Roche aux Pucelles*[6] where he learns the fate

---

[1] *Die Abenteuer*, 61. *Meraugis*, ll. 2648–2653: 'En toz tens servent de pledier. —/ De quoi? De ce qui a esté? —/ Non pas, ja n'en sera parlé / Par eles, ne ja n'avront pes; / Ainz i tienent toz tens lor plez / De ce qui est a avenir.'

[2] *Die Abenteuer*, 62.   [3] Loc. cit.

[4] In the *Lancelot* there is no quest of Merlin, but in the Vulgate *Merlin* continuation Arthur, having had no news of Merlin for seven weeks, sends knights in quest of him. Gauvain eventually finds the place where Merlin is imprisoned and speaks to him, just as does Baudemagus in the *Suite du Merlin* (*Vulgate Version*, II, 416–62).   [5] See above, 73–5.

[6] Gaheriet, like Meraugis, walks round the rock to try and find a way up (*Meraugis*, ll. 2656–9; *Die Abenteuer*, 125).

awaiting him—how he will be slain the same day as his brothers Agravain and Guerrehes. The damsels refuse at first to free Gauvain and Le Morholt, but relent when Gaheriet threatens to behead their brother who lives nearby. Thus by inventing a narrative which leads successive characters to the *Roche aux Pucelles*, our author succeeds in giving a theme, purely incidental in his source, a structural function; for the repeated references to the future sorrow of Logres not only contribute to the general atmosphere of gloom hanging over the kingdom, but reinforce the links between the beginning and the end of the Arthurian epic.

The Perron du Cerf

The episode of the *Perron du Cerf* is interwoven with the *Roche aux Pucelles* story.[1] Le Morholt together with a squire and a damsel come to a *quarrefour* in a forest where there is a *perron* with a large wooden cross in front of it.[2] On the *perron* is inscribed in red letters that here one may see part of the adventures of the Holy Grail and that no one may see these adventures without being killed or wounded until the coming of the Good Knight who will end them.[3] While the companions are discussing what to do, two knights arrive who, without saying a word, point their lances at the cross, then draw their swords and engage in a fierce combat, after which they silently embrace each other and go. Then a stag followed by four *levriers* 'whiter than snow' comes running to the cross. The *levriers* tear up the stag and drink so much of its blood that they cannot move. A dragon swallows the *levriers* and then lies down by the stag to warm it. After a while the dragon becomes restless and rolls about in agony. It then falls down from the *perron* and from its mouth issue forth the four *levriers*, all still alive. The stag, which has regained life 'par l'eschaufement du serpent', now runs off into the forest. The *levriers* follow it, 'glatissant et refaisant greigneur noise que ne feissent autres dix',[4] while the dragon goes off in another direction. When Le Morholt and his companions

---

[1] *Die Abenteuer*, 48–52, 69–71, 73–4.

[2] 'Droit ou milieu de ces ·iiii· voies avoit une grant croix de fust vielle et ancienne et ung perron de marbre tres devant la croix' (*Die Abenteuer*, 48). In the miniature, however, the cross is on top of the *perron*, not in front.

[3] 'Sur cest perron puet l'en veoir avenir des merveilles du Saint Graal grant partie'. Aprés redisoient: 'Ja nul ne demourra cy pour veoir de ces merveilles qui n'y soit mort ou mehaignés ou navrés a tout le moins jusqu'a tant que le Bon Chevalier y vendra qui mettra a fin les aventures' (*Die Abenteuer*, 48–9).

[4] *Die Abenteuer*, 50.

PLATE 3

Gauvain and Le Morholt at the *Roche aux Pucelles*

from MS. B.N. fr. 112, *Livre* II, f. 35v

PLATE 4

Yvain, his damsel and a squire asleep by the *Perron du Cerf*
from MS. B.N. fr. 112, *Livre* II, f. 38r

have seen this adventure, they lie down by the *perron*, but shortly afterwards the damsel and the squire are killed by a lance, while Le Morholt is badly wounded.[1] Later, when Yvain comes to the *Perron du Cerf*, the whole adventure takes place again although this time not much of it can be seen: 'ne du dragon ne du cerf ne des levriers ne virent riens pour l'obscureté du temps'.[2]

This incident, like so many others, was not invented 'de toutes pièces'. It is the result of a combination of two originally separate motifs—the theme of the *Perron du Cerf* and that of the avenging lance. Whereas the latter is, of course, a commonplace in the *Estoire del Saint Graal* and *Queste*,[3] the origin of the former is less certain. It is probably modelled on the episode of the yelping beast in *Perlesvaus* or Gerbert's continuation of Chrétien's *Perceval*.[4] In Gerbert, Perceval finds one day in a clearing 'une croix molt bele de fust'. By the cross are two hermits, one of whom beats the cross, while the other prays. Suddenly there jumps out of a bush 'une beste grant a merveille' within whose belly her young are yapping like dogs. After running a while, the *beste* breaks into two and the whelps within her issue forth and devour her. They then go mad and kill each other. In the *Perlesvaus* account, which is very similar, a knight and a damsel sit at either end of the cross holding vessels of gold. The beast is frightened by the sound of the whelps within her and takes refuge by the cross. The whelps tear her to pieces, but are unable to eat her flesh and flee into the forest 'autressi comme tuit enragié'. Two priests then appear, one beating the cross, while the other prays.

There are obviously striking similarities between the Gerbert–*Perlesvaus* and the *Roman du Graal* versions. In both we find the same

---

[1] See also above, 132.

[2] *Die Abenteuer*, 69.

[3] Our author may have had in mind the story of Alfasim's misfortune in the *Estoire del Saint Graal* (*Vulgate Version*, I, 288–9). One night when Alfasim was sleeping in the Grail castle, a fiery man appeared and told him that no one may sleep here. Then he struck him with a lance through the thighs as a punishment for his presumption (see also above, 18).

[4] *Perlesvaus*, ed. Nitze, Chicago (1937), ll. 5486–6026; Gerbert de Montreuil, *La Continuation de Perceval*, ed. M. Williams, CFMA (Paris, 1925), ll. 8296–8427). According to Bruce (*Evolution*, I, 292–3) Gerbert is later than 1220. A. Stanton (*Gerbert de Montreuil as a writer of Grail romance*, Chicago, 1942) dates Gerbert's continuation 1226–1230. The *Perlesvaus* is sometimes placed as early as 1212 (see Nitze, ed. cit., II, 73–89), though it may have been written after the Vulgate Cycle. Nitze (II, 133–41) suggests that the *Perlesvaus* account of the yelping beast is the source of Gerbert.

combination of details—a cross by which there are two figures acting mysteriously, a beast running for refuge to the cross and dogs tearing up the beast. There are also differences, but these seem largely due to the fact that our author remodelled his borrowings to integrate them in his own work. Whereas in Gerbert and in *Perlesvaus* the incident has a specific allegorical meaning,[1] in the *Roman du Graal* it represents one of the 'marvels of the Holy Grail' which only the Good Knight can end. This means the adventure has to be capable of repetition and therefore the stag and *levriers* have to be kept alive. Hence the introduction of the dragon who resuscitates the stag and removes the *levriers* until they are required for the whole round to start again. The theme of the avenging lance is added to bring out the author's conception of the Grail adventures as divine retribution.[2]

Mark's first invasion of Logres

The *Queste* episodes added by our author reveal the same method of composition.[3] Here as elsewhere he supplies 'motive and circumstance'[4] where his sources fail to do so and integrates his borrowings in the romance as a whole. A good example is provided by the story of Mark's first invasion of Logres,[5] which has been adapted from the First Version of the prose *Tristan*. After mentioning that Arthur's kingdom had been greatly impoverished by the Quest of the Grail, the First Version of the prose *Tristan* says that for this reason Mark invaded Logres, abducted Yseut who together with Tristan had found refuge in Joieuse Garde, and besieged Arthur in Camalot, but finally returned to Cornwall 'hontosement':

Et por ochaison de celle qeste et des preudomes qi mors estoient, vint puis li rois Marc a grant force de gent et entra dedenz le roiaume de Logres, et destruit granz partie de la Grant Bertaigne, et torna en feu et en flamme, et assist le roi Arthur dedenz Kamaalot ou il le cuidoit prendre a force. Mais il s'en parti hontosement; et a cele fois conquist il ma dame Yseult que Tristan li avoit toloite, et la retorna en Cornuaille.[6]

At a later point the First Version of the *Tristan* gives in outline the

---

[1] See Nitze, ed. *Perlesvaus*, II, 137–8.   [2] See above, 133, n. 2.

[3] For the episodes which make up the continuation of the *Suite du Merlin*, see above, 78–84.

[4] Vinaver, *Works*, III, 1271.

[5] MS. B.N. fr. 343, ff. 61a–72c; *D*, II, §§ 445–84; Sp. *D*, Chs. CCXXX–CCLIX.

[6] MS. B.N. fr. 755, f. 158d; Löseth, *Analyse*, § 495.

account of Mark's invasion, saying that Arthur was only saved by the timely arrival of Galaad and his three companions, Palamedes, Esclabor and Artus le Petit.[1] Now the *Roman du Graal* not only uses the episode to motivate and balance Mark's second invasion of Logres after Arthur's death, but has elaborated it and removed some of its obscurities.[2] How, for instance, did Galaad come to hear of Arthur's distress, and why did the other knights of the Round Table not come to Arthur's rescue? To elucidate this, the author inserts into the account of the death of Perceval's sister a passage in which, shortly before dying, she tells Galaad to return to Camalot and help Arthur, 'car sachiez que li rois Artus a grant besoing que vous vegniez a lui, et sachiez se vous demourez gueres a venir la, si grant doumage en avendra qui ne sera pas amendé legierement'.[3] Galaad meets Palamedes, Esclabor and Artus le Petit who follow him to Camalot,[4] but the other knights of the Round Table do not hear of Mark's invasion in time to be of any use to Arthur.[5] The prose *Tristan's* statement that Mark returned to Cornwall in shame has similarly been clarified in the *Roman du Graal* by the addition of a fresh incident. We are told that after his defeat Mark came to the abbey where Galaad and Pharan were resting. Seeing Galaad's shield hanging on the wall, Mark decided to avenge himself by giving Galaad and Pharan the poison he had intended for Tristan. Pharan died, but Galaad survived and exposed Mark's treachery before all the monks.[6]

[1] MSS. B.N. fr. 757, ff. 252c–d; 760, ff. 109a–c; 1463, f. 87d; 1628, ff. 239a–d; Bodleian, MS. Douce, 189, ff. 65a–b. Cf. Löseth, *Analyse*, § 534, n. 5. MS. B.N. fr. 755 breaks off before it reaches this point.

[2] The Second Version of the prose *Tristan*, which incorporated from the *Roman du Graal* the whole *Queste* section, including Mark's invasion of Logres, reproduces the latter episode with the same details as the *Roman du Graal*. Löseth thought that the briefer account of Mark's invasion as found in the MSS. of the First Version of the prose *Tristan* must be an abridgement of the more detailed account found in the Second Version of the *Tristan* (see *Analyse*, 372, n. 5: 'Ici le texte de 772, etc., se rencontre avec celui de 757, qui donne de l'invasion, du siège etc., un récit abrégé...'). There can be no doubt, however, that the shorter version of Mark's invasion preceded the more detailed narrative.

[3] MS. B.N. fr. 772, f. 370a.   [4] MS. B.N. fr. 343, ff. 63a–64b.

[5] Agravain, Gaheriet and Mordred were on their way to Camalot when they learnt from Galaad of Mark's defeat (MS. B.N. fr. 772, f. 383b). Similarly, Keu, Brandelis and Gauvain left the quest of the Grail 'pour le roy secourre', but changed their plans when Gaheriet told them of Arthur's victory (MS. B.N. fr. 772, f. 383c). Hector and Meraugis, too, intended to go to Camalot, but on hearing that the battle was over went instead with Galaad to the Chastel Felon (MS. B.N. fr. 772, f. 385b).   [6] MS. B.N. fr. 343, ff. 70b–72c.

Palamedes

The story of Palamedes is similarly based on the First Version of the prose *Tristan,* but it too has been adapted to the author's design. As in the *Tristan,* Palamedes is Tristan's rival for Yseut's love, but whereas in the *Tristan* the theme serves primarily to motivate Tristan's love,[1] in the *Roman du Graal* it is subordinated to Palamedes' conversion which becomes the culmination of his career.[2] The circumstances in which Palamedes falls in love with Yseut have moreover been modified to make the Palamedes story more coherent within its new context. In the prose *Tristan,* Palamedes first sees Yseut while she is still in Ireland.[3] In the *Roman du Graal* he does not meet her until much later, after she has taken refuge in Joieuse Garde:

Et sachiez que aventure l' (i.e. Palamedes) avoit la semaine devant aporté a la Joieuse Garde ou il avoit veu la reine Yseut. Et por la grant biauté qu'il avoit veue en li l'avoit il adonc amee de si grant amor qu'il n'amoit autretant ne lui ne autrui.[4]

Finally the account of Palamedes' death at the hands of Gauvain, referred to but not related in the First Version of the prose *Tristan,*[5] rounds off the Palamedes story and at the same time serves to intensify the feud between Arthur's and Ban's lineage.[6]

[1] Vinaver, *Works,* I, lxxi, including n. 2.
[2] See above, 104–9.
[3] Löseth, *Analyse,* § 31. See also above, 20.
[4] MS. B.N. fr. 343, f. 83c. The prose *Tristan* MSS. have the same reading as MS. B.N. fr. 343, but *D,* II, § 369, has: 'E quem saber quiser em qual guisa amou primeiramente Iseu e quanto fêz e sofreu por ela, a grande estória de Tristam lho dirá. Mais esta vez sabede que passava pela Joiosa Guarda e viu Iseu, e pola grã beldade que lhe viu, renovou-xe-lhe o amor que dela havia e começou de crecer mais e mais, assi que nom amava tanto si, nem outra rem nom no fazia desesperar de haver seu amor, senom que Tristan era uũ dos fremosos cavaleiros do mundo e uũ dos melhores' (Lacuna in Sp. *D*).
[5] MS. B.N. fr. 757, f. 262d.
[6] See above, 146. The treatment of the *beste glatissant* theme is no less significant. The First Version of the prose *Tristan* briefly describes the *beste,* but Palamedes who hunts it never completes his quest, for 'encore n'estoit mie li termes q'il la peust a fin mener' (MS. B.N. fr. 757, f. 236a). The *Roman du Graal,* on the other hand, substantiates the theme and makes it a coherent part of the romance by linking it up with the Grail. When at the beginning of the *Suite* Arthur first sees the *beste glatissant* Merlin explains that it is a Grail adventure. In the *Queste* section Palamedes accompanied by Galaad and Perceval succeeds in

The feud between Arthur's and Ban's lineage

Some minor incidents, seemingly without significance, gradually introduce the theme of the feud between Arthur's and Ban's lineage. In the
Vulgate there are no signs of discord before the *Mort Artu*, but the
Roman du Graal in order to strengthen the sense of continuity between
the various sections of the romance already announces the theme in
the *Queste* portion. When the five 'cousins de la Deserte' encounter
Galaad and Blioberis,[1] they attack them at once although they are
knights of the Round Table, for they hate all those who belong to
Ban's lineage: 'Et pour la grant chevalerie qu'ilz savoient en eulx,
hayoient ilz de mortel haine le parenté le roy Ban, pour ce qu'ilz
estoient plus amés et plus chier tenus du roy Artus que cilz n'estoient.'[2]
After Galaad and Blioberis have killed the five cousins, they come to
a forester's house where three brothers, all companions of the Round
Table and excellent knights, but envious of Ban's people, decide to
ambush Galaad in the hope of bringing shame to Ban's line: 'Et se
nous l'avions desconfit, le parenté le roy Ban qui tant le loe en seroit
honteux et vergoigneux a tousjours mais.'[3] The three brothers are,
of course, defeated, and to take vengeance challenge two other knights
of Ban's lineage, Darubre and Acorant le legier. Darubre pleads that
as they are all knights of the Round Table they may not fight with each
other, but the three brothers insist and in the ensuing combat all five
knights are killed. Darubre's last words as he sees his opponents die
foreshadow and sum up the downfall of the Round Table: 'Ganemor,
or n'avés vous mie trop gaigné en ce que vous nous assaillistes, car
vous en estes mort et nous aussi.'[4]

Similarly, the account of Artus le Petit's death added to the *Mort
Artu* section not only strengthens the connexion between the latter
and the Post-Vulgate *Queste*, but completes the theme of the feud
between Ban's and Arthur's lineage and underlines the tragic folly that
caused it. When after the battle of Salisbury Plain Blioberis rides
through Logres he encounters Artus le Petit and the latter challenges
him immediately to a combat. Blioberis tries to dissuade him from it

killing this monster and the story of its origin is related by King Pellean (see
above, 125–6). In this way the theme is integrated in the work as a whole and by
running intermittently through its different sections helps to unify them.

[1] MS. B.N. fr. 112, *Livre* IV, ff. 125c–128b; *D*, II, §§ 399–408; Sp. *D*, Chs.
CCXVI–CCXXV, 242b–246b.

[2] MS. B.N. fr. 112, *Livre* IV, f. 125d.

[3] Ibid., f. 126d.   [4] MS. B.N. fr. 112, *Livre* IV, f. 128b.

but, like Gauvain, Artus le Petit only realizes his folly when it is too late.[1]

The foregoing analysis could easily be extended, but from what has been said it is clear that the author's treatment of his material reveals a desire to produce a coherent whole. He skilfully combines originally unconnected themes to form a unified narrative—the history of Arthur's adventurous kingdom—and gives his romance form and shape by making extensive use of parallel episodes, deliberately inventing long sequences of events to balance and complete incidents taken over from his sources. The methods he used are the same as those of the other prose romance writers. Indeed, the significance of the *Roman du Graal* lies largely in the fact that its genesis is characteristic of the whole development of medieval prose fiction. As Vinaver first realized, behind the complex texture of the prose romances lies a constructive approach, a constant striving to produce more coherent and more spacious compositions 'by building up and lengthening sequences of episodes'.[2] Successive *remanieurs* did not add episodes haphazardly, but endeavoured to complete the earlier romances and give them greater cohesion by linking up previously unrelated events. These tendencies which, as we have seen, are evident both in the *Roman du Graal* and in its main sources, the Vulgate Cycle and the First Version of the prose *Tristan*,[3] continue also to shape the later prose romances and account for their ever-increasing volume. The *Palamède*, for instance, written shortly after the *Roman du Graal*, provides the early history of the characters of the older generation referred to in the Vulgate Cycle, the prose *Tristan* and the *Roman du Graal*, and attempts to complete themes left unfinished in these romances. An interesting example is the story of Esclabor. The First Version of the prose *Tristan* states that Esclabor is Palamedes' father, but does not assign to him any part in the narrative. The *Roman du Graal*, on the other hand, contains a considerable number of adventures bringing in Esclabor and includes an account of his death. The *Palamède* completes the process by relating in detail Esclabor's adventures before he came to Logres.[4] Moreover, like the other cyclic com-

---

[1] *D*, II, §§ 674–6; Sp. *D*, Chs. CCCCXXIX–CCCCXXXI, 327b–328b.

[2] Vinaver, 'The Dolorous Stroke', *Med. Aev.*, XXV (1956) 180.

[3] See above, 16–21.

[4] Löseth, *Analyse*, §§ 630–1. The Second Version of the Post-Vulgate *Queste*, which is probably later in date than the *Palamède*, also attempted to fill in this

positions, the *Palamède* developed in stages. In its original form it began with Arthur's reign, but a later writer turned it into the story of *Guiron le Courtois*[1] and not only added a prehistory of Britain as well as a detailed account of life in Utherpendragon's time, but invented a new conclusion. Later, yet another *remanieur* (the author of the *Guiron* contained in Turin, MSS. L–I–7, L–I–8 and L–I–9) expanded the *Palamède* still further. He replaced the 'Introduction' contained in MS. B.N. fr. 358 by a version which prepared even better for later events,[2] and remodelled the ending so as to round off the whole romance. He borrowed material from a variety of sources, the Vulgate Cycle, the prose *Tristan* and the earlier versions of the *Palamède* and *Guiron*, but he did not simply juxtapose the various incidents. The story of the Dame de Malohaut provides a typical example. In the *Lancelot* proper she is loved by Galehaut, Lancelot's friend, but we are not told anything about her earlier life, and so the authors of the *Palamède* and the first version of *Guiron* were free to make her into the wife of a new character, Danain le roux.[3] Now the Turin redaction incorporates both themes, but links them up by means of a remodelled account of Danain's imprisonment in the Vallee des Faus Soulaz. In the first version of the *Guiron* (MS. B.N. fr. 362)[4] Danain after being freed from the Vallee des Faus Soulaz continues to go in quest of adventures,[5] but in the Turin version he returns home to his wife, falls ill and dies within a month. The way is thus open for the later episode of the Dame de Malohaut's life, her friendship with Galehaut: 'Et Danayn demoura a Maloaut, et luy print une maladie si forte qu'il couvint que ains qu'il fust ung mois il morut, dont ce fut dommage, car moult avoit esté bon chevalier. Si mena moult grant dueil la dame de Maloaut et fit ensepvelir son seigneur en la maistre eglise de Maloault moult honnorablement. Et depuis fut la dame moult

---

lacuna (see *D*, I, §§ 123–8). For a summary of the *Palamède* MSS. in Paris, see Löseth, *Analyse*, §§ 620–43; for an account of the London, Florence and Vatican *Palamède* MSS., see the references given above (8–9, n. 2) in connexion with the *Tristan* MSS. in these libraries.

[1] Contained in MSS. B.N. fr. 358–363. Cf. my article in *Med. Aev.*, XXXIII, no. 2 (1964) 89–101.

[2] Brit. Mus. Add. MS. 36673 contains the same version as Turin MS. L–I–7.

[3] *Vulgate Version*, III, 266 ff.; Löseth, *Analyse*, 448.

[4] The MSS. of the first version of *Palamède* all break off before dealing with the delivery of Danain.

[5] Löseth, *Analyse*, 463.

aymee de Galeot, le seigneur des Loingtaines Isles, le filz a la belle geande, ainsi que le compte devise.'[1]

Other writers, still more ambitious, combined the Alexander cycle with the Arthurian romances so as to produce a comprehensive history of the world as did the author of *Perceforest*.[2] But in all cases the principles of composition underlying the development of the various prose romances are the same. If the *Roman du Graal* forms a more coherent and unified whole than either the Vulgate Cycle or the prose *Tristan*, or some of the later romances, it is not because the author uses different techniques, but because he handles them more skilfully and limits himself to fewer themes. It is only when we come to Malory that the general trends are reversed, for Malory, as Vinaver has made it clear,[3] far from trying to link up the Arthurian stories as did the French prose writers, attempted to unravel their various interwoven strands and produce a series of short, self-contained narratives each with a definite beginning and end, in which the characters themselves and not the preceding tales determine the action.[4]

[1] Turin, MS. L–I–9, f. 6a. Also in MS. B.N. fr. 112, *Livre* II, f. 60a, which has borrowed the episode from a MS. related to the Turin MS. On the relationship of the Turin MS. to MS. B.N. fr. 112, see my article 'Part III of the Turin Version of Guiron le Courtois: a hitherto unknown source of MS. B.N. fr. 112' in *Medieval Miscellany presented to Eugène Vinaver*, Manchester, 1965.

[2] See Jeanne Lods, *Le roman de Perceforest* (Genève: Droz; Lille: Giard, 1951), 38–94.

[3] See Vinaver, *Works*, I, xlviii–lxxxv; III, 1265–77, 1398–1404, 1417–24, 1432–7, 1572–81, 1600–12; *The Tale of the Death of King Arthur* (Oxford, 1955), vii–xxv; *King Arthur and his Knights* (The Riverside Press, Cambridge, U.S.A., 1956), viii–xiii.

[4] According to Pickford, *Évolution*, 186–201, 291–5, the compiler of MS. B.N. fr. 112, although linking up the various Arthurian romances, produced really, like Malory, a series of short self-contained tales. I do not share this view and hope to discuss in a separate article the position of MS. B.N. fr. 112.

CHAPTER IX

The New Arthuriad

AT first sight the *Roman du Graal* might seem to be simply a remodelled cycle of Arthurian romances, reduced in length by the omission of the greater part of the *Lancelot* proper. Indeed many critics have maintained that the author's sole purpose was to produce a shortened version of the cycle. Thus Bruce writes:

It is not likely that the Pseudo-Robert cycle, from its inception, was cast in the form of a trilogy, yet in all the extant fragments of the cycle, such is assumed to be its structure. Now, in endeavouring to account for this particular form which the work eventually received in the manuscript tradition, it is to be observed, first of all, that its author plainly designed to make the new cycle shorter than the old (the Vulgate). On this account, although accepting the *Lancelot* in a general way, as belonging to the same cycle of romances, he did not actually include it in his series. Furthermore, in carrying out his plan of shortening the whole, his own predilections evidently suggested to him that he could best sacrifice the *Mort Artu* . . .[1]

But this does not explain why the various branches were thoroughly revised. The essential difference between the Vulgate Cycle and the *Roman du Graal* is, in fact, not one of length but of spirit and structure.

The Vulgate Cycle of Arthurian romances grew up in stages. The original romance, the *Roman de Lancelot du Lac*, a trilogy consisting of the *Lancelot* proper, the *Queste del Saint Graal* and the *Mort Artu*, is built up on the opposition between the courtly and the religious ideals ('la chevalerie teriene' and la chevalerie celestiele'). It is concerned primarily with the adventures and character of Lancelot, and its three sections, each characterized by its own spirit, correspond to the three periods of Lancelot's life: the *Lancelot* proper which deals with Lancelot's youth and incorporates a modified version of Chrétien's *Charrette*, is an apotheosis of the courtly ideal.[2] Only

---

[1] *Evolution*, I, 463–6. Cf. P. Zumthor, *Histoire littéraire de la France médiévale VIe–XIVe siècles*, Paris, P.U.F., 1954, 253, § 467.

[2] It excuses Lancelot and Guenevere because of the ennobling effects of their love, and many a passage is an apology for their adultery. Thus when Lancelot and Guenevere have consummated their love for the first time, the damsel of the Lake assures Guenevere that there can be no wrong in loving *le seignor et la flor*

towards the end, in the *Agravain* section, do discordant notes enter
and foreshadow the next phase, that of the *Queste*, in which the
traditional values are reversed: earthly chivalry is condemned and
'virtuous love becomes sinful'.[1] For the *Queste*, written by a man
steeped in the teachings of Saint Bernard of Clairvaux, is really a
treatise on grace, with hardly a line not intended for doctrinal exposition.[2] It preaches the ideal of Christian asceticism, and its object is to
show how those who had risen highest in the world of Arthur's court
sink lowest in that of the Grail. Lancelot is treated 'as a symbol of
earthly chivalry desperately and sincerely attempting to approach a
higher ideal',[3] and his ultimate failure is as important a part of the story
as Galaad's success. The *Mort Artu*, which relates how Lancelot, after
his return from the *Queste*, relapsed into sin and so brought about the
destruction of Arthur's kingdom, but was finally converted and died
'en odeur de sainteté',[4] completes the 'story of Lancelot'.

It is certain that none of the sections of the *Roman de Lancelot*
could, at the time of composition, have been conceived as part of an epic
of Arthur.[5] Arthur and the history of his kingdom are only of secon-
dary importance: the real hero throughout is Lancelot. Arthur owes
him both the renown of his court and his very kingdom which, without
Lancelot's intercession, he would have lost to Galehaut.[6] The *Lancelot*
proper goes so far as to blacken Arthur's character, showing him up
to disadvantage whenever Lancelot appears at his noblest.[7] In the

---

de tot cest monde: '... Ne li peciés del siecle ne puet estre menés sans folie, mais
moult a grant raison de sa folie que raison i troeve et honor. Et se vous folie poés
trover en vos amors, ceste folie est a honerer sor toutes autres, car vous amés le
seignor et la flor de tot cest monde, si vous poés de ce vanter que onques mais
dame ne pot faire ce que vous poés, car vous estes compaigne au plus preudome
et dame au millor chevalier du monde...' (*Vulgate Version*, III, 418, ll. 33–9).

[1] Vinaver, *Malory* (Oxford, 1929) 74.
[2] See E. Gilson, 'La mystique de la grâce dans la *Queste del Saint Graal*', *R*, LI
(1925) 321–47.
[3] Vinaver, *Malory*, 75.
[4] Cf. Lot, *Étude*, 10.
[5] Cf. Vinaver, *The Tale of the Death of King Arthur*, ix–x.
[6] *Vulgate Version*, III, 210–15, 223, 231–50.
[7] Thus immediately after the long account of Lancelot's noble nature, Arthur
is reproached by a black friar for his failure to help Ban (*Vulgate Version*, III, 33–
40, 45–7), while later, after Lancelot's first great exploit, his conquest of the
Dolorous Guard, Arthur has two warning dreams and is humbled by a holy man
who rebukes him for all his shortcomings (*Vulgate Version*, III, 119–200, 215–23).
Again Arthur's stupid love affair with the enchantress Camille and the false

Queste and the *Mort Artu*, too, the dominant figure is Lancelot, and it is not without significance that the latter ends not with the death of Arthur, but with that of Lancelot.[1] Despite this, however, the *Roman de Lancelot* contains sufficient Arthurian events to be interpreted as a partial history of Arthur's kingdom, and it was in fact so interpreted by later *remanieurs* who attempted to complete the story by the addition of two further branches, the *Estoire del Saint Graal* and the *Estoire de Merlin*. The former, differing vastly in spirit from the *Queste* and frequently in contradiction with the rest of the cycle,[2] serves as a prologue to the *Queste* and supplies the history of Logres in its pre-Christian and pre-Arthurian days. The *Estoire de Merlin* bridges the gap between the end of the *Estoire del Saint Graal* and the beginning of the *Lancelot* proper by dealing with the story of Arthur's kingdom from its beginnings down to Lancelot's birth; but there are chronological discrepancies between the two,[3] and the author, interested above all in pseudo-history, made his account into a series of uninspired chronicles, completely out of harmony with the rest of the work.[4]

The Vulgate Cycle thus contains a number of different themes—courtly love, religious mysticism and pseudo-history. Two of the branches, the *Merlin* and the *Mort Artu*, give between them a fairly coherent account of the beginning and end of Arthur's kingdom, but there is no unifying idea running through all the branches and the whole lacks organic or 'epic unity'.[5]

The *Roman du Graal* is, on the other hand, a far more homogeneous and closely-knit whole. Many of the discrepancies between the *Estoire del Saint Graal* and the rest of the work which mar the Vulgate have been avoided, and the links between the other sections have been strengthened. The Post-Vulgate *Queste* runs without a break into the Post-Vulgate *Mort Artu*, and the *Suite du Merlin*, far from being a

---

Guenevere episode are clearly intended to tarnish his reputation and enhance Lancelot's (*Vulgate Version*, III, 409–10, 425–7, IV, 10–19, 44–82).

[1] On Lancelot's place in the *Queste*, see Pauphilet, *Études*, 130.

[2] See above, 160–8.

[3] On the chronological discrepancies between the *Merlin* and the *Lancelot* proper, see A. Micha, 'Les sources de la Vulgate du *Merlin*', *MA*, VII (1952) 330.

[4] On the *Estoire de Merlin* see A. Micha, 'La guerre contre les romans', *R*, LXXII (1951) 310–23; 'Les sources de la Vulgate du *Merlin*', *MA*, VII (1952) 299–345; 'La composition de la Vulgate du Merlin', *R*, LXXIV (1953) 200–20; 'La Suite-Vulgate du *Merlin*', *ZRPh.*, LXXI (1955) 33–59.

[5] Vinaver, *Malory* (Oxford, 1929) 93.

perfunctory addition like the Vulgate *Merlin* continuation, is an integral part of the work and foreshadows and prepares for many of the themes of the Post-Vulgate *Queste* and *Mort Artu*. The various sections form in fact an indissoluble whole.[1]

But not only is the structure of the *Roman du Graal* much tighter than that of the Vulgate Cycle; its subject matter, too, is more uniform. The *Roman du Graal* is an attempt to create out of the several branches of the Arthurian Cycle a unified romance centring upon Arthur rather than Lancelot. The author realized that the Vulgate contained the Arthurian epic in embryo, but that it was essentially a romance of Lancelot. In his endeavour to develop the theme of Arthur and his adventurous kingdom he had to reduce Lancelot's and Guenevere's part in the *Mort Artu* and cut out most of the *Lancelot* proper, keeping only a few episodes necessary for a smooth transition to the *Queste*.[2] Lancelot remains, of course, an important character in the story, but he no longer overshadows Arthur: as the Lancelot-Guenevere theme recedes, Arthur and the land of Logres come to the fore. A large part of the narrative concerns Arthur directly and he is, for the first time, given the 'importance and the dignity of a real hero'.[3] He is no mere abstract centre of the Round Table, but an active ruler, keenly aware of the high office of kingship. He realizes that he is king by the grace of God and recognizes no one as his overlord except his Creator—witness his energetic reply to the twelve messengers from Rome when they ask him to do homage to the Emperor:

Signeur, je ne ting onques de Roume nule chose, ne ja ne quier que j'en tiegne. Et chou que je tieng, je le tieng de Dieu seulement, qui en ceste poesté et en ceste grasce me mist, au destruisement de m'ame se je n'i faich chou que je doi, et au sauvement se je i tieng le peule come peres le doit tenir. A chelui dont, signour, qui en ceste hautesce me mist, sui je tenus que je li rende treu de toutes les hounours qui en sa baillie m'avenront, mais a nul autre je n'i sui tenus, car nus autres ne me mist en possession.[4]

---

[1] On the links between the *Suite du Merlin*, the Post-Vulgate *Queste*, Post-Vulgate *Mort Artu* and *Estoire del Saint Graal*, see above, Chs. V, VI, VII.

[2] On the treatment of the *Lancelot* episodes, see 213–14. On the Post-Vulgate *Mort Artu*, see 146.

[3] Vinaver, *Malory* (Oxford, 1929) 91. The words which Vinaver applied to Malory's Arthur are equally applicable to the Arthur of the *Roman du Graal*.

[4] Huth MS., f. 86c; Huth *Merlin*, I, 180. In the Vulgate *Merlin* Arthur also refuses to do homage to the Emperor, but his reply there to the messengers lacks the religious tone which it has in the *Suite* (*Vulgate Version*, II, 426, ll. 1–20).

He is just and generous to his people,[1] ever ready to defend them against all. When the five kings invade Logres and his barons advise Arthur to wait until Pellinor arrives with reinforcements to aid him, he refuses to delay, for he would be failing in his duty:

'Coument! fait il, signour, volés vous que je aille chi sejornant et demourant et mi anemi iront ma terre reubant et preant et prendant mes hommes? Certes mauvaisement garderoie le peuple que Diex m'a mis entre les mains, se je n'en ostoie les roubeours et les felons. Saichiés vraiement que je ne serai ja mais aise devant que je lour soie a l'encontre. Et certes se jou avoie la moitié de gent mains que je n'ai, si assamblerai jou a eus se je les truis, car autrement ne mousterroie jou pas que je deusse estre sires, se jou ne les ostoie de toutes autres subjections fors de la moie.'[2]

His sense of responsibility to his kingdom is equalled only by his personal bravery. When in his fight with Accalon his sword breaks, Arthur shows not the least dismay, but continues to defend himself with courage.[3] In the war against Mark, he fights so valiantly that even his enemies praise him for his valour,[4] while in the last battle against the traitor Mordred, Arthur does not as in the Vulgate lament his fate, but encourages his companions.[5] With all this he has a sense of humour,[6] is courteous, humble[7] and full of human sympathy.[8] But the episode which indicates perhaps best the importance which the *Roman du Graal* attaches to Arthur is the account of the institution of the Round Table at Camalot. The Vulgate Cycle has very little to say on the subject. According to the *Lancelot* proper the Round Table, the

[1] See Huth *Merlin*, II, 209.

[2] Huth MS., f. 187b–c; Huth *Merlin*, II, 159–60.

[3] Huth *Merlin*, II, 205–6.

[4] Et il estoit de grant force et grant hardement, si se defent tant bel et tant bien que nus nel voit qui ne die: 'Voiremant est ce li rois Artus.' Et si enemis meimes le prisent et le loent de la grant defense qu'il voient en lui (MS. B.N. fr. 343, f. 62c).

[5] On Arthur's character in the Post-Vulgate *Mort Artu*, see above, 150–1.

[6] When Rion's messengers demand his beard, Arthur smiles and remarks that Rion must have made a mistake for he is too young to have a beard (Huth *Merlin*, I, 202). Cf. Arthur's reply in the Vulgate, where he is simply angered (*Vulgate Version*, II, 412, l. 38–413, l. 1).

[7] When Arthur learns how reluctantly Pellinor jousted with Giflet, he remarks: 'Par Diu, fait li rois, vaillans est li chevaliers et bien est gracieus et de chevalerie et de cortoisie. Pleust ore a Dieu que je le resamblaisse' (Huth MS., f. 88a; Huth *Merlin*, I, 184).

[8] When Arthur finds himself in Domas' prison, he is more grieved for his companions than for himself (Huth *Merlin*, II, 185). Again, when Arthur hears of Gallin's distress, he offers at once to defend his rights (*Die Abenteuer*, 96).

glory of Arthur's kingdom, hardly belongs to Arthur at all: Guenevere
brings it with her as part of her dowry and apparently can claim it as
her own.[1] The Vulgate *Merlin* mentions briefly that after Arthur's
marriage (which took place in Carmelide) the Knights of the Round
Table, 'qui tout estoient de foi homme al roy Leodegan', accompanied
him and Guenevere to Logres;[2] but no ceremony marks the transfer
of the Round Table to Arthur's court: on the contrary, there is at first
a great deal of rivalry and even ill-feeling between the Knights of the
Round Table and the others,[3] which does not cease until Gauvain is
made 'sires et maistres et compaignons de la Table Roonde'.[4] After
Leodogan's death, which coincides with the end of Arthur's wars
against the Saxons, the Knights of the Round Table decide to remain
in Logres.[5] The *Roman du Graal* has replaced these scattered remarks
by a detailed narrative clearly intended to glorify Arthur and his
kingdom. When Merlin goes to Carmelide to ask for Guenevere's
hand, Leodogan offers at once to send to Arthur his most treasured
possession, the Round Table. He explains that he has not replaced the
fifty companions of the Round Table who had died since Utherpendragon's death, for a hermit had told him that a worthier king would
soon do so. After summoning the remaining hundred companions,
he tells them of his decision to send them to Arthur who would be
able to complete their number and maintain them in greater honour
than he ever could. The companions rejoice at this news and thank God
for their good fortune. Three days later they set out for Logres.
Arthur welcomes them in so splendid a fashion 'k'il se tenoient a
boin euré de che qu'il estoient cele part venu'.[6] The day of the wedding
is fixed and many *preudommes* assemble at court. On Arthur's request
Merlin fills all the vacant seats at the Round Table except two. He
explains the significance of the *Siege Perilleus* and then introduces the
hundred companions to their forty-eight new brothers: ' "Veschi vos
freres que je vous ai esleus. Et Nostre Sires meche pais et concorde
entre vous aussi comme il fist entre ses apostles." Et lors les fist tous

[1] *Vulgate Version*, IV, 13, l. 41–14, l. 1 and 14, ll. 21–26: '... Et se vous ne
volés ce faire, ma dame vous desfent de par Dieu et de quan que vient de par lui,
que vous des ore mais en avant ne teigniés l'onor que vous o lui presistes en
mariage, chou fu la Table Reonde, mais envoiés li aussi bien garnie de chevaliers
comme sez peres le vous charga, et ne maintenés plus la Table Roonde en vostre
ostel, car vous n'i avés nul droit, ne a vous n'afiert elle pas.'

[2] *Vulgate Version*, II, 314, ll. 26–27.

[3] Ibid., 302–8, 322–34, 382.   [4] Ibid., 334, ll. 17–18.

[5] Ibid., 450   [6] Huth *Merlin*, II, 64. Cf. *infra*, 228–41.

entrebaisier.'[1] When all are seated, the Archbishop of Canterbury gives them his blessing, while the other *clergiés* pray that they should live 'en boine pais et en boine concorde aussi coume frere germain pueent estre et doivent'.[2] Thereafter Merlin asks the knights to rise and do homage to Arthur, 'qui est vostre compains de ceste table'.[3] As soon as they have vacated their seats, their names are found inscribed therein, indicating God's pleasure at the establishment of the Round Table in Logres:

Ceste chose tinrent il a grant merveille tout li sage houme, et disent que se che ne fust chose qui a Nostre Signeur pleust, ja tel merveille ne fust avenue. Et li compaignon de la Table Reonde vinrent maintenant devant le roi et li firent hommage. Et il les rechut comme ses houmes de par sa terre et coume ses hommes de par la Table Reonde. Et il en estoit compains ensi comme li autre, car Merlins l'[i] avoit mis pour la bonté de chevalerie qu'il sentoit en lui, et l'avoit assis droit au commenchement de la table.[4]

The task the author of the *Roman du Graal* set himself was clearly to write the Epic of Arthur—the story of the rise and fall of the *roiaume aventureus*. This accounts among other things for some features of his treatment of the Grail theme. In the Vulgate Cycle the *Queste* holds ideologically a central position: it serves to show the vanity of the courtly ideal—the triumph of heavenly over earthly chivalry. Its culmination is the spiritual experience of the Grail knights, for the author conceives of the quest as a quest for union with God—'li encerchemenz des grans secrez et des privetez Nostre Seignor et des grans repostailles'.[5] Now in the *Roman du Graal* the *Queste* is not an occasion for doctrinal exposition, but essentially a chapter in the story of Logres. Its main object is to relate how Galaad, the good knight, ended the adventures inaugurated by Balain's Dolorous Stroke. Our author is not so much interested in Lancelot's inability to achieve the Quest as in the Grail adventures themselves, which he interprets as divine punishment for Balain's unwitting transgression in wounding Pellean and touching the Holy Lance.[6] A deliberate contrast is worked up between Balain, the 'man born on earth to destroy people',[7] and Galaad, the redeemer; and the healing of Pellean, purely incidental in

---

[1] Huth *Merlin*, II, 67.   [2] Loc. cit.   [3] Loc. cit.
[4] Huth MS., f. 149d; Huth *Merlin*, II, 68. Cf. *infra*, 236.
[5] Vulgate *Queste*, 19, ll. 20–2.
[6] For details, see above, 129–37.
[7] Huth *Merlin*, I, 254: 'hom nés sour terre pour destruction de gent'.

the Vulgate, becomes as much an integral part of the final scene at Corbenic as the communion of the chosen knights.

To give the impression that he is writing a continuous history of Logres, the author of the *Roman du Graal* does not confine the *Queste* section to the adventures of the Grail knights, but adds such episodes as Mark's first invasion of Logres and the exploits of Tristan, Palamedes, the Conte de Bedoin and others, performed at the time of the great Quest. At the same time, many of the original Vulgate episodes are remodelled. The author of the Vulgate was concerned primarily with the *senefiance* of his narrative, its symbolical meaning which he endeavoured to explain when it was not self-evident. The result is an account which is on the whole vague and improbable. The author of the *Roman du Graal*, on the other hand, was interested first and foremost in the substance of the narrative. His primary aim was to tell the 'adventures of Logres'. He cuts out or shortens some of the theological disquisitions, removes some of the mystical manifestations, and adds small realistic touches here and there. A typical example is furnished by the incident of the Boiling Fountain. In the Vulgate the episode is very brief. All the writer says is that one day Galaad found the Boiling Fountain in the *forest perilleuse*. 'Et si tost come il i ot mise la main, si s'em parti l'ardor et la chalor, por ce que en lui n'avoit onques eu eschaufement de luxure.'[1] The Post-Vulgate expands this reference into an account which has a certain narrative interest.[2] One day when it was very hot Galaad comes to the *forest perilleuse* where he meets a knight accompanied by a squire and a damsel. The latter complains of thirst, and the squire who goes in search of a fountain comes by chance upon the Boiling Fountain. Unfortunately, however, he forgets to notice whether the water is hot or cold, and when the damsel bends down to drink, she slips and is scalded to death. The knight attempts to pull her out, but cannot keep his hands in the water. Galaad now knows that this is the Boiling Fountain and prays to God that its waters should cool at his coming. When the people of Arthur's court hear that Galaad has ended this adventure, they realize that it is not 'par chevalerie, mes par miracle de Nostre Seignor'.[3]

Equally characteristic are the alterations made in some of the episodes involving Lancelot. In the course of his voyage, Lancelot

[1] Vulgate *Queste*, 263, ll. 30–2.
[2] MS. B.N. fr. 343, ff. 100c–101a; *D*, II, §§ 578–80; Sp. *D*, Chs. CCCLIV–CCCLV, 295a–b.
[3] MS. B.N. fr. 343, f. 101a.

comes upon 'une roche vielle et anciane'.[1] The purpose of this incident in the Vulgate is to remind Lancelot that his 'pechié mortel' has prevented him from being the best knight in the world, but that if he will henceforth be 'chaste in thought and deed', he will find 'pity and forgiveness in Him who is all pity'.[2] All the *Queste* needed as background was a vague and mysterious island and an anonymous *preudhome* to advise Lancelot. The concrete setting did not really interest the Vulgate. In the Post-Vulgate *Queste*[3] the old man is identified with 'li rois Galegantis', Lancelot's maternal grandfather,[4] and the unexpected meeting between grandfather and grandson is explored and acquires a dramatic interest. Lancelot is blamed for his sin, but in a much more subtle and less abrupt manner: the grandfather compares his own long and chaste life with Lancelot's sinful existence. When Lancelot departs, a final human touch is added: 'et sachiez que au departir plore li uns et li autre, car bien pensent que il ja mes ne s'entreveront'.[5]

These particular modifications may not obscure the meaning of the original, but if necessary our author does not hesitate to sacrifice the *sens* in order to give an episode greater verisimilitude. Thus in describing Lancelot's visit to Corbenic,[6] the *Roman du Graal* does not mention the two lions guarding the entrance, which in the Vulgate serve to test Lancelot's faith;[7] Lancelot disobeys the voice and enters the Grail Chamber, not because he sees within a mystical Mass, but simply because there is no one about 'qui le peust destorber d'entrer leienz'.[8] Most of the supernatural manifestations preceding Lancelot's trance

[1] Vulgate *Queste*, 246–9.

[2] Ibid., 248, ll. 26–30.

[3] MS. B.N. fr. 343, ff. 72d–74b; *D*, II, §§ 510–12 (not in Sp. *D*).

[4] The identification of Galegantis as Lancelot's grandfather on the maternal side is peculiar to our romance. In the Vulgate Cycle, Helaine, Lancelot's mother, is, as here, King Ban's wife and the sister of King Boort's wife, but her father is not named. As for Galegantis, he is described in the *Mort Artu* as one of Arthur's most loyal knights (*La Mort le Roi Artu*, 217, ll. 20–1). Two of the MSS. of the *Mort Artu* (B.N. fr. 342 (*D*) and Palatinus Latinus 1967 (*V*)) make Galegantis of royal lineage: 'car moult estoit Gelegantins boins chevaliers et gentius hom, si comme cil ki avoit esté fius de roi et avoit tous jours esté molt loiaus enviers son segneur le roi Artu' (*La Mort le Roi Artu*, 217, § 189, variant 6).

[5] MS. B.N. fr. 343, f. 74a.

[6] MS. B.N. fr. 343, ff. 90d–92b; *D*, II, §§ 539–45; Sp. *D*, Chs. CCCXV–CCCXXI, 280a–282a.

[7] Vulgate *Queste*, 253–4; MS. B.N. fr. 343, f. 90c–d.

[8] MS. B.N. fr. 343, f. 91a; Vulgate *Queste*, 254–6.

are also omitted, as well as Lancelot's reflections, by means of which in the Vulgate he realizes the significance of his adventure. A hermit explains in a few words to Pelles the reason for Lancelot's trance.[1] During his trance Lancelot is recognized by Pelles' daughter (represented as dead in the Vulgate),[2] whose grief is described in some detail. Similarly, when Lancelot discovers that his hairshirt has been removed from him, he is no less distressed than in the Vulgate, but he does not dare to ask for it 'de honte. Por ce la lesse il a cele foiée.'[3]

One of the effects of rationalization is the abandonment of the all-important notion that Corbenic is visible only to knights in a state of grace. The castle remains inaccessible, it is true, but in a manner of a castle in a fairy tale: Thanabus, an enchanter, who lived at the time of Utherpendragon, had built it in such a way that no one could find it

se aventure ne l'i amenast et cheance. Et s'i eust esté cent foiz, ja por ce n'i asenast plus tost. Et se aucuns qui la voie seust i voxist mener chevalier estrange, ja mes n'i assenast, se aventure nel feist.[4]

Yet it would be wrong to conclude that the *Roman du Graal* is wholly secular in spirit. Without being the expression of any particular doctrine, it has a clear religious overtone.[5] Some of the most significant Vulgate episodes, such as the communion of the chosen knights at Corbenic and Galaad's ecstatic vision in Sarraz, have been taken over with comparatively few changes.[6] The author realizes that the Grail is a symbol of grace[7] and at several points says that no one can succeed in the Quest unless he has served his Creator loyally. When Hector arrives at Corbenic and all the doors and windows close of their own accord, King Pelles explains that this always happens at the approach of those

qui en la Queste del Saint Grahal se sunt mis sanz aler a confession. Il se funt apeller serjant de Sainte Eglise et il ne [le] sunt mie, si lor mostre ceienz Nostre

---

[1] MS. B.N. fr. 343, f. 91c–d; Vulgate *Queste*, 257–8.

[2] Vulgate *Queste*, 259, ll. 21–4; MS. B.N. fr. 343, f. 91b.

[3] MS. B.N. fr. 343, f. 91d; Vulgate *Queste*, 258, ll. 24–7.

[4] MS. B.N. fr. 343, f. 90d.   [5] Cf. above, 115–16.

[6] For the treatment of the final scene at Corbenic, see above, 109–12.

[7] In speaking of the Maimed King, the Post-Vulgate says that he had been a long time in the Holy Chamber, 'ne n'i avoit eu sostenance, se ce n'estoit de la grace de Nostre Seigneur ou del Saint Vessel' (MS. B.N. fr. 343, f. 103a). At another point the Post-Vulgate remarks that those in Corbenic 'avoient ja... esté serviz de la grace del Saint Vessel' (MS. B.N. fr. 343, f. 91d).

Sires tout apertement, car quant il viennent ceienz, [si] voelent entrer en cest palais, qui palais aventureux est apellez, les huis meemes se cloent encontre els et les fenestres ausint.[1]

Galaad makes a similar remark when he and his companions reach the 'palleis aventureux':

'Bel seignor, dit Galahaz, or poez ci veoir la prouvance de nos oevres. En cest paleis ne puet nul chevalier errant entrer, s'il ne s'est auques maintenuz en ceste Queste com chevalier de Sainte Eglise doit faire vers son Creator. Se nos somes chevalier del Sainte Grahal, les portes nos aouvrent. Se nos nel somes, ce est noient de l'entrer,'

to which Palamedes replies:

Ha! Dex... conseilliez nos de ceste afaire, car sanz vostre merci n'i valt noient mortex chevalerie.[2]

The characters may not always be as assiduous in their religious practices as in the Vulgate, but there are many references to prayer and confession, and sin by all standards is condemned. In the incident where Galaad, Hector and Meraugis are imprisoned in the Chastel Felon, Galaad reassures his companions that He whom they served in this Quest will deliver them, 'car il est li pastours qui delivre ses oeilles de touz perilz'.[3] Before meeting Mark in battle, Galaad goes to hear Mass[4] and tells Artus le Petit and Esclabor that God will help them 'se nos avom nostre esperance en lui'.[5] Simeu, we are told, was almost damned for his *pechié*, but pardoned because of Galaad's goodness.[6] The magician from Barbarie loses all his power in the presence of 'so holy a man as Galaad', and because in his youth he had renounced his Creator and become 'sers de l'ennemi', he is carried off to hell by flaming hands.[7]

---

[1] MS. B.N. fr. 343, f. 91d.
[2] Ibid , f. 102b. Cf. the incident where Gauvain and Gaheriet arrive at Corbenic. A damsel tells them that they cannot enter, 'qu'a Nostre Seignor ne plaist mie que vos i entroiz. Par ce poez vos conoistre que vos ne L'avez pas si bien servi en ceste Queste com vos deussiez'. Gauvain thereupon curses the castle, but Gaheriet assures him that it is not the castle's fault but their own: 'Sire, ce dit Gaheriet, nos n'en devom mie le chastel blasmer, mes nos meemes qui les mauveses oevres fesom, pour qoi [nous n'i poom avoir honor nule foiz]' (MS. B.N. fr. 343, ff. 92d–93a).
[3] MS. B.N. fr. 772, f. 386c.
[4] MS. B.N. fr. 343, f. 67c.
[5] Ibid., 68a.   [6] Ibid., f. 65d.   [7] Ibid., f. 88c–d.

When Mark has given Pharan and Galaad poison Galaad has a vision in which he learns that Pharan has died 'pour ce qu'il gissoit en mortel pechié', but that he has been saved, 'pour ce que li Haut Mestre te trouva en bone vie'.[1] Samaliel has lived on 'pain et eive' since he was knighted, and though anxious to avenge his father's death on Arthur, refrains from doing so as it would be 'la greignor dolor et le greignor pechié qui onques avenist el roiaume de Logres'.[2] When Perceval's sister fetches Galaad from the hermitage to which he came after his encounter with Eliezer, the hermit begs Galaad to pray for him, 'car je sçay bien que je suis assés plus pecherres que je ne deusse'.[3] Similarly, when Palamedes leaves Corbenic, he implores Galaad to intercede for him with *Nostre Sires*: 'Por Deu, s'il est ensint que aventure ne nos rascemble, toute voies te souviegne de moi. Tu m'ostas de dolor et de pechié ou je estoie et me mis en voie et en bone aventure. Et por ce te requier je que tu pries por moi que Nostre Sires ne m'oblie, ainz m'amaint a tel fin que l'ame de moi truist la joie pardurable aprés la mort del cors.'[4]

There is in the *Roman du Graal* no 'double esprit' such as we find in the *Lancelot-Graal*. Though the *Suite du Merlin* has been described as a collection of purely romantic adventures, 'of the same general kind as the adventures of the *Lancelot*, by which they were manifestly inspired',[5] it has, in reality, a religious 'colour' similar to that of the Post-Vulgate *Queste*. Now that the episode of the Dolorous Stroke can be read in its entirety in the Cambridge MS., it is clear that for the author of the *Suite du Merlin*, as for the author of the Post-Vulgate *Queste*, the Grail was a holy object which no unworthy person could behold. When Balain was about to enter the Grail Chamber a voice warned him not to do so, just as in the *Queste* a voice warned Lancelot.[6] When later on, after the Dolorous Stroke, Merlin approached the Grail Chamber he immediately knelt down and prayed. Though anxious to help Balain and King Pellean who were both lying in the Grail Chamber, Merlin knew that he was not worthy of entering so holy a place and looked round for 'un provoire', whom he instructed to put on 'lez armez Jhesu Crist', . . . 'car auterment n'i doit nus entrere por le

[1] MS. B.N. fr. 343, f. 71c.
[2] Ibid., f. 82a.   [3] MS. B.N. fr. 112, *Livre* IV, f. 124d.
[4] MS. B.N. fr. 343, f. 104b–c.
[5] Bruce, *Evolution*, I, 464. See also ibid., I, 463.
[6] Cambridge MS., f. 270d; MS. B.N. fr. 343, f. 91a; Vulgate *Queste*, 255, ll. 9–11. Cf. above, 205.

saintisme lieu, s'il ne porte lez enseignez Jhesu Crist'.[1] In the other portions of the *Suite du Merlin*, too, there is, as in the Post-Vulgate *Queste*, a constant preoccupation with sin. Before his fight with the giant Aupartis, Gaheriet hears Mass and does penitence as a hermit had suggested: 'Et quant il fu armés, il se fist confés au preudomme de tous les pechiés dont il se sentoit coulpable vers Nostre Seigneur. Et cil ly encharga tel penitence comme il cuidoit qu'il peust faire par dejoste le travail des armes'.[2] Similarly, when Arthur is about to face Lot's army, Merlin advises him to confess all his sins, as this would help him more than anything else:

Rois, ne te desconforte, car Nostre Sires te secourra. Et bien sachiés qu'Il ne te mist pas en si haute segnourie pour oster t'en si delivrement, se tu trop ne Li mesfais. Ore chevauce tout asseur et ordene tes gens au miex que tu savras. Et je te di que Nostre Sires te fera hui le grignour hounour qui piecha mais avenist a roi pecheour. Et je voel que tu te rendes confés de toutes les choses dont tu te sens coupables vers Nostre Signour. Et je te di que che est une chose qui moult te pourfitera et moult te porra aidier.[3]

Tor's mother's injunctions to her son before leaving him likewise recall the spirit of the *Queste*. She reminds him that just as God has raised him to his high position, He has the power to lower him again. He should, therefore, not forget Him, but guard his soul so as to render it intact to his Creator:

Biaus fius, vous avés esté norris en povreté. Se Nostre Sires vous aimme tant qu'Il vous mette en la boine euurté et en la hautece, pour chou ne L'oubliés vous pas, car bien sachiés qu'Il vous oublieroit. Car tout ensi que Il est poissans de vous soushaucier, aussi est Il poissans de vous abaissier et de metre a nient. En ceste chose vous devés vous regarder et prendre essample; ne Il ne vous bailla que une ame a garder: se vous cele Li rendés, dont vous tenra Il a preudomme et a vrai chevalier, et se vous la metés en autrui garde et en la saisine de l'anemi, certes miex vous venroit que vous fuissiés laboreres de terre et povres aussi coume sont vo autre frere.[4]

When Balain laments the death of his companion a hermit tells him that it is wrong to make such grief, 'se n'estoit seulement pour repentance de ses pechiés. Pour tele chose doit on plourer, ne mie pour autre.'[5] Gallinor, assuring Gaheriet that he has told him the truth about his adventure, adds: 'se Dieu me face pardon de mes pechiés au jour de

[1] Cambridge MS., f. 271d. *Infra*, 248.   [2] *Die Abenteuer*, 121.
[3] Huth MS., f. 111d; Huth *Merlin*, I, 249.
[4] Huth MS., f. 177c–d; Huth *Merlin*, II, 135.   [5] Ibid., II, 9.

la mort'.[1] The damsels of the *Roche aux Pucelles*, we are told, desist from doing too much harm by their enchantments 'pour doubtance de pechié'.[2] When Gauvain and his brothers are determined to avenge their mother's death on Gaheriet, Lamorat points out that it is not for them, but for God to take vengeance: 'Car pour ce, se vostre frere occist par son pechié et par sa mesaventure sa mere et la vostre, ne l'en devés pas traire a mort, car la vengeance n'en est pas a vous a prendre, mes a Dieu.'[3] Morgain, after being prevented by Yvain from killing her husband, King Urien, realizes that had she been successful, she would have lost her soul: 'Et certes j'estoie si courechie que anemis m'avoit si sousprise que je ne savoie que je faisoie. Et Dieus t'amena pour sauver ton pere et moi, car jou l'euusse occhis, et m'arme en fust dampnee a tous jors mais.'[4] Yvain himself would readily have slain his mother for her treachery, but refrains from doing so as he does not wish to lose his soul for such an 'anemi' as she is.[5] Similarly Merlin refuses to reveal to Arthur the name of the child that will one day destroy Logres, for he would be damned if through him an innocent creature were killed: 'Mais quel chose que la terre i gaaignast, jou i perderoie trop, car je i perderoie l'ame de moi, dont il m'est ore plus que de tout che païs. Et pour chou le vous celerai jou. Je voel miex m'ame sauver que la terre.'[6] Nor will Merlin help Arthur hide his 'pechié de la femme le roi Loth', for to do so he would have to dispose of three people, and if he did this he would sin 'mortelment'.[7] For the same reason, too, Merlin will not use his enchantments to ward off his own death: 'Mais des moies choses sui je si contrebatus par enchantemens que je n'i sai metre conseil, car les enchantemens qui sont fait ne puis je desfaire se je ne voel m'arme perdre; mais certes mieus vaurroie je que mes cors fust tornés a honte par auchune traïson que l'ame de moi fust perdue.'[8]

Illicit love, in particular, is severely condemned in the *Suite du Merlin*, just as it is in the Post-Vulgate *Queste*. Gaheriet summarizes

---

[1] *Die Abenteuer*, 108–10.

[2] Ibid., 80.

[3] *La Folie Lancelot*, 17, ll. 734–7. When Niviene asks Merlin to tell him the nature of Arthur's sin, Merlin refuses for the same reason: 'Che ne vous doi je pas, fait il, descouvrir, car che n'apartient pas a moi ne a vous. A chelui en apartient qui des grans pechiés prent venganche a sa volenté' (Huth *Merlin*, II, 153).

[4] Huth *Merlin*, II, 214.

[5] Loc. cit.

[6] Huth *Merlin*, I, 159.

[7] Huth *Merlin*, I, 162–3.

[8] Ibid., II, 152.

the doctrine of the *Suite du Merlin* when he explains why he killed his mother, the Queen of Orkney:

'J'en ay fait, fait il, ce que l'en doit faire de royne qui par maleureuse luxure fait honte a ses enfans et a tout son lignage. Et celle chose fera, se cuide je, chastier les haultes dames des grans desloyaultés qu'elles font.'[1]

Other references are equally revealing. When Baudon's damsel fell in love with another knight, and Baudon's friend, Gallinor, discovered this, he threatened to kill the lovers unless they promised 'que ja mais en cellui pechié ne cherroient'.[2] Again in the *Suite du Merlin* as in the *Lancelot* Morgain is represented as a wicked character, but in our romance alone Morgain's wickedness, reflected in her ugliness, is significantly attributed to her *luxure:*

Mais sor toutes celes qui le jour i furent em porta le pris et l'ounour de biauté Morgue, la fille Igerne. Et sans faille elle fu bele damoisiele jusques a celui terme que elle commencha aprendre des enchantemens et des charroies; mais puis que li anemis fu dedens li mis, et elle fu aspiree et de luxure et de dyable, elle pierdi si otreement sa biauté que trop devint laide, ne puis ne fu nus qui a bele le tenist, s'il ne fu enchantés.[3]

In the incident dealing with the revelation of Tor's parentage the author likewise condemns sinful love. Tor is ashamed for his mother,[4]

---

[1] *La Folie Lancelot*, 5, ll. 172–5. In the First Version of the prose *Tristan*—source of this episode—Gaheriet and his brothers likewise disapprove of their mother loving Lamorat, but their reason there is simply that Lamorat is the son of the man who slew their father: '... Aprés ces deus morz estoit la haine renovelee por la royne [d'Orchanie] qui mere estoit Gauvain et aux autres freres, car la roine avoit en Lamorat si mis son cuer por la proesce qu'elle savoit en lui qu'elle n'amoit riens du monde autant come elle fesoit lui. La dame estoit de grant biauté et por ce l'amoit Lamorat de tout son cuer. Tuit li frere monseigneur Gauvain qui ceste chose savoient vraiement en estoient trop courrociez *et a grant desdaing lor tornoit de ce que lor mere c'estoit abandonee au filz de celui qi lor pere avoit ocis...*' (MS. B.N. fr. 757, f. 54b–c). In our romance Gaheriet and his people are clearly angered because Lamorat loves the Queen *charnellement* without marrying her: 'Si en estoient tous ceulx du parenté doulent, car ilz tenoient ceste chose a grant despit, *mesmement pour ce que Lamorat ne l'avoit pas espousee, et si estoit ung povre chevalier*'. *La Folie Lancelot*, 2, ll. 50–2.

[2] *Die Abenteuer*, 108.

[3] Huth *Merlin*, I, 166. In the Vulgate *Merlin* continuation Morgain is described as very beautiful (*Vulgate Version*, II, 338, ll. 16–21), but in the *Lancelot* proper she is represented as ugly (*Vulgate Version*, IV, 124, l. 25) without the author making any attempt to explain why Morgain became ugly.

[4] Huth *Merlin*, II, 72–3.

and when she is brought to court to certify that Pellinor and not her 'baron' is Tor's father, she admits her sin, but reproaches Merlin for making it public:

> Merlins, or voi ja bien que vous n'estes mie dou tout de la maniere as autres dyables. Che savons nous que li autres dyables vaurroi[en]t tous jours que li pechi[é] de chascun fuissent repost et celé, si que il n'en issist ja de la bouce au pecheour, se che n'estoit par gap et par eschar, et vous volés que jou descuevre le mien; si le descoverrais, mais sachiés que ja Dieus ne vous en savra gret, car vous ne le faites mie pour l'amour de [Dieu] ne pour moi amender, fors pour moustrer vostre savoir.[1]

The Pelleas-Arcade story, on the face of it a typically courtly episode, also serves to condemn courtly love. When Gauvain and Arcade assemble *charnelment* the author says that they have committed *pechié grant et orrible*.[2] Even Pelleas who loves Arcade loyally feels that in loving her he is serving *l'ennemy*:

> Ha! Jhesu Crist, pour quoy souffristes vous onques que je nasquisse, quant ma destinee est si dure qu'il convient que je fine ma vie en duel et en tristesse et que je perde la vie de moy? Sire, mauvés guerdon vous rendray des biens que vous m'avez fait en cest siecle, car je me suis si fort enlaciés aux oeuvres de l'ennemy que je ly ay ja baillee et octroié ce que je vous devoie rendre, ce est l'a[m]e de moy.[3]

Nor is it without significance that when Arcade finally accepts Pelleas, they marry at once.[4]

Certain incidents are not only anti-courtly in spirit, but distinctly anti-feminist. When Balain discovers his friend's damsel in the arms of another man and, what is more, an ill-favoured one, he exclaims:

> Ha! feme, moult est honnis qui en toi se fie,[5]

subsequently adding:

> Ha! Diex, tant a ore bien choisi come feme. Et ja Diex ne m'aït se je ne li faich veoir apertement, a chelui qui tant a hui esté a mal aise, *si verra come grant folie che puet estre de metre trop son cuer en feme!*[6]

---

[1] Huth *Merlin*, II, 133.

[2] *Die Abenteuer*, 32.

[3] MS. B.N. fr. 112, *Livre* II, ff. 27a–b; *Die Abenteuer*, 34–5.

[4] *Die Abenteuer*, 40.

[5] Huth *Merlin*, II, 39.

[6] Huth MS., f. 138c; Huth *Merlin*, II, 40.

Similarly, when Gauvain is deserted by the damsel accompanying him, his friend makes the following uncourtly observation:

'Sire, fait le chevalier, or est ainsi; de ce ne vous chaille, telle est la maniere de femme qu'elle ne regarde mie nulle chose fors que a sa volenté.'[1]

Later Gauvain encounters the knight who took his damsel, defeats him in battle and then proceeds to tell the damsel how wrong she had been in leaving him. The damsel readily admits her error, but Gauvain refuses to have anything more to do with her.[2]

The episodes adapted from the *Lancelot* (those dealing with Lancelot's third madness) are no exception. Far from treating Lancelot's love as ennobling as does the *Lancelot*, our author sees in it a source of misfortune. Lancelot's *folie* is for him not an expression of the tragic nature of his love, but a punishment for his sin:[3] as if to underline Lancelot's humiliation the *remanieur* dwells on the pathetic aspects of his madness. A number of characters recognize Lancelot, and all regret the shame and dishonour to which he has come.[4] Even a dwarf weeps over him 'moult tendrement'.[5] When Erec discovers Lancelot asleep by a fountain, dressed in rags, head shorn and face blackened, he does not trust his eyes at first, for he cannot believe that God could have allowed such great shame to befall the flower of all chivalry:

'Ja Dieu ne m'aïst, fait il, se je ja croiray, se Dieu plaist, que Dieu ait souffert a avenir au meilleur chevalier du monde si grant mescheance comme ceste me semble, ne Il ne sera ja si villains qu'Il l'ait consenti, car ce seroit la greigneur douleur que je onques veisse a avenir... Ja Dieu ne m'aïst, se je ja mais

---

[1] *Die Abenteuer*, 24.
[2] Ibid., 40. That illicit love is for our author a source of evil is suggested also by his treatment of the theme of Merlin's love for King Urien's wife, Morgain. Merlin, who normally always had Arthur's welfare at heart in all he did, was so much in love with Morgain that although she did not return his affection, he helped her to flee after she had stolen Arthur's scabbard, and then did his best to win back Arthur's goodwill towards her by inventing a false story (Huth *Merlin*, I, 270-1). The story of Merlin's love for Niviene does not need to be discussed here, as of course in all versions it is treated in an anti-courtly spirit.
[3] It is perhaps not without significance that at the point where the Vulgate remarks that Lancelot's health did not improve despite all Bliant's efforts, our romance adds 'car a Nostre Seigneur ne plaisoit mie' (*Vulgate Version*, V, 396, l. 14; *La Folie Lancelot*, 39, ll. 162-3).
[4] In the Vulgate, Lancelot is not recognized until shortly before his recovery; hence no one pities him and he does not become a pathetic figure (*Vulgate Version*, V, 400).
[5] *La Folie Lancelot*, 45, l. 408.

P

baioye a honnour avoir, se si grant deshonnor estoit avenue a cellui qui de toutes honnours deust estre sires.'[1]

Later, when Lancelot comes to Corbenic, our romance alone relates how Lancelot fled whenever he saw the Grail approaching, for the devil within him who had caused his madness could not remain in the same place as so holy a thing as the Grail.[2] Lancelot himself, too, is acutely aware of his disgrace. When he has been restored to sanity and learns of his great misfortune, he wishes to spend the rest of his days in some far corner of the earth in tears and sorrow so that no one should ever again hear of him, 'ne chevalerie n'avra honte ne deshonor par moy si comme elle a eu a ceste foiz'.[3]

The Post-Vulgate *Mort Artu* has the same ascetic overtones as the other sections of the *Roman du Graal*. In the Vulgate Cycle there is a contradiction between the last two branches; for Boors, one of the three chosen knights in the *Queste*, not only condones Lancelot's adultery in the *Mort Artu*, but actively encourages his friend and urges the Queen to take Lancelot back after their misunderstanding.[4] The *Roman du Graal* avoids this contradiction. Although it keeps the theme of Lancelot's relapse into sin, it does not represent Boors as Lancelot's accomplice: when Boors hears of Lancelot's love for the Queen he is deeply grieved and leaves the court.[5] On the other hand, the Post-Vulgate reproduces in full the account of Lancelot's pious death, and in the epilogue which it adds to complete the Arthur story there is much emphasis on the virtue of repentance. After Lancelot's death, Blioberis and Boors join the Archbishop of Canterbury to do 'penance' for the rest of their lives. On the way to their hermitage, 'tout a pié et bien povrement', they encounter Meraugis de Porlesgues to whom the Archbishop explains that they are 'pecheurs qui faisons la penance du pechié et des males euvres que nous avons en cest siecle faiz. Et bel nous pourroit estre se, par ceste petite paine, povons noz ames sauver.'[6] When pressed further to say who he is, the Archbishop admits that

---

[1] *La Folie Lancelot*, 55, l. 390–56, l. 404.

[2] *La Folie Lancelot*, 62, ll. 31–9.

[3] Ibid., 67, ll. 275–6. In the Vulgate where Lancelot also retires to an island his reason for doing so is not that he is ashamed of himself, but that he has offended the Queen and may not return to Logres without her permission (*Vulgate Version*, V, 401, ll. 13–17).

[4] *La Mort le Roi Artu*, 56–60, 67, 130–1. See also Frappier, *Étude*, 224–6.

[5] *D*, II, § 626: 'Boorz morou tanto na côrte atá que entendeu que Lançalot amava a raîa e pesou-lhi em muito.'

[6] MS. B.N. fr. 340, f. 205f. *Infra*, 265.

although he is a hermit now, he was Archbishop of Canterbury until the day of the dolorous battle on Salisbury Plain: 'Et pour celle douloureuse journee que je vis me mis je en hermitaige, et des lors je y ay demouré jusques a ores, et encore y demourray se Dieu plaist toute ma vie.'[1] Meraugis is so impressed that they have given up *chevalerie* to serve God, that thereupon he too renounces earthly chivalry:

Beaux seigneurs, puis que je vois que vous avez laissié chevalerie pour le service de Nostre Seigneur, et je la laisse, car aussi grant mestier ay je de m'ame sauver comme entre vous avez, ne ja mais ne quier armes porter se trop grant besoing ne le me fait faire.[2]

The *joie de vivre* so characteristic of the early part of the *Lancelot* proper is completely absent from the *Roman du Graal*. Of all the ways in which the author could have dealt with the Arthur story he chose to treat it from a tragic angle. There is in this new Arthuriad no real characterization, and it depends for its effect not on the development of the characters (who indeed do not develop), but solely on the 'rhythm of its structure, on the inner harmony of its composition'.[3] The author knew that it was possible to convey a sense of finality and inevitable tragedy through purely structural means—the suggestive use of prophecies, the skilful repetition of themes in reverse—and he used these devices not only to give his Arthuriad form and shape, but also to bring out its different emotional phases. Logres is for him the *roiaume aventureux*, the kingdom doomed to mischance.[4] From the beginning an atmosphere of gloom and foreboding hangs over Logres and emphasizes the twin themes of death and *mescheance*. A series of tragic happenings punctuate the early history of the kingdom. First Varlan accidentally causes the partial blighting of the land; then Balain strikes the Dolorous Stroke which devastates three kingdoms and inaugurates the fearsome adventures of Logres. Arthur's knights, too, are dogged by *mescheance*. After the establishment of the Round Table in Camalot Merlin prophesies that shame and defeat will befall the best of them, 'car toute jour lour avenra, [quant] il seront lassé et travillié et il se

---

[1] Ibid., f. 206a. *Infra*, 265.   [2] MS. B.N. fr. 340, f. 206a. *Infra*, 265.

[3] Vinaver, 'Flaubert and the Legend of Saint Julian', *BJRL*, XXXVI (Sept. 1953) 204. Vinaver is the first to have indicated how the thirteenth-century prose writers made use of purely structural means to give their works an emotional content. See in particular art. cit., 228–44, and 'King Arthur's Sword or the Making of a Medieval Romance', *BJRL*, XL (March 1958) 513–26.

[4] Cf. above, Ch. VI, 149–55.

deveront reposer, qu'il les estevera combatre as chevaliers qui seront froit et reposet, et pour chou seront il souvent outré'.[1] One after another is fated to perish through mischance after bringing misfortune to others—Balain and his brother, Pellinor, Lamorat and Drian, Erec and Gaheriet—not because they are deserving of punishment, but because they are the chosen victims of destiny. As Merlin explains to Pellinor when the latter allowed his daughter to be devoured by lions: 'Mais certes, je ne di mie que che soit par vos oevres que vous soiiés si mescheans, ains le voit on toutdis par costume que Nostre Sires envoie plus tost as preudommes et as vassaus corous et anuis en cest monde qu'il ne fait as mauvais. Et chou est la chose qui plus vous doit reconforter seur ceste mesqueanche.'[2] There is a continual contrast of joy and sorrow, and the characters learn of their tragic destiny in an hour of triumph. When Balain alone of Arthur's knights succeeds in untying the knot of the magic sword he is told that unless he returns it to its bearer he will ere the year is up slay with it the man he loves most in this world.[3] Gaheriet, after being knighted by Arthur, is warned by a fool that he will cause his mother's untimely death.[4] Pellinor, after being crowned, kneels before the altar and prays 'od larmes et o plors' that he may not die *par mesqueanche*, whereupon a voice replies: 'Rois Pellinor, tout aussi coume faudras a ta char te faurra ta char, et che sera pour coi tu morras plus tost.'[5] Later, when Pellinor is holding a great feast at Montor and wearing his royal robes, a fool prophesies that the 'fieus del roi ochis' will take his crown from him.[6] Arthur himself is not spared, and from the moment he unwittingly commits a mortal sin which he and his kingdom will have to expiate the theme of his death and of the future destruction of Logres is constantly in the foreground, casting shadows even over the most joyous occasions. When all are rejoicing over the discovery of Arthur's parentage Merlin announces that Giflet will be the last man to see Arthur alive, and that when he leaves him the greatest misfortune there ever was will befall Logres. At this Arthur is filled with grief: 'A cest mot commencha li rois a penser durement, que il aperchoit maintenant que c'estoit de sa mort dont Merlins parloit, si en fu tous escommeus a cele fois.'[7] Shortly after he has obtained his good sword Escalibor Arthur has a divine

---

[1] Huth *Merlin*, II, 97. [2] Ibid., II, 128.
[3] Ibid., I, 217. [4] *Die Abenteuer*, 93, and above, 71–3.
[5] Huth *Merlin*, II, 130–1.
[6] Ibid., II, 129. The prophecy relates of course to Gauvain's slaying of Pellinor. Cf. above, 75–8. [7] Ibid., I, 178.

vision warning him that nothing can prevent the 'evil child' from destroying Logres,[1] and in the midst of Arthur's greatest joy, his marriage to Guenevere, Merlin speaks again of his death:

'Or m'avés bien paiiet, Merlins, fait li rois, qui en ma grant joie me ramentevés mon grant duel.' 'Je le fais, che dist Merlins, pour chou que se en toutes tes grans joies te souvenoit de cele dolereuse jornee, tu en seroies plus humelians vers ton Creatour, qui en ceste hauteche te mist ou tu ies et plus t'en douteroies, si em pecheroies mains que tu ne feras.'[2]

But with the coming of the Good Knight who ends the adventures of Logres the shadows seem to recede and the completion of themes begun in the earlier parts of the story produces a sense of relief. First there is the arrival at Camalot of the 'perron' with the sword in it reserved for Galaad, which Merlin had dispatched from the *Isle de Merveilles* after Balain's death.[3] Then there follow the numerous episodes in which Galaad brings healing and comfort to all those he meets, just as Balain had brought sorrow and destruction. He alleviates the suffering of Simeu, Moïs and Mordrain as foretold in the *Estoire del Saint Graal* and comforts Cayphas who has been living on a desert island since the time of Joseph of Arimathea,[4] while Perceval's sister heals the leprous damsel whom Balain's companion had failed to cure.[5] The culminating point is the final scene at Corbenic when Galaad heals King Pellean whom Balain had maimed. It is the moment of greatest joy in the history of Logres, and to emphasize this the two episodes, the maiming and the healing of Pellean, have been developed into two contrasting parallel movements each of which gives meaning to the other.[6]

After the final scene at Corbenic, however, when Galaad's mission has been completed and the Grail has left Logres, the gloom of the early portion sets in again. The *reprise* of themes in reverse is now accompanied by a renewed darkening of tone, and there is a feeling of impending disaster as the prophecies of long ago are fulfilled one by one. As soon as Arthur's knights have returned to court dissension

[1] Ibid., I, 203.

[2] Ibid., II, 66. After Merlin's entombment, the twelve damsels on the Roche aux Pucelles keep the theme of the tragic destiny of the 'adventurous kingdom' before the reader by continually prophesying the end of the various characters (see *Die Abenteuer*, 63, 64, 125).

[3] Huth *Merlin*, II, 59-60.   [4] See above, 161-2.

[5] Huth *Merlin*, II, 13-19; MS. B.N. fr. 772, ff. 368c-370b; *D*, II, §§ 433-9.

[6] See above, 129-37.

breaks out among them and Lancelot's adultery is revealed.[1] In the Vulgate the full implication of this discord is not immediately apparent, but in the Post-Vulgate its meaning is clear from the outset, for Merlin's remark at the beginning of Arthur's reign that Logres will be feared as long as Arthur's knights 'vaurront estre a un acort'[2] is present in the reader's mind. The discovery of Lancelot's adultery is the more ominous because we still have in mind Merlin's prophecy before Arthur's marriage that if he loved Guenevere any less he would be well advised to take another wife.[3] Thereafter in rapid succession the other predictions are realized, and each time the contrast with earlier parallel scenes added by our author brings out their meaning and completes the pattern. When Lancelot comes to rescue the Queen from the pyre Gaheriet, Agravain and Guerrehes are all slain as prophesied.[4] The episode is derived from the Vulgate, but acquires a new significance in that it recalls how Hector once told Gaheriet that Lancelot would rather give up his life than let any harm come to Gaheriet.[5] In the same way Gauvain's grief at the death of his beloved brothers[6] appears the more poignant in the Post-Vulgate as it immediately brings to mind two contrasting episodes earlier in the narrative: the scene where Gaheriet, yet too young to be knighted, weeps tenderly when Gauvain is wounded during his quest of the white stag,[7] and the episode in which Gauvain endeavours to avenge his mother's death on Gaheriet.[8] The battle round the pyre is followed by an account of the election of new knights to the Round Table to fill the seats of Lancelot, Hector and Boors, and the knights slain in the combat.[9] The episode is again based on the Vulgate,[10] but has been so elaborated as to form a contrast with the earlier joyous ceremony when on the day of Arthur's marriage the Round Table was set up in Camalot.[11] The symmetry is deliberate, and the Round Table, from first signifying the unity of Arthur's knights, now becomes a tragic reminder of their broken loyalty. A similar effect is achieved in a later episode when the Pope, who threatens to excommunicate Arthur if he does not let the Queen return to court, is

---

[1] *D*, II, § 626 (Lacuna in Sp. *D*).
[2] Huth *Merlin*, II, 68.   [3] Ibid., II, 61.
[4] *D*, II, §§ 638–9; Sp. *D*, Chs. CCCCI–CCCCII.
[5] *La Folie Lancelot*, 8.
[6] *D*, II, §§ 642–3; Sp. *D*, Chs. CCCCVI–CCCCVII.
[7] Huth *Merlin*, II, 93.   [8] See above, 74–5.
[9] *D*, II, §§ 650–1; Sp. *D*, Chs. CCCCXIV.
[10] *La Mort le Roi Artu*, 113–14.
[11] Huth *Merlin*, II, 65–8; *infra*, 230–6.

replaced in the Post-Vulgate by the Archbishop of Canterbury who many years before presided over Arthur's wedding.[1] After Arthur's victory over the Romans,[2] which for one brief moment recalls his earlier successes, Mordred's part as prophesied at the beginning of the Arthuriad at last becomes clear to Arthur, and the curse which he utters on slaying his son ironically recalls the curse he once laid upon the unknown child destined to cause the destruction of Logres.[3] There is now no doubt that the end of the 'adventurous kingdom' is close at hand, and from here to the end of the romance the feeling of finality is reinforced by a further series of incidents each of which completes some early episode invented by our author. Arthur's agonizing night in the Noire Chapelle is followed by the *reprise* of the theme of Arthur's enchanted sword: Arthur asks Giflet to cast the sword he once obtained from a hand in a lake back into this same lake.[4] When Giflet has accomplished his task Arthur bids him leave, and this incident too is already foreshadowed at the beginning, when Merlin prophesied that after Giflet has left Arthur, not of his own accord, but on Arthur's bidding, no one would ever see Arthur again 'si ce n'est en songe'.[5] With the passing of Arthur yet another prophecy—that just as Arthur came into this world *par aventure*, so he shall die *par aventure*—is fulfilled, and the fulfilment gives the romance a sense of completion such as we do not find in the Vulgate Cycle where there are no references to Arthur's adventurous birth and death.[6] Finally, in the closing act of the Arthurian epic, Mark, the oldest man alive, invades Logres after Lancelot's death and destroys the Round Table, the symbol of Arthur's former glory, thus repeating in reverse the pattern of his first invasion of Logres during the *Queste*, and providing an ironic contrast to the episode of the newly crowned Mark, barely aged seventeen and Arthur's faithful vassal, helping him to defeat his most formidable enemy, King Rion.[7] All that the author found in his sources was a brief outline of the middle episode.[8] The other two he invented himself

---

[1] *La Mort le Roi Artu*, 129; *D*, II, § 656; Sp. *D*, Ch. CCCCXIX; Huth *Merlin*, II, 67–72.　　　　[2] *D*, II, § 661; Sp. *D*, Ch. CCCCXXII.

[3] *D*, II, § 667; Huth *Merlin*, II, 139.

[4] See Vinaver, 'King Arthur's Sword or the Making of a Medieval Romance', *BJRL*, XL (March 1958) 522–6, and above, 174–6.

[5] Huth *Merlin*, I, 177–8; *D*, II, § 679; Sp. *D*, Ch. CCCCXXXIII; *La Mort le Roi Artu*, 224–5.

[6] See above, 153–4.　　　[7] Huth *Merlin*, I, 230–3.

[8] See above, 190–1. The incident of Arthur's war with Rion is adapted from the Vulgate *Merlin* continuation, but the latter does not mention Mark.

and thereby created a remarkable succession of scenes which through their similarities and contrasts give meaning to this last of all tragedies to befall the 'adventurous kingdom'.

One of the features of the *Roman du Graal* which has hitherto puzzled critics most is the reference to its tripartition. The suggested divisions cut across the traditional Vulgate branches, the first part ending in the midst of one of Balain's adventures. Gaston Paris thought that the desire to make the three parts equal in length was the determining factor and that the third part alone had a logical beginning. Sommer, on the other hand, suggested that the scribe of the Huth manuscript deliberately displaced the beginning of the second part because, having copied the *Joseph* and the *Merlin* from a different manuscript than the *Suite du Merlin*, he could not retain the original divisions of the 'book'.[1] Wechssler, Brugger, Bruce and Pickford were likewise unable to find a reason for the division indicated in the Huth manuscript and took it to be purely arbitrary,[2] due perhaps to some scribe who happened to copy the work in three volumes.[3] But if we

[1] Huth *Merlin*, I, lxii ff.; Sommer, *ZRPh.*, XXXII (1908) 325–6; *R*, XXXVI (1907) 380; *Die Abenteuer*, xviii, xxi–xxii. Sommer's theory has been disproved by the discovery of the Cambridge MS. where the *Merlin* is preceded by the *Estoire del Saint Graal*, and the division between the first and second parts occurs at the same point as in the Huth manuscript.

[2] Wechssler, 8–9; Brugger, *ZFSL*, XXII, 114–17; *ZFSL*, XXXIV, 111–22; Bruce, *Evolution*, I, 468, n. 35, and 473–8.

[3] Pickford, *Évolution*, 69–71. In fact, Pickford does not believe that there ever existed a Post-Vulgate romance which can be reconstructed with the aid of the redactional indications: 'S'il n'est pas permis de juger de telles indications comme absolument dénuées de sens, il faut avouer que dans leur contexte actuel, leur vraie signification ne nous apparaît pas bien clairement… Toute confusion ne disparaîtrait-elle pas si l'on considérait que les divisions et les annotations proviennent d'une séparation matérielle d'une copie, une copie répartie entre trois tomes, dont chacun était composé d'un nombre à peu près égal de feuillets? La phrase *mon signeur de Borron… devise son livre en trois parties* signifierait alors que le roman était conservé en une série de trois volumes. Que la division ne réponde pas à une trilogie arthurienne bien établie est une chose claire, car les textes ne s'accordent pas entre eux pour les changements d'un livre à un autre. La *Demanda* portugaise parle même de la tripartition, bien qu'elle n'ait conservé que la dernière partie du cycle' (*Évolution*, 69–70). It is true that the scribes of the fourteenth and fifteenth centuries frequently divided the prose romances into 'volumes' and 'books' on account of their length. Thus we find the following rubric in one of the manuscripts of the *Guiron* (MS. B.N. fr. 361): '*Cy commence la table des rubrices de la premiere partie de ce tiers volume de Guiron de Cortois, lequel pour la grosseur d'icellui il a esté neccessaire de le mectre en deux volumes.*' But the references of the

regard the *Roman du Graal* as a romance rather than a succession of 'branches' with Arthur as its central figure, the work will fall logically into three parts corresponding to the three periods in the history of Logres. The first part is the story of Logres before the beginning of the *aventures*; it naturally includes a history of the Grail,[1] for it is the Grail which produces the marvels of Logres, and ends when Balain sets out on the quest which is to lead him to the Grail castle where, with the Holy Lance, he is to strike the Dolorous Stroke and so inaugurate the marvels of Logres. The second part shows us Logres labouring under the spell which the *Dolorous Cop* has cast upon it, while the last part begins with the news of the arrival of the Good Knight who will end the adventures of Logres, and includes not only the *Queste* proper, but also an account of the destruction of the kingdom. Pre-Arthurian history—*l'Estoire del Saint Graal*—thus becomes symmetrical with the account of the misfortunes which befall Logres after Arthur's death.

Many of the difficulties raised by the *Roman du Graal* are solved once we see it for what it is: a unified work in which the various themes of its sources coalesce to form a single story—that of the *roiaume aventureux*, which is also that of the Grail. Even the *Estoire del Saint Graal*, which presumably had a separate existence before the later parts were written,[2] is not thought of as a separate and detachable 'branch', but simply as the opening chapter of a longer story. And the name by which the whole romance is often referred to in the *Suite du Merlin*, *L'Estoire dou Saint Graal* or *La Haute Escriture del Saint Graal*,[3] is perhaps the best yet found to describe the author's intentions.

Roman du Graal can be explained on aesthetic grounds. Moreover, far from it being the case that our texts 'ne s'accordent pas entre eux pour les changements d'un livre à un autre', the Huth and Cambridge MSS. both state *at the same point* that the Second Part begins with Balain's quest of the invisible knight and ends with the beginning of the *Queste del Saint Graal* (see above, 61–2). On the other hand, I fail to see the point of Pickford's statement that *even* the Portuguese *Demanda* has references to the tripartition. If, as is clear, the Post-Vulgate *Queste-Mort Artu* forms the third part of the *Roman du Graal*, we should indeed expect to find in it references to the fact that it is the '*postomeira parte*'.

[1] I.e. the *Estoire del Saint Graal*.

[2] I.e. the *Suite du Merlin* and the Post-Vulgate *Queste-Mort Artu*.

[3] For references, see 11, n. 1.

APPENDIX I

Chronological Evidence

The date of the 'Roman du Graal'

Since much of the material in the *Roman du Graal* is drawn from the Vulgate Cycle (written *c.* 1215–30)[1] and the First Version of the prose *Tristan* (written *c.* 1225–30),[2] the year 1230 can be considered a *terminus a quo*. G. Paris, who did not realize that the *Suite du Merlin* was dependent on the Vulgate, dated it as early as 1225–30.[3] J. D. Bruce, on the other hand, places what he calls the 'pseudo-Boron cycle' between 1230 and 1250.[4] C. E. Pickford too seems to assign a late date to the *Suite du Merlin*, suggesting that it may have been written after the *Palamède*.[5] His reason for this view is that Hervi de Rivel and King Lac, who are made knights of the Round Table in the *Suite du Merlin*, play an important part in the *Palamède*. But this argument does not take into account the fact that Hervi de Rivel figures already in the Vulgate Cycle, while King Lac is mentioned in Chrétien's *Erec*. On the other hand, there is evidence to suggest that the *Roman du Graal* was written not only before the Second Version of the prose *Tristan*,[6] which incorporated the First Version of the Post-Vulgate *Queste*[7] and one of the incidents of the *Suite du Merlin*, the death of the Queen of Orkney,[8] but also before the *Palamède*, which was in existence before 1240.[9] Not only does the redactor of the *Palamède* Prologue, as Gaston Paris first pointed out, appear to have read the passage in the *Suite du Merlin* where our author claims that his companion at arms Helie wrote the *Conte du Brait*,[10] but there is at the beginning of the *Palamède* a precise reference to the final episode of the Post-Vulgate *Mort Artu*, the destruction of Camalot by Mark after Arthur's death:

Et pour che que li rois Artus l' (i.e. Camalot) ama toutes voies sour toutes

---

[1] For references to the dating of the Vulgate Cycle, see above, 5, n. 1.

[2] See Vinaver, *Études*, 23.   [3] Huth *Merlin*, I, lxix.

[4] *Evolution*, I, 479, n. 70.   [5] *Évolution du roman arthurien*, 66.

[6] The Second Version of the prose *Tristan* probably belongs to the second half of the thirteenth century (see Vinaver, *Études*, 28–30).

[7] See above, Ch. IV.   [8] See above, 78

[9] In a letter dated 5 February 1240, the Emperor Frederick II thanks one of his officials, the *secretus* of Messina, for sending him the book of *Palamède* which formerly belonged to Johannes Romanzorius (see Ward, *Catalogue of Romances*, I, 336, and Bruce, *Evolution*, II, 21, including n. 4).

[10] See Huth *Merlin*, I, xxxiii–xxxv.

autres chités, la destruit puis toute et la desoula li felons rois Marc de Cornouaille
aprés [la mort] le roi Artus. Misire Robert de Borron mi compaignon en commencha a dire en son livre cele destruction et celui destruiement, et commencha
a dire la descorde del roi Artus e [de] misire Lancelot et de celui lingnage. Mais
a ceste fois m'en tairai dusqu'a tant que li point viegne del deviser, et retournerai
a ma matire des ore mes.[1]

Two of the *Palamède* MSS. (Arsenal 3325 and Brit. Mus. Add. 12228)
make the allusion to the Post-Vulgate *Mort Artu* even more specific. As we
saw earlier, the author of the Post-Vulgate *Mort Artu* omits most of the
details of the war between Arthur and Lancelot.[2] Now MSS. Arsenal 3325
and Brit. Mus. Add. 12228 add after the word *lingnage* that because Robert de
Boron did not give a detailed account of the war between Arthur and Lancelot,
the author of the *Palamède* will do so; then these two MSS. go on to explain
that Arthur would not have been defeated if Tristan and Palamedes had been
alive at the time:

Por ce qe li rois Artus l'ama toute sa vie sor toutes autres citez, la destruit puis
toute e desola li felons rois Mars de Cornoaille aprés la mort le roi Artus. Missire
Robert de Borron comença adonc en son livre cele destruction e cel deseritemant,
e comença a dire la descorde del roi Artus e de missire Lancelot dou Lac e de
celui lignage. *Mes por ce q'il ne devisa pas apertemant tout celui fet e les granz
ovres qi a celui tens furent fetes entre les compeignons le roi Artus et entre misire
Lancelot del Lac,* le deviserai ge en cest mien livre tout apertemant, se Dex me
done tant de vie, e la grace de mon seignor le roi Henri, qe ge viegne a celui
point (*Add. 12228 adds:* que ge doie cestui fait conter). E sachent tuit qe cele
estoire est mout delitable a escouter e a oïr. Et por ce pramet ge a monseignor *f. 66a*
le roi Henri qe ge le deviserai tout apertemant, qar la furent ovres sanz faille qe
bien doivent savoir tuit bon home qi entendent a pris et a honor. La ont (*Add.
12228:* ot) feites chevaleries. La fu moustree force contre force apertemant, e
gentilece contre gentilece. A celui point se pot bien plaindre li haut linhage le roi
Artus qe li bons Tristains n'estoit mie vis, e qe li preuz Palamedes estoit morz.
Se cist tres dui (*Add. 12228:* cil dui tres) bons chevaliers fussent en vie adont,
bien eust li rois Artus a celui point mis touz ces enemis au desouz. Mes cil dui
buen chevaliers, e non mie buen tant seulement, mes tres buen, estoient ja morz,
einsint cum ge vos deviserai en cest mien livre apertemant. Mes a ceste foiz m'en
terai dusqu'a tant qe li point viegne del deviser, e retornerai a ma matire des
ore mes.[3]

Since the remark to the effect that Robert de Boron did not relate all the

---

[1] MS. B.N. fr. 350, f. 6a; B.N. fr. 338, f. 9a; B.N. fr. 355, f. 72b; B.N. fr. 356,
f. 10c; B.N. fr. 359, f. 25d; Arsenal 3447, f. 21a; Turin MS. L-I-7, f. 56a–b. Cf.
Löseth, *Analyse*, § 630, including n. 5.

[2] See above, 146.

[3] Arsenal MS. 3325, ff. 8d and 61a (the leaf that should follow f. 8d has been
misplaced and inserted after f. 60d, with the result that it bears the number 61);
Brit. Mus. Add. 12228, f. 16d.

exploits *qi a celui tens furent fetes entre les compeignons le roi Artus et entre misire Lancelot del Lac* is in keeping with what we know of the Post-Vulgate *Mort Artu*, it would seem to show that the author of the *Palamède* knew this work.

If, then, we regard the allusion in the *Palamède* as the *terminus ad quem*, the *Roman du Graal* must have been composed between 1230 and 1240.

The date of the Second Redaction of the Post-Vulgate Queste (Z)

The second redaction of the Post-Vulgate *Queste* (*Z*) may be later in date than the prose *Tristan Queste*, for a number of details in *Z* appear to be derived from certain manuscripts of that work. When the compiler of the Second Version of the prose *Tristan* incorporated into his work the Post-Vulgate *Queste* (*Y*), he expanded it by the addition of episodes taken over from the First Version of the prose *Tristan*, and traces of some of these appear in the *Demanda*. For instance, after reproducing the Vulgate account of Arthur's visit to church, the *Tristan Queste* borrows from the First Version of the prose *Tristan* a second account of Arthur's visit to church.[1] Now the *Demanda*, while dealing only once with Arthur's visit to church, bases its account of the episode on the Vulgate, but remodels and expands it with details from the prose *Tristan* account of Arthur's second visit to church. Thus while in the Vulgate Arthur's raiment is not described,[2] the *Demanda* and the second prose *Tristan* account say that Arthur wore his crown and coronation robes.[3] Again, at a later point, after the coming of

---

[1] See above, 91, n. 5.

[2] The Vulgate *Queste* (3, ll. 22–3) only has: 'Et li rois ert alez au mostier por oïr la messe a grant compaignie de hauz homes'.

[3] Sp. *D*, Ch. VI, 165b (*D*, § 8 has omitted some sentences):

El rey fue estonce a oyr la
gran missa a la yglesia con
gran conpaña de caualleros,
que marauilla era de lo ver;
*y el traya estonce corona
e vestio aquellos paños con
que fuera reynado*, e la
reyna otrosi;

*y este guarnimento era tan
rico, que no era sino
marauilla.*

MS. B.N. fr. 755, f. 155a (the
MSS. of the Second Version of
the *Tristan* have the same reading):

Li rois issi de sa chambre
*sa corone d'or en sa teste
vestu de drapeau reals ou
il avoit esté sacrez*. Il
fait devant lui aporter
s'espee et son ceptre......
Aprés eus vont li compaignons
de la Table Reonde, deux et
deux, *si richement
apareillié que ce est
merveille del veoir.*

Galaad, the prose *Tristan Queste* inserts another incident from the First Version, including a passage which occurs in the *Demanda*[1] and in which Arthur rebukes Yseut for her apparent reluctance to let Tristan leave her.

These particular agreements between the prose *Tristan* and the *Demanda* could, of course, be explained on the hypothesis that both used independently the First Version of the prose *Tristan*. There is, however, another episode, the account of Tristan's arrival in the field where the tournament is being held, which suggests clearly that this is not the case. Most of the manuscripts of the prose *Tristan Queste* reproduce the incident verbally from the First Version of the prose *Tristan*, but five of the manuscripts, *THLCJ*, and the *Demanda* greatly expand the account, and the *Demanda* gives exactly the same details as do the French MSS. In the manuscripts of the First Version of the prose *Tristan* and in MSS. *ABFGKMPRUVW*[2] Tristan simply arrives in the field, is welcomed by the people and told that the adventure of the Siege Perilous has been ended. In the *Demanda* and MSS. *THLCJ*, however, Tristan rides towards the field in great haste:[3]

e vinha tam toste, como se tôdolos diaboos do inferno viessem depós êle	Mes bien sachiez *qu'il venoit adonc si grant erre parmi la praierie comme se la foudre le chaçast.*

The king recognizes Tristan's shield and points it out to Lancelot who goes to meet Tristan:

E *el-rei*	*Li rois* qui encor estoit es prez et qui avoit resgardé le borhordeiz o grant compaignie de barons et de chevaliers, se resgarde adont, et
catou o scudo	maintenant *qu'il vit l'escu* que mesire Tristan portoit, il le recognoist, si est assez plus liez et plus joieus qu'il n'estoit devant, car il cognoist veraiement que ce est misire Tristan.
e mostrou-o a Lançalot que cabo dêle stava, e disse-lhe: 'Ora soom ledo e hei grãm sabor, ca vejo aqui viir	*Il le moustre maintenant a Lancelot qui delez lui estoit, et li dist:* 'Or ferons joie. *Vez ci Tristan, le neveu*

---

[1] Cf. Ch. IV, 92.

[2] MSS. B.N. fr. 755, f. 157a, 757, f. 158b, 12599, f. 462c–d; *P*, f. 335b; *V*, f. 80c; *G*, ff. 181d–182a; *K*, f. 169a; *W*, f. 250c; *R*, f. 358d; *A*, f. 567d; *B*, f. 101c; *F*, f. 149d; *U*, f. 155d.

[3] *D*, I, § 23–4; Sp. *D*, Chs. XXI–XXII, 170b–171a; MSS. *T*, ff. 196d–197a; *H*, ff. 420a–b; *C*, f. 204b–c; *J*, f. 5d; *L*, f. 387b–d.

Tristam, *o sobrinho de rei Mars* de Cornualha,

ca bem conheço aquêle scudo, que nom vi depois que me fêz muito pesar.'

E Lançarot começou a ferir *o cavalo das sporas e foi* *contra êle, e disse-lhe, de* *tam longe como pôde entender* que o poderia ouvir: 'Dom Tristam, *vós sejades o* benvindo.' *E Tristam,* que o conhoceu, *salvou-o* e abraçou-o.

le roi *March,* un des chevaliers de mon hostel qui plus fet a prisier de chevalerie. *Je le cognois bien a l'escu.'*

Et lors hurte Lancelot *cheval des esperons et li vient* *a l'encontre et li crie de si* *loing con il le puet entendre:*

'*Misire Tristan, bien soiez vous* *venuz.' Et misire Tristan* s'arreste tout maintenant, *et li rent son* *salu.*

Arthur welcomes Tristan as soon as he arrives and tells him that he alone was needed in order to complete the Round Table:

Em todo êsto, aque-vos *el-rei saiu contra êle, ca* *muito era ledo da sua vinda,*

e disse-lhe: 'Dom Tristam, vós *sejades o benvindo.' E Tristam* *salvou-o mui ensinadamente.* *El-rei lhe disse: 'Dom Tristam,* *eu soom mui ledo da vossa vinda,* *ca nom falecia nhuũ dos* *companheiros da Távola Redonda,* *fora vós.'*

Li rois vint atant cele part *liez et joianz de sa venue,* car de grant cuer amoit Tristan, *si li dist que bien fust il* *venuz.* 'Sire, Dex vous doint honour,' fet Tristan. 'Tristan, fet li rois, *mout sui liez de vostre venue,* *car de touz les compaignons de* *la Table Roonde ne nos failloit* *fors que vous seul.'*

Finally, the other companions join them and all rejoice over Tristan's arrival:

Quando os cavaleiros virom que aquêle era Tristam com que elrei falava, foram pera alá *mui ledos e com mui grã prazer* *da sua viinda...* *Grande foi a alegria e o prazer* *que todos com Tristan houverom.*

Atant assemblent illuec li compaignon qui

mout furent liez de sa *venue.* *Grant est la joie que li* *compaignon de la Table* *Roonde firent.*

It is probable, therefore, that the *remanieur Z* of the Post-Vulgate *Queste* (*Y*) knew a manuscript of the Second Version of the prose *Tristan* closely

related to MSS. *THLCJ* and borrowed from it a few details at the beginning
of the *Queste*.[1]

---

[1] Another possibility is that the Post-Vulgate *Queste* (*Y*) incorporated from
the First Version of the prose *Tristan* the account of Arthur's second visit to
church and of Tristan's arrival in the field, changed the details of the latter
episode and was incorporated in this form into the Second Version of the prose
Tristan. Some manuscripts of the latter then used a manuscript of the First
Version of the prose *Tristan* in addition and replaced the account of Tristan's
arrival in the field by the one from the First Version of the *Tristan*.

APPENDIX II

Extracts from the 'Roman du Graal'

In the following pages will be found four extracts from the *Roman du Graal*. The text has in all cases been established along conservative lines. Abbreviations have been expanded in accordance with the normal graphies of the extracts. The modern distinction of 'i', 'j', 'u', and 'v' has been observed and the use of capital letters has been regularized, as well as the division of words. The acute accent has been used to distinguish final accented 'e' from mute 'e'. It has also been used where 'ee' has been reduced to 'e'. The diaeresis has been used to distinguish two vowels in hiatus from the diphthong represented by the same graphy. The cedilla has been used as in modern French. Unless stated to the contrary, all emendations have been indicated by the use of square brackets. A short note precedes each extract.

The establishment of the Round Table at Camalot, Arthur's marriage and the knighting of Tor (from the Siena MS. of the 'Suite du Merlin')

The establishment of the Round Table in Camalot, the story of Arthur's marriage and the knighting of Tor are found in the Huth, Cambridge and Siena MSS. of the *Suite du Merlin*, as well as in the 1535 Spanish *Baladro*; the 1498 edition of the *Baladro* contains only the last incident.[1] We have reproduced the text of the Siena fragment as it is the oldest MS. of the *Suite du Merlin* so far come to light and contains a state of the text closer to the original than either of the other two manuscripts.[2] All variants from the Huth and Cambridge MSS. have been given, but only selected readings from the Spanish *Baladro*.[3]

The Siena fragment is the only manuscript of the *Suite du Merlin* written mainly in Francien. The language of the Huth scribe has a strong Picard colouring, while that of the Cambridge MS. is distinctly Anglo-Norman. The Siena MS., in contrast, has only a few linguistic peculiarities. The most

---

[1] Huth *Merlin*, II, 64–72 (ff. 148a–151a); Cambridge MS., ff. 281a–283b; Bonilla, 1535 *Baladro*, Ch. CCCI–CCCVI (122a–125b); Bohigas, 1498 *Baladro*, II, 87, l. 60–90, l. 158.

[2] See my article in *R*, LXXXI (1960) 188–98.

[3] The *Baladro* readings are taken from the 1535 edition; readings from the 1498 edition have only been included if they differ from those of the 1535 one.

significant of these is the non-differentiation of *ei* ($<$ *ę* tonic free and *e* + *jod*) to *oi* in a large number of words.[1] This is a characteristic of Western French.[2] Other Western features are the reduction of *ie* to *e* in *chevaucherent*,[3] the form *montes* for *moutes*,[4] the *-ur* ending in *ennur*,[5] the *-om* ending in *avom*, the form *tis* for the nominative second person singular possessive pronoun and the forms *mi*, *si* for the nominative singular of the first and third persons possessive pronoun before a word beginning with a consonant.[6] On the other hand, the raising of the second vowel to *i* in *conissieʒ* (beside *conoissoit*), the reduction of *iee* to *ie* in *comencie*, and the differentiation of *eau* to *iau* in *noviaux*, *biaus* and *viaut* (beside *velt*) are characteristic of the Picard dialect.[7] Another Northern form is *carruie*, where velar *k* has been retained before Gallo-Roman *a*. Other points to note are that *ueu* is not differentiated to *ieu*, but develops to *eu* in *leu* ($<$ *lueu* $<$ *locum*);[8] *a* followed by *n'* intervocalic is written with a palatal glide in *compaignon*, *compaignie*, *gaaignerieʒ* and *Bretaigne*;[9] closed *o* tonic free has remained undiphthongized before *r* in *greignor*, *meillor* (beside *meilleur*), *ennor* (beside *enneur*), *creator* and *douçor*;[10] closed *o* tonic has the graphy *u* in *sun* and *mult*; *vus* is found beside *vos*; *ei*, *e* and *ai* are used interchangeably to denote open *e*;[11] *l* is used as a graphy for *u* in the diphthong *eu* (derived from *e* plus velar vocalized *l*), as in *els*, *cels*, *apparels*, *velt*, *mielʒ*; *an* is used for *en* in *anvoie* (beside *envoia*). Finally in the

---

[1] Thus we find: mei, sei, tei (*beside* toi), seit (*beside* soit), aveit (*beside* avoit), esteit (*beside* estoit), deveit (*beside* devoit), beneisseiz (*beside* benoissoiz), deit honnireit, abaissereit, sereit, porteit, aleit, meteit, vesteit, faiseit, enveisure, reis (*beside* rois), orendroit, veirs, dreit (*beside* droit), fei, quei, reiaumes (*beside* roiaume), seir, ainceis.

[2] See M. K. Pope, *From Latin to Modern French* (Manchester University Press, 1934), §§ 230 i, 1326 vi.

[3] See ibid., §§ 512 and 1326 i.

[4] See ibid., § 464.

[5] In Western French the diphthong *ou* ($<$ *o* tonic free) was not differentiated to *eu*, but levelled to *u* (see Pope, § 1326 v).

[6] We find in the text: tis filz, tis cuers, mi filz, si filz (cf. Pope, § 853).

[7] See Pope, §§ 1320 v, vii, viii and 501. It should be noted, however, that the reduction of *iee* to *ie* and the differentiation of *eau* to *iau* are very common also in Francien texts of the later O.F. period.

[8] Localization doubtful (see Pope, § 557).

[9] This development is fairly common in late texts and is not dialectal (cf. Pope, §§ 1322 xxiii, 1325 xiii, 445).

[10] While the *-or* ending is common in Eastern texts, it is found also frequently in late Francien texts (cf. Pope, §§ 230 ii, 1322 xviii).

[11] Thus we find: mauveis, leisse, neistra, paleis *beside* palés, pleit, devrei, avrei, leienz (*beside* laienz), feit (*beside* fet), fere, afere, pes, vet, baisa, maistre, maigre (cf. Pope, §§ 717, 966).

second person plural of the present subjunctive the etymological *-oiz* ending is found in *sachoiz* (beside *sachiez*), *tenoiz*, *entramoiz*, *benoissoiz*.[1]

The various texts have been designated by the following sigla:

S—Siena fragment
C—Cambridge MS.
H—Huth MS.
D—1535 Spanish *Baladro*
B—1498 Spanish *Baladro*
M—Micha's transcript of the Siena fragment in *R*, LXXVIII (1957) 37–45.[2]

Trois* jorz sejorna Merlin leienz entre lui et sa compaignie. Et quant i, *f. 1a* vint au departir, li rois plora [plus] por les compaignons de la Table Reonde q'il ne fit por sa fille, si les baisa chascun par sei et sa fille aprés. Et s'il ot nul bel joel ne nule bele enveiseure, sachoiz qu'il en envoia au roi

5 Artus. Atant se departirent del roi li message qui la damoisele en menoienti et orent en leur compaignie cels de la Table Reonde, si errerent tant q'il vindrent el roiaume de Logres, et oïrent dire que li rois sejornoit a Londres. Il chevaucherent cele part. Et quant il furent auques pres, Merlin manda au roi qu'il venoit ou tot tel compaignie: bien se gardast q'il venist

---

[1] The *-oiz* ending persisted longest in the Eastern region (see Pope, § 908)
[2] Micha's transcription contains a number of errors, which will be indicated ir the variants.

* The Siena fragment begins in the middle of a sentence: 'li doint force e. pooir qu'il vus puisse maintenir a enneur de lui et de vos'.

[1] *H* laiens Merlins; entre *not in H*; trois .. compaignie *not in C*; second et *not in H*; *HC* quant che (*C* ceo) vint.

[2-3] *H* ploura moult pour les compaignons de la Table Reonde, plus qu'il ne fesist pour sa fille, *C* plura mult tendrement pur les compaignons de la Table Reonde, plus pur eus que pour sa fille, *D* e quando se ouieron de partir, lloro el rey *mas* por los caualleros de la Mesa Redonda que no por su hija. *S as emended is probably the original reading*, plus *dropping out before* por *by homoeoarcheion*. *CH go back to a badly elaborated reading: their common source inserted* moult (tendrement) *after* ploura *and then placed* plus *after* Reonde, *but in doing so produced a non-sequitur. C further altered the text by adding* pur eus *after* plus *and changing* q'il ne fit por sa fille *to* que pour sa fille.

[3] *M* que ne fit.

[4] *H* s'il i ot; *H* biel jovenchiel; *M* enveisure; *H* sachiés, *C* sachez; *H* il les envoia, *C* il envoia; *C* au roi Arthur en present e par chierté.

[5] *C* s'en partirent; *C* que; *C* en mainent.   [6] *H* ichiaus de la Table.

[7] *H* ou roiaume; *C* sojornoit a Logres.

[8] *C* e il chevauchoient; *M* onque pres.

[9] *C* venist; *H* o tele, *C* atut tel; se *not in C*.

10 encontre liement et a grant feste. Et quant li rois oï parler que li compaignon de la Table Reonde venoient a sa cort por demorer avec lui, si en fu
tous liez, car il ne desiroit riens del siegle autant com ce q'il les eust en sa
compaignie. Lors eissi de Londres ou tot grant gent et ala encontre, si les
reçut toz ou reiste grant ennur. Et si grant joie leur fit et si grant feste qu'il
15 se tenoient a bien euré de ce qu'il estoient cele part venu. Li aparels des
noces fu fez et li termes mis et li jors nomez qu'eles seroient. Et Merlin dist
au roi:

— Rois, eslis de tote ta terre les meilleur cinquante chevaliers que tu i
savras, et se tu sez aucun chevalier preudome de cors et vassal, ne leisse
20 mie por povreté que tu ne l'i metes. Et se aucuns qui seit bien gentis hom
et de haut lignage i velt estre et il ne seit tres bons chevaliers, garde que
tu ne sueffres ja // qu'il i seit, car il seux, puis q'il ne sereit de grant *f.* 1*b*
chevalerie, honnireit et abaissereit tote l'autre compaignie.

— Merlin, fet li rois, vos conissiez mielz chascun que ge ni faz, et les
25 boens chevaliers et les mauveis. Vos meismes eslissiez cels que vos quide-
roiz qui mielz en soient digne.

---

¹⁰⁻¹¹ *H* li compaignie de la T. R., *C* li chevalier de la T. R.

¹¹ *H* venoit; *CH* lui, il en fu.

¹² *C* mult lez; *C* riens tant au siecle com. *M* rien.

¹³ *C* issi de Logres; *H* a tout; *C* od tut grant compaignie; et ala encontre *not
in C.*

¹⁴ *M* ou mult grant; *H* rechuit tous a moult grant hounour, *C* resceut tuz a
mult grant joie et a mult grant honur, *D* recibio-los con tan gran honra. *Godefroy
has* 'roiste' *only in the sense of* 'escarpé', 'rude', 'raide'. *The ei spelling of S is
probably a Western feature. There are no other examples, as far as I know, of*
'roiste' *being used in the sense of* 'moult'; *H* lour fist; et si grant joie. . feste *not in*
C; *C* si qu'il se tenoient.

¹⁵ *C* estoient la venu.

¹⁶ *C* lui termes; *M* nomez qu'eles sero[n]t feites et.

¹⁸ *S—the MS. does not write* cinquante *in full, but has* .l.; *H* les cinquante
millours; cinquante *not in C.*

¹⁸⁻¹⁹ *C* tu saveras.

¹⁹ *C* si tu; *H* auchun povre chevalier, *C* aucun chevalier povr; *C* qui soit
preudome; *H* et de vasselage; *M* prudome.

²⁰ *CH* por sa poverté (*H* povreté), *D* por toda su pobreza; *C* si aucun; hom
not in CH.

²¹ *C* de grant lignage; i *not in CH*; *C* e veut.

²² *C* gardez que vus ne soffrés; *H* qu'il i soient; *H* car uns seuls, *M* car il
feire puis.

²²⁻³ *C* puis qu'il n'est bons chevaliers honieroit, *H* de si grant chevalerie; *H*
abaisseroit toute chevalerie de la compaignie.

²⁴ *C* conoissez; *CH* jeo (*H* je) ne fais.

²⁵ *C* si eslisiez vus meismes ceus; *C* qui vus quidiez; *H* cuideriés, *M* cuideroiz.

²⁶ *C* qui meuz vaillent e qui plus i sont dignes d'estre mis.

— Or, fet Merlin, puis que vos sor mei metez cest afere, je l'acheverai en
tel maniere que ge n'en devrei estre blasmez. Et je les avrei tost esleuz si
qu'il seront mis en leur sieges le jor que vos feroiz vos noces. Et en tel
30 maniere sera la feste doblee: et de vos noces et de la Table Reonde qui sera
enterine.

Lors manda li rois par son roiaume toz les preudomes qui tenoient de
lui terre qu'il venissent au jor nomé a Chamahaloth a la feste de sa femme.
Et cil vindrent au plus esforciement q'il porent. Et quant il furent venu, li
35 rois dist a Merlin:

— Pensez de la Table Reonde.

— Si ferai je, fist Merlins.

Et lors commença par leienz a eslire les chevaliers, cels q'il conoissoit a
plus preudomes. Et quant il en ot esleu dusqu'a quarante et uit, il les mist a
40 une part et leur dist:

— Des ore mes covient il que vos vos entramoiz et tenoiz chiers come
freres, car por l'amor et por la [douceur] de cele table ou vos seroiz assis
vos neistra [el cuer] une si grant joie et une si grant amistié que vos en
lerroiz voz femes et voz enfanz por estre l'un avec l'autre, et por user
45 ensemble voz jovences. Et neporquant, ja vostre table ne sera a mon tens
del tot parfete ne asoumee devant que a cest leu se vendra aseoir li boens

---

27 HC ore soit (C sait): H et puis que vous dou tout vous en metés sour moi
de cest, C puis que vus vus en mettez sor moi; cest afere not in C.

28 H que ja n'en devrai; H tous esleus.

29 H ferés, C freez; et not in C.

30 et not in C; C doble; et en tel. . vos noces not in H; M doble; CH et de ceo
que la haute table; qui not in CH.

30-31 C serra entiere e emplie; D y en tal guisa sera la honrada fiesta acabada.

32 C a atant mandé; C tuz les barons qui; H de li tenoient, C de li tienent;
M prudomes.

33 H en la terre de Camalaoth; C a la feste de ces noces, D a sus bodas.

34 H cil i vindrent, C e il vindrent; M ou; H il i furent.

35 C dist Merlins; H fait Merlins.

38 C e li rois comence; C les meillors chevaliers; cels not in C; C as plus.

39 en not in C; M prudomes; H jusques a; S—quarante et uit. The MS. has
·xlviii·.

40 C lor dist, H lors mist.

41 C vus covient; H entramés, C entreamez; H et vous tenés chiers, C e aiez
chier l'un vers l'autre com frere.

42 S por la dolor, C la douçur, H la douchour, D por el sabor; H serés, C serrez.

43 C naistra el quer, H naistera es cuers, D crescera en vuestros coraçones. The
emendation of S is based on C.

44 C larrés, H lairés.

45 C vos jovens; H nonpourquant.

46 C en ceste leu.

chevaliers, li meillors des boens, cil qui metra a fin les perilleuses aventures
del roiaume de Logres la ou tuit li autre faudront.

    Et lors vient as cent et cinquante sieges de fust que li reis Artus aveit fet
50 fere toz noviaux, si vint au siege dou mi leu et le mostra au roi Artus // et *f.* 1c
a toz les autres qui leienz estoient, chevaliers et dames et leur dist:

    — Vez ci le Siege Perilleus. [Aiiés le bien en memoire aprés ma mort
que je ensi l'ai apelé.

    Li rois demande a Merlin:
55   — Merlin, pour coi l'avés vos apelé perilleus?]

    — Sire, por ce qu'il i a si grant peril que ja chevalier ne s'i aserra qui
ne muire ou qui ne seit mahaigniez dusqu'a tant que li tres boens chevaliers
viendra qui metra a fin les merveilleuses aventures dou roiaume de Logres.
Cil s'i aserra et repossera, mes ce ne sera mie lonc tens.

60   — Et coment avra il non? dit li reis.

    — Sire, ce ne vos descovrerai ge pas, car vos ne gaaigneriez riens se vos
orendreit le saviez, mes tant vos di je bien que cil de cui il istra n'a encor
pas deus anz d'aage.

    — Donc ne sera ce a piece, ce dit li reis, que cil chevaliers viegne qui
65 deit cest siege acomplir.

    — Veirs est, ce dit Merlin. Ge meimes me tenisse a bien eurez se ge
peusse celui veoir qui l'acomplira, car en cest paleis avra adonc joie si

---

[47] *H* li mieudres des boins; *H* chis qui; *C* a fin les merveilles aventures.

[49] *S*—cent et cinquante. *The MS. has* ·c·l; *HC* vint; *C* vint Merlin a cent e cinquante; *C* fust qu'il avoit fait.

[50] *C* vient; *HC* d'en mi leu; *H* les moustra.

[51] *H* estoiens; *C* dames e damoiseles.

[52-5] *H* 'Veschi le Siege Perilleus. Aiiés le bien en memoire apriés ma mort que je ensi l'ai apielé.' Li rois demande a Merlin: 'Merlin, pour coi l'avés vous apielé perilleus?' *C has the same homoeoteleuton as S, but D agrees with H.*

[56] *C* se aserra; *H* n'i muire; *CH* qu'il.

[57] *CH* ni soit; *H* jusques a tant, *C* desques autant; tres *not in C.*

[58] *H* tres merveilleuses.

[59] *H* s'i assaiera, *C* se aserra; *C* e li apposera.

[60] *CH* dist.

[61] sire *not in CHD*; *H* n'i gaaignieriés, *C* n'i gaignerez; *C* si orendroit.

[62] *H* n'a pas encore.

[62-3] *C* de qui il naistra n'est encore pas de mult grant aage, ne point de femme n'a. *D agrees with SH.*

[64] *H* dist, *C* fait li rois; *H* chis chevaliers.

[64-5] *C* veigne qui ceste siege doit emplir.

[65] *H* cesti siege; *S* siegne *for* siege.

[66] *CH* dist; *H* je endroit de moi me tenisse; *C* m'en tenisse.

[66-7] *C* si jeo puis.

[67] *HC* chelui (*C* celi) jour veoir que che (*C* qu'il) sera acompli, *D* aquel dia ver que sera conplida; *H* en cest païs avera anon, *D* en esta tierra.

grant que devant ne aprés n'avra autretele. Et entre celui jor et l'autre ou
tu orras noveles de ton grant [duel], avra grant terme. Mes aprés celui jor
70 que ge te devis ne vivras tu mie longuement, car li granz dragons que tu
veïs en ton songe te metra a destruiement.

— Or m'avez bien paié, Merlin, fet li reis, qui en ma grant joie me
ramente[v]ez mon grant duel.

— Je le faz, dit Merlin, por ce que [se] en totes tes granz joies te
75 sovenoit de cele dolereuse jornee, tu en seroies plus humilianz vers ton
Creator qui en ceste hautece te mist ou tu ies, et plus t'en doteroies, si en
pecheroies mains que tu ne feras.

Ensint dist Merlin au rei. Et quant il ot esleuz les quarante et uit
chevaliers, il apela les autres cent chevaliers et [leur] dist:
80 — Veez ci voz freres, que je vos ai esleuz. Nostre Sire mete pes et
concorde entre vos ausint com il fist entre ses apostres.

Et lors les fist toz entrebaisier et apela les evesques et les arcevesques
dou païs et dist:

— Il covient que vos beneisseiz ces sieges ou // cist preudome seront, *f.* 1*d*
85 et il est bien droiz, car maint chevalier de haute vie et de glorieuse a Deu et
au siegle s'i aserra encor. Por ce est il bien dreiz que vos le [leu] benoissoiz,
et Nostre Sire, par sa grace et par sa douçor, s'il Li pleit, l[e] saintefiera.

---

[68] *H* ni aprés; *C* aprés li ni avera; jor *not in H*; et l'autre *not in C*; ou *not in H*.

[69] *CH* grant doel (*H* duel), *D* gran pesar; *C* ou tu averas noveles; *C* grant
terre; *M* aura terme; jor *not in CH*.

[70] *C* car li serpent que tu voies. *D* la gran serpiente.

[71] *H* en destruisement, *M* destruiment.

[72] Merlin *not in C*; *C* que en ma.

[73] *H* ramentevés, *C* rementivés, *S* ramenteriez. *The verbs* ramentever *and*
ramenter *have the same sense, but the conditional of S is clearly an error.*

[74] *CH* jeo le fais; *C* fait Merlin, *H* che dist Merlins; *H* pour chou que se (*C also
omits* se); totes *not in C*.

[75] *C* cele grant doloruse jornee; *C* en serras.

[76] *C* creature; *C* tu es; *C* t'en douteras.

[77] *C* e en peccheras; que tu ne feras *not in C*.   [78] *CH* ensi.

[78-9] *S does not write the numbers in full, but has* ·xlviii· *and* ·c·.

[79] cent chevaliers *not in C*; chevaliers *not in H*; *S* et les dist; *CH* lor (*H* lour) dist.

[80] *H* veschi; *H* et Nostre Sires; *H* meche.

[81] entre vos *not in C*; *H* aussi comme, *C* autresi com; *HC* apostles.

[83] *CH* lor (*H* lour) dit, *D* dixoles.

[84] *H* que vous il couvient que poursingniés et benissiés *C* il covient que vus
purseignés e benissiez, *D* conuiene que los bendigays e los santiguays; *S* ou ou;
H cil preudoume; *M* ou cest.

[85] *H* il en est; *H* que maint; *H* et a Dieu.

[86] *C* e encore; *C* si est il; *M* asserra; *H* que vous le lieu benissiés, *C* que vus
benoissez le leu, *D* e tanbien el lugar.

[87] *S* la saintefiera, *CH* le saintefiera.

Lors fit les chevaliers asseoir chascun en son leu et fit metre par devant
els la Table Reonde. Et li arcevesqes de Cantorbiere fit maintenant desus
90 els la beneizon, et li autre clergié qui la estoient assemblee firent oreison et
priere a Nostre Seigneur que Il des or en avant les tenist en bone pes et en
bone concorde, ausi com frere germain doivent estre. Quant li clergié
orent ce fet, Merlin fit drecier ces chevaliers et dit:
— Il covient que vos faciez homage au rei Artus qui est vostre compainz
95 de ceste table. Et quant vos li avriez fet homage, il vos jurera sor sainz
qu'il des or en avant vos maintendra a si grant ennor com il porra tot son
aage.
Et il responnent que de ce fere sunt il tuit apareillié, si se drecierent
erramment et s'en alerent dreit vers le rei por lui fere homage. Et en ce
100 qu'il avoient leur sieges voidiés, Merlin regarde ça et la et trove en
chascun siege le non de celui qui assis s'i estoit. Et disoient les letres: 'Ci
deit seoir cil, et ci endroit cil autres.' Et ensi estoit seigniez chascun siege,
ne mes cil de mi leu et li darreeins. En ces deus n'avoit encor [nu]lui assis.
Et quant Merlin vit les letres, il dist as barons qui laienz estoient:
105 — Par fei, seigneur, merveilles poez ci veoir bien apert, qu'a Nostre
Seigneur plest que einsint soient assis cist preudome com nos les avom
ordenez, car il i a en chascun siege envoié le non tot escrit de celui qui ci
doit seoir. Beneoite soit l'eure que // ceste oevre fu comencie, car de cest *f. 2a*
s[i]gne ne puet venir se trop bien non.

⁸⁸ *CH* fist.
⁸⁹ *H* Cantorbile, *C* Cantorbire, *D* Conçurbel; *C* fist; *H* fist sour eus maintenant; *M* arcevesques.
⁹⁰ qui la estoient assemblee *not in H*.
⁹² *H* frere germain pueent estre et doivent; *C* doivent estre bon ami; *C* la
clergié. *D* assi como a buenos hermanos devian ser.
⁹³ *CH* fist; *C* adrescier; *S* cest chevaliers, *CH* les chevaliers, *D* todos los
caualleros; *CH* dist.   ⁹⁴ *C* compaignes.
⁹⁵ table *not in H*; *H* et quant et quant; *H* avrés, *C* averez.
⁹⁸ *CH* respondent; *CH* sont il tut (*H* tout) prest.
⁹⁹ dreit *not in CH*; *C* s'en alerent tuz vers le roi; *C* li faire.
¹⁰¹ *C* chescun lieu; s'i *not in H*; s' *not in C*.
¹⁰² *H* endroit seoir chis autres; et ci endroit cil autres *not in C*; *H* singniés,
C seigné.
¹⁰³ *C* ne mais que cil, *H* ne mais chis; *CH* d'en mi leu; *H* li darrainniers, *C* li
daarraine; *S* encor celui assis, *HC* encore nului (*C* nuli), *D* no auia seydo ninguno
en ellas.
¹⁰⁴ *C* voit.   ¹⁰⁵ ci *not in C*; *H* apertes.
¹⁰⁶ *HC* ensi; *H* chi preudoume, *C* cil p.; *M* cest.
¹⁰⁷ tot escrit *not in C*; *H* qui i doit, *C* qui se doit.
¹⁰⁸ beneoite soit l'eure *not in H*; *H* lors que ceste œvre.
¹⁰⁹ *S* sagne, *H* signe, *M* seigne; *C* car il n'en poet venir; *C* si trop grant bien,
H se tres bien.

110 Quant cil dou palés oïrent ceste novele, il corrurent et ça et la par les sieges por veoir se ce esteit voirs. Et quant il l'aparçurent, il distrent: 'A Nostre Seigneur pleit ceste compaignie et granz biens en avendra. Beneoiz soit par cui ele fu comencié, car toz li reiaumes de Logres en sera cremuz et redotez tant com il voudront estre a un acort.'

115 Ceste chose tindrent a grant merveille tuit li sage home et distrent que se ce ne fust chose qui a Nostre Seigneur pleust, ja tel merveille ne fust venue. Et li compaignon de la Table Reonde vindrent maintenant devant le roi et li firent homage. Et il les reçut com ses homes de par sa terre et com ses homes de par la Table Reonde. Et il en estoit compainz ausi com

120 li autre, car Merlin l'i aveit mis por la bonté de chevalerie qu'il sentoit en lui, et l'aveit assis dreit el comencement de la table. Quant ceste chose fu ensin faite, Gauvain, qui estoit assez biax damoisiaux, vint au roi son oncle et li dit:

— Sire, ge vos requier por Deu que vos me doigniez un don.

125 Et il li otroie, se ce est chose qu'il puisse avoir.

— Sire, montes merciz, fet Gauvain. Or m'avez mult servi a gré. Et savez vos de quei? De cei que vos me feroiz chevalier au jor de vostre grant joie, c'est au jor que vos esposeroiz la vaillant Guenievre.

Et li rois dit que ce li pleist bien, puis qu'il le viaut.

130 Celui seir veilla Gauvain a la maistre eglise de Saint Estiene de Camahaloth et avec lui dusqu'a dis autres damoisiaux que li reis deveit toz fere

---

110 _C_ cil del païs oïrent; _C_ ces noveles; _CH omit_ et _before_ ça.   111 _C_ si ceo.
111 _H_ quant il aperchuirent, _C_ il aparceurent ceo; _C_ si distrent, _H_ il disent.
112 _C_ avient.
112–13 _C_ e benoit soient tut cil par qui conseille ele comença, _H_ par cui conseil ele commencha, _D_ e bendito sea por cuyo consejo fue começada.
114 _C_ doutés; _H_ vaurront; _C_ estre ami a un acord.
115 _H_ tinrent il; home _not in C_; _H_ disent.
116 _C_ si ceo; _C_ que a Nostre S; _C_ n'en fust.
117 _CH_ avenue.
118 _C_ resceust.
119 com ses homes _not in C_; _H_ ensi.
120 _H_ l'avoit; _C_ de la chevalerie que en lui estoit (qu'il sentoit en lui _not in C_).
122 _CH_ ensi; _C_ fait; assez _not in CH_.
123 _CH_ dist.
124 _C_ requere; _C_ doignez.
125 _C_ si ceo; _H_ que il le puisse, _C_ qu'il poet avoir ne faire, _DB_ si era cosa que pudiesse fazer.
126 _H_ sire, grans merchis, _C_ sire, vostre merci; _C_ fait il.
127 _C_ de ceo, _H_ de chou; _HC_ ferés.
128 c'est _not in H_; c'est au jor _not in C_; _H_ espouserés, _C_ espuserez.
129 _CH_ dist; _H_ plaisoit; _H_ veult, _C_ veut.
130 _H_ Estevene, _C_ Esteven, _D_ Esteuan, _B_ Ostiano; _C_ desques a _H_ jusques a.
131 _S does not write_ dis _in full, but has_ ·x·; _C_ ·xx· autres; _C_ qui.

chevaliers por l'amor de Gauvain, son neveu. A l'endemain, si tost com li
rois fu levez et li baron comencie//rent a assembler el palés, atant e vos *f. 2b*
laienz venir seur un maigre et las roncin trotant un vilain qui amenoit un
135 suen fil juene enfant de l'aage de quinze anz seur un povre jument. Il vint
el palés tot ensint monté com il estoit entre lui et sun fil et se mist entre les
barons, n'il ne trova home qui la porte li contredeist. Et il comença a
demander li quex estoit li reis Artus. Et uns vallez saut avant, si li mostre.
Et cil s'en vet dusqe pres de lui tot ensi monté com il estoit, et si filz
140 ausi. Et cil salue le roi et dit oiant toz cels de la cort:

    — Rois Artus, a toi m'anvoie la bone renomee qui cort de tei et pres et
loing, car tuit dient communelment que nus ne vient a tei si desconseillié
que tu nel conseilles, ne nus n'est si hardiz [de toi demander aucun don que
tu ne soies aussi hardis] de doner, por quei tu soies puissanz d'avoir ce que
145 l'en te demande. Et por ceste novele que l'en m'en a dite sui ge venuz a
tei que tu me doignes un don tel com gel te demanderai. Et saches que cil
dons ne te puet de riens nuire.

    Li reis regarde le vilain qui si sagement parole, si se merveille q'il
viaut requerre. Et li vilains li dit tote voies:
150   — Rois, doinras me tu ce que ge te demande?

    — Certes, oïl, ce dit li reis, por quei ge soie puissanz del doner.

---

[132] *C* l'amur G.; son neveu *not in C.*

[133] *C* lui baron.

[134] laienz *not in H*; *C* un maigre rouncin las e trottant.

[135] *CH* jovene; *S does not write quinze in full,* but *has* ·xv·; *CH* une povre;
C il vient laienz.

[136] el palés *not in C*; *H* ensi, *C* ausi; *C* entre li.

[137] *C* ces barons; *HC* barons et ne trouva; *H* contredist, *C* contredesit (*sic*).

[138] *H* est li rois; *HC* et li moustre.

[139] tot *not in C*; *C* issi montez; *HC* ses fius (*C* filz).

[140] *C* e il salue; *CH* dist.

[141] *H* Artus, a vous m'envoie.

[142] *H* communaument; *C replaces* communelment *by* apertement; *H* vient si
desconsilliés a toi.

[144] *HC* hardis de toi (*C* a) demander auchun (auchun *not in C*) don que tu ne
soies aussi hardis dou donner; *D agrees with CH. The omission in S has been caused
by a saut du même au même; H* pour coi, *C* pur que.

[145] *H* chou que on te, *C* ceo que home te; *H* que on on, *C* que hom m'a dite.

[146] *H* tel que je le te, *C* tel com jeo le te; *C* sachez; *H* chis dons.

[147] de *not in CH.*

[148] *C* si s'en merveille, *H* si s'esmerveille; *CH* que il veut.

[149] *CH* dist.

[150] *H* rois, me donras tu por coi je sui cha venus? *DB* rey Artur (Artur *not in
B*), darme has lo (*B* por lo) que a ti (a ti *not in B*) vine?; *C* rois, tut vois dorras.

[151] *CH* oïl, dist; *C* puis que (*in place of* por quei); *C* jeo en soie; *H* de douner,
C du doner.

Et cil saut erraument de son roncin et l'en vet baisier le pié, et autresi fet li filz, et l'en mercient ambedui. Et lors dit li vilains au roi:

— Savez vos, sire, qe vos m'avez doné? Que vos feroiz hui en cest jor 155 mon fil chevalier, que vos ci veez, et li ceindrez l'espee au costé ainceis que a Gauvain vostre neveu.

Et li rois li otroie tout en sorriant et dit:

— Je le te doig, mes ge te pri que tu me dies qui t'a doné cest conseill, car il ne me semble mie que tu deussez baer a si haute chose com est 160 chevalerie, ne tis filz ne s'en deust ja entremetre.

— Certes, sire, fet li preudom, ausint me semble il, mes mi filz qui ci est m'en feit parler ou // je voille ou non, car a ma volenté ne baast il ja a si *f. 20* grant chose com est ceste, ainz fust home laborant ausint com sunt si frere et vesquist de son travaill ausint com font si autre parent. Mes il onques por 165 parole que je li die ne s'i velt consentir ne acorder for a estre chevalier.

Et li rois dit que ceste chose tient il a grant merveille. Et puis redemande au vilain:

— Di mei tot ton estre et quanz enfanz tu as.

Et cil respont:

170 — Sire, je le vos dirai. Sachiez que je sui uns laboranz de terre et main ma carruie, et en laborant et en coutivant ma terre aquier je mon vivre et le sostenemenz de mes enfanz.

---

[152] *H* et cil si saut errant, *C* erraument jus; *CH* et li vait; *C* baisier le soulier.
[153] *CH* fist son filz (*H* ses fiex), *D* su hijo; *second* et *not in H*; *CH* dist.
[154] *H* sire, savez vous que vous m'avés douné? Vous m'avés douné que vous ferés, *C* vous m'avez doné? Ceo est que vus ferez, *D* Señor, sabed que don os demando: que fagays, *B* Señor, la merced, que os pido es que fagays; en cest jor *not in C*.
[155] *H* que vous veés ichi; *C* caindras; *C* ainz que; *M* cendrez.　　[156] a *not in H*.
[157] en *not in H*; *CH* dist.
[159] *H* car il me samble que tu ne deusses pas baer; *C* tu le deussez; est *not in C*.
[160] *CH* tes filz (*H* fiex); *C* ne se deust.
[161] sire *not in CH*; *CH* aussi; *H replaces* semble il *by* fait il; *M* prudom; *HC* mes fiex (*C* filz).
[162] *H* m'en parole voelle ou non, *C* m'en somont voil jeo ou non, *D* mas mi fijo me faze fablar, *B* mas mi fijo me lo faze fazer; *S* ill; *H* baast il pas; ja *not in H*.
[163] com est ceste *not in C*; *C* ausi; ausint *not in H*.
[164] *C* travail si com, *H* aussi coume; autre *not in C*.
[164–5] *H* onques pour chose que je li deisse; *DB* de cosa que le diga.
[165] *C* ne se veot; consentir ne *not in C*.
[166] *first* et *not in H*; *H* dist; *C* tint.
[168] tot *not in H*.
[170] *C* sachez; *C* jeo sui home laborans.
[170–1] *C* maine jeo meisme ma carue.
[171] en laborant. . aquier je *not in C*; *H* acquier jou le vivre, *C* gaigne le vivre.
[172] *C* le sustenance de moi e de mes enfanz.

— Et quanz enfanz as tu? dit li rois.

— Sire, ge en ai treize. Li doze laborent por leur vivre et se tienent a
175 ma maniere, mes cist ne s'i viaut acorder en nule guise, ainz dit q'il ne sera
ja se chevalier non. Ne sai dom cist corages li puet avenir.

Et lors commencent a rrire tuit li baron dou palés qui ceste parole
entendirent. Et li rois qui mult estoit sages, ne ne tient mie ceste chose a
gas, dit au vallet:
180 — Biaus amis, viaus tu estre chevaliers?

Et cil respont:

— Sire, il n'a riens el monde que ge desirasse autant com estre chevalier
de vostre main et estre compainz de la Table Reonde.

— Or te face Dieus preudome, ce dit li rois, que tu bees a mult greignor
185 chose que ti autre frere ne font. Et certes tu ne [me] requiers chose que ge
ne te face. Et ge quit se gentillece ne te venist d'aucune partie, ja tis cuers
ne se traisist a si haute chose com est chevalerie. Or doinst Deus qu'elle i
soit bien enploiee, car il n'avra hui chevalier fet ceienz devant que tu [le]
soies.
190 Et li vallez l'en mercie mult.

A ces paroles vint laienz Gauvain et si compeignon. Et quant li rois les
vit, si les apela mult bel et les fit avant venir, si fit aporter robes et armeures *f. 2d*
et espees et les fit toz vestir, // le vallet avant et Gauvain et les autres

---

¹⁷³ *H* dist.

¹⁷⁴ sire *not in CH*; *C* e li ·xii·; *S does not write treize in full, but has* ·xiii·; *C* en
labourent; *H* pour pour.

¹⁷⁴⁻⁵ *C replaces* se tienent a ma maniere *by* sont a ma volunté.

¹⁷⁵ *H* mais icil; *C* ne se volt; *CH* dist; ne *not in C*.

¹⁷⁶ ja *not in CHD*; *C* si; *H* chis corages; *CH* puet venir.

¹⁷⁷ *S* lors lors; *H* tout a rire li baron, *C* a rire tut cil du palais.

¹⁷⁸ *C* parole oïrent; *M* entendent; *CH omit one* ne; *C* tint.

¹⁷⁹ *H* si dist, *H* ainz dit.

¹⁸² sire *not in C*; *C* certes, oïl, il n'est riens; ge *not in C*; *H* desire, *C* tant desir
com.

¹⁸⁴ ce *not in CH*; *H* dist, *C* fait li rois; *C* car tu; *M* prudome; mult *not in H*.

¹⁸⁵ *C* frere ne beent; *first* et *not in H*; *CH* ne me requeres (*H* requiers).

¹⁸⁶ *C* quit si de gentilesse, *H* cuic que se; *HC* tes cuers (*C* quers).

¹⁸⁷ *H* ne te traisist, *DB* tu coraçon no te traeria (*B* incitaria); est *not in CH*;
H comme a chevalerie; *H* Diex que il soit.

¹⁸⁸ *CH* il n'i; *C* averoit; *H* chevalier chaiens fait, *C* hui cainz fait chevalier;
HC tu le soies.   ¹⁹² *C* apele; *C* fist.

¹⁹²⁻³ *H* biel et lour dist: 'Venés avant et aportés reubes et dras et armes et
espees.' Et lour fist tous vestir reubes, et le vallet; *C* e lor fist tost vestir des robes
e dona armes tut avant au vallet e a Gauvain e puis as autres; *DB* llamo-los e
fizolos venir ante si, e hizolos (*B* fizolos) vestir de (*B* paños e de) armas, e al
moço (*B* al nino labrador) ante, y despues a Galuan, e despues (despues *not in B*,
a los otros.

aprés. Et au tens de lors estoit costume en la Grant Bretaigne que quant
195 l'en faiseit chevalier novel l'en li vesteit cote de samit blans et puis le
hauberc, et li meteit l'en l'espee en la main. Et en tel maniere aleit il oïr la
messe en quel que leu q'il fust. Et quant il avoit oïe messe et il s'en deveit
revenir, adonc li ceingnoit cil l'espee qui chevalier le devoit fere. En tel
maniere com alors estoit costume furent atorné li novel chevalier. Et
200 alors estoit li jorz que li rois Artus devoit esposer sa feme et li chevalier de
la Table Reonde se devoient entrefiancier que ja mes ni faudront li uns as
autres, ainz s'entreporteront leial compaignie tant com il vivront. Li rois
fu apareilliez et la reine ausint et li novel chevalier et li autre, si alerent en
tel maniere a la mestre iglise de la cité a tel joie et a tel feste que ge ne vos
205 savroie tenir comte de greigneur. A cele feste ot rois et dux et comtes tant
que ce ne fu se merveille non. Et fu celui jor la reine sacree avec li rei
Artus en la cité de Camahaloth, et porterent ambedui corone. Et a celui
tens sanz faille estoit la reine Genievre la plus bele damoisele que l'en
seust en tot le monde. Et quant la messe fu chantee et il furent issuz del
210 mostier et venu el paleis, li rois demande au vilain:

— Comment as tu non?

— Sire, je ai non Arés li vachierz.

— Et tis filz coment a non?

---

194 *H* des lors, *C* de donc; *C* costume el realme de Logres e en tut la Grant
Bretaigne.

194–5 *H* quant on, *C* quant hom.

195 *H* nouviel on le, *C* novel home le; *H* viestoit tout de blanc samit, *C* vestoit
d'un samit blanc, *D* vestian saya de xamete blanco, *B* vestian de xamete sobre
el armes.

196 *C* le hauberc desus; *H* metoit on, *C* mettoit home; *C* s'espee; et *not in C*;
H en tel maniere aloit on oïr le messe en tel maniere.

197 *C* la messe on que ceo fust, *H* en quel conques lieu que; *H* quant il l'avoit
oïe; *M* avoit oï [l]e messe; messe *not in HC*.

198 *H* venir; et il s'en devoit revenir *not in C*; *C* donc; *C* s'espee.

199 *H* lors, *C* adonc.

200 *H* et adont estoit, *C* e adonc fust; *C* devoit estre espusee a Guenievre e li
chevalier.

201 ja mes *not in H*; *C* ne faudroient, *H* que il ne faurront; *C* lui un a l'autre.

202 *C* s'entreporteroient.

203 *H* et tout li nouviel chevalier; *C* lui autre.

204 de la cité *not in H*.

205 *H* tenir parole de tel gringnour, *C* tenir parole de greignor joie; *C* out dux
e rois e contes.

206 *C* ceo ne fust; *C* si merveille; *H* la roine Gennevre. *DB* la reyna Ginebra.

208 *C* estoit sanz faille; *H* que on seust, *C* home seust.

209 *C* par tut le monde; *H* et il fu issus.

212 *H* j'ai a non. *D* Dares el Barquito, *B* Ares el Vaquero.

213 *CH* tes fiz (*H* fiex).

— Sire, il a non Tor.
215   — Or avra non, ce dit li rois, Tor, li filz Arés.
Si li dit a tel eur qe puis ne li cheï cist nons. Et lors prent l'espee que cil
porteit et li done la colee.

The Dolorous Stroke (*from MS. Cambridge Add. 7071, ff. 269c–272a*)

Until the discovery of the Cambridge MS. in 1945 by Professor Vinaver, the
greater part of the episode of the Dolorous Stroke was known only through
the 1535 Spanish *Baladro** and Malory's adaptation. The Huth MS. has a
lacuna for the greater part of the narrative.

Most of the Cambridge MS. was copied in the fourteenth century, but
some leaves, including those containing the Dolorous Stroke episode, date
from the fifteenth century. The language of both scribes is distinctly Anglo-
Norman. In transcribing the text, no attempt has been made to rationalize the
spellings. Variants from the *Baladro*, and the Huth MS. as far as extant, have
only been given when they help us to establish the text of the Cambridge
MS. As the graphy *vus* predominates, *v'* has always been expanded to *vus*.
The following sigla have been used:

C—Cambridge MS.
H—Huth MS.
Sp. *D*—Spanish *Demanda del Sancto Grial*.

Cele nuit fut mult a aise li Chevalier as ·ii· Espeez et mult bien harber-
giez, et fu mult liez de cez novellez qu'il avoit laeinz apresez. Au matin, si
tost cum il fu ajorné, il se leva et oï messe laeinz meismes ou il avoit une
petite chapele. Aprez s'arma et monta en son chival et se mist au chimin
5   enter lui et la damoisel et son oste. Ensi chivalchierent ensambel tout la
semaine, et l'auter aprez, sannz aventour trover que ome doie en conte

---

214 *H* a a non; sire il a non *not in C.*
215 *H* avra a non, dist; ce dit li rois *not in C*; *H* li fiex a Arés, *C* Tor, filz Arez.
216 *HC* si le dist; *HC* chaï, *M* n'en cheï, *H* chis, *C* cil, *M* cest.
217 *H* chis portoit; *S* breaks off in the middle of a sentence: 'Et sachent tuit
cil qui ceste estoire escoutent que li premiers hom qui done colee a chevalier
novel.'

* Bonilla, 1535 *Baladro*, Chs. CCLXXX–CCLXXXV, 108a–112a. The 1498
Baladro omits this portion of the narrative. For the portion of the episode only
in *C*, variants have been given from Sp. *D*.

1 The following corresponds to Huth *Merlin*, II, 23–8 (ff. 132b–134a); *Le
roman de Balain*, 73–80. The text is published by permission of the Syndics of
the Cambridge University Library.

metter, e tant qu'il vindrent au joure devisé au chastel ou li roi Pelleanz
tenoit sa court, e entrent laeinz tout droit a eure de prime. La fest estoit par
tiel manier establé que nus chevalier ne puet entrere en la court s'il n'amaine
10 sa molier ou s'amie, e s'il i venist auterment, il n'i peut entrere en nule
maniere. Li Chevalier as ·ii· Espeez enter lui et sa damoisel entrerent
dedenz, et li ostez remist dehors pour ceo qu'il n'avoit oveque lui // *f.269*
damoisel nule, si en paisa mult a son compaignon. E si tost cum il fu laeinz
entrez, il trova si grant compaignie dez chevaliers cum se tout cil de
15 reialme de Logrez i fussent assemblé. E maintenant que cil de l'ostel le
roie le virent armé, il lui corourunt a l'encontre et le firent discendre et le
menerent en un dez chambrez de laeinz et sa damoisel oveque lui, si le
dezarmerent errament et lui aporterent a vestir robe novel tiel qui fu
covenabel, car assez en i avoite laeinz. Il le menerent el palaiz seoire
20 avoque lez autrez chevaliers, mais onques s'espee ne lui porront oster qu'il
ne la chainsist, et dist qui tex estoit la custome de son païs que nus
chevalier ne mengoit en estrange lieu, mesme[me]nt en si haut lieu cum
en court de roie, qu'il n'eust s'espee chainte; e se il ne li voloient suffrire a
faire le custome de son païs, il s'en irroit ariere la dont il estoit venus. Et
25 pour celui chose lui suffrirent il. Mult fu grant le chevalerie que li roie
Pellehanz out laieinz assemblé. E quant ceo vint a eure de disner que lez
tablez furent misez, chacuns s'asist fors cil qui devoient servire. E fu en
tiel manier la fest establie que chacuns chevaliers oute dejoste lui s'amie
assis, e lors commencerent a servir par laeinz mult biel et mult richement.
30 Lui Chevalier as ·ii· Espees commencha a demander a un chevalier qui
dejoste li seoit a destrere:

— Ditez moi, liquex est Garlam, li freres le roi Pelleham?

Et li chevalier lui mostre et dit:

— Veez le uns la, chele grant rous chevalier a cele soor chevelour, li
35 plus merveillous chevalier del siecle.

— De quoi est il merveillous? dist cil as ·ii· espeez, ainsi coun [se] il nel
seust mie (e ceo demandoit il por ceo qu'il en seut miex la verité).

— Quant ceo est chose, fait li chevaliers autres, qu'il est armés, nus ne
le puet vir tant cum il se vuelle celer.

40 — Par foie, fait [il], mervailes me distez! Ceo ne porroi jeo mie croire
que ceo fust voirs.

— Si est, fait lui autrez, sachiez le verraiment.

— Ore me ditez, fait li Chevalier as ·ii· Espeez, si il vus mesfaisoit tant
qu'il eust mort deservie, coment vus en ven//geriez vus quant vous *f270a*
45 l'arriez perdu si tost cum il serroit armés?

— Par foi, fait cil, s'il m'avoit mesfait, jeo le prenderoie la ou jeo le
troveroie, fust armé ou desarmé.

---

[36] *C* ainsi counsail nel.
[40] *H* fait il.

— Vus ne le poez trover armé, einsi cum vus mesmes le me ditez.

— Et jeo dezarmé le prenderoi, fait cil.

50 — Voire, ma[i]s se vus estez armez et il est desarmez, et vus mettez maine a lui, touz li sieclez vus en tendra a honie et recreant.

— En acune manier, fait cil, se covendroit il vengier, si vus en ai dit che que jeo en feroie, ne auterment nel puet nus faire.

Lors commence li Chevalier as ·ii· Espees a penser, et quant il a grant 55 pechie pensé, il regarde celui qui le chevalier occist en son conduit, si en est tant a mal eise que nus plus, car se cist li escape a cest fois, il ne [le] quid ja mais reveoire. E se i l'occist en cestui point devant le roi Pellehan et devant toute l'assemblé, il ne voit mie comment il peust de laeinz escaper qu'il ne soit occhis et decopés s'i avoit le proesche a ·vi· lez 60 meillors chevaliers del monde. De cest chose ne siet il quele connsail il doie prender, car, se i l'occist en cest point, il ne puet escaper sanz mort, et se il li eschape, il ne le quide ja mais recoverer.

Cez ·ii· chosez le mettent en si grant pensee et en si grant distreche qu'il ne boit ne mangue, ainz pense totz voiz. Si durra cil pensiers tant que tuit 65 li més furent venu sor la tabel, si s'en peust bien a celui point lever ainsi cum il i estoit assis, qu'il n'avoit ne beu ne mangié. De cest chose s'en fu mult bien prise garde Garlam li rous qui aloit servant par lez tablez, et bien ot veu qu'il n'i out beu ne mangié, si le // tint a mult grant mervaille. Il *f.270b* quida bien qu'i le laissast par despit. Lors s'acoste de lui et hauche le 70 paulme et lui donne grant colpe en la fache, si que ele en devint toute vermaile, et puis li dist:

— Dreschiez vostre teste, sir chevalier, et mengiez ausi cum lui auter, car li seneschax le commande. E deait [ait] qui vus apris a seoir a tabel de preudhome quant vus ne faistez fors penser.

75 Quant li Chevalier as ·ii· Espees voit que cil l'a ensi feru, il est tant dolens qu'il en piert tout sez sens et toute sa mesure, si respont:

— Garlam, ce n'est mie le premiers dols que tu m'as fait.

E cil respont:

— Si t'en venge, quant tu porras.

80 — Si ferrai jeo, fait cil, assez plus tost que tu n'osieriez quidier.

Il met la main a l'espee et dit:

— Garlam, veez ici le chevalier que tu as fait venir aprés toi de la court le roi Artu a grant painez et a grant travaile, mais ja mais preudhome ne ferras a tabel de roi, ne n'occiras chevalier en traïson.

85 E maintenant le fiert de l'espee par mie la teste si durement qu'il le

---

[50] *C* il estez desarmez.

[56] *H* ne le cuide.

[64] *C* si durai—*the scribe has expunged* durai *and written* durra *over it.*

[73] *H* et dehait ait qui.

por[f]ent dusqu'a la pointrine, si l'abate a terre. Et lors s'en crie:

— Ostez, ore poez prendre du sanc Garlam a la garisson de vostre fil.
Lors redist a la damoisel:

— Damoisel, baillez moi le tronchon de coi le chevalier fu ferus devant
90 lez pavillons.

E ele li baille, cum cele qui l'avoit mis dejoste lui. Et il le prent et saut
fors de la tabel, et en fiert Garlam qui a tere gisoit mors si du[r]ement qu'i
li perce ambezdeus lez costez. E lors dit si haut que tuit le porent oïr:

— Ore ne m'en chaut que home face de moi, car jeo ai bien ma queste
95 achevé.

A cest mote liev grant la noise en la court. Li un et lui auter s'escrient:

— Prenez le, prenez le!

Et li rois meismez qui touz [estoit] dervez de son frere que om li avoit
devant lui occhis, s'ezcrie:

100 — Prenez le moie, // mais gardés que vous ne l'occhiez!   *f. 27*

E cil as ·ii· espees respont:

— Sir rois, ne commandez pas que home me pregne, mais vous meismez
me venés prendre, et vus le devez bien faire, ceo m'est avis, car om vus
tient, ceo sai jeo bien, a un dez bons chevaliers del monde.

105 Li rois sanz faile estoit mult bons chevaliers et mult preudehomez vers
Dieu, ne home ne savoit en tuit le Grant Bretaingne a ceolui tans nul
prinche que atant fust amez de Nostre Seignor. Il fu esmeus de [i]re et de
mautalent por la mort de son frere et por lez paroleɜ du chevalier, si dist
que voirement le vengera il, s'il peust. Lors saut de la tabel et dit a [tous]
110 lez autreɜ:

— Gardez que nus de vus ne soit si hardis que nus i mette la maine, car
je touz seus en quit mult bien venir a chief.

Lors curt a une grant perche de fust qui estoit en mi la sale et le prent, si
le lieve contermont, si curt sus a celui qui tenoit l'espee traite, non mie
115 cele dont il out la damoisele delivré a cort, mais un autre. E quant il veit le
roie venir vers lui, le fust levé, il nel refuse pas, ainz dres l'espee. E li rois
le susprent a un travers, si fiert en l'espee si durement qu'il le brise par
devant le helte, si que li brace li chiet a tere e li heus* li remaint en la
main. Quant cis as· ii· espeeɜ voit cest aventour, il n'est pas petite esbahis,
120 si saute erraument en un chambre, car il i quid trover armeure acun.
Mais quant il est venus, il n'i troeve ne ce ne quoi, et lors est il plus esbaïs

---

[86] *C* porraent, *H* il le fent tout jusques. *H* s'escrie.

[98] *H* tous estoit derves.

[107] *C* esmeus de ure, *H* ire.

[109] *C* dit a ceus lez autres, *H* dist a tous les autres.

[118] * *At this point there is a lacuna of some two folios in the Huth MS. (see Huth
Merlin,* II, 27).

[121—4] et lors... plus qu'en l'autre *not in Sp. D.*

que devant, car il voit que lui rois le sueut touz voiez le fust levé. E il saut
encor en un autre chambre qui estoit encore plus long, mais il n'i troeve
nient plus qu'en l'autre, fors tant qu'il voit bien que lez chambrez sont
125 [les] plus belez du monde et lez// plus richez que onque mais vaist. Et il *f. 270d*
regarde, si voit l'uis overte de la tierce chambre qui estoit encore plus
loing, si s'adresche cele part por entrer dedenz, car il i quid totez voiez
trover aucune armoure, dont il se peust defender vers celui qui de prez
l'en chace. E quant il veut entré dedenz, il out une vois qui li crie:
130   — Mar i entrez, car tu n'es mie dignez d'entrer en si haut lieu.

Il entent bien la voice, mais pur ceo ne laisse il pas sa voie, ainz se fiert
en la chamber et troeve que ele est si bele et si riche qu'il ne quidast mie
qu'en toute le monde eust sa paraille de biauté. La chamber estoit quarré
et grans a mervaille et soef flerant ainsi cum se toutez lez espicez du monde i
135 fussent aporteez. En un lieu de la chamber avoit un tabel d'argent mult
grante [et] haute par raison, et seoit sor ·iii· pilerez d'argent. E desus la
tabel, droit en mi lieu, avoit un orçuel d'argent et d'or, et dedenz cele
orçuel estoit une lance drescie, la point desoz et le haut desuz. E qui
regardast a mult la lanche, il merveillaist coment ele tenist droite, car ele
140 n'estoit apoié ne d'un part ne d'autre.

Lui Chevalier as ·ii· Espeez [r]egarde le lanche, mais il ne [la] conoist pas
trez bien, si s'adresse cele parte et ot un auter voiz qui li escrie mult haute:
      — Ne la touchie, pechierez!

Mais il ne laisse onques por ceste parole qu'il ne preigne la lance as ·ii·
145 mains et fiert le roie Pelleham qui ja estoit deriere lui si durement qu'il li
trenche ambdeuz lez quissez. E il chiet a tere, qu'il se sent navrez trop
durement. E lui chevaliers retrait a lui la lanche et la remette ariere en
l'orchuel ou il l'avoit prise. Et si tost cum ele i refu, ele se tint ausi droit
cum ele faisoit devant. Quant il out ceo fait, si s'en turne grant erre vers le
150 palais, qu'i lui sambel qu'il soit mult bien vengiez, mais ains qu'il fust
venus, commencha touz li palais // a tramblere, et ausi fierent toutez lez *f. 271a*
chambres de laeinz et toute li mure cro[ll]oint ausi durment con se il
deuissent maintenant verser et depeschier. E tout cil qui el palaice se seoint,
estoient si esbaï de cest mervaille qu'il n'i avoit si preu qui s'i peust tenir en
155 estant, ainz comenchierent a caoir lui un ça et lui autrez la, ansi cum c'il

---

[136] Sp. *D* puesta en quatro pies de plata.

[136-7] Sp. *D* e sobre aquella mesa auia un gran bacin do oro.

[138] et le haut desuz *not in Sp. D.*

[139-40] Sp. *D* maravillarse ya, ca no estaua fincada, ni acostada, ni assentada
a ninguna parte.

[141] *C* legarde.

[141-2] Sp. *D* mas no la miro bien, e el fue por la tomar, e dixole vna boz.

[149] *C* fe faisoit.

[152] *C* crossoint. Sp. *D* y de se levantar tan fieramente como si se quisiessen caer.

R

fussent toute morte. Et avoient tutez lez oex cloz, car il ne gardoient l'eure qu'il fondissent tout en abisme. E pour ceo qu'il veoient que li palais crolloit et trambloit si durement cum s'il deust erranment verser, quidoient il ben que la finz del monde fust venue et qu'il deussent maintenant morir.

160 E lors vint entr'ex une voiz ausi grosse que un bosine, qui dist apertment: 'Ore comenchent lez aventurez et lez mervaillez du roialme aventurus, qui ne remandero[n]t devant que chierement sera achaté che que la Seintim Lanche ont atouchez lez mains ordes et cunchiés et ont navré lez plus preudhome dez princez; si en prendra li Haus Maistres sa venjanche sor

165 cheus qui ne l'ont pas deservi.' E cest vois fu oïs par tuit le chastel, si en furent si esponté tuite cil del palaice, qu'il s'en pasmerent trestuit. Et dist le verrai estoire qu'il [ju]rent en paumeison ·ii· nuis et ·ii· jours. E de chele grant paour en morut ele palais plus de ·c·; dez autrez qui ele chastel estoient et non pas ele palais, en morust assez de paour. Et lui auter

170 [furent] mahaigné et quassé, car plusurs dez maisonz de la ville caïrent et grant partie dez murez versa au croille que lui chasteaux fist, si out par laeinz de chevaliers et de villains assez bleschiez. Et de tiex i out qui n'orent nul mal, mais sannz faile onques n'i ote si hardi en tuit la vile qui es ·ii· primiers jors osast entrere el palais; ne encore ne feussent il pas

175 entré si ne fust Merlin qui vint el chastel pour veoir la grant dolour qui i estoit avenu et de povrez et de richez, car il savoit // bien que sanz grant *f.* 27 mervaile avenir ne serrot pas fais le cols de la Lanche Vengeresse. Quant il vint el chastell, si lez trova si malades et si disconfortez que li pieres ne puet aidier au fil, ne le fiex au pier. Et de ceus qui estoint li plus saine, n'i ot

180 nul si hardi qui osast entriere el palais, car bien quidoient chascun que tout cil qui i fussent, [furent] mort. E quant Merlin fu venus, il lor demanda que cil de la forteresche fasoient, et il s'escrient a un voiz:

— Sir, nus ne savoms riens, ne n'i asoms aler, car par le palais quidons nus bien que cest dolor nus soit avenu.

185 — Ha! fait il, vous estez la plus mauvais gent et la plus coarde que jeo onques mes vais, qui n'osez la sus aler por veoir coment li rois Pellehans,

---

156–7 Et avoient... abisme *not in Sp. D.*

162 *C* remanderoit.

164–5 Sp. *D* y el gran Maestro tomara dende Vengança, assi que lacereran por ende de los que lo merescieren.

167 *C* qu'il virent en paumeison.

167–9 Sp. *D* e dize la verdadera historia que estuuieron a muerte dos dias e dos noches, a bien murieron de los del palacio la mitad, tanto ouieron gran pauor.

169–70 Sp. *D* e los otros del castillo fueron muchos feridos e muertos.

170–2 car plusurs... bleschiez *not in Sp. D.*

180–1 Sp. *D* ca bien pensaua que todos los del palacio eran muertos.

181 Sp. *D* e quando Merlin fue entre ellos.

186 *C* n'osez aler p lasus. *The scribe has expunged* aler p.

vostre liegez sirez, le fait, ou s'il est mors ou s'il est vifs. Venez ent aprés moi et jeo irrai devant, si veroms coment il li est.

— Alez, font il, et nous vous sivroms.

190   Lors vint Merlin a la port de la palaice et enter dedenz et troeve a l'entré le porter et ·ii· sarganz qui gisoient mort, cum cil qui estoient tuit dequassé de un pan dez quarraux de la tor qui estoient sor eux queoit.

— Chez ·iii·, fait Merlin, poez vous prendre et metter lez en tiere, car il n'avront ja mais mestier de mire, a che q'il sont devié plus a de un jore.

195   Et om lez prent. Et Merlin s'en revait avant et troeve en la court bien ·cc· que chevaliers que sarganz qui tout gisoient a tiere, lui un mors de paour et li autre ou de piere ou de fust qui sor eus estoient queu. E lui auter gisoient non mie mort, mais il estoient encore ausi cum [en] paumeison, car il quidoient bien que tuit dis veut durrer la mervaille qu'[i]l avoient
200 veu. Cheuz qui estoient en vie fist Merlin redrescher et lez reconforta mult et lor dist:

— Levez vous, car vous // n'avés mes garde. La tempest est fallie dont *f.* 271c la granz poors vouz vient.

E cil respondent:

205   — Sir, ditez vouz voire?

— Oïl, fait il, soiez vouz tout asseuré.

Lors se dreschirent cil qui [dreschier] s'en porrent, et lui autre qui n'avoient tant de poire qu'il s'adressaschent, furent portee en la vile pour garir et por repasser. Et Merlin s'en vait el grant palais. E quant il fu
210 venuz amount, il trove en mi la sale gisant plus de ·vii·ᶜ· que chevaliers que damoisels que esquierz, si en i avoit plusurs mors, ne li plus fors n'avoit tant de pooir qu'il se puet dreschier en seant, ainz estoient ainsi cum tuit mort. E Merlin lor dit si haut qu'il [l]e puent bien entendre:

---

[189] *C* aalez.

[191] Sp. *D has* e as otras gentes muertas *instead of* et ·ii· sarganz.

[193] *C* Merlin fait Merlin. Sp. *D* e Merlin dixo: estos podes soterrar, que son muertos.

[193-5] car il n'avront... prent *not in Sp. D.*

[195-6] Sp. *D* e fallo ay de cavalleros, dueñas, donzellas, escuderos e servientes, bien dozientes muertos.

[199] *C* qu'el avoient.

[202-3] Sp. *D* e dixoles que no ouiessen pauor, que ya quedada era aquella mala ventura.

[204-6] e cil... asseuré *not in Sp. D.*

[207] *C* cil qui dreschirent s'en porrent. Sp. *D* y estonce de leuantaron los que se pudieron leuantar.

[207-8] et lui autre... s'adressaschent *not in Sp. D.*

[209-21] Et Merlin s'en vait... lez autrez la *not in Sp. D.*

[211] *C* si en avoit i avoit—*the scribe expunged the first* avoit.

[213] *C* qu'il se puent.

— Levez sus vouz qui gisez et estez en vie. La tormente est remesse qui
215 vous a mis en cest torment.

Quant cil orent cest parole, il se dreschent en lor seant et oe[v]rent lor
oex, ansi cum gent qui veignent de songe, et demandent:

— Ha! Diex, est encore failli le tempeste?

— Oïl, fait Merlin, dresciez vouz touz et soiez asseuré.

220 Lors se dreschent cil qui faire le porrent; cheus qui faire ne le purrent, si
lez en portent lez uns ça et lez autrez la. E Merlin s'en vait toutez lez voiez
avant de chambre en chambre et tant qu'il vint pres de la chamber ou la
sainte lanche estoit et li Sainz Vasseax que ome apeloit Grale. E il s'agenoile
erraument et dist a cheus qui dejoste lui estoient:

225 — A! Diex, tant fist fole hardement li chaitifs pechierz maleaventur[u]z,
qui de sez mainz ordeez et vilainz, cunchiees de vileté et de l'ort venim de
luxure, atoucha si haut fust et si prechieus cum jeo voie la, et en mehaigna
si preudhom cum li roiz Pellehans estoit. Ha! Diex, tant sera chier vendus
cil grante utragez et cil granz forfais, et tant l'aceteront chier cil qui ne
230 l'avoient // pas deservi, et tant en sofferont encore painez et travax lui *f. 2*
preudhome et lui bon chevalier del roialme de Logrez, et tantez mervaillez
et tantez aventurez perillleusez en avendront encore pour cest Dolerouz
Colp qui a est[é] fais.

Einsi dist Merlin mult en plorant et del quer et dez oex. E quant il out
235 fait sez priers et sez oreisonz devant l'uis de la chamber telez cum il lez
savoit, il se dresche en son estant et demande a ceus qui environ lui
estoient:

— A il en vostre companie nul provoire?

— Oïl, font il, un moine blanc.

240 Et Merlin l'apele et lui dit:

— Sir, si vouz avez lez armez Jhesu Crist, si vous en armez.

— Jeo nes ai pas, fait il, mais jeo sai bien qu'elez sont en une chambre de
chains, car jeo meismez lez i mis le jore qui le grant dolor avint en cest
chastelle.

245 — Sir, fait Merlin, alez lez prendre et vouz en revestez, si entrez laienz
en cele chamber, car auterment n'i doit nus entrere por le saintisme lieu,
s'il ne porte lez enseignez Jhesu Crist.

Li preudhomes pense bien que Merlin le dist voirz, si fait che qu'i lui
loe. Et quant il est touz aparaillez ansi cum c'il vausist messe chanter,
250 Merlin le dist:

— Sir, ore p[oe]z bien entrere asseure, car bien estes armez pur entrere

---

[216] *C* oeirrent lor oex.

[241-7] Sp. *D* has shortened this passage to: Señor, si soys de Jesu Christo,
reuestidvos y entrad en esta camara, do ninguno no deue entrar, tanto es santo
lugar, si no traxere las armas de Jesus Christo.

[251] *C* proz.

en un saintisme lieu. Entrés laeinz, si [m'ostez] le chevalier que vus i
troverez et le roi Pelleham, et si lez mettez defors, si que nus lez en puissoms
porter la ou nus vaudroms.

255 Et cil le fait tut einsi que Merlin li loe, si en oste le chevalier qui encore
gisoit* en paumeison, si le baille Merlin. Et Merlin l'apele par son droit
non et li dist:
— [B]aalin, oever lez oex.
Et il dist:
260 — Ha! Diex, ou sui jeo?
E il dist:
— Tu es encore chiez le roie Pelleham ou tu as tant fait que touz li
sieclez qui te conistra t'en arra dez or mais et portera male veillanche.
Li chevalier ne respont a rienz que Merlin lui die, car il se sent bien
265 coupablez de ceo que lui mette sus, mais il demande coment il s'en porra de
laeinz issir, car bien a sa quest achievé, si cum il dist. E Merlin dist:
— Sivés moi, et jeo vus conduira tant que vouz soiez hors de cest
chastell, car se cil de cest chastel // vous conissoient, et il savoient del *f.272a*
male qu'il ount suffiert que ceo ensi est par vous, nus ne vous porroit
270 garandire qu'il ne vus detrenchassent toute ainz que vus fuissiez venus as
portez.
— Et la damoisel qui chaiens vint avoque moi, fait li chevalier, savez
vouz en novele?
— Oïl, voire, fait Merlin, vus la poez veoire mort en mie cele palais.
275 Tant a ele gaigné en che qu'ele vus fist cumpaignie que vus l'avez morte!
Li chevaliers est mult dolens de cez novelez que Merlin lui dist, car il
voit bien que toute est verité de quant qu'il li conte, si dist a Merlin qu'il le
main hors de laienz, car il n'i a mais que demurer quant la damoisel est
morte.
280 — Chertez, fait Merlin, ja nel me deissiez vus, si le ferroie jeo, car jeo
ne vaudroie pas encore que vus morussiez.
Lors s'adresse li chevalier de la chambre ou il gisoit encore et Merlin le
maine hors del palais. Et quant il vindrent en mie la court, assez troverent
dez maladez et d'enfers et de mors. Et Merlin dit au chevalier:
285 — Toute cest damage as tu fait chaienz. Ore garde coment tu as
esploitié.
— [Ore est] il ensi, fait lui chevaliers. Puis qu'il est fait, il ne peust mais
remanoir.
— Voirs est, fait Merlin.

---

²⁵² C si mostrez; Sp. D e sacad un cauallero.
²⁵³⁻⁴ si que... vaudroms *not in Sp. D.*
²⁵⁶ * *The lacuna in the Huth MS. ends at this point (see Huth Merlin,* II, 27);
H baille a Merlin.
²⁵⁸ C Gaalin.   ²⁷² H et de la damoisiele.   ²⁸⁷ H ore est ensi.

The final scene at Corbenic (from MS. B.N. fr. 343, ff. 102a–104b)

The only extant French MS. which contains the Post-Vulgate version of the final scene at Corbenic is MS. B.N. fr. 343, a fourteenth-century MS. copied in Italy. The Portuguese *Demanda do Santo Graal*[1] gives a faithful translation of the episode, but the Spanish *Demanda del Sancto Grial* has replaced the incident by the one familiar from certain MSS. of the Vulgate *Queste*. The language of MS. 343 is on the whole Francien, but contains a number of orthographical features characteristic of texts copied by Italian scribes.[2]

A considerable portion of the incident is based on the corresponding scene in the Vulgate *Queste*. To indicate the extent of the borrowing from the Vulgate, all passages based on the latter have been placed in italics. In the footnotes, the relevant sections from the Vulgate are given.[3] The Vulgate phrases not in 343 are in italics.

All emendations based on the Portuguese *Demanda* have been indicated by the use of pointed brackets. Other emendations have been placed in square brackets.

The following sigla have been used:

N—MS. B.N. fr. 343
D—Portuguese *Demanda do Santo Graal.*

[L]i compaignon, quant il orent grant piece demoré sor le lac et il orent *f.* 10 veues les merveilles qui devant els estoient avenues et il virent que la beste ne retornoit de souz l'ieve ou ele s'estoit mise, il dient entr'els:
— Mult est ceste aventure merveilleusse.
5   Et Galahaz dit:
— Cist lac est mult changiez, qui ensint estoit devant froiz ⟨et⟩ or est chalz. Ceste merveille ne remandra mie a nostre tens. Or nos poom de ci partir, car ceste aventure sanz faille est finee. Ja mes par ceste beste ne sera travailliez nus, car ja mes de ci en avant ne sera veue. Or est avenu ce que
10 je vos di hui matin. Ceste aventure est achevee en quelque maniere. Ja mes nus hom n'en verra plus que veu en avons. Palamedes en doit avoir l'onor et la victorie, et nos que en avom esté compaignon, l'en devom

---

[1] *Demanda do Santo Graal*, II, §§ 585–94.
[2] I am preparing a critical edition of the Post-Vulgate *Queste* for the SATF, and a discussion of the linguistic peculiarities of MS. 343 will be included in this edition.
[3] The readings from the Vulgate *Queste* are taken from MS. B.N. fr. 120.

[6] *D* éste lago é mui cambado, ca ante era frio e ora é caente;
[7] *N* merveille re ne.
[9] *N* avenue.
[10] *N* acheevee.

porter tesmoing. Or beneïssom Nostre Seignor de ce qu'il nos a mostré
ceste merveille.

15   Et il si funt.

[A]prés ceste parole, sanz plus de demorer, se partirent li troi compaignon de devant le lac et vindrent a un hermitage ou il se desgeunerent,
et jurent la nuit leienz por els repouser. Aprés ce chevauchierent enscemble
tuit troi grant tens et trouverent plusors aventures dont cil de Beron ne
20   raconte riens, mes li Braiz le devisse. Tant chevachierent en tel maniere
querant aventures et pres et loing qu'il vindrent a Corbenic.

[E]t quant Galahaz vit le chastel et il le reconut, il dit:

— Hé! Corbenic, tant vos ai quis et tant me sui travailliez por vos
trouver, tant ai erré et nuit et jor por ce que je veisse les hautes merveilles
25   qui dedenz sunt. Beneoit soit li Sires qui a souffert que je vos voie aprés
le[s] granz merveilles et les granz aventures, dom il m'a delivré sain et
haitié a l'onor de chevalerie.

[Q]uant li autre dui compaignon entendent que ce estoit Corbenic, ou il
sevent veraiement que li Sainz Graaux estoit por quoi il se sunt si longue-
30   ment travaillié, il en tendent lor mains vers le ciel et beneïssent Nostre
Seignor, car or lor est avis qu'il aient lor queste afinee. Et Galahaz // lor *f.*102*b*
dit:

— Volez vos que nos entrom orendroit en Corbenic ou [n]os atendom
plus?

35   — 〈Sire, dit Perceval, ja par mon conseil n'atendrom plus.〉 Puis que
Dex nos a ensi pres amené, alom dedenz, si verom que Dex nox i voudra
faire. Nos somes encor geun. Se a Nostre Seignor plesoit que nos peussom
recouvrer a la haute viande que nos oümes jadis a Camaalot, je ne queroie
en avant.

40   Et Galahaz respont adonc:

— Nostre Sires ne regart mie a noz pechiez, mes a nos volentez et a sa
misericorde.

[L]ors chevauchierent tant qu'au chastel vindrent et entrerent dedenz.
Et la ou il passoient par mi les rues, cil de leienz disoient:

45   — Veez ci des chevaliers aventureux qui en la Queste del Saint Grahaal
se sunt tant travaillé.

Tant chevauchierent li chevalier par mi le chastel qu'il vindrent a la
mestre forteresce, tres devant le palleis aventureux, qui mult estoit riches
et merveilleux a veoir.

---

[19] *N* ne re raconte—*the scribe has expunged* re.

[33] *N* vos atendom.

[35] *D* Senhor, disse Persival, já per meu conselho nom atenderemos mas,
pois que Deus nos i chegou tam preto, vaamos i (*the recurrence of the word* plus
caused the sentence in brackets to fall from N).

[41] *N* mes la nos volentez.   [48] *N* forforteresce.

50   — Bel seignor, dit Galahaz, or poez ci veoir la prouvance de nos oevres. En cest paleis ne puet nul chevalier errant entrer, s'il ne s'est auques maintenuz en ceste Queste com chevalier de Sainte Eglise doit faire vers son Creator. Se nos somes chevalier del Sainte Grahal, les portes nos aouvrent. Se nos nel somes, ce est noient de l'entrer.

55   — Ha! Dex, dit Palamedes, conseilliez nos de ceste afaire, car sanz vostre merci n'i valt noient mortex chevalerie.

[Q]uant il furent descendu, il ne regardent onques a lor chevaux, ainz les lessent aler quel part qu'il voloient, ne il n'avoit home leienz qui de riens les aresnast. Et quant il sunt venu dusqu'a la porte del paleis, il
60 voient qu'ele s'aouvri a l'encontre d'els, non mie por ce que mortex hom meist la main, mes por ce que ensint plesoit a Nostre Seignor, qui bien conoissoit les oevres et la pansee de chascun. Quant il se furent mis el paleis, maintenant reclost la porte aprés els, si qu'il se virent leienz en-serré. Et Galahaz lor dist:

65   — Ostom noz armes. Par armes n'entrames nos mie ceienz, mes par la merci de Nostre Seignor, qui melz nos porra ceienz valoir que ne feroient totes les armeures del monde.

Et il le funt tout ensint com il lor enseigne.

[Q]uant il sunt desarmé en une des chambres de leienz et il sunt venu
70 el paleis, il voient devant els dusqu'a noef chevaliers qui tuit estoient compaignon de la Table Reonde, et les avoit leienz aportez aventure celui jor meemes. Et se auc[u]ns me demandoit qui estoient li noef chevalier, je diroie que li uns estoit messire Boorz de Gaunes, li autres // Melians de *f.*10ː Danemarche, qui Galahaz avoit fait chevalier el comencement de sa
75 chevalerie. Et se cil de Berron n'a mie fait granment parole de Melian en ceste Queste, ne l'en blasmez mie, qu'il ne l'a mie lessié por ce que Meleanz ne feist multes merveilles en ceste Queste, ainz l'a lessié por ce que si livres ne fust trop granz. Mes qui les prouesces de lui vouldra apertement savoir, si voie le Brait, car iluec les devise messire Helies. Li autres aprés
80 avoit nom Helianz li blanc, et li quarz Artuz li petit, et li quinz Merangis de Prolesguez. Li sestes avoit nom Claudin, le filz le roi Claudas, bon chevalier et de bone vie. Li septimes avoit nom Lambegues, qui avoit esté niés Pharan. Cil estoit viell chevalier, mes mult estoit de glorieusse vie et de bone. Li autres avoit nom Pinabel de l'Ille, et li autres Persides li
85 Galois.

[C]il estoient noef chevalier qui aventure avoit leienz aportez por metre a fin la haute aventure del Saint Grahal. Et quant il s'entreconurent, sachiez que assez firent grant joie li uns as autres.

---

⁶⁰ *N* alouvri.

⁷² *N* aucins.

⁷⁹⁻⁸⁰ *N* aprés savoit.

⁸³ *N* cil estoit nies viell—*the scribe has expunged* nies.

— Ha! sire Dex, dit Galahaz, beneoit soiez vos, quant il vos plaist que
90 je voie ensemble vos douze chevaliers. Or cuit je bien que en ceste venue
sera menee a fin celle oevre dont l'e[n] a si lonc tens parlé par le roiaume de
Logres.

Il s'entrebaissent et demandent li uns as autres nouvelles de la Queste,
et il en dient ce qu'il en sevent. Et se vos adonc i fuissiez, la adonc peussiez
95 oïr conter maintes belles merveilles et maintes belles aventures. La ou li
compaignon estoient enscemble en tel maniere, atant e vos vers els venir
un viel home qui lor dist:

— Li quex de vos est Galahaz?

Et il li mostrent.

100 —Messire Galahaz, dit li preudom, mult avons longuement vos atendu
et mult avom desiré vostre venue tant, Deu merci, que or vos avom.

Venez aprés moi, si verrai si vos estez tel com li preudome vos tesmoignent.

Lors s'en torne dusqu'a la chambre dom il estoit devant oissuz. Et
Galahaz s'en vait toutevoies aprés lui, si vont tant de chambre en chambre
105 en tel maniere qu'il vindrent dusqu[e] la ou li rois Mahaigniez gisoit, et ce
estoit en la chambre meemes ou estoit li Sainz Graaux.

— Messire Galahaz, dit li preudom, je ne vos puis en avant de ci faire
compaignie, car je ne sui pas digne d'entrer leienz. Entrés i por la guerisson
del Roi Maahigné qui leienz a longuement travaillié, non mie por sa
110 deserte, mes por le pechié d'autrui.

Et il se siegne // maintenant et comande mult a Nostre Seignor et entre *f.* 102*d*
leienz, et voit maintenant en mi leu de la chambre, qui mult estoit granz
et riche, la table d'argent et le Santime Vessel si hautement et si bel aorné
com ⟨n⟩ostre estoire a ja autre foiz devisé. Il ne s'ose pas aprouchier del
115 Saint Vessel, car il ne li est pas avis qu'il en soit digne, mes i l'encline et
aore de cuer parfont, a lermes et a plors, et il voit tres desus la table
d'argent celle meemes lance dont la santime car Jhesu Crist avoit esté
navree. Et ele estoit mise en l'air, la pointe desouz et li fust desus, et pendoit si merveilleussement que mortex hom ne peust pas veoir qui la
120 sostenoit. Et sachiez que ele rendoit par la pointe gotes de sanc qui
cheioient en un mult riche vessel d'argent assez espessement, mes aprés ce
que eles estoient venues el vexel, ne pooit nus savoir que li sanz devenoit.

[Q]uant Galahaz voit ceste merveille, il pense bien maintenant que ce
est sanz faille la Lance Aventureuse, celle meemes dont li filz Deu soufri
125 mort, si s'agenoille devant et est mult grant piece en prieres et en oroisons,
tant liez de ce que Dex li a souffert qu'il voie ceste chouse apertement,
qu'il em plore de la joie qu'il en a et en beneïst Nostre Seignor et glorifie.

---

[105] *N* dusqua.   [111] *N* sieegne.
[114] *N* vostre, *D* nossa estoria.
[125] *N* piece en muers prieres—*the scribe has expunged* muers.

[E]t la ou il estoit en tel maniere a genolz, il escoute et ot une voiz qui li dist:

130 — Galahaz, lieve sus et prent cel vessel desouz cele lance et t'en va au roi Pellan et l'adente desus ses plaies, car ensint est aterminee sa guerison.

Il le fait tout ensint com il li fu comandé, mes quant il ot pris le vessel, il vit que la Lance s'en ala sus vers le ciel et s'esvanoï en tel meniere qu'il n'ot puis si hardi en toute la Grant Bertaingne qu'i osast dire qu'il veist la 135 Lance Vencherresse.

[I]l prent le vessel, ne ne voit riens dedenz, et si cuidoit il veraiement qu'il i deust avoir grant foison de sanc por les gotes qu'il i avoit veu cheoir si espessement. Et il dit adonc:

— Ha! sire Dex, tant sunt les vos vertuz merveilleuses.

140 [L]a chambre ou il estoit estoit granz a merveilles et faite esquarie et si richement qu'en tout le mont ne peust l'en pas trouver chambre de greignor biauté. Et li rois Pellians, por cui Dex avoit fait maint bel miracle et qui avoit ja demoré / / en la chambre qu'il ne s'en estoit oissuz *f.* 103* plus avoit de quatre anz, ne n'i avoit eu sostenence, se ce n'estoit de la 145 grace de Nostre Seignor ou del Saint Vessel, il estoit tex atornez qu'il n'avoit puis sainté de soi drecier, ainz gisoit toute voies.

[Q]uant il vit Galahaz qui tenoit le vessel de la Lance, il li crie si com il puet:

— Filz Galahaz, vien ça et pens[e] de ma guerison, puis que Nostre Sire 150 a establi que je doie guerir en ta venue.

Quant Galahaz entent le roi qui ce li dit, il set maintenant que ce est li rois Pelleans, qe touz li monz pleignoit si durement.

[L]ors s'en vait droit a lui, le vessel entre ses mains. Et cil joint les mains encontre le Saint Vessel et descouvre ses cuisses et dit:

155 — Veez ci li Doloreux Cop que li Chevaliers as Deus Espees fist. Par cestui cop sunt maint mal avenu. Ce me poise.

Et les plaies estoient encor ausint fresches com le jor memes qu'il avoit esté feruz. Et Galahaz adente le vessel ou il cuidoit bien qu'il n'eust riens et au verser qu'il fist, il vit cheoir sor les plaies trois goutes de sanc. Et 160 maintenant li escha le vessel des mains et s'en ala tout contremont, ausint cum vers le ciel, que cil qui entre ses mains le tenoit n'ot pooir d'els retenir.

---

140 *N* faites.

144 *D also has* quatre anz, *but according to the Suite du Merlin, the adventures of Logres and hence Pellean's wound were to last twenty-two years (see Huth Merlin,* I, 280). *It is very probable, therefore, that* quatre *is a corruption of some bigger number.*   145 *N* et il estoit (et *not in D*).

149 *N* pensa.   161 *N* cum vers vers.

162-3 els retenir: *the pronoun* els *is plural although it refers to a singular noun,* le vessel. *D, on the other hand, has a singular pronoun:* 'que nom houve poder de o

[E]n tel maniere com je vos devisse avint de la Lance Vencheresse, que
ele se parti del roiaume de Logres voiant Galahaz et s'en ala es ciex, si com
165 la veraie estoire le tesmoigne. Et ausint fist li // vaxiaux qui desoz avoit *f.* 103*b*
lonc tens demoré. De cellui, sanz faille, ne savom nos tres bien s'il s'en
alla es ciez, mes a la volenté Nostre Seignor en avint qu'il ne fu puis nus
mortex hom en Engletere qui osast dire por verité qu'il le veist.

[L]i rois Pelleanz se senti erraument touz sains des plaies qui si lonc
170 tens li avoient duré et il cort erraument a Galahaz et l'acolle et li dit:

— Filz Galahaz, saintime chose et gracieusse, droite rose et droit lis, lis
me rescemble[s] tu droitement, car tu es virges et nez de toutes ordures de
luxure. Rose me rescemblez tu voirement, car tu es plus bel que autre et
meillor et plains de bones odors et de totes les vertuz del monde. Tu es li
175 arbres noviauz que Jhesu Crist a garni de tout les bons fruiz que cuer
mortex porroit avoir.

Tex paroles dist li rois Pelleans de Galahaz quant il vit qu'il estoit gueriz.
Et quant il fu venuz devant le Saint Grahal et il ot iluec demoré grant piece
em prieres et en oroissons, il s'en oissi de la chambre entre lui et Galahaz
180 et dist:

— Filz Galahaz, puis que Nostre Sires a eu de moi si belle merci, ja
mes n'istrai de son servisse. Je m'en vois de ci, que ja a home ne a feme ne
parlerai plus a ceste foiz, ainz me rendrai a un hermitage qui pres de ci est,
et ilec ueserai le remanant de ma vie, car je voi bien que de servir Nostre
185 Seignor viennent li plus bel guerredon del monde et li meillor.

Et lors vient as autres compa//ignons qui leienz estoient et les bessa *f.* 103*c*

---

teer.' *It is not desirable, however, to emend. There is the possibility that the author
had the* Lance Vencheresse *as well as the* vessel *in mind and therefore deliberately
wrote* els. *This conjecture would seem to be borne out by the fact that in the following
sentence both the Lance and the vessel are mentioned. D could well have altered the
original.*   [170] *N* il lor cort—*the scribe has expunged* lor.

[171-6] *In the Vulgate, the Maimed King does not speak to Galaad, but the above
passage can be traced to the Vulgate account of the healing of Mordrain. Pellean's
and Mordrain's speeches are so similar that there can be no doubt that the former is
based on the latter. The following is Mordrain's speech reproduced from* MS. B.N.
fr. 120, f. 563b (*cf.* Vulgate Queste, 262, l. 29–263, l. 9): Et se dreça en son seant
tout esraument et dist a Galaad: 'Ha! sergant Dieu et vray chevaller de qui je ay
longuement attendue la venue, embrace moy . . . car tu es aussi nés et aussi
vierge sur touz aultrez chevallers comme [est] la fleur de lis en qui virginité
est signifié et [qui est] plus blance que toutes aultres. Tu es lis en virginité et tu
es rose, droitte flour de bonne vertu et en couleur de feu, car le feu du Saint
Esperit est si en toy espris et si alumés que ma char qui toute estoit morte...'

[172] *N* lis me rescemble tu droitement lis me rescemble tu droitement (*duplication*)

[186-7] *In the Vulgate, Pellean does not at any point kiss the Grail knights, but
Josephés gives Galaad the* 'baiser de paix' *and bids him* 'qu'il baisast aussi touz
ses freres' (MS. B.N. fr. 120, f. 564b).

touz, les uns aprés les autres, et ⟨lor⟩ conte la belle merveille que Nostre
Sires a fait leienz de lui en la venue de Galahaz, et il rendent graces et
loenges a Nostre Seignor. Et li rois s'en vait maintenant qu'il n'ot home
190 ⟨el⟩ chastel qui s'en aperceust et tant fait qu'a l'ermitage vient, si se met
leienz et i demora puis bien dem⟨i⟩⟨a⟩n et plus el servise de Nostre Seignor et demena leienz si bone vie et si glorieuse, tant com il i vesqui, que
Nostre Sires fist puis por la soe amor maint bel miracle et mainte belle
merveille que nostre livre ne devisse mie.

195   Et li douz compaignon qu'il ot lessiez el paleis aventureux, quant il
orent ilec demoré dusqu'a hore de vespres et Galahaz lor ot conté ce qu'il
avoit veu de la Lance Vencheressce et del vessel ou le santime sanc cheoit,
la ou il lor contoit cele bele merveille qu'il avoit veue, atant e vos une
voiz qui entr'els descendi, qui lor dist:

200   — Chevaliers plainz de foi et de creance, esleuz sor touz autres chevaliers
pecheors, entrez leienz en la chambre del Saint Vessel, si verroiz la belle
merveille que Nostres Sires vos mostrera et seroiz repleniz de la viande
que vos avez tant desirree.

Quant il entendent ceste voiz, il s'agenoillent tuit et plorent de joie et de
205 pitié et rendent loenges et merci a Nostre Sires de cele bele aventure qui
promisse lor est, et aprés redient a Galaz:
— Sire, alez avant et ⟨n⟩os conduissiez.

Et il se met avant, puis qu'il l'en prient, et aprés lui s'en vait Perceval et
puis Boort, et tuit li autre aprés. Et quant il sunt en la chambre venuz et il
210 voient la riche table d'argent sor quoi li Sainz Vexiaux // estoit, il n'i a cil *f.* 103*d*

---

187 *N* lors conte, *D* contou-lhis.

190 *D* no castelo.

191 *N* demain et plus, *D* e morou i mais de uũ meo ano.

189–94 ff. *In the Vulgate, the Maimed King also retires to a hermitage after being
healed, but there is no suggestion that he slipped away without being noticed (see*
Vulgate *Queste,* 272, ll. 3–7).

200–3 chevaliers... desiree: *compare with this Josephés' words in the Vulgate
as he invites the knights to sit by the Grail table:* 'Sergans Jhesu Crist, qui vous
estes travaillié pour veoir partie des merveilles de cest Saint Vaissel, asseés vous
devant ceste table, si serés repeu de la plus haulte viande et de la plus doulce
dont oncques chevailliers mengassent, et de la main meismes a Nostre Sauveour,
si povés bien dire que de bonne heure vous estes travaillié, car vous en recevrés
huy le plus hault loier que oncques chevalliers receussent' (MS. B.N. fr. 120,
f. 564b; Vulgate *Queste,* 269, ll. 25–31).

204–6 il s'agenoillent... lor est: *compare with this the Grail knights' reaction in
the Vulgate on hearing Josephés' words:* 'Et ceulz s'assieent maintenant a la table
a moult grant paour et plourerent si tendrement que leurs faces en sont toutez
mouilliees des lermes qui des yeulz lour chieent' (MS. B.N. fr. 120, f. 564b;
Vulgate *Queste,* 269, l. 33–230, l. 2).

207 *N* vos conduissiez, *D* guiade-nos.

qui bien ne conoise qe c'e[st] li Sainz Graaux, si s'agenoille chascuns tant
liex et tant joieux de ce qu'il i voient, qu'il ne lor est pax avis qu'il doient
ja mes morir.

[Q]uant il estoient en oroisons en tel maniere com je vos devis, il
215 regardent desus la table d'argent et voient un home vestu tout de blanc,
mes sanz faille le vis de lui ne pooient il pas veoir, car il estoit de si tres
grant clarté plain que li oil terien des chevaliers, qui mortex estoient, nel
pooient regarder, ainz es[b]loïsoit et defailloit la veue de chascun a
regarder la merveille celestiele. Li hom qui si estoit clers com je vos devis,
220 quant il fu venuz sor la table d'argent, il dist:
— Venez avant, chevaliers plains de foi, filz de Sainte Eglise, si [s]eroiz
repeu de la viande que vos tant avez desirré. Et tu Galahaz, filz que je ai
trouvé plus loial serjant et meillor que nul autre chevalier, vien avant.

Et cil se lieve de genolz ou il estoit, si ⟨estoit la clarté si⟩ tres grant qu'a
225 paine pooit il veoir a soi conduire. Et cil li dit:
— Oevre la bouche!

Et cil la oevre, et il li done une oblee, et autretel fist a chascun, mes bien
sachiez qu'il n'i avoit nul d'els, quant il recevoit celui don, a cui il ne fust
bien avis que l'en li metoit en la bouche un hom tout vif. Et en ce qu'il
230 l'usoit si esbaïz qu'il ne savoit qu'il deust dire, il ne cuidoit pas estre en
terre mes en ciex, dom il n'i avoit celui qui plus n'eust joie en sun cuer que
mortex hom ne porroit penser. //

[Q]uant il furent ensint repeu, come je vos cont, de la dolce viande et de *f.* 104a
la glorieuse del Saint Grahal, il se remetent a genolz devant la table d'argent
235 et comence li uns a demander a l'autre coment il se sentoit, et chascuns
respont a son compaignon qui ce li demande:

---

212 *N* qu'il li voient.
218 *N* esoloisoit.
221 *N* feroiz repeu.
223 *N* vient.
221–3 venez... vien avant: *compare with this Christ's words in the Vulgate as he invites the knights to partake of the* 'haulte viande': 'Mes loiaux sergans et mes vrays filx, qui en mortel vie estes devenuz espiritueulx, qui m'avés tant quis que je ne me puis maiz envers vous celer, ains couvient que vous veés partie de mes repostaillez et de mes secrés... Or tenés et recevés la haulte viande que vous avés si long temps desiree et pour quoy vous estes tant travaillié' (MS. B.N. fr. 120, f. 564b–c; Vulgate *Queste*, 270, ll. 5–16).
224 *D* mas a claridade era tam grande (*homoeoteleuton in N*).
226–7 œvre... chascun: *In the Vulgate Galaad also receives communion first:* 'Lors prist il meismez le Saint Vaissel et vint a Galaad. Et cil s'agenoille et il li donne son Sauveour. Et il le reçoit joieulx et [a] jointes mains, et aussi fist chascun des aultres' (MS. B.N. fr. 120, f. 564c: Vulgate *Queste*, 270, ll. 16–19).
234 *N* tatable.
233–43 *The Vulgate describes the spiritual experience of the Grail knights more*

— Je me sent raempli de si glorieuse viande et de si dolce que je sai bien que ce n'est mie viande de pecheor mes ⟨de juste⟩; ne ceste viande n'est mie ter⟨riene⟩ mes espiritel, por quoi je di que onques mes a mon
240 escient chevaliers pecheor n'orent si haut guerredon de lor servise a lor vie com ⟨n⟩ os avom ci receu. Des nos tiegne en si haute vie des or en avant, s'il Li plaist, car iceste viande n'est pas sanz faille viande terriene, mes joie et grace esperitex.

Et ausint dist chaschuns des autres, et lors se remist a genolz devant la
245 table d'argent et furent em prieres et en oroisons dusque vers mie nuit, tant liez et tant joianz que de lor joie ne vos porroit nus mortex homs dire la some.

[E]ntor la mie nuit, quant il orent requis a Nostre Seignor qu'il les conseillast a sauveté de lor ames en quel que leu qu'il allassent, lors descendi
250 e[n]tr'els une voiȝ qui lor dist:

— Mi filȝ, non pas ⟨mi⟩ fillastre, mi ami non pas mi guerier, issieȝ de ceienȝ et aleȝ la ou aventuire vos conduira, mes de bien faire onques ne vos ratenez, car vos en recevroiz haut loier en la fin de vos chevaleries.

Et puis dit a Galahaz:
255 — Por ce voil je que tu t'en ailles le matin droit vers la mer, et illuec

briefly: 'Ne il n'en y a nul d'eulx a qui n'en fust avis que on li meist la piece en semblance de pain en sa bouche. Quant il orent toulz [receu] la haulte viande qui tant leur sembloit doulce et merveillieusse qu'il leur estoit avis que toutez les souatumes du monde que on pourroit nommer de langue fussent entrees dedens leurs corps, Cil qui ainsi lez ot repeuz dist a Galaad' (MS. B.N. fr. 120, f. 564c; Vulgate *Queste*, 270, ll. 19–25). *In the Vulgate, after the knights have received communion, Christ explains the significance of the* 'Saint Graal' *and tells Galaad that he will see it* 'apertement' *in Sarraȝ. This detail is not in 343.*

238 *blank in N, but D has* nom é de pecadores mas *de justos.*

239 *N* n'est mie terminee mes, *D* nom é terreal.

241 *N* vos avom, *D* nos.

248 ff. *From here to the end of the scene, the Post-Vulgate consists largely of passages taken over from the Vulgate, with changes in order and minor differences in phraseology. All passages borrowed from the Vulgate have been placed in italics. The words in the Vulgate which differ from 343 have also been italiciȝed.*

251 *D* meus filhos, ca nom meus enteados.

248–52 MS. B.N. fr. 120, f. 564d; Vulgate *Queste*, 272, ll. 8–13: Entour mie nuit quant il orent grant piece *prié* Nostre Seigneur que il *par sa pitié leȝ conduisist* a sauveté de leurs ames en quel que lieu que il alassent *maiȝ, et* lors descendi une voix entr'eulx qui dist: 'Mes filz *et* non pas mes fillastres, mes amis *et* non pas mes guerroiers, yssiés de ceans et alés la ou *vous cuidiés mieulȝ faire et tout ausi comme* aventure vous conduira.' *It should be noted that in the Vulgate this passage is found at a later point, after Christ has told the Grail knights what they are to do the following morning.*

255–7 MS. B.N. fr. 120, f. 564c; Vulgate *Queste*, 271, ll. 11–15: 'Et pour ce veul je que tu aillez le matin a la mer et illuec trouveras la nef ou tu preis l'espee aux

trouveras la nef ou tu preis la spee as estranges ranges. Et por ce que tu
n'ailles seus, voel je que tu menes avoec toi Perceval et Boorʒ.
    — Ha! beauz, doz *Sire, fet Galahaʒ, por quoi ne souffreʒ vos qu'il viegnent*
tuit avec moi?
260   — *Por ce, fet il, que je le faʒ en scemblance de mes apostres. Car tout ausi*
com il mangerent avoec moi le jor de la Cene, tot ausi mangieʒ or avec moi a la
table del Saint Grahal. Et esteʒ ausi douʒ apostre, et je sui le troʒoimes par
desus, qui doie estre vostre mestre. Et tot ausi com je les departi et fis aler par
universe terre *praaichier la veraie creance, tot ausi vos depart je, les uns ça et*
265 *les autres la, et morroiʒ tuit en ceste servisse fors uns seus.*
    [Q]*uant il* entendent ceste parole, il responnent tuit a une voiz: *f.*104*b*
    — *Pere de*[*s*] *ciex, beneoit soies tu qui nos dignes tenir a filʒ. Or voiom nos*
bien que nos n'avom pas perdu nos paines.
    Lors s'en issent de la chambre et s'en viennent el grant paleis qui paleis
270 aventureux estoit apellez, si s'entrebesent et acollent por ce qu'il voient
bien qu'a departir les couvient. Et plore li un sor l'autre, por ce qu'il ne
sevent pas s'il s'entreverunt ja mes. Et il dient adonc a Galahaz:
    — *Sire, sachoiʒ que nos n'eumes onques si grant joie com* nos avom de ce

---

estranges ranges. Et pour ce que tu n'ailles seul veul je que tu maines avec toy
[Perceval] et Boort.' *In the Vulgate, Christ says this in person after the Grail*
knights have received communion and he has explained what the Grail is. There
follows Christ's command to Galaad to heal the Maimed King.
    [258-65] MS. B.N. fr. 120, f. 564c; Vulgate *Queste*, 271, ll. 19–29: 'Ha! sire, fait
Galaad, pour quoy ne souffrés vous que ilz viengnent touz avecques moy?' 'Pour
ce, fait [il], *que je ne le vueil mie*, et je le fas en semblance de mes apostres. Car tout
aussi comme il mengierent avec moy le jour de la Cene, tout aussi mengiés vous
ore avec moy a la table du Saint Graal. Et estes douze apoustres et je sui le treziesme
par dessus vous qui doy estre vostre pere (Vulgate *Queste* vostre mestres et
vostre pastres). Et tout aussi comme je lez departi et fis aler par universel *monde*
pour preschier la vraye evangile (Vulgate *Queste* loi) tout aussi vous depart je les
uns ça et lez aultrez la, et morrés touz en cestui service fors que *li ung de vous.*'
    [266-8] MS. B.N. fr. 120, f. 564d; Vulgate *Queste*, 272, ll. 13–16: Et quant il *oent*
ce, si respondent toulz a une voix: 'Peres des cieulz, benois soies tu qui nous
daingnes tenir a tes filz *et a tes amis.* Or veons nous bien que nous n'avons pas
perdu nos paines.' Lors s'en issent *du palais… In the Vulgate, this passage follows*
immediately after the one beginning 'Entour mie nuit… conduira'.
    [269-70] *In the Vulgate, there is no special Grail Chamber as in the Post-Vulgate.*
The Grail scene takes place in the 'palais', *and on leaving the knights go at once into*
the courtyard, where they take leave of each other (Vulgate *Queste*, 272, l. 17–273,
l. 5).
    [270-2] *The corresponding passage in the Vulgate is much shorter:* 'Quant vint
au departir, si s'entrebaisierent comme freres et pleurerent moult tendrement et
dient a Galaad' (MS. B.N. fr. 120, f. 564d; Vulgate *Queste*, 272, ll. 24–6).
    [273-4] sire… feste: *The corresponding passage in the Vulgate is almost the same:*
'Sire, sachiez vraiement que nous n'eusmes onques si grant joye comme *alors*

que nos vos avom tenu compaignie a ceste haute feste. A si haute joie ne si
275 haute viande ne seront ja mes chevaliers apellez com nos [avom] esté.
Iceste est la deriene feste del roiaume de Logres. Mes encontre la grant
joie que nos avom eu, eussom nos grant duel de cest departiment. *Mes nos
veom* qu'a faire le couvient et *que li departirs plaist a Nostre Seignor.*
— *Seignor, fait il, se vos amieʒ ma compaignie, autant aim je la vostre. Mes*
280 *vos veeʒ bien qu'a* departir nos estuet et tenir chascun sa voie, se aventure ne
nos rascemble. *Por ce vos comant je a Nostre Seignor et vos pri que, se vos a*
la cort le roi reveneʒ, salueʒ moi le roi Artuz et *monseignor Lancelot, mon*
pere, et touʒ les compaignons *de la Table Reonde.*
Et il dient que, s'il viennent cele part, qu'*il ne l'oblierunt mie.*
285 [A]tant se regarnirent de lor armes qu'il avoient lessiees et viennent aval
en la cort, si lor avint si que chascun trouva son cheval appareillié. Et quant
ce fu chose que Galahaz fu montez et il tint son escu et son glaive,
Palamedes, qui mult estoit tendres de cest departement, vint a lui et
l'embrace par mi ⟨la jambe⟩ armee et li comence a besier le pié et a plorer
290 trop tendrement et li dit tout em plorant:
— Hé! Galahaz, santime chose, car neite, home beneuré, cist departement que je faz de toi m'ocit, car je ai doutance et paor qu'a Nostre Sire ne
plaise que ja mes te revoie. Por Deu, s'il est ensint que aventure ne nos

---

que nous seusmes que nous vous tenrions compaignie' (MS. B.N. fr. 120, f. 564d;
Vulgate *Queste*, 272, ll. 26–8).

[274] *N* a ceste haute feste a si haute feste a si haute joie, *D* sabede que nunca
tam grã prazer houvemos como des que fomos em vossa companha em esta tam
grã festa e este tam glorioso manjar. *The second* 'haute feste' *in N is spurious.*
What has happened is clear enough: having written 'a si haute' *the scribe brought in*
'feste' *by contamination with* 'a ceste haute feste'.

[276–8] Mes encontre... Seignor: *These sentences are similar to the corresponding*
ones in the Vulgate: 'Ne oncques n'eusmes si grant dueil que nous avons de ce que
nous departons ja de vous. Mais nous veons *bien* que cilz departement plaist a
Nostre Seigneur, et pour ce nous en couvient souffrir sans dueil faire' (MS. B.N.
fr. 120, f. 564d; Vulgate *Queste*, 272, ll. 28–31).

[279–84] seignor... oblierunt mie: *This passage is almost identical with the corre-*
sponding one in the Vulgate: 'Biaux seigneurs, fait il, se vous amissiez ma compaignie, autretant amasse ja la vostre. Mais vous veés bien qu'*il ne puet estre*
que li [uns] *tiengne compaignie a l'autre.* Pour ce vous commans je a Dieu et vous
pri que se vous venés a la court le roy *Artus,* que vous me salués monseigneur
Lancelot mon pere et *ceulʒ* de la Table Ronde.' Et il dient que s'il viennent celle
part, il ne l'oublieront mie (MS. B.N. fr. 120, f. 564d; Vulgate *Queste*, 272,
l. 32–273, l. 6).

[285–6] atant... appareillié: *In the Vulgate, the knights mount before taking leave*
of each other, but the wording is similar: 'Lors s'en issent du palais et viennent en
la court aval et treuvent armes et chevaulx, si montent esraument' (MS. B.N.
fr. 120, f. 564d; Vulgate *Queste*, 272, ll. 17–19).

[289] *blank in N; D* abraçou-lhi a perna.

rascemble, toute voies te souviegne de moi. Tu m'ostas de dolor et de
295 pechié ou je estoie et me mis en voie et en bone aventure. Et por ce te
requier je que tu pries por moi que Nostre Sires ne m'oblie, ainz m'amaint
a tel fin que l'ame de moi truist la joie pardurable aprés la mort del // cors. *f.* 104*c*
  Et Galahaz respont:
    — Je ne vos oblierai pas, ne vos n'obliez mie moi.
300   Et lors se partirent tuit et s'en issent de Corbenic, qu'il ne trouvent
home qui de riens les aresnast. Galahaz, Perceval et messire Boorz s'en
vont d'une part et li autre d'autre. De ces trois compaignons que Nostre
Sires ascembla devisse cil de Borron coment il lor avint, et coment
Galahaz devia ⟨et⟩ Perceval, et coment messire Boorz revint a la cort le roi
305 Artus. Des autres noef compaignons qui a celle aventure avoient esté ne
devisse il riens, fors que de Palamedes. De celui sanz faille devise il coment
messire Gauvain l'ocist et par quel desloiauté. Des autres ⟨uit⟩ qui voudra
oïr coment il morurent et qu'il trouverent, si preigne l'estoire del Brait, car
messire Helies le devise iluec tout apertement. Si lesse or li contes a parler
310 d'els touz et retorne a Palamedes.

Guenevere's death and Mark's second invasion of Logres (from MS. BN. fr.
340, ff. 205a–207c)

The greater part of the Post-Vulgate *Mort Artu* is known only through the
Portuguese and Spanish *Demandas*, but two of the episodes, Guenevere's
death and Mark's second invasion of Logres after the death of Lancelot,
have been preserved in French in one of the manuscripts of the compilation
of Rusticien de Pise, MS. B.N. fr. 340. The Vulgate *Mort Artu* refers only
briefly to Guenevere's death,[1] and includes, of course, no account of Mark's
adventures.[2]
  The following sigla have been used:

M—MS. B.N. fr. 340
D—Portuguese *Demanda do Santo Graal*
Sp. *D*—Spanish *Demanda del Sancto Grial.*

Guenevere's death

  Or dit li comptes que quant la royne Genievre se fut mise en religion et *f.* 205*a*
elle eust prins draps de nonnain pour la doubtat ce et paour qu'elle avoit

---

[304] *D* e como Galaaz e Persival morrerom.
[307] *N* autres VIIII, *D* dos outros oito.

[1] *La Mort le Roi Artu*, 229, ll. 22–30.
[2] Guenevere's death is found in *D*, vol. II, §§ 687–9, and in Sp. *D*, Ch.
CCCCXLI–CCCCXLIII, 331b–332a; Mark's second invasion of Logres is
found in *D*, II, §§ 699–706, and in Sp. *D*, Chs. CCCCLI–CCCCLV, 335b–338b.

S

que les filz Mordret ne la feissent mourir, elle avoit aprins a avoir tous les
deduis et toutes les aises du monde. Dont il advint que quant il lui
5 couvint souffrir les durtez et les travaulx et les mesaises de la religion, elle,
qui ce n'avoit pas accoustumé ne ne pot endurer, cheÿ maintenant en une
maladie si grant que nul ne la veoit qui n'eust en lui greigneur esperance de
mort que de vie. Elle avoit avecques soy une damoiselle gentil femme et de
hault lignage qui lui faisoit toute voies compaignie et s'estoit leans rendue
10 pour l'amour de lui. Celle damoiselle avoit esté amie Gifflet, le filz Dou. Et
pour ce que la royne avoit ja ouÿ dire a aucunes gens que Gifflet avoit tenu
plus longuement compaignie au roy Artus que a nul autre chevalier,
amoit elle tant la compaignie de celle damoiselle que elle ne s'en povoit
saouler. Et s'entrereconfortoient assez et plouroient moult souvent quant
15 // elles recordoient entre elles deux la grant haultesce ou elles avoient esté *f.* 205
et le grant povoir, et ores estoient a ce menees que elles s'estoient laiens
rendues pour poour de mort. La royne, la meismes ou elle estoit en sa
maladie, ne se povoit tenir que elle ne regretast Lancelot et qu'elle ne
deist aucune foiz:

20   — Haa! messire Lancelot, tant vous m'avez oubliee. Je ne peusse ja
maiz cuidier que vous me laississiez si longuement en autrui servage
comme vous m'y avez laissiee. Se vous regardissiez vostre prouesse et
vostre valour et le grant povoir que Nostre Sire vous a octroié, alors vous
souvenist bien de moy. Vous eussiez vengié la mort le roy Artus et
25 conquesté le royaume de Logres et moy delivree du douloureux servage et
de la subgection ou je sui mise pour paour de mort.

Telz paroles disoit la royne de Lancelot la ou elle gisoit au lit. Et la
damoiselle qui devant lui estoit la reconfortoit a son povoir et l'asseuroit et
lui disoit que elle ne s'esmaiast, car bien sceust elle vraiement que Lancelot
30 ne demourroit mie qu'il ne venist en la Grant Bretaigne, car cil du
royaume de Logres, li uns et li autres, l'aloient ja consuivant. Et la royne
lui respondoit:

    — Il demeure trop et je doubte que cil demourer ne me doint la mort.

En celle abbaie ou la royne demouroit en telle maniere avoit une dame
35 rendue de long temps. Et avoit celle dame amé Lancelot trop merveilleusement. Et pour le dueil qu'il l'avoit reffusee s'estoit elle leans rendue. Elle
haioit la royne de tout son // cuer pour ce que Lancelot l'amoit et
l'avoit refusee, si pensa que puis qu'elle son courroux ne pourroit vengier *f.* 20c
vers Lancelot, elle s'en vengeroit a la royne. Un jour vint a l'amie Gifflet
40 qui gardoit la royne, si lui dist et fist semblant que elle voulsist que la royne
ne les ouïst:

    — Haa! damoiselle, dist elle, mauvaises nouvelles vous aport. Messire
Lancelot du Lac qui ça venoit pour le royaume de Logres conquerre (et

---

[37] *M* Lanceloit.

advenoit avecques lui le greigneur peuple du siecle) est perillez en la mer
45 et toute sa compaignie.

— Par Dieu, dist l'amie Gifflet, c'est grant dommage. Mais comment
savez vous que ce soit verité?

— Je le sçay bien, dist la dame. Cil meismes qui celle grant douleur vit
appertement le me dist.

50   La royne qui se gisoit si malade comme je vous compte, quant elle
entendi celle nouvelle, elle en fut tant dolante qu'a pou que elle n'yssy du
sens, si cela son dueil pour celle qu'elle vit devant lui, mais maintenant
quant elle s'en fut partie, elle dist trop dolante:

— Haa! [mer], amere chose et maudicte, plaine d'amertume et de
55 doulour, non saichant et mescongnoissant, morte m'avez quant vous a
Genievre la plus vraie amant de toutes dames avez tolu ses amours.

De ceste nouvelle fut la royne si dolante et si triste qu'elle ne voult
puis mengier ne boire, ains fut quatre jours en tele maniere que nul n'en *f.205d*
povoit parole traire. Au quint jour vindrent leans autres nouvelles // qui
60 vraies estoient, car ung varlet dist que Lancelot, sans faille, estoit arrivez
en la Grant Bretaigne a si grant gent et a si bonne chevalerie qu'il ne
trouveroit ja homme qui lui peust contretenir. La damoiselle qui la royne
gardoit, quant elle oït ces nouvelles, elle vint devant sa dame moult liee et
moult joieuse et lui dist:

65   — Dame, nouvelles vous aport. Messire Lancelot est en la Grant
Bretaigne a si grant gent qu'il avra en bien peu d'eure conquis le royaume
de Logres. Ce dient ceulz qui bien le scevent.

La royne qui pres estoit de la mort et qui a paines povoit mais parler,
quant elle entendi ceste parole, elle respondi a grant paine et dist ainsi
70 comme elle puet:

— Damoiselle, a tart le m'avez dit. Ne me vault neant sa venue, car je
sui a la mort. Mais toute voies, pour ce que Lancelot est l'omme du monde
que je plus oncques amay et que je plus aime, vous prie je que vous faciez
pour la moye amour et pour la sienne une chose je vous requerray.

75   Et celle lui creante qu'elle le fera a sa requeste, mais qu'elle en ait le
povoir.

— Or vous diray donc, fait la royne, que vous ferés. Je voy bien et
congnoiz que je suis a la mort venue et sans que je ne puis vivre pas
jusques a demain. Et avec ce vous di je que je ne fus oncques maiz si liee de
80 nouvelle que je oïsse que je suis de la venue de Lancelot. Maiz d'autre part
trop me poise durement de ce que je ne le puis veoir ains que je trespasse
de ce siecle, car il m'est bien advis que m'ame en feust plus a aaise. Et toute
voies pour ce que je vueil qu'il sache et voye appertement // que de sa *f. 205e*

---

⁵⁴ *D* Ai, mar amargoso e maldito.
⁵⁸ *D* III dias.
⁵⁹ *D* ao quarto dia.

venue m'est bel et que je muir de dueil de lui et que je volentiers l'eusse
85 veu se je eusse le povoir, vous requier je que tout maintenant que je seray
desviee, prenez mon cuer et le traiez hors de mon corps et le portez a
Lancelot en cest heaume meismes qui jadis fut siens. Et quant vous
serés a lui venue, presentez lui de par moy et lui dictes que en remem-
brance de noz amours lui envoye je le cuer qui onques ne l'oublia.
90   Cellui jour meismes trespassa la royne Genievre. Et tout ainsi comme
elle l'avoit commandé le fist la damoiselle. Mais de tant lui mesavint
qu'elle ne pot Lancelot trouver et pour ce ne mist elle pas tres bien a fin la
besoigne que sa dame lui avoit enchargié. Si en laisse ores li comptes atant
a parler et retourne a parler de la mort au roy March.

Mark's second invasion of Logres

Or dit li comptes que *quant le roy Boort*, qui avoit esté a l'enterrement
Lancelot et moult ententivement *escoutoit* l'arcevesque de Cantorbiere
toute la vie de Lancelot, *il respont:*
        — *Sire, puis qu'il a esté jusques en la fin avec vous, je sui cil qui // en lieu f. 205*
5 *de lui vous tendray compaignie tant comme je vivray, car ja maiʒ sans faille*
ne me partiray de penance, ains m'en yray avecques vous, ains useray en
vostre compaignie le remenant de ma vie.
        Et l'arcevesque en mercie Nostre Seigneur de ceste belle aventure, et
autressi fait Blioberis. *A l'endemain se partit du chastel de la Joieuse Garde*
10 *li roys Boort, et en envoya son chevalier et son escuier, et demanda a ceulx*
de Gaunes qu'ilʒ feïssent tel roy comme ilʒ voulssient, qu'il ne revenroit ja
maiʒ. Puis s'en ala avec l'arcevesque et avec Blioberis tout a pié, bien

---

³ *M* Lanceloit.
⁶ *D* e viverei em vossa companha.
¹⁻⁹ *The passage in italics is based on the Vulgate Mort Artu* (ed. Frappier,
1936, 238 l. 2–7): Et li arcevesques li dist erranment la vie de Lancelot et la fin
de lui; et quant li rois Boorz ot bien escouté, il respont: 'Sire, puis qu'il a esté
avec vos jusqu'en la fin, je sui cil qui en leu de lui vos ferai compaignie tant com
ge vivrai; car ge m'en irai avec vos et userai le remenant de ma vie en l'ermitage.'
Et li arcevesques en mercie Nostre Seigneur molt doucement.
¹¹ *M* et qu'il ne revenroit.
⁹⁻¹² *The passage in italics is based on the Vulgate Mort Artu* (ed. Frappier,
238 l. 8–12): A l'endemain se parti li rois Boorz de la Joieuse Garde, et en envoia
son chevalier et son escuier, et manda a ses homes (MS. *D* a ciaus de Gaunes)
qu'il feïssent tel roi comme il voudroient, car il ne revendra jamés. Einsint s'en ala
li rois Boorz avec l'arcevesque et avec Bleobleeris et usa avec eus le remanant de
sa vie por l'amour de Nostre Seigneur.
¹² *From* tout a pié *onwards our text is unique. None of it is found in the Vulgate*
which ends at this point with the words: 'Si se test ore atant mestre Gautiers Map de

povrement au regart de sa haultesce et de sa gentillesce. Un jour qu'ilz
s'en aloient a leur hermitaige leur advint qu'ilz encontrerent en une
15 valee Meraugis de Porlesgues, qui estoit armez de toutes pieces. Quant
il vit les trois preudommes, il ne les recongnut mie. Toutevoies lui en
prinst pitié, pour ce que tous nuz piez aloient, et bien ressembloit a leurs
corsages et a leurs manieres qu'ilz eussent esté gent de grant parage et de
grant affaire. Lors vient devant eulx tout ainsi armez comme il estoit et
20 leur demande:
— Quelz gens estes vous?
Et l'arcevesque, qui assez savoit, respont:
— Nous sommes pecheurs qui faisons la penance du pechié et des
males euvres que nous avons en cest siecle faiz. Et bel nous pourroit estre
25 se par ceste petite paine povons noz ames sauver.
Lors le commence Meraugis a aviser et tant qu'il lui est advis qu'il
l'eust aucune foiz veu, mais il ne le puet mie tres bien congnoistre. Et
pour ce lui dist il:
— Je vous pri par la foy que vous devez a Dieu // en qui service vous *f.* 206a
30 estes mis que vous me diez qui vous estes.
Et li arcevesque lui respont:
— Je sui hermites ainsi comme vous povez veoir, mais je fus jadis
arcevesque de Cantorbire, et l'estoie encore le jour que la douloureuse
bataille fut en la plaine de Salebieres, dont le royaume de Logres est
35 encores honnis. Et pour celle douloureuse journee que je vi me mis je
en hermitaige, et des lors je y ay demouré jusques a ores, et encore y
demourray se Dieu plaist toute ma vie.
— Et qui sont ces autres deux? dist Meraugis. Pour Dieu, ne le me
celez mie.
40 Et il lui en dit la verité sans riens celer. Quant il entend celle parole, il
en devient tout esbahis de la merveille qu'il en a, car il ne cuidast ja maiz
que si hault chevalier et de si grant afaire se meist si curieusement ou
service de Nostre Seigneur, si sault erramment jus de son cheval et dist:
— Beaux seigneurs, puis que je vois que vous avez laissié chevalerie
45 pour le service de Nostre Seigneur, et je la laisse, car aussi grant mestier
ay je de m'ame sauver comme entre vous avez, ne ja mais ne quier armes
porter, se trop grant besoing ne le me fait faire.
Et lors oste son escu et son heaume et son haulberc et toutes ses
armeures et les laisse em my le chemin, et dit que il leur fera compaignie
50 tant comme il vivra. Et quant les trois preudommes voient ceste chose,
ilz en font grant joie et en mercient Nostre Seigneur, si accueillent leur

l'*Estoire de Lancelot,* car bien a tout mené a fin selonc les choses qui en avindrent,
et fenist ci son livre si outreement que aprés ce n'en porroit nus riens conter qui
n'en mentist de toutes choses.' (ed. Frappier, 238 l. 13–16).
[40] *M* ilz entendent, *D* Quando Meraugis esto ouviu, foi maravilhado.

chemin et font tant qu'ilz vinrent a leur hermitage. Et Meraugis leur commence a demander se ilz savoient nulles nouvelles de monseigneur Lancelot. Et cilz lui en dirent teles comme ilz en savoient et lui comptoient *f. 206b*
55 comment ilz avoient long temps demouré en cel her // mitaige. Et il tint ceste chose a grant merveille, car il ne cuidast pas aaisieement que si envoisiez chevalier comme Lancelot se peust a hermitage tenir comme li preudomme li content. Et quant ce fut chose qu'il fut sceu par mi le royaume de Logres que Lancelot du Lac estoit trespassez du siecle, assez
60 en furent dolent pluseurs preudeshommes, car sans faille c'estoit le chevalier du monde qui plus avoit esté amez de privés et estranges. La nouvelle de sa mort fust tost espandue par toute la Grant Bretaigne et par mi Gaule et aussi ou royaume de Gaunes et de Benvic; cilz de la Petite Bretaigne le sceurent, cilz d'Escoce, cilz d'Irlande et cilz de Cornouaille.
65 Le roy Marc, qui encores demouroit en Cornouaille et qui estoit de si merveilleuse viellesce que a cellui temps il n'avoit ou monde nul roy de son aage, il chevauchoit forment et bien tenoit sa terre, si qu'il ne doubtoit voisin qu'il eust; mais de tant estoit son parages abaissiez que Tristan son nepveu estoit mort ja avoit plus de ·vii· ans passez, et la royne Yseult
70 autressi. De la royne estoit le roy Marc moult dolans, car il l'avoit tous diz amee trop merveilleusement; mais de la mort de son nepveu n'estoit il pas dolent, maiz liez. Quant il oïst parler de la mort Lancelot, il en fut trop joieux, si dist:

— Or ne voy je mais qui me puist contredire que je n'aie le royaume de
75 Logres, puis que cil du parenté le roy Ban sont mort; et meesmement la mort de cestui seul le me donne, car a son vivant n'en peust nul a chief venir.

Lors assembla toute la gent qu'il peust avoir et pres et loing et tant que *f. 206c* moult ot grant gent avecques lui. Et il se mist // maintenant en mer et
80 tant fist qu'il arriva en la Grant Bretaigne. Quant ilz furent venuz a terre et ilz orent osté leurs armes, le roy Marc dist adoncques:

— Or sui je venuz en la terre ou j'ay plus receu honte et dommage que je ne fis oncques en lieu du monde. Or ne vueil je que ja maiz soye tenuz a roy, se je ne m'en venge a cestui point.

85 Lors fist un commandement a ses felons et a ses cruelz que onques en la Grant Bretaigne n'avoit esté autretel fait a roy crestien, car il commanda a tous ceulx qui avec lui estoient venuz qu'ilz n'espargnassent ne homme ne femme qu'ilz trouvassent, mais tous meissent a mort.

— Ne je ne vueil, fait il, que riens que li roys Artus ait esdifié remaigne
90 mais soit destruit; ne eglise nulle n'y soit espargniee, car ja tant n'en sarez destruire que je ne face esdifier mieulx et aussi richement que elles

---

[69] ja.. passez *not in D*; Sp. *D* mas auia de vn ano.

[86-7] *M* commanda avec tous (*contamination with* avec lui *of the next line*).

[89] *M* vueil riens fait il.

furent oncques. Et je faiz ceste destrucion faire, pour ce que je ne vueil
mie que aprés ma mort n'apere mie riens que li roys Artus ait fait en son
vivant.

95 Cest commandement fist le roy Marc, dont le royaume de Logres fut
presque destruit tout. Quant ilz se furent mis au chemin, ilz s'en alerent
sus et jus destruisant la terre par tout la ou ilz venoient et tant qu'ilz
vindrent entour mie nuit a la Joieuse Garde, si entrerent dedens la ville en
emblee et destruirent adonc le chastel si nettement que aprés eulx ne
100 remest se petit non. Quant le roy Marc sceust que laiens estoit le corps
Lancelot, il ala veoir la lame dessoubz quoy il avoit esté mis. Et // quant il *f.* 206d
la vit si riche et si merveilleuse, il dist:
— Lancelot, moult me feistes ja mal tant comme vous vesquistes, ne
revengier ne m'en puis. Puis que je mal ne vous peus faire a vostre vie,
105 je m'en revengeray atant comme je pourray.
Lors fist despecier la lame qui tant estoit riche et precieuse que tout le
royaume de Cornouaille ne peust pas esleger la valour et la fist gecter en
mi le lac, dont nul ne la peust puis trouver ne traire. Le corps de Lancelot
trouva il aucques tout entier, car il n'y avoit gueres de temps qu'il avoit
110 esté mis en terre, si en fist greigneur cruaulté qu'il ne deust, car il fist
erranment un grant feu appareiller et y fist gecter le corps de Lancelot et
les os de Galehas, si fut en pou d'eure tout ars et tourné en cendre, que l'en
n'y peust trouver ne char ne os, si vous di que en la place ou ce fut fait
peust l'en veoir maint preudomme qui de ce furent moult courrouciez.
115 Quant il ot le chastel destruit en tele maniere comme je vous ay compté,
il s'en parti et tant fist qu'il vint en la place de Kamaalot a si grant compaignie de gent comme il menoit. Cil de leans qui trop pou avoient gent
et qui estoient de grant cuer et de grant renommee, quant ilz virent le roy
Marc devant la ville, ilz dirent que ilz ne s'i lairoient ja assegier, ains s'en
120 istroient hors et se combatroient aux gens le roy Marc. Et a qui Dieux
vouldroit donner l'onneur de la bataille, que il l'eust. Lors issirent tous
armez hors un matin et se combatirent encontre le roy March, mais ilz
estoient si petit de gent qu'ilz furent tuit si oultreement occis qu'il n'en
escheppa nul. Et ce sans faille les fist mourir // qu'ilz estoient de si grant *f.* 206e
125 cuer qu'il n'en n'y ot nul qui voulsist fouïr. Le roy Marc entra en la ville
et destruit le plus de la cité. Et quant il vint devant la Table Reonde et il
vit le lieu Galehas, il dist:
— Ce fut le lieu de cellui qui destruit en un seul jour et moy et le
royaume de Saxoigne. Je destruiray pour l'amour de li la Table Reonde,
130 son lieu premierement et tous les autres aprés.
Tout ainsi comme il le dist le fist il faire, car il fist adonc la Table
Reonde destruire si merveilleusement qu'il n'y remest siege entier; et
cellui siege que l'en appelloit le Siege Perilleux et dont tant de merveilles
estoient avenues, fist il premierement destruire.
135 A cellui point qu'il ot destruite la cité ainsi comme je vous compte, vint

devant lui un chevalier du royaume de Cornouaille, qui moult avoit tous
jours haÿ le roy Artus et ceulx du parenté le roy Ban. Cil dist:

— Sire, vous n'avez neant fait, se vous ne mettez a mort le roy Boort
et Blioberis et l'arcevesque de Cantorbie et Meraugis de Porlesgues. Cilz
140 furent compaignons de la Table Reonde et demourerent en ceste terre.
S'ilz vous eschappent ainsi et ilz peuent gaires recouvrer, ilz feront encores
dommage a ceulx qui remaindront en cest regne de vostre part.

Le roy Marc enquist que c'estoit, et cil lui devisa tout l'estre des quatre
compaignons.

145   — Ce n'a mestier, dist li roys Marc. A ceulx couvient que je me venge
mon courroux. Pensez de les querre tant qu'ilz soient trouvez, que ceulx
qui les m'amerra, je // leur donray terre et honnoureray si largement qu'il *f.* 206*
se tendra a bien paié de cellui service.

De celle promesse que le roy Marc avoit faite s'esmurent maint cheva-
150 lier et commencierent a cerchier les hermitages du royaume de Logres
pour savoir s'ilz peussent trouver ceulz qu'ilz vont querant. Au lignage
du roy Marc y avoit ·iiii· chevaliers qui s'estoient mis en celle queste, et
estoient frere de pere et de mere. Un jour qu'ilz chevauchoient ainsi leur
advint qu'ilz approchierent de l'hermitage ou les ·iiii· compaignons
155 demouroient. Et lors trouverent devant une fontaine Meraugis qui se
dormoit, vestu moult povrement, maigre et pale et changié durement, car
assez avoit souffert mesaise. Quant ilz le virent, ilz l'esveillierent pour
demander lui nouvelles de ce qu'ilz aloient querant. Et il leur dist:

— Cy devant les pourrez trouver. Et je suis Meraugis, li uns des
160 quatre.

— Voire, dirent ilz, or nous y menez.

Et il si fist. Quant ilz virent les deux compaignons qui tant avoient esté
preudomme aux armes et puissans, et ores s'estoient mis du tout au
service Nostre Seigneur, ilz en orent pitié moult grant, si issirent hors
165 de l'hermitaige et distrent entr'eulx:

— Que ferons nous?

Si s'acorderent entr'eulx qu'ilz ne les occiroient mie, mais ilz le feroient
savoir au roy Marc. Atant se departirent de l'hermitage, qu'ilz ne dirent
riens aux compaignons de ce pour quoy ilz estoient // la venus. Quant ilz *f.* 207*a*
170 furent revenuz au roy Marc, ilz [li] distrent ce qu'ilz avoient trouvé.

— Voire, dist le roy Marc, ci a bonnes nouvelles.

Lors prinst avecques soy l'un des quatre chevaliers et dist:

— Menez moy la ou ilz sont.

Et il dist que volentiers le feroit. Il se parti de sa compaignie tous
175 armez, qu'i[l] ne le fist savoir a nul fors a cellui qui le conduit. Et il haioit
les quatre compaignons si mortelement qu'il les veut occirre tous ·iiii·

---

¹⁵⁴ *M* approchierent ainsi (*contamination with* chevauchoient ainsi).
¹⁷⁰ *D* disserom-lhe.   ¹⁷⁶ *M* veet,

de sa main. Et quant il fut venuz a l'hermitaige, il trouva leans un chevalier du parenté le roy Ban, qui tout maintenant estoit descenduz et estoit encore armez, si le congnoissoient moult bien les ·iiii· compaignons.

180 Cilz chevaliers avoit nom Paulars, bon chevalier a merveilles et avoit quis cellui hermitaige bien deux ans et plus, pour ce qu'il avoit oÿ dire que monseigneur Boort y est et Blioberis. Encores faisoient ilz joie de ce que ilz s'estoient entretrouvez, quant le roy Marc, qui la hors estoit descenduz, entra leans tout a pié si armé comme il estoit. Il ne le[s] salua pas, ains

185 dist:

— Li quelz de vous est Boort de Gaunes et Blioberis?

Ilz saillent avant et dient:

— Ce somes nous. Que vous plaist, sire?

— Il me plaist, fait il, tel chose qui a dommage vous tournera. Savez

190 vous qui je sui? Je sui le roy Marc de Cornouaille, qui ça sui venus pour moy vengier, et vous n'en povez eschapper sans mort.

Lors met la main a l'espee. Et quant l'arcevesque voit qu'il veult occirre les deux cousins, // il se met devant le coup. Et le roy Marc le *f.* 207*b* fiert par mi la teste si durement qu'il le rue mort. Quant Paulart voit ceste

195 chose, il sault sus iriez et dolens et dist au roy Marc:

— Roy Marc, felon et desloial, tu as fait la greigneur desloyauté que onques maiz roy fist. Mais tu t'en repentiras, se je puis.

Lors met la main a l'espee et court sus au roy Marc. Et il estoit chevalier de grant force, si le fiert si merveilleusement que le heaume de la coiffe

200 de fer ne le garentist qu'il ne lui fende jusques aux dens, et le corps chiet a terre. Et quant l'autre qui le roy avoit amené a l'hermitaige voit ceste chose, il crie mercy et dist qu'il ne le occie pas.

— Donc me creanteras tu, dist Paulart, que tu de ceste nouvelle ne diras riens en lieu ou tu ailles.

205 Et cil lui creante, si s'en part atant. Et les compaignons prennent le corps le roy March et le mettent en terre devant l'ermitaige. Ilz ne l'oserent en terre benoite mettre pour ce qu'ilz savoient bien qu'il avoit esté un des plus desloial roy du monde. En tele maniere comme je vous devise mourut le roy March. Grant parole n'en fut mie de sa mort pour ce que

210 pou de gent le savoient, mais depuis fu il sceu comment il en estoit avenu. Les compaignons demourerent leans toute leur vie et userent leur aage ou service de Nostre Seigneur. Si s'en taist atant cil de Borron, que plus n'en devise, car bien a mené a fin selon son advis toutes les choses que il avoit proposees en son livre. Mais qui vouldra veoir et savoir les comptes qu'il

215 a entrelaissiez a dire par // lieux, si praigne l'istoire del Brait et de Tristan, *f.* 207*c*

---

[177] *M* quant quant.

[179] *M* encore desarmez si le, *D* mas era ainda armada, Sp. *D* y estaua avn armado.

[184] Sp. *D* e no los saluo (*not in D*).   [215] *M* de la Brait.

car par ces deux livres pourra il tout appertement veoir toutes les choses
du Saint Graal, celles qui de latin sont translatees en françois. Et sachent
tous que sans ces deux livres ne puet l'en enterinement savoir les aventures du Saint Graal, mais qui les avroit avec cestui livre, adonc pourroit
220 il estre certain des merveilles du Saint Graal.

BIBLIOGRAPHY

I. Manuscripts[1]

(a) *Suite du Merlin*

LONDON, BRITISH MUSEUM

1. *Additional MS. 38117*

A volume consisting of 226 vellum leaves (220 × 290 mm.) written in double columns of 37 lines each. Folio 1 is missing; one leaf is missing after f. 101 and two after f. 113. Illuminated initials, miniatures and some borders.[2] Bound in purple velvet on old boards. First quarter of the fourteenth century. (For a history of the MS., see Chapter I above.)

The prose *Joseph* occupies ff. 1–18c, the prose *Merlin* ff. 18d–74a and the *Suite du Merlin* ff. 74a–226b of the new foliation. According to the old foliation, which took no account of the missing leaves, the *Joseph* occupies ff. 1–19c, the *Merlin* ff. 19c–75a and the *Suite du Merlin* ff. 75a–229b. The *Suite du Merlin*, which is incomplete at the end, breaks off with the following colophon: *Si laisse ore atant li contes a parler et de l[a] dame et del roi et de toute la vie Merlin, et devisera d'une autre matiere qui parole dou Graal, pour chou que c'est li commenchemens de cest livre.*

CAMBRIDGE, UNIVERSITY LIBRARY

2. *Additional MS. 7071*

A volume of 343 vellum leaves (340 × 220 mm.) written in double columns of 44 lines each. Two illuminated initials (ff. 1r and 159r); also blue and red initials. Fourteenth century, but folios 269–73, 276 and 335–43 were inserted in the fifteenth century. Folios 158v and 273v are blank. Bound in sheepskin over wooden boards; two clasps and bosses are missing. For a history of the MS. see Chapter I above and Vinaver, *Works*, III, 1277–80.

A version of the *Estoire del Saint Graal* related to that edited by E. Hucher (*Le Saint Graal*, Le Mans, 1875–8, 3 vols.) occupies ff. 1–158b, the prose *Merlin* ff. 159a–202d, the *Suite du Merlin* ff. 202d–343b. The latter, which is incomplete, breaks off with the following words: *e la damoisele deschent maintenant que ele vient pres de la crois. E ele le maine au perron e li moustre lettres vermeillez qui estoient entallez dedenz cil pierre. Sire, fait il, si vous.* This

---

[1] This list includes only the texts of the *Roman du Graal*. Details of other texts cited in the study are given in the footnotes.

[2] On the miniatures in MS. 38117, see R. S. and L. H. Loomis, *The Arthurian Legends in Medieval Art*, New York, 1938, 100 and figs. 254–7.

corresponds to p. 48 of the 112 fragment edited by Sommer, *Beihefte zur ZRPh.*, XLVII.

ITALY, SIENA, STATE ARCHIVES

3. *An unnumbered MS.*

This consists of two parchment folios (290 × 210 mm.) written in double columns of 47 lines each. Alternate red and blue initials. Thirteenth century. The two folios contain the portion of the *Suite du Merlin* corresponding to Huth *Merlin*, II, 64–72. See above, Ch. I, 25; Appendix II, 228–41.

PARIS, BIBLIOTHÈQUE NATIONALE

4. *Fonds français 112*

Three volumes bound in one, containing respectively 248, 301 and 233 vellum leaves (440 × 310 mm.) written in double columns of 50–55 lines each. Coloured and illuminated initials, borders, miniatures[1] and red rubrics. Bound in seventeenth-century red morocco with the arms of France embossed on the cover. Compiled in 1470 by Micheau Gonnot (cf. *La Folie Lancelot*, p. L). The manuscript was formerly the property of Jacques d'Armagnac, duc de Nemours, comte de la Marche, who was executed in 1477, and then of the family of Montejehan. Jacques d'Armagnac's signature, now partly erased, is found in *Livre* II, f. 248r, and *Livre* IV, f. 233r. The emblem and motto of the family of Montejehan ('Loyauté a Montejehan') are in *Livre* IV, f. 1r.

The scribe of MS. 112 attempted to produce as complete an Arthuriad as possible and included in his work episodes from most of the Arthurian prose romances in existence at the time—the Vulgate Cycle, the Post-Vulgate *Roman du Graal*, the prose *Tristan* and the *Palamède*. For an analysis of the content of MS. 112, see Pickford, *Évolution*, 297–319 and my article 'Part III of the Turin Version of *Guiron le Courtois*, a hitherto unknown source of MS. B.N. fr. 112', in *Medieval Miscellany presented to Eugène Vinaver*, Manchester, 1965.

Livre II, ff. 17b–58b, contain the fragment of the *Suite du Merlin* first identified by Wechssler in 1895. It begins at a point corresponding to Huth *Merlin*, II, 228, and ends after the completion of the triple adventures of Gauvain, Yvain and Le Morholt.

Livre III, ff. 214c–220b, 240a–275c and 281a–282c, contain the hitherto unidentified continuation of the *Suite du Merlin* published under the title of *La Folie Lancelot*.

---

[1] On the miniatures in MS. 112, see Loomis, *The Arthurian Legends in Medieval Art*, 109–111 and figs. 297–8.

5. *Fonds français 12599*

Roman de Tristan. Consists of 511 vellum leaves (272 × 190 mm.). Red and blue initials; also illuminated initials, miniatures and borders. Several pages are torn. Folios 106v–107r are blank. Folios 1–106b and ff. 222a–320c are written in double columns of 50 lines each by an Italian scribe named Oddo (his signature is found on ff. 63r and 71r); ff. 107c–221d and 320d–500d are in another hand and are written in double columns of 42 lines each. Folios 501a–511d are also written in double columns of 42 lines each, but appear to be the work of the scribe Oddo. Bound in brown calf with the figure XVIII on the back. Second half of the thirteenth century. The volume was purchased by the Bibl. Nat. in 1843 from the bookseller Tosi of Florence; previously it belonged to the bookseller Gianfilippi of Verona (see A. Limentani, *Dal Roman de Palamedes ai Cantari di Febus-el-Forte*, Bologna, 1962, CV–CVI).

The manuscript contains fragments from several prose romances: ff. 1–16b —fragment of the *Palamède* in French; ff. 16b–38d—fragment of the *Palamède* in Italian (see Löseth, *Analyse*, 488–9 and § 636; published by Limentani, op. cit., 1–188). Folios 39b–100c, 107c–221d and 321a–511d— portions of the prose *Tristan* (Löseth, *Analyse*, §§ 59–71, 202–282a, 338b– 417 and 538–568); ff. 101a–106b contain a number of small fragments, mainly of the prose *Tristan* (see Pickford, *Erec*, 10). Folios 269a–320c— a peculiar version of the *Queste del Saint Graal* (Löseth, *Analyse*, §§ 291a middle to 299a).

Folios 221d–268c contain the hitherto unknown continuation of the *Suite du Merlin* published under the title of *La Folie Lancelot*.

(*b*) The Post-Vulgate *Queste*

PARIS, BIBLIOTHÈQUE NATIONALE

6. *Fonds français 343*

A volume consisting of 113 numbered parchment folios (390 × 280 mm.) the last of which has remained blank. Written in double columns, in a single Italian hand of the end of the fourteenth century. The normal number of lines to each column not containing miniatures is 55 (columns with miniatures may have as few as 7). Between folios 9a and 24d are coloured initials; else-where the initials have not been filled in. There are in all some 123 miniatures, but many of them have remained in outline. There is a border on f. 1a which has not been filled in. The illustrations are the work of a Lombard artist.[1] The volume is bound in seventeenth-century red morocco, with the arms of Louis XIV embossed on the covers and the title (*Lancelot du Lac*) inscribed in gilt letters on the spine. The manuscript was once the property of certain

---

[1] For a description of the miniatures in MS. 343, see Loomis, *The Arthurian Legends in Medieval Art*, 118–20 and figs. 328–34.

of the Dukes of Milan. The name Galeazzo Maria Sforza, fifth Duke of Milan, is found several times on f. 113v, written as follows:

$$\overline{\text{GA}} \quad \overline{\text{MA}} \qquad\qquad \overline{\text{GAZ}} \quad \overline{\text{MAR}}$$
$$\qquad\qquad\qquad \text{or}$$
$$\text{DVX} \quad \overline{\text{ME}} \qquad\qquad \text{DVX} \quad \overline{\text{MED}}$$

$$\overline{\text{QVI}}$$

The manuscript remained in his family until Louis XII acquired the Sforza library at Pavia (1499–1500).[1]

Folios 1–60v reproduce the Vulgate *Queste* up to the point where Galaad and Perceval separate at the *forest d'Aube* (i.e. 1–246, l. 6 of Pauphilet's edition of the *Queste del Saint Graal*). Folios 105r–112v contain the beginning of the ordinary *Mort Artu* (i.e. 1–34, l. 7 of Frappier's 1936 edition of the *Mort le Roi Artu*).

A large section of the Post-Vulgate *Queste* is found on ff. 61r–104v. It begins with the account of Mark's first invasion of Logres: *Li contes dit et la veraie estoire que li rois Marc de Cornouaille avoit bien oï dire que Tristan si niés estoit venuz el roiaume de Logres…* It breaks off in the middle of the account of Palamedes' combat with Lancelot: '*Ce cuit je bien,' dit Hestor, 'et neporquant lou je que vos vos en gardoiz.' Et il se drece maintenant et cort a sez armez. Et quant il est armez et montez, il dit: 'Pieça mes.'* (f. 104d).

7. *Fonds français 112*

(See also 4 above.) *Livre* IV of the MS. contains a version of the *Queste del Saint Graal* made up of sections of the Vulgate *Queste*, the Post-Vulgate *Queste* and the prose *Tristan*.

The portions derived from the Post-Vulgate *Queste* are: *Livre* IV, ff. 84d–128b, 146d–152c, 179d–180c.

8. *Fonds français 116*

Lancelot del Lac. A volume consisting of 158 vellum leaves (340 × 493 mm.) numbered 577–735. Written in double columns of 50 lines each. Coloured and illuminated initials, miniatures, borders.[2] Red rubrics explain the miniatures and serve as chapter headings. Bound in seventeenth-century red morocco with the arms of France on the covers. Fifteenth century. The MS. belonged formerly to Jacques d'Armagnac, comte de la Marche, whose

---

[1] Like so many of the other MSS. which came to France by way of Louis XII, MS. B.N. fr. 343 has written on it 'Pavye, Au roys Loys XII' (bottom right hand corner, f. 112v).

[2] On the miniatures in MS. 116, see Loomis, *The Arthurian Legends in Medieval Art*, 110–11.

emblem is painted on f. 678r, and whose signature, now partly eradicated, is on f. 735v. Subsequently the MS. passed into the hands of Jehan de Chabannes, as is evident from the inscription on f. 735: *Le troisiesme jour de Juing mil CCCC IIII*^{XX} *et seize fut donné ce livre a mon filz monseigneur de Chastillon sur Loin par moy Jehan de Chabannes.*

The MS. forms the fourth volume of a complete version of the Vulgate Cycle (MSS. 113–16). It contains part of the *Lancelot* proper, the *Queste del Saint Graal*, the *Mort Artu*. After the end of the *Queste* (ff. 673b–676c), the MS. has some episodes taken over from the prose *Tristan*.

Folios 676c–677d contain an incident adapted from the Second Version of the Post-Vulgate *Queste*—that of the *Olivier vermeil* (Portuguese *Demanda*, §§ 201, 206): *Comment messire Lancelot du Lac arriva a l'ermitage de l'olivier vermeil et la nuyt songia Lancelot que Tristan et la royne Yseut venoient a luy tous embrasez du feu.*

9. *Fonds français 340*

Le romant de Meliadus et de Tristan son filz et aussi de Lancelot du Lac, compilé par maistre Rusticiens de Pise (first fly leaf). Consists of 207 vellum leaves (330 × 420 mm.) written in columns of three, 54–58 lines to each column. Red rubrics, coloured initials, miniatures. Bound in brown calf over wooden boards, with the arms of France on the covers and the figure IX. End of the fourteenth or beginning of fifteenth century. According to the inscription on f. 207v, the manuscript belonged once to Prigent de Coictivy: *Ce livre est a Prigent, sire de Rais, de Coictivy et de Taillebourg, conseillier et chambellan du corps du roy et admiral de France.*

Folios 1–79c, 110d–121e contain Rusticien de Pise's compilation (Löseth, *Analyse*, §§ 620–9, 639–43); folios 79c–110d contain a fragment of the *Palamède* (Löseth, p. 446n); folios 121e–204f contain a portion of the prose *Tristan* which follows partly the First Version and partly the Second Version (Löseth, *Analyse*, §§ 252–344); folios 205a–207c contain a fragment of the Post-Vulgate *Mort Artu* (see below, no. 32).

Folios 17e–18e contain an incident adapted from the Second Version of the Post-Vulgate *Queste*—Dalides' adventure with Galaad (Magne, *Port. D*, I, §§ 74–80): *Comment Galaad jousta au filz son hoste oultre son gré, car il se vouloit esprouver a Galaad, mais Galaad l'abatit tout mort si comme l'istoire le raconte. Et de cellui coup fu Galaad mult courouciez pour l'onneur qu'il lui avoit faite en son hostel.*

10. *Fonds français 355*

Le rouman de Meliadus (explicit). Consists of 413 vellum leaves (405 × 283 mm.) written in double columns of 60 lines each. Coloured and illuminated initials, one miniature on f. 13, red rubrics. Formerly bound in sheepskin over wooden boards; now bound in red morocco with the arms of

France on the covers. Fourteenth century, but some folios, including f. 1, date from the fifteenth century. The manuscript contains the compilation of Rusticien de Pise (ff. 1–64v) and part of the *Palamède* (ff. 65r–413v). Folio 16a–16e contains the same version of Dalides' adventure as MSS. B.N. fr. 340 and 1463 (see nos. 9 and 11): *Comment Galaad jouste au filz son oste outre son gré, car il se vouloit esprouver a Galaad, mes Galaad l'abati tout mort, si comme l'istoire le nous raconte ci aprés. Et de ce cop fu mult Galaad courociez pour l'onneur que li avoit faite en son ostel.*

11. *Fonds français 1463*

Compilation of Rusticien de Pise. A volume consisting of 106 vellum leaves (213 × 305 mm.) written in double columns of normally 41 lines each. Coloured initials, miniatures and some red rubrics. Bound in brown calf with the letter N on the spine. Thirteenth century. The MS. contains part of the compilation of Rusticien de Pise (ff. 1–87d) and part of the First Version of the prose *Tristan* (ff. 87d–106a).

Folio 26a–27a contains the same version of Dalides' adventure as MSS. 340 and 355 (see above, nos. 9 and 10): *Ci comance des chevaleries de monseigneur Galeat et comant il mist a mort Dalides.*

12. *Fonds français 97*

Le romant de Tristant (explicit). Consists of 555 vellum leaves (457 × 350 mm.) written in three columns, 62 lines to each column. Red and blue initials; also illuminated initials, miniatures and a border on f. 1r. Bound in seventeenth-century lemon morocco, with the arms of France on the covers. Beginning of the fifteenth century.

The prose *Tristan Queste* begins on f. 416d and ends after Boors' return to Camalot (f. 555f).

The sections derived from the Post-Vulgate *Queste* are: ff. 416d–426f, 485f–535d, 543c–554f and 555c–e.

13. *Fonds français 99*

Le rommans de Tristan et de la royne Yseult la blonde, royne de Cornoaille (explicit). Consists of 775 numbered vellum leaves (415 × 305 mm.) written in double columns of 44–46 lines each. Red rubrics, miniatures,[1] illuminated borders and coloured and illuminated initials. Bound in seventeenth-century red morocco with the arms of France on the covers. The copy was completed on 8 October 1463 by Micheau Gonnot de la Brouce, *prestre, demeurant a Crousant*, as is stated on f. 775v (cf. above, no. 4). The volume was once the property of Jacques d'Armagnac, comte de la Marche, whose name, now partly eradicated, can be read beneath that of the scribe.

---

[1] On the miniatures in MS. 99, see Loomis, *The Arthurian Legends in Medieval Art*, 109 and figs. 292–5.

The prose *Tristan Queste* begins on f. 561a. It ends after Sagremor's return to court with Tristan's shield (f. 775b). Many passages in the *Queste* section have been revised. The same alterations are found in Chantilly MS. 647 and Pierpont Morgan MS. 41.

The sections derived from the Post-Vulgate *Queste* are: ff. 561a–579b, 699b–754d and 766c–774b.

14. *Fonds français 101*

Le Livre de Tristan et la royne Yseult de Cornouaille et le Graal. Consists of 400 vellum leaves (460 × 320 mm.) written in double columns of 52 lines each. Coloured and illuminated initials, miniatures[1] and a few borders. Red rubrics explain the miniatures and serve as chapter headings, but often the space for the rubrics has not been filled in. Bound in seventeenth-century lemon morocco with the arms of France on the covers. Fourteenth century.

The prose *Tristan Queste* begins on f. 198c. It ends after the account of Boors' return to Camalot (f. 400a). A considerable number of passages have been omitted in the *Queste* section so as to shorten the narrative. The same omissions are found in MS. B.N. fr. 349.

The sections derived from the Post-Vulgate *Queste* are: ff. 198c–215c, 303c–375d, 386d–398d and 399c–d.

15. *Fonds français 336*

Le Rommant de Tristan et de Yseut (explicit). Consists of 335 vellum leaves (370 × 260 mm.) written in double columns of 44 lines each. Alternate red and blue initials; illuminated initials and miniatures.[2] Red rubrics explain the miniatures and serve as chapter headings. Bound in seventeenth-century red morocco with the arms of France on the covers. Dated in the *explicit* 17 April 1400.

The prose *Tristan Queste* begins on f. 95c. It ends after Boors' return to Camalot (f. 354c), which is followed by an epilogue. Large passages in the prose *Tristan Queste* have been replaced by the corresponding episodes in the Vulgate *Queste* (cf. nos. 22, 23, 28, 29).

The sections derived from the Post-Vulgate *Queste* are: ff. 95c–113b, 228d–315b, 331a–352b, 353c–354b.

16. *Fonds français 349*

Roman de Tristan. Consists of 628 vellum leaves (385 × 270 mm.) written in double columns of 52 lines each. Spaces have been left for illuminated initials

---

[1] On the miniatures in MS. 101, see Loomis, *The Arthurian Legends in Medieval Art*, 104 and figs. 269–76.

[2] On the miniatures in MS. 336, see ibid., 105 and figs. 277–8.

T

and miniatures. Bound in seventeenth-century red morocco with the arms of France on the covers. Fifteenth century.

The prose *Tristan Queste* begins on f. 380c. It ends after Boors' return to Camalot (f. 628b). The text contains the same omissions as MS. B.N. fr. 101 (see above, no. 14).

The sections derived from the Post-Vulgate *Queste* are: ff. 380c–401b, 510d–597a, 611a–626a and 627b–d.

17. *Fonds français 758*

Roman de Tristan. Consists of 447 vellum leaves (320 × 230 mm.) written in double columns of 38–41 lines each. Folios 72–382 are in a different hand from the rest of the MS. On ff. 1, 71 and 383–447 are red initials; between ff. 72 and 382 are red initials decorated with blue, and blue initials decorated with red. There is one miniature at the beginning of the *Queste* section. Bound in seventeenth-century lemon morocco. Folios 72–382 are of the thirteenth century, ff. 1–17 and 383–447 of the fourteenth.

The prose *Tristan Queste* begins on f. 142c. It agrees with MS. B.N. fr. 772 as far as the beginning of the account of Boors' return to Camalot (f. 382d). From f. 383a onwards the MS. reproduces the Vulgate *Mort Artu* (see Löseth, *Analyse*, § 407, and Frappier, *La Mort le Roi Artu* (1936), xviii and xxxiii–xxxv.

The sections derived from the Post-Vulgate *Queste* are: ff. 142c–163a, 265a–349d, 363b–381d and 382d.

18. *Fonds français 772*

Roman de Tristan. Consists of 417 vellum leaves (320 × 230 mm.), written in double columns of 40 lines each. Coloured and historiated initials, miniatures[1] on ff. 96r and 190r. The first 339 folios are in a different hand from the rest. Bound in seventeenth-century lemon morocco. The volume belonged formerly to the library of Châtre de Cangé. On the bottom of f. 1a is a coat of arms which, according to Cangé's note written beside it, recalls the ownership of Antoine de Croy (died 1475). P. Paris (*Les Manuscrits françois*, VI, 129–30) thinks that the coat of arms in question is more recent.

There is a lacuna after f. 402 which extends from Löseth, *Analyse*, §§ 550–7 middle. The prose *Tristan Queste* begins on f. 190b. The MS. breaks off just before the end, during the account of Boors' return to Camalot (f. 417d).

The sections derived from the Post-Vulgate *Queste* are: ff. 191b–209c, 311b–390c, 405a–416b and 417b–d.

---

[1] On the miniatures in MS. 772, see Loomis, *The Arthurian Legends in Medieval Art*, 100.

19. *Fonds français 24400*

Roman de Tristan. Consists of 248 numbered paper leaves (265 × 205 mm.) written in double columns of 36–38 lines each. Folios 243–4 are in a different hand from the rest. Red initials. Bound in seventeenth-century red morocco with the arms of Cardinal de Richelieu on the covers. Sixteenth century. The volume was formerly no. 460 of the Sorbonne library.

The MS. contains only a portion of the prose *Tristan Queste*, with which it begins. The opening words are: *Qui en telle maniere est perdue, elle est bien perdue, quant nulz ne la voit fors nos deus.* This corresponds to Löseth, *Analyse*, § 399. With the account of Boors' return to Camalot (f. 188d), the MS. differs from all other prose *Tristan* MSS. After relating a long series of adventures not found in the other MSS. (*Analyse*, §§ 571a–619), MS. 24400 ends with a summary of the *Mort Artu* (ff. 247c–248b).

The sections derived from the Post-Vulgate *Queste* are: ff. 86a–159a, 170d–187d, 188d and 239c–241d.

CHANTILLY, MUSÉE CONDÉ

20. *MS. 647 (formerly 317)*

Le Rommans de Tristan et de la Royne Yseult la blone royne de Cornoaille (*explicit*). Consists of 280 vellum leaves (445 × 310 mm.) written in double columns of 45 lines each. Contains many coloured and illuminated initials and miniatures executed by Evrard d'Espingues. Red rubrics. On the fly leaf are painted the arms of Montmorency, while inset in the initials are the arms of Jean de Mas, seigneur de l'isle. The scribe Gilles Gassien, *natif de la ville de Poictiers*, has left his signature at the end of the volume after the *explicit*. Bound in seventeenth-century red morocco with the arms of Bourbon Condé on the covers. Second half of the fifteenth century. The third of a set of three volumes of the prose *Tristan*. All three volumes were formerly owned by Jean du Mas.

The MS. contains only the prose *Tristan Queste*. It ends after Sagremor's return to court with Tristan's shield (f. 280a). The text of the *Queste* has been somewhat revised. The same alterations are found in MS. B.N. fr. 99 and Pierpont Morgan 41.

The sections derived from the Post-Vulgate *Queste* are: ff. 4c–24a, 181d–255(bis)b and 263d–278c.

DIJON, BIBLIOTHÈQUE MUNICIPALE

21. *MS. 527 (formerly 300)*

Roman de Tristan. Consists of 163 parchment folios (420 × 320 mm.) written in double columns of 55 lines each. Coloured and illuminated initials, miniatures, borders. The miniatures are the work of one of the miniaturists in Jean Mansel's *atelier* (see *La Miniature Flamande, le Mécénat de Philippe le*

Bon, Bruxelles (1959) 60–2). Many of the original miniatures have been cut out, however, and were replaced by others in the seventeenth century together with the missing portions of the text which were added on the verso of the miniatures (see ff. 45a, 52d, 105b, 106d, 112c, 117b, 120c, 125b, 125d, 138a, 146d, 150d, 154c, 156a, 158a, 161d). Bound in calf. The volume belonged in the seventeenth century to Nicolas Moreau, *sieur d'Autueil, general de France, à Paris*, who has recorded his ownership on the last folio (f. 167b). Fifteenth century.

The volume contains only the prose *Tristan Queste*. It ends after Boors' return to Camalot.

The sections derived from the Post-Vulgate *Queste* are: ff. 1a–13d, 81b–139b, 147c–162a and 162d–163a.

BRUSSELS, BIBLIOTHÈQUE ROYALE

22. *MS. 9086*

L'ystoire de messire Tristan de Loenois et de la roine Yseut de Cornoaille (*explicit*). Consists of 335 paper leaves (400 × 280 mm.) written in double columns of 34–36 lines each. Red initials. Bound in calf. On the verso of the second fly leaf is a coat of arms surrounded by the *collier* of the *Toison d'or* and the following inscription:[1] *Ce livre est* [?] *de Nassau, nommé Englebert le vert. Quiconque requis le trouvera, sy le rendra ou le feu de Saint Antoine, l'ardera. Ce sera moy Nassau.* Beneath this inscription is a second one:[2] *Moy seul Chimay.*[3] The first inscription enables us to date the manuscript. Englebert, Count of Nassau-Dillembourg, born 17 May 1451, was made a knight of the *Toison d'or* in 1473 and died at Brussels 31 May 1504 (see Ulysse Chevalier, *Répertoire des sources historiques du Moyen Age, bio-bibliographique*, Paris, 1905, vol. I, 1327a). The MS. was therefore very probably written in the second half of the fifteenth century. From the paleographical evidence it also appears that the MS. dates from the fifteenth century.

The manuscript is the first of two volumes containing portions of the prose *Tristan*.[4] The second volume (Brussels MS. 9087), consisting of 438

---

[1] The slip of paper bearing the inscription has been glued on to the page.

[2] This inscription has also been glued on to the page.

[3] The de Croy family, who were lords of Chimay, had a large collection of MSS. Chimay, mentioned in the Brussels *Tristan*, may be Charles, prince de Chimay, who died in 1527. For an account of the library of the de Croy family, see Marcel van Houtryve, 'Un manuscrit de l'Histoire *d'Olivier de Castille* dans la Bibliothèque des Croy', in *Fin du moyen age et renaissance, . . . offerts à Robert Guiette*, Anvers (de Nederlandsche Boekhandel), 1961, 115–20.

[4] R. Curtis, 'An unnoticed family of Prose *Tristan* manuscripts', *Modern Language Review*, XLIX (1954) 429, states wrongly that Brussels MSS. 9086–7 contain a complete version of the prose *Tristan*.

paper leaves, contains the beginning of the prose *Tristan* as far as Löseth, *Analyse*, § 192. Both volumes, together with other MSS., were removed after the fall of Brussels, 1746, from the Bibliothèque royale de Bourgogne and were taken to Paris where they remained until 7 June 1770. The stamp of the Bibliothèque Royale in Paris is still visible on the MSS.

The first volume (MS. 9086) contains only the prose *Tristan Queste*. It begins at the same point and with the same words as does MS. Brit. Mus. Egerton 989: *Or dit le compte et la vraie histoire du Sainct Grael le devise que quant messire Tristan de Loenoys se fut party de ses compaignons de la Table Ronde qui la Queste du Sainct Greal avoit juree...* (= Löseth, *Analyse*, § 398). The *Queste* ends after Boors' return to Camalot (f. 334a). Then follows the same epilogue as in MS. Egerton 989.

MSS. Brussels 9086, Egerton 989 and Vienna 2537 are very closely related. Their versions of the *Queste* are in all respects identical: all three have the same revised accounts of Palamedes' conversion and of the final scene at Corbenic, and like MSS. B.N. fr. 336 and Vienna 2540 they replace large sections of the prose *Tristan Queste* by episodes from the Vulgate *Queste*.[1]

The sections derived from the Post-Vulgate *Queste* are: ff. 175d–280a, 301a–331a and 332d–334a.

LONDON, BRITISH MUSEUM

23. *Egerton MS. 989*

L'istoire de messire Tristan de Leonn et de la royne Yseut de Cornouille (*explicit*). Consists of 465 paper leaves (292 × 205 mm.), 26–37 lines on each side. Red initials. The leaves are badly worm-eaten. Bound in nineteenth-century light brown calf. According to the *explicit* the MS. was written 21 October 1475. The first folio bears the following inscription: *A Anne de Graville de la succession de feu monseigneur l'admyral, mil Vc et XVIII.* Ward (*Catalogue of Romances*, I, 362) thinks that the admiral in question is Louis Malet, Sire de Graville, admiral of France in 1486, deceased 30 October 1516.

The volume contains only the prose *Tristan Queste*. It begins the narrative at the same point as does Brussels MS. 9086 (see above, no. 22): *Or dit le compte et la vraye hystoire du Saint Grael le devise que quant messire Tristan de Lionnoys se fut party de ses compaignons de la Table Ronde qui la Queste du Saint Greal avoit juree...* The *Queste* ends after Boors' return to Camalot. Then follows the same epilogue as in Brussels MS. 9086.

The sections derived from the Post-Vulgate *Queste* are: ff. 230r–393r, 425r–462r and 463v–464v.

24. *Additional MS. 5474*

Roman de Tristan. Consists of 305 vellum leaves (358 × 246 mm.) written in double columns of 47–49 lines each. Coloured initials, miniatures and a

---

[1] I propose to deal with the relationship of these five MSS. in an article.

border and an illuminated initial on f. 1r. Incomplete at the beginning and end. Folio 139 is mutilated. There are lacunæ after ff. 11d, 264d and 266d, indicated in the manuscript by a marginal note (*yssi a faulte*). Bound in eighteenth-century red morocco. Beginning of the fourteenth century. At the beginning of the volume is a modern French 'Mémoire' indicating that it belonged formerly to an anonymous family who received it from the abbey of Fontfrede in Languedoc. At the end of the 'Mémoire' are the following words: *Aujourd'huy le Manuscript est a vendre*. In the Register of Sloane and Additional Manuscripts, the MS. is entered as 'purchased of a French Emigrant'. According to Ward (*Catalogue of Romances*, I, 359), the volume was purchased before 1810.

The prose *Tristan Queste* begins on f. 164c. It ends in the midst of the account of Sagremor's return to court with Tristan's shield (f. 305d).

The sections derived from the Post-Vulgate *Queste* are: ff. 164c–178a, 232c–283c and 293b–305d.

25. *Royal MS. 20 D II*

Li roman de Tristan et d'Iseult la bonde de Cornoalle (*explicit*). A volume consisting of 315 vellum leaves (335 × 234 mm.) written in double columns of 40–50 lines each. Coloured initials and 58 historiated initials at the beginning of sections. According to Ward (*Catalogue of Romances*, I, 361), the volume was written in the Netherlands. On the verso of the first fly leaf are two fifteenth-century references to ownership: *Cest livre cy est a Gorge Nessefeld* and *C. Hermanville*, followed by some verses written upon Charles Hermanville and a song with the burthen *De bien servir*. On the same page is written also in a sixteenth-century hand 'entier en tout Kirkeby'. Prigent de Coictivy, who was admiral of France in 1439, has left on f. 1b his signature together with his mottos *a belle merciis* and *dame sans per* (cf. no. 9, above). A modern binding (half leather). Beginning of the fourteenth century.

The prose *Tristan Queste* begins on f. 176b. It ends after the account of Sagremor's return to Arthur's court with Tristan's shield (f. 315b).

The sections derived from the Post-Vulgate *Queste* are: ff. 176b–191d, 223a–291d, and 302a–311a.

ABERYSTWYTH, N.L.W.

26. *MS. 5667*

L'estoire de Tristran et du Graal (*explicit*). Consists of 523 vellum leaves (355 × 250 mm.) written in double columns of 41 lines each. Miniatures, illuminated initials, a grotesque on f. 286a. According to the description by Professor Edward Bensly in the Annual Report for 1928 of the National Library of Wales, the type of ornament is that of a Parisian atelier of the early fourteenth century. The Visconti arms are painted at the foot of f. 89a. The main body of the manuscript is in a hand of the early fourteenth century;

ff. 1–85 are of a later date. Folios 85v, 86, 87 and 326v–334v are blank. Bound in green morocco. The volume was purchased by the N.L.W. at Sotheby's Sale, December 1927. It previously belonged to M. Jean Bloch of Paris. On the first and last folios is a small stamp of the Château de la Roche Guyon Bibliothèque. The prose *Tristan Queste* begins on f. 241c with a miniature. It ends after Boors' return to Camalot (f. 523d). The sections derived from the Post-Vulgate *Queste* are: ff. 241c–263b, 387c–483d, 500a–521d and 523a–b.

NEW YORK, PIERPONT MORGAN LIBRARY

27. *MS. 41*

Le roman de Tristan et Artus. Consists of 282 vellum leaves (430 × 330 mm.) written in double columns of 53 lines each. Decorated with coloured and illuminated initials and miniatures. Bound in seventeenth-century French calf with a double C monogram. Second half of the fifteenth century. According to Seymour de Ricci (*Census of Medieval and Renaissance Manuscripts in the United States and Canada*, vol. II (1937) 1372), the manuscript belonged formerly to Peter le Neve although it cannot be traced to his sales catalogues (London, 22 Feb. and 19 March 1731). Later the volume was given by G. Vertue to Bishop Warburton. In 1780 it was sold by Payne to G. L. Way, and in the latter's sale (London, 1881) to B. Quaritch. By 1894 the manuscript was in the possession of an American collector, John E. Kerr (see *Modern Language Notes*, IX, 1894, cols. 36–40). In 1903 the whole of the Kerr collection entered the Pierpont Morgan Library. The prose *Tristan Queste* begins on f. 151b. It breaks off on f. 282d in the midst of the account of Lancelot's visit to Corbenic. The *Queste* of this MS. is closely related to that of MSS. B.N. fr. 99 and Chantilly 647. The sections derived from the Post-Vulgate *Queste* are: ff. 151b–165c, 231a–277d and 278a–282d.

VIENNA, STAATSBIBLIOTHEK

28. *MS. 2537*

Le rommant de Tristan et de Yseult (*explicit*). Consists of 492 vellum leaves (477 × 335 mm.) written in double columns of 64–68 lines each. Red rubrics, 144 large miniatures, borders, coloured and illuminated initials. The decorations are the work of a Paris atelier of the first quarter of the fifteenth century.[1]

---

[1] For a detailed description of the miniatures and a number of reproductions, see H. J. Hermann, *Die Westeuropäischen Handschriften und Inkunabeln der Gotik und der Renaissance . . .* vol. 3, *Französische und Iberische Handschriften der ersten Hälfte des XV. Jahrhunderts* (Leipzig, 1938) 44–64.

The manuscript is written in several different hands. There is a table of contents on ff. 1–3v; the text begins on f. 4r. Bound in eighteenth-century red morocco with the arms of Prince Eugène de Savoie on the covers and on the spine. First half of the fifteenth century. On f. 196v, in the left hand margin, are the names of two sixteenth-century owners of the manuscript, Lefresne and Lefourne. Later the manuscript came into the possession of Prince Eugène de Savoie, on whose death (21 April 1736) Princess Victoria de Savoie acquired it. She subsequently bequeathed the whole of Prince Eugène's library to the Emperor Charles VI (1737). In 1809 Napoleon took the manuscript, together with many others,[1] to Paris, but they were all returned to Vienna in 1814–15. The stamp of the Bibliothèque Impériale is still to be seen on ff. 1 and 429v.

The prose *Tristan Queste* begins on f. 331c. It ends after Boors' return to Camalot (f. 492a). There follows an epilogue. For the *Queste* of this MS., see above, no. 22.

The sections derived from the Post-Vulgate *Queste* are: ff. 331c–342c, 414a–467a, 477b–490d, 491b–d.

29. *MS. 2540*

Li roumans de Tristan et de Yseult (*explicit*). Consists of 243 vellum leaves (490 × 350 mm.) written in double columns of 67 lines each. Miniatures, coloured and illuminated initials. Bound in brown morocco. The *explicit* on the last folio supplies the date: *Explicit li Roumans de Tristan et de Yseult que fu fait l'an mil CCCCLXVI veille de Noel.* That is, the manuscript was completed 24 December 1466. It forms the second of two volumes containing a complete version of the prose *Tristan.*

The prose *Tristan Queste* begins on f. 76b. It ends after Boors' return to Camalot (f. 243d). There follows an epilogue. The *Queste* of this manuscript is closely related to that of MS. B.N. fr. 336, etc. (see above, nos. 15, 22, 23 and 28).

The sections derived from the Post-Vulgate *Queste* are: ff. 76b–88a, 164b–218a, 228c–242b, 243a–c.

30. *MS. 2542*

L'estoire de monseigneur Tristan et del Saint Graal (*explicit*). Consists of 504 vellum leaves (460 × 340 mm.) written in three columns of 60 lines each. Red rubrics, coloured and historiated initials, some borders, musical annotations. Bound in eighteenth-century red morocco with the arms of Prince Eugène de Savoie on the covers and on the spine. Fifteenth century. The volume was formerly owned by Jacques d'Armagnac, comte de la Marche, as is indicated by the note following the *explicit*: *Ce livre de Tristan est au duc de*

---

[1] Cf. below, no. 30.

Nemours, conte de la Marche. P. Jacques pour Carlat (cf. nos. 4 and 13). Subsequently the manuscript was acquired by Prince Eugène de Savoie. From him the manuscript passed to Princess Victoria de Savoie and then to the Emperor Charles VI (cf. no. 28). The volume, like Vienna MS. 2537, was taken to Paris by Napoleon in 1809, but was returned to Vienna in 1814–15. The stamp of the Bibliothèque Impériale is on ff. 1r and 500v.

The prose *Tristan Queste* begins on f. 353e. It ends after Boors' return to Camalot (f. 500f).

The sections derived from the Post-Vulgate *Queste* are: ff. 353e–366b, 432e–481e, 490c–499e, 500c–d.

TURIN, UNIVERSITY LIBRARY

31. *MSS. L–I–7–9*

These three fifteenth-century volumes, badly damaged in the fire of 1904, consist respectively of 237, 339 and 362 parchment folios (430 × 285 mm.) written in double columns of 54–55 lines each and illustrated by Evrard d'Espingues. They contain a complete version of *Guiron le Courtois* (see my article referred to in number 4 above). Part III of the romance preserved in L–I–9 is incomplete at the beginning due to the loss of several folios, and begins with two episodes borrowed from the Post-Vulgate *Queste*— Esclabor's account of how the *beste glatissant* killed eleven of his twelve sons (f. 1a) and the story of the birth of the *beste* (ff. 1b–3b). The first of these incidents is not found in French in any other manuscript and is known only from the Portuguese *Demanda*, I, §§ 125–6; the second episode corresponds to MS. B.N. fr. 112, *Livre IV*, ff. 150d–152c. The first episode, very fragmentary, consists of the following short passage: *f. 1a bottom* (the top half of the folio has been destroyed): Il n'a ou monde... qui l'eust oÿ qu'il n'en fust... Que vous dirois je? La voix leur fut si horrible et si malle qu'il n'y ot cellui d'eulx qui en selle se peust tenir et cheïrent a terre tous en pamoison. Quant Esclabor revint de pamoison et se trouva feru d'ung glaive par my le corps, mais non mie comme navré a mort, si regarde entour soy et voit que tous ses filz estoient...

The second episode, also fragmentary, begins:

[*F. 1b bottom*]...tant belle chose...avoit ung frere...aage... a louer soe jeunesse et... Il estoit tant beaulx et tant sages et tant gracieux de toutes choses que... la congnoissoit qu'il ne s'esmerveille de sa vie et de son estre. Il estoit moult bien lettrés, mais encores l'estoit la... [*f. 1c bottom half*] elle avoit en ung sien escrin et se partit de sa chambre et de ses damoiselles et s'en ala ou verger son pere devant une fontaine. Et la ou elle se vouloit occire... douleur finer, adont luy apparut ung ennemy... [*f. 1d bottom*] vraiement... son frere jusques... nos... 'Ne... fait cil, ou vous faictes ce que je vous requiers.' Celle qui estoit plaine de peché et de mal aventure, quant elle oÿt la requeste de l'enmy, elle refusa moult. Et nepourquant au derrenier elle s'accorda a quel que peine… mallement pour ce qu'il luy sambloit home de grant beauté et de grant valeur… [*f. 2a top half destroyed and bottom half covered with paper; f. 2b top half destroyed*]… plusieurs fois… qu'elle sentoit… parcreu. [*Miniature followed by the rubric*: Comment le roy Ypomenes fit livrer son filz aux chiens qui le devorerent]. Ainsi mist le roy Ypomenes son filz en prison par la desloyaulté de sa fille. Le damoisel s'excusoit bien… [*f. 2c bottom*]… Il dist a sa seur oyant son pere et oyant tous ses barons qui la estoient, leur dist il: 'Tu scez bien que tu me fais morir a tort et que je n'ay mye desservy ceste mort que tu me fais souffrir. Si ne me poise mie tant de l'angoisse comme il fait de la honteuse mort a quoy tu me fais livrer. Tu me fais honte sans desserte, si ne m'en vengeray mie, mais cellui m'en vengera qui scet prandre les grans vengances et les merveilles des grans desloyaultés du monde. Et a la naissance de la chose que tu as dedens ton ventre apperra bien que ce ne fu mie de moy, car oncques de homme ne de femme ne issit si merveilleuse chose comme il istra de toy. Ennemy l'engendra, ennemy le conceupt, et ennemy en istra en semblance d'une beste la plus diverse qui oncques fut veue. Et pour ce que tu as chiens as livree ma char avra celle beste dedens son ventre chiens qui toutes voyes yront glatissant en memoire et en reprouche des bestes a qui tu me fais livrer. Celle beste… (*the top half of ff. 2d–3b has been destroyed and the rest is illegible*).

(*c*) The Post-Vulgate *Mort Artu*

Paris, Bibliothèque Nationale

32. *Fonds français 340*

See no. 9 above. Folios 205a–207c contain two of the incidents of the Post-Vulgate *Mort Artu*—Guenevere's death and Mark's second invasion of Logres. (See Appendix II, 261–70.)

(*d*) *Estoire del Saint Graal*[1]

Rennes, Bibliothèque Municipale

33. *MS. 255*

A volume consisting of 275 vellum leaves written in three columns of 45 lines each. Coloured and illuminated initials, miniatures. Bound in calf. Thirteenth century.

The *Estoire del Saint Graal* occupies ff. 1–100c. Its opening words are: *Cil qui se tient et juge au plus petit et au plus pecheor de toₓ les altres pecheors…* The last words are: *Si se test ore atant li contes de totes les lingniees Celydoine*

---

[1] I include in this list only the Rennes MS., as it is the nearest extant representative of the *Estoire* of the *Roman du Graal*. For a complete list of the MSS. of the *Estoire del Saint Graal*, see B. Woledge, *Bibliographie des romans et nouvelles en prose française antérieurs à 1500*, 72–8.

qui de lui oissirent et retorne a une autre branche que l'en apele l'estoire de Merlin, que il covient ajoster a fine force avec l'estoire del Graal, por ce que branche en est et i apartient, et commence messires Roberʒ de Borron cele branche en tel maniere. The rest of the MS. contains the prose *Merlin* (ff. 101a–135e) and part of the *Lancelot* proper (ff. 137a–275f). F. 136 is blank.

2. Printed Texts of Portions of the 'Roman du Graal'

BOGDANOW, F. (ed.). 'The version of the *Queste del Saint Graal* contained in MS. B.N. fr. 343 (ff. 61–104)' (typewritten M.A. thesis, Manchester, 1953).

—— *La Folie Lancelot, a hitherto unidentified portion of the Suite du Merlin contained in MSS. B.N. fr. 112 and 12599, Beihefte ʒur ZRPh.*, 109 (Max Niemeyer Verlag, Tübingen, 1965).

LEGGE, M. D. (ed.). *Le roman de Balain*, with an Introduction by Eugène Vinaver (Manchester University Press, 1942).

MICHA, A. 'Fragment de la *Suite-Huth du Merlin*', *R*, LXXVIII (1957), 37–45.

PARIS, G., and ULRICH, J. (eds.). *Merlin, roman en prose du XIIIe siècle, publié... d'après le manuscrit appartenant à M. Alfred H. Huth*, SATF (Paris, 1886), 2 vols.

PICKFORD, C. E. *Erec, roman arthurien en prose, publié pour la première fois d'après le ms. fr. 112 de la Bibliothèque Nationale* (Genève: Droz; Paris: Minard, 1959). [An edition of MS. 112, *Livre* III, ff. 240b–243d, 247d–251a, 262d–268a, 271a–272b, and *Livre* IV, ff. 101b–114a.]

SOMMER, H. O. 'The *Queste* of the Holy Grail forming the third part of the trilogy indicated in the *Suite du Merlin* Huth MS.', *R*, XXXVI (1907), 573–9. [Unreliable transcription of MS. B.N. fr. 343, ff. 102a–104b.]

—— *Die Abenteuer Gawains, Ywains und Le Morholts mit den drei Jungfrauen aus der Trilogie (Demanda) des Pseudo-Robert de Borron. Die Fortsetʒung des Huth-Merlin nach der allein bekannten HS. Nr. 112 der Pariser National Bibliothek, Beihefte ʒur ZRPh.*, XLVII (Halle, 1913).

3. Portuguese and Spanish Translations

LISBON, TORRE DO TOMBO

1. *MS. 643*

Livro de Josep Abaramatia intetulado a primeira parte da Demanda do Santo Grial ata a presente idade nunca vista. Treladado do propio original por ho doutor Manuel Alvareʒ corregedor da Ilha de Sã Miguel. Deregido ao muy alto e poderoso principe El Rei dom Joãho ho 3º deste nome, El Rrey nosso Senhor (f. 1r). A paper manuscript consisting of 311 leaves, 29 lines on each side.

Copied in the sixteenth century by Manuel Alvarez who dedicated the volume to King John III of Portugal (1521–57). In his dedication (ff. 1r–2r) Manuel Alvarez explains that his book is a translation or transcription of an illuminated parchment manuscript two hundred years old which he found at Riba d'Ancora in the possession of a very old lady at the time when his father was the King's *corregidor* in Entre Douro e Minho. He remarks also that he has removed certain obsolete words. As appears from the final colophon of the MS., the present copy is derived from a version executed in 1313 by Juan Bivas on the order of a certain João Samches, *mestre escolla* at Astorga: *Este livro mamdou fazer João Samches mestre escolla d'Astorga no quimto ano que o estado de Coimbra foy feito e no tempo do papa Clememte que destroio a ordem del Temple e fez o comcilio geral em Biana e pos ho emtredito em Castela e neste ano se finou a rainha dona Costamça em São Fagumdo e casou o ymfamte Dom Felipe com a filha de Dom A[ffonso] ano de 13XII[I] anos* (f. 311v). The name of the translator, Juan Bivas, is found on ff. 123v and 199r. The same name is also found in the fragmentary Spanish *Josep* as well as in the Spanish *Demanda*.

The opening words of the Portuguese *Josep* are: *Aquelle que se tem e nomea por menor e por mais pecador em começo desta istoria encomendo saude a todos aquelles que crem e tem fee na santa trindade, no padre e no filho e no spirito santo* (f. 2r).

2. 'Um episodio do *Josep ab Aramatia*' by J. J. Nunes, in *Crestomatia arcaica*, 4th edition. Livraria Classica editora, Lisbon, 1953, 108–15. Also in *Revista Lusitana*, X, 223–37.

3. *Spanish Grail Fragments: El Libro de Josep Abarimatia, La Estoria de Merlin, Lançarote*, edited from the unique MS. by Karl Pietsch. Modern Philology Monographs of the University of Chicago, 2 vols., 1924, 1925. [Edition of the Spanish Grail fragments contained in MS. 2–G–5 of the Palace Library, Madrid.]

4. *El Baladro del sabio Merlin con sus profecias*, Burgos: Juan de Burgos, 1498. [The only extant copy is now in Oviedo University Library.]

5. *El Baladro del Sabio Merlin segun el texto de la edicion de Burgos de 1498*, edicion y notas de Pedro Bohigas, 3 vols., Barcelona, I, 1957, II, 1961, III, 1962.

6. *La Demanda del Sancto Grial con los maravillosos fechos de Lanzarote y de Galaz su hijo. Segunda parte de la Demanda del Sancto Grial*, Toledo, Juan de Villaquiran, 1515. [A unique copy is in the British Museum, bound up with the 1535 edition of the *Baladro*. See below, no. 7.]

7. *La Demanda del Sancto Grial.* Primera Parte: *El Baladro del sabio Merlin con sus profecias.* Segunda Parte: *La Demanda del Sancto Grial con los maravillosos fechos de Lanƶarote y de Galaƶ su hijo,* Sevilla, 1535. [Three complete copies are known still to exist: in the National Library of Madrid, the Advocates' Library, Edinburgh, and the Bibliothèque Nationale, Paris. A fourth copy of the 1535 *Baladro,* bound up with the 1515 *Demanda,* is in the British Museum. See above, no. 6.]

8. *La Demanda del Sancto Grial.* Primera Parte: *El Baladro del Sabio Merlin.* Segunda Parte: *La Demanda del Sancto Grial con los maravillosos fechos de Lanƶarote y de Galaƶ su hijo. Libros de Caballerias.* Primera Parte: *Ciclo arturico,* por Adolfo Bonilla y San Martin, Nueva Biblioteca de Autores Españoles, 6, Madrid, 1907. [Reprint of the 1535 *Baladro* and *Demanda.*]

9. *A historia dos cavalleiros da Mesa Redonda e da Demanda do Santo Graal,* Vienna, Staatsbibliothek, MS. 2594. A volume consisting of 199 parchment folios, written in double columns of 42–43 lines each. Fifteenth century.

10. *A historia dos cavalleiros da mesa redonda e da demanda do santo Graal,* ed. Karl von Reinhardstöttner, Berlin, 1887. [Edition of the first 70 folios of the Portuguese *Demanda.*]

11. *A Demanda do Santo Graal,* por Augusto Magne, Rio de Janeiro, Imprensa Nacional, 1944, 3 vols. [First complete edition of the Portuguese *Demanda.*]

12. *A Demanda do Santo Graal, reproduçao fac-similar e transcrição critica do codice 2594 da Biblioteca Nacional de Viena,* por Augusto Magne, Rio de Janeiro, Imprensa Nacional, 1955. [First volume of the 2nd edition of the Portuguese *Demanda.*]

4. MALORY

VINAVER, EUGÈNE, ed. *The Works of Sir Thomas Malory,* Oxford, Clarendon Press, 1947; reprinted 1948, 3 vols. *The Tale of King Arthur* is in I, 1–180. This is the first edition to be based on the Winchester MS. For an account of the latter, as well as of Caxton's edition, see I, lxxxvii–xci, and III, 1647–51.

— *The Works of Sir Thomas Malory,* Oxford, Clarendon Press, 1954. The *Tale of King Arthur* occupies 1–133.

CRITICAL WORKS[1]

BALAGUER, P. BOHIGAS, *Los Textos españoles y gallego-portugueses de la Demanda del Santo Grial*, *RFE*, Anejo VII (Madrid, 1925).

— 'El *Lanzarote* español del manuscrito 9611 de la Biblioteca Nacional', *RFE*, XI (1924), 282–97.

— 'Más sobre el *Lanzarote* español', *RFE*, XII (1925), 60–2.

— review of Rodrigues Lapa, *A Demanda do Santo Graal*, *RFE*, XX (1933), 180–5.

— 'La visión de Alfonso X y las *Profecías de Merlin*', *RFE*, XXV (1941), 383–98.

— 'Origines de los Libros de Caballeria' in *Historia general de las Literaturas Hispanicas*, ed. G. Diaz Plaja, I (Barcelona, 1949), 526–7.

— *El Baladro del Sabio Merlin segun el Texto de la edicion de Burgos de 1498*, 3 vols. (Barcelona, 1957, II, 1961, III, 1962). The critical study is contained in III, 129–94.

BOGDANOW, FANNI, 'The rebellion of the kings in the Cambridge MS. of the *Suite du Merlin*', *UTSE*, XXXIV (1955), 6–17.

— 'The character of Gauvain in the thirteenth century prose romances', *Med. Aev.*, XXVII (1958), 154–61.

— 'Pellinor's death in the *Suite du Merlin* and the *Palamedes*', *Med. Aev.*, XXIX (1960), 1–9.

— 'Essai de classement des manuscrits de la *Suite du Merlin*', *R*, LXXXI (1960), 188–98.

— 'The Spanish *Baladro* and the *Conte du Brait*', *R*, LXXXII (1962), 383–399.

— 'The relationship of the Portuguese *Josep Abarimatia* to the extant French MSS. of the *Estoire del Saint Graal*', *ZRPh.*, 76 (1960), 343–75.

— 'The *Suite du Merlin* and the Post-Vulgate *Roman du Graal*', Ch. 24 in Loomis, *Arthurian Literature in the Middle Ages* (Oxford: Clarendon Press, 1959, 1961).

BREILLAT, P., 'La *Quête du Saint Graal* en Italie', *Mélanges d'archéologie et d'histoire publiés par l'École française de Rome*, LIV (1937), 274–6, 282–5.

BROWN, A. C. L., 'Balin and the Dolorous Stroke', *MPh.*, VII (1909), 203–6.

— 'The Bleeding Lance', *PMLA*, XXV (1910), 1–59.

BRUCE, JAMES DOUGLAS, *The Evolution of Arthurian Romance from the beginnings down to the year 1300* (*Hesperia*, Ergänzungsreihe: Schriften

[1] This list comprises in the main only works dealing with the *Roman du Graal*. Studies dealing with aspects of the Vulgate Cycle have only been included if they have a bearing on the *Roman du Graal*. For a detailed bibliography of the Spanish *Baladro* and the Spanish and Portuguese *Demandas*, see Balaguer, *Los textos españoles*, 24–9.

zur englischen Philologie, 8 and 9) (Göttingen: Vandenhoeck & Ruprecht, and Baltimore: The John Hopkins Press, 1923; 2nd edition with a bibliographical supplement by A. Hilka, 1928), 2 vols., I, 458–482, II, 136–41.

BRUCE, JAMES DOUGLAS, 'The development of the Mort Arthur theme in medieval romance', *RR*, IV (1913), 429–34.

— 'Mordred's incestuous birth', in *Medieval Studies in memory of Gertrude Schoepperle Loomis* (Paris: Champion, and New York: Columbia University Press, 1927), 197–208.

— 'The composition of the Old French Prose *Lancelot*', *RR*, IX (1918), 355–8.

— 'Pelles, Pellinor and Pellean in the Old French Arthurian romances', *MPh.*, XVI (1918), 113–28, 337–50.

— Introduction to his edition of *Historia Meriadoci* and *De Ortu Waluuani* (Hesperia, Ergänzungsreihe: Schriften zur englischen Philologie, 2) (Göttingen: Vandenhoeck & Ruprecht, and Baltimore: The John Hopkins Press, 1913), xxxvii–xlv.

BRUGGER, E., 'L'Enserrement Merlin. Studien zur Merlinsage', *ZFSL*, XXIX (1906), 56–140; XXX (1906), 169–239; XXXI (1907), 239–81; XXXIII (1908), 145–94; XXXIV (1909), 99–150; XXXV (1910), 1–55.

— review of A. C. L. Brown, 'The Bleeding Lance', *ZFSL*, XXXVI (1911), 187–90.

— review of J. D. Bruce, 'The development of the Mort Arthur theme in medieval romance', *ZFSL*, XLVII (1925), 98–105.

— review of H. O. Sommer, *Die Abenteuer Gawains, Ywains und Le Morholts mit den drei Jungfrauen*, *ZFSL*, XLVII (1925), 105–10.

— review of K. Pietsch, 'Concerning MS. 2-G-5 of the Palace Library at Madrid', *MPh.*, XI (1913), *ASNSL*, 133 (1915), 229–30.

— 'Das arturische Material in den *Prophecies Merlin* des Meisters Richart d'Irlande', *ZFSL*, LXI (1938), 346–51; LXII (1939), 60–5.

— 'Der schöne Feigling in der arthurischen Literatur', *ZRPh.*, LXI (1941), 41; LXIII (1943), 172–3; LXV (1949), 350–3, 390–6, 348 n. 1, 359 n. 2.

BRUMMER, RUDOLPH, *Die erzählende Prosadichtung in den romanischen Literaturen des XIII. Jahrhunderts*, vol. I (Berlin: Stundenglas-Verlag, 1948), 154–63.

CORONEDI, P. H., 'La leggenda del san Graal nel romanza in prosa di Tristano', *AR*, XV (1931), 83–98.

ENTWISTLE, W. J., *The Arthurian Legend in the Literatures of the Spanish Peninsula* (London & Toronto: Dent; New York: Dutton, 1925), 133–81.

FERRIER, JANET, M. *Forerunners of the French Novel* (Manchester University Press, 1954), 7–21, 104–8.

FRAPPIER, JEAN, *Étude sur la Mort le Roi Artu* (Paris: Droz, 1936; 2nd revised edition, Geneva: Droz, and Paris: Minard, 1961).

FRAPPIER, JEAN, *La Mort le Roi Artu, roman du XIIIe siècle*, TLF (Geneva: Droz, and Lille: Giard, 1954; 2nd ed., Geneva: Droz, and Paris: Minard, 1956), xvi–xvii.

— 'Le Graal et la Chevalerie', *R*, LXXV (1954), 165–210.

GARDNER, EDMUND G., *The Arthurian Legend in Italian Literature* (London: Dent, and New York: Dutton, 1930), 205–6.

GILSON, ÉTIENNE, 'La mystique de la grâce dans la *Queste del Saint Graal*', *LI* (1925), 321–47; reprinted in *Les Idées et les Lettres* (Paris: J. Vrin, 1955), 59–91.

GOLTHER, W., *Parzival und der Gral in der Dichtung des Mittelalters und der Neuzeit* (Stuttgart: Metzlersche Verlagsbuchhandlung, 1925), 103–5.

GRÖBER, GUSTAV, *Grundriss der Romanischen Philologie*, II. Band, 1. Abteilung (Strasbourg: Trübner, 1902), 997–1000, 1006; II. Band, 2. Abteilung (Strasbourg, 1897), 438–9, 213–15.

HEINZEL, RICHARD, *Über die französischen Gralromane* (Denkschriften der kaiserlichen Akademie der Wissenschaften, Philos. Hist. Klasse, XL, Vienna, 1891), 31, 68–9, 162–71.

HIBBARD, L. A., 'Malory's Book of Balin', in *Medieval Studies in memory of Gertrude Schoepperle Loomis* (Paris: Champion, and New York: Columbia University Press, 1927), 175–95.

HILKA, A., 'Die Jugendgeschichte Percevals im Prosa-Lancelot und im Prosa-Tristan', *ZRPh.*, LII (1932), 513–16.

JEANROY, A., review of L. A. Paton, *Studies in the Fairy Mythology of Arthurian Romance*, *R*, XXXIV (1905), 117–21.

KLOB, OTTO, 'Beiträge zur Kenntnis der spanischen und portugiesischen Gral-Litteratur', *ZRPh.*, XXVI (1902), 169–205.

KRAPPE, A. H., 'La naissance de Merlin', *R*, LIX (1933), 12–33.

LÖSETH, E., *Le roman en prose de Tristan, le roman de Palamède et la compilation de Rusticien de Pise, analyse critique d'après les manuscrits de Paris*, Bibl. de l'École des Hautes Études, fasc. 82 (Paris, 1891).

— *Le Tristan et le Palamède des manuscrits français du British Museum. Étude critique*, Videnskabs-Selskabets Skrifter II. Hist. Filos. Klasse, 1905, no. 4 (Christiania, 1905).

— *Le Tristan et le Palamède des manuscrits de Rome et de Florence*, Videnskabs-Selskabets Skrifter II. Hist. Filos. Klasse, 1924, no. 3 (Christiania, 1924).

LOOMIS, ROGER SHERMAN, *Celtic Myth and Arthurian Romance* (New York: Columbia University Press, 1927), 128, 135–6, 212, 250–9, 308, 339, 348.

— *Arthurian Tradition and Chrétien de Troyes* (New York: Columbia University Press, 1949), 45, 69, 102, 106–8, 189, 191, 261, 289, 295, 306, 318, 329, 340, 380, 382, 422, 425, 454.

— 'L'Esplumeor Merlin again', *BBSIA*, 9 (1957), 79–83.

— *Arthurian Literature in the Middle Ages, a Collaborative History*, edited by R. S. Loomis (Oxford: Clarendon Press, 1959, 1961).

LOT, F., *Étude sur le Lancelot en prose*, Bibl. de l'École des Hautes Études, fasc. 226 (Paris: Champion, 1918; reprinted with a supplement in 1954), 77, 79–81, 204–55, 284.

LOT-BORODINE, MYRRHA, 'Le symbolisme du Graal dans l'*Estoire del Saint Graal*', *Neophilologus*, XXXIV (1950), 65–79.

— 'Les apparitions du Christ aux messes de l'*Estoire* et de la *Queste del Saint Graal*', *R*, LXXII (1951), 202–23.

— 'Les grands secrets du Saint-Graal dans la *Queste* du pseudo-Map', in *Lumière du Graal: Études et textes présentées sous la direction de René Nelli* (Paris: Les Cahiers du Sud, 1951), 151–74.

— 'Le double esprit et l'unité du *Lancelot* en prose', in *Mélanges... offerts à M. F. Lot* (Paris: Champion, 1925), 477–90; reprinted as an Appendix to the revised edition of Lot's *Étude* (Paris: Champion, 1954), 443–56, and in her *De l'amour profane à l'amour sacré* (Paris: Nizet, 1961), Ch. VI.

— *De l'amour profane à l'amour sacré* (Paris: Nizet, 1961), Chs. VI and VIII.

MARTINS, MARIO, 'O livro de José de Arimatia da Torre do Tombo', *Broteria (Revista contemporâne de cultura)*, Lisbon, LV, fasc. 4 (1952), 289–98; reprinted in Martins' *Estudos de Literatura medieval* (Braga: Livraria Cruz, 1956), 30–57.

— *Estudos de literatura medieval* (Braga: Livraria Cruz, 1956), Ch. II, '*A Demanda do Santo Graal*' (34–47).

MARX, JEAN, *La Légende Arthurienne et le Graal* (Paris: Presses Universitaires de France, 1952), 169–72, 179.

— 'Le personnage de Merlin dans le *Roman de Balain*', in *Fin du Moyen Âge et Renaissance, Mélanges de Philologie française offerts à Robert Guiette* (Anvers: Nederlandsche Boekhandel, 1961), 65–9.

MICHA, ALEXANDRE, 'L'épreuve de l'épée', *R*, LXX (1948–9), 37–50.

— 'Deux sources de la *Mort Artu*', *ZRPh.*, LXVI (1950), 369–72.

— 'Les sources de la Vulgate du *Merlin*', *MA*, VII (1952), 325 n. 33.

— 'Deux études sur le Graal. II: Le livre du Graal de Robert de Boron', *R*, LXXV (1954), 316–52.

— 'Les manuscrits du *Merlin* en prose de Robert de Boron', *R*, LXXIX (1958), 78–94, 145–75.

— 'L'Esprit du Lancelot-Graal', *R*, LXXXII (1961), 357–78.

— 'La Table Ronde chez Robert de Boron et dans la *Queste del Saint Graal*', in *Les Romans du Graal dans la littérature des XIIe et XIIIe siècles* (Colloques Internationaux du Centre National de la Recherche Scientifique, III, Paris: Éditions du CNRF, 1956), 119–36.

MOISES, MASSAUD, 'O processo dialético-narrativo na *Demanda do Santo Graal*', *RI*, ano III, no. 26 (1951), 65–9.

— 'A *Demanda do Santo Graal*', *RH*, VI (1951), 275–81.

— 'A Margem da *Demanda do Santo Graal*', *RH*, XXI (1955), 319–22.

MOISES, MASSAUD, 'A concepção medieval da vida expressa na *Demanda do Santo Graal'*, *RI*, ano III, no. 30 (1951), 99–110.

MUIR, L., 'The Questing Beast', *Orpheus*, IV, fasc. 1–2 (1957), 24–32.

NITZE, W. A., 'The Beste glatissant in Arthurian Romance', *ZRPh.*, LVI (1936), 409–18.

— 'The Esplumoir Merlin', *Spec.*, XVIII (1943), 69–79.

PARIS, GASTON, Introduction to *Merlin, roman en prose du XIIIe siècle, publié avec la mise en prose du poème de Merlin de Robert de Boron d'après le manuscrit appartenant à M. Alfred Huth*, SATF (Paris, 1886), 2 vols.

— review of Karl von Reinhardstöttner, *Historia dos cavalleiros da Mesa Redonda e da demanda do Santo Graal*, *R*, XVI (1887), 582–6.

— review of Wechssler, *Über die verschiedenen Redaktionen des Robert von Borron zugeschriebenen Graal-Lancelot-Cyklus*, *R*, XXIV (1895), 472–5.

— *La Littérature française au moyen âge (XIe–XIVe siècle)* (Paris: Hachette; 5th edition, 1914), §§ 60, 62, 63.

PATON, LUCY ALLEN, *Studies in the Fairy Mythology of Arthurian Romance*, Radcliffe College Monographs, no. 13 (Boston: Ginn, 1903; 2nd edition, enlarged by a Survey of Scholarship on the Fairy Mythology since 1903 and a Bibliography by R. S. Loomis, Burt Franklin Bibliographical Series XVIII, New York: Burt Franklin, 1960), 13–24, 121–3, 197–200, 204–47, 294–8.

— *Les Prophécies de Merlin, edited from MS. 593 in the Bibliothèque Municipale of Rennes*, Modern Language Association of America, Monograph Series, no. 1, 2 vols. (New York: Heath, and London, Oxford University Press, 1926–7), II, 275, 297–300, 302–3.

PAUPHILET, ALBERT, 'La *Queste du Saint Graal* du MS. Bibl. Nat. fr. 343', *R*, XXXVI (1907), 591–609.

— *Études sur la Queste del Saint Graal attribuée à Gautier Map* (Paris: Champion, 1921).

— *La Queste del Saint Graal, roman du XIIIe siècle*, CFMA (Paris, 1923, 1949), vii–viii, xi–xii.

— *Le Legs du Moyen Âge. Études de littérature médiévale* (Melun: Librairie d'Argences, 1950), 175–6, 212–17.

— review of F. Lot, *Étude sur le Lancelot en prose*, *R*, XLV (1918–19), 514–534.

PICKFORD, C. E., *L'Évolution du roman arthurien en prose vers la fin du moyen âge d'après le manuscrit 112 du fonds français de la Bibliothèque Nationale* (Paris: Nizet, 1960), 60–77, 86–109, 119–21.

— 'La priorité de la version portugaise de la *Demanda do Santo Graal'*, Bulletin Hispanique, LXIII (1961), 211–16 (Annales de la Faculté des Lettres de Bordeaux, LXXXIIIe année).

PIDAL Y BERNALDO DE QUIROS, ROQUE, *Noticias de libros peregrinos*. Numero 30. *El Baladro del sabio Merlin con sus profecias* (Madrid, 1950).

PIEL, JOSEPH M., 'Anotações criticas ao texto da *Demanda do Graal'*, *Biblos*, XXI (1945), 175–206.

PIETSCH, KARL, 'Concerning MS. 2–G–5 of the Palace Library of Madrid', *MPh.*, XI (1913), 1–18.

ROACH, W., *The Didot-Perceval according to the Manuscripts of Modena and Paris* (Philadelphia: University of Pennsylvania Press, 1941), 6–7 n. 6.

RODRIGUES LAPA, M., *A Demanda do Santo Graal. Prioridade do texto português* (Lisboa, 1930).

— 'La *Demanda do Santo Graal*. Priorité du texte portugais par rapport au texte castillan', *Bulletin des Études Portugaises*, publié par l'Imprimerie de l'Université de Coimbra et l'Institut français en Portugal (Coimbra, 1931), 137–60.

— *Lições de Literatura Portugueses, época medieval, 3a ediçao revista e acrescentada* (Coimbra: Editora Limitada, 1952), 210–33.

SOMMER, H. O., 'The Queste of the Holy Grail, forming the third part of the trilogy indicated in the *Suite du Merlin*, Huth MS.', *R*, XXXVI (1907), 369–462, 543–90.

— 'Galahad and Perceval', *MPh.*, V (1907–8), 295–322.

— 'Zur Kritik der altfranzösichen Artus-Romane in Prosa: Robert und Helie de Borron', *ZRPh.*, XXXII (1908), 323–37.

— *Die Abenteuer Gawains, Ywains und Le Morholts mit den drei Jungfrauen aus der Trilogie (Demanda) des Pseudo-Robert de Borron. Beihefte zur ZRPh.*, XLVII (Halle: Niemeyer, 1913), ix–lxxxix.

TIEMAN, HERMAN, 'Zur Geschichte des altfranzösischen Prosaroman', *Romanische Forschungen*, LXIII (1951), 306–28.

VETTERMANN, ELLA, *Die Balen–Dichtungen und ihre Quellen, Beihefte zur ZRPh.*, LX (Halle: Niemeyer, 1918).

VINAVER, EUGÈNE, *Études sur le Tristan en prose: les sources, les manuscrits, bibliographie critique* (Paris: Champion, 1925).

— *Le Roman de Tristan et Iseut dans l'œuvre de Thomas Malory* (Paris: Champion, 1925), 99–109.

— 'The Prose *Tristan'*, Ch. 26 in *Arthurian Literature in the Middle Ages, a Collaborative History*, ed. R. S. Loomis (Oxford: Clarendon Press, 1959, 1961).

— *Malory* (Oxford: Clarendon Press, 1929), 130–4, 142.

— Introduction to *Le Roman de Balain*, edited by M. D. Legge with an Introduction by E. Vinaver (Manchester University Press, 1942), ix–xxx.

— *The Works of Sir Thomas Malory*, ed. by E. Vinaver (Oxford: Clarendon Press, 1947, 1948), 3 vols., I, xlviii–lv; III, 1265–80, and Notes to the *Tale of King Arthur* in III, 1281–1359 (in particular p. 1292, n. 39, l. 1–41, l. 14, p. 1306, n. 78, ll. 22–7, p. 1311, n. 85, ll. 4–21, p. 1313, n. 85, l. 27–86, l. 6, p. 1317, n. 92, ll. 14–21.

— 'La genèse de la *Suite du Merlin'*, *Mélanges de Philologie romane et de*

Littérature médiévale offerts à Ernest Hoepffner (Paris: Les Belles Lettres, 1949), 295–300.

VINAVER, EUGÈNE, 'Flaubert and the Legend of Saint Julian', *BJRL*, XXXVI, no. 1 (September 1953), 228–44.

— *The Tale of the Death of King Arthur by Sir Thomas Malory*, ed. E. Vinaver (Oxford: Clarendon Press, 1955), viii–xi, xx–xxi.

— *King Arthur and his Knights. Selections from the Works of Sir Thomas Malory* (Boston: The Riverside Press, Cambridge, U.S.A., 1956), viii–xiii, xiv, xvii.

— 'The Dolorous Stroke', *Med. Aev.*, XXV (1956), 175–80.

— 'King Arthur's Sword or the Making of a Medieval Romance', *BJRL*, XL, no. 2 (March 1958), 513–26.

— 'A la recherche d'une poétique médiévale', *Cahiers de Civilisation Médiévale, Université de Poitiers*, IIe Année (1959), 1–16.

VISCARDI, ANTONIO, 'La Quête du Saint Graal dans les romans du moyen âge italiens', in *Lumière du Graal: Études et textes présentées sous la direction de René Nelli* (Paris: Les Cahiers du Sud, 1951), 279–81.

WECHSSLER, EDUARD, *Über die verschiedenen Redaktionen des Robert von Borron zugeschriebenen Graal-Lancelot-Cyklus* (Halle, 1895).

— *Die Sage vom heiligen Gral in ihrer Entwicklung bis auf Richard Wagners Parsifal* (Halle, 1898), 124–9.

WHITEHEAD, FREDERICK, 'On certain episodes in the Fourth Book of Malory's Morte Darthur', *Med. Aev.*, II (1933), 199–216.

WILSON, R. H., 'The Rebellion of the Kings in Malory and in the Cambridge *Suite du Merlin*', *UTSE*, XXXI (1952), 13–26.

— 'The Cambridge *Suite du Merlin* re-examined', *UTSE*, XXXVI (1957), 41–51.

WOLF, FERDINAND, *Über Raoul de Houdenc und insbesondere seinen Roman Meraugis de Portlesguez* (Denkschriften der kaiserlichen Akademie der Wissenschaft, Philos. Hist. Klasse, vol. XIV), Vienna (1865), 183–94.

WRIGHT, THOMAS L., 'The Tale of King Arthur', in *Malory's Originality*, ed. R. M. Lumiansky (Baltimore: The Johns Hopkins Press, 1964), pp. 9–66.

ZENKER, R., review of E. Vettermann, *Die Balen-Dichtungen und ihre Quellen*, *ASNSL*, 141 (1921), 150–61.

ZUMTHOR, PAUL, 'La délivrance de Merlin', *ZRPh.*, LXII (1942), 370–86.

— *Merlin le Prophète. Un thème de la littérature polémique de l'historiographie et des romans* (Lausanne: Imprimeries Réunies S.A., 1943), 115–58, 179–222, 231–59.

— 'Merlin dans le Lancelot-Graal. Étude thématique', in *Les Romans du Graal aux XIIe et XIIIe siècles* (Colloques Internationaux du Centre National de la Recherche Scientifique III) (Paris: Éditions du CRNS, 1956), 149–66.

Index of Manuscripts